BAHAMAS

OFFSHORE INVESTMENT AND BUSINESS GUIDE

VOLUME 1

STRATEGIC AND PRACTICAL INFORMATION

International Business Publications, USA
Washington DC, USA - Bahamas

BAHAMAS

OFFSHORE INVESTMENT AND BUSINESS GUIDE

VOLUME 1 STRATEGIC AND PRACTICAL INFORMATION

UPDATED ANNUALLY

Cover Design: **International Business Publications, USA**

We express our sincere appreciation to all government agencies and international organizations, which provided information and other materials for this guide

2018 Edition Updated Reprint International Business Publications, USA
ISBN 1-4330-0370-8

This guide provides basic information for starting or/and conducting business in the country. The extraordinary volume of materials covering the topic, prevents us from placing all these materials in this guide. For more detailed information on issues related to any specific investment and business activity in the country, please contact Global Investment Center, USA
Please acquire the list of our business intelligence and marketing reports and other business publications. We constantly update and expand our business intelligence and marketing materials. Please contact the center for the updated list of reports on over 250 countries.

For additional analytical, business and investment opportunities information,
please contact Global Investment & Business Center, USA
at (703) 370-8082. Fax: (703) 370-8083. E-mail: ibpusa3@gmail.com
Global Business and Investment Info Databank - www.ibpus.com

Printed in the USA

For additional analytical, business and investment opportunities information,
please contact Global Investment & Business Center, USA
at (703) 370-8082. Fax: (703) 370-8083. E-mail: ibpusa3@gmail.com
Global Business and Investment Info Databank - www.ibpus.com

BAHAMAS

OFFSHORE
INVESTMENT AND BUSINESS
GUIDE

VOLUME 1
STRATEGIC AND PRACTICAL INFORMATION

TABLE OF CONTENTS

BUSINES AND DEVELOPMENT PROFILES

BASIC PROFILE

Capital and largest city	Nassau 25°4′N 77°20′W
Official languages	English
Recognised regional languages	Bahamian Creole
Ethnic groups (2016)	90.6% African 4.7% European 2.1% Mixed 1.9% other
Demonym	Bahamian
Government	Unitary parliamentary constitutional monarchy
• Monarch	Elizabeth II
• Governor-General	Dame Marguerite Pindling
• Prime Minister	Hubert Minnis
Legislature	Parliament
• Upper house	Senate
• Lower house	House of Assembly
Independence	
• from the United Kingdom	10 July 1973
Area	
• Total	13,878 km^2 (5,358 sq mi) (160th)
• Water (%)	28%
Population	
• 2017 estimate	372,000 (177th)
• 2010 census	351,461
• Density	25.21/km^2 (65.3/sq mi) (181st)
GDP (PPP)	2017 estimate
• Total	$9.374 billion
• Per capita	$25,173
GDP (nominal)	2017 estimate
• Total	$9.172 billion
• Per capita	$24,630
Gini	57 high
HDI (2014)	0.790 high · 55th
Currency	Bahamian dollar (BSD) (US dollars widely accepted)
Time zone	EST (UTC−5)
• Summer (DST)	EDT (UTC−4)
Drives on the	left
Calling code	+1 242
ISO 3166 code	BS
Internet TLD	.bs

The Bahamas known officially as the **Commonwealth of The Bahamas**, is an archipelagic state within the Lucayan Archipelago. It consists of more than 700 islands, cays, and islets in the Atlantic Ocean and is located north of Cuba and Hispaniola (Haiti and the Dominican Republic); northwest of the Turks and Caicos Islands; southeast of the US state of Florida and east of the Florida Keys. The capital is Nassau on the island of New Providence. The designation of "the Bahamas" can refer either to the country or to the larger island chain that it shares with the Turks and Caicos Islands. As stated in the mandate/manifesto of the Royal Bahamas Defence Force, the Bahamas territory encompasses 470,000 km^2 (180,000 sq mi) of ocean space.

The Bahamas is the site of Columbus' first landfall in the New World in 1492. At that time, the islands were inhabited by the Lucayan, a branch of the Arawakan-speaking Taino people. Although the Spanish never colonised The Bahamas, they shipped the native Lucayans to slavery in Hispaniola. The islands were mostly deserted from 1513 until 1648, when English colonists from Bermuda settled on the island of Eleuthera.

The Bahamas became a British Crown colony in 1718, when the British clamped down on piracy. After the American War of Independence, the Crown resettled thousands of American Loyalists in the Bahamas; they brought their slaves with them and established plantations on land grants. Africans constituted the majority of the population from this period. The Bahamas became a haven for freed African slaves: the Royal Navy resettled Africans here liberated from illegal slave ships; American slaves and Seminoles escaped here from Florida; and the government freed American slaves carried on United States domestic ships that had reached the Bahamas due to weather. Slavery in the Bahamas was abolished in 1834. Today the descendants of slaves and free Africans make up nearly 90% of the population; issues related to the slavery years are part of society.

The Bahamas became an independent Commonwealth realm in 1973, retaining the British monarch, then and currently Queen Elizabeth II, as its head of state. In terms of gross domestic product per capita, The Bahamas is one of the richest countries in the Americas (following the United States and Canada), with an economy based on tourism and finance

GEOGRAPHY

Location: Caribbean, chain of islands in the North Atlantic Ocean, southeast of Florida
Geographic coordinates: 24 15 N, 76 00 W
Map references: Central America and the Caribbean

Area:
total: 13,940 sq km
land: 10,070 sq km
water: 3,870 sq km

Area—comparative: slightly smaller than Connecticut
Land boundaries: 0 km

Coastline: 3,542 km

Maritime claims:
continental shelf: 200-m depth or to the depth of exploitation
exclusive economic zone: 200 nm
territorial sea: 12 nm

Climate: tropical marine; moderated by warm waters of Gulf Stream

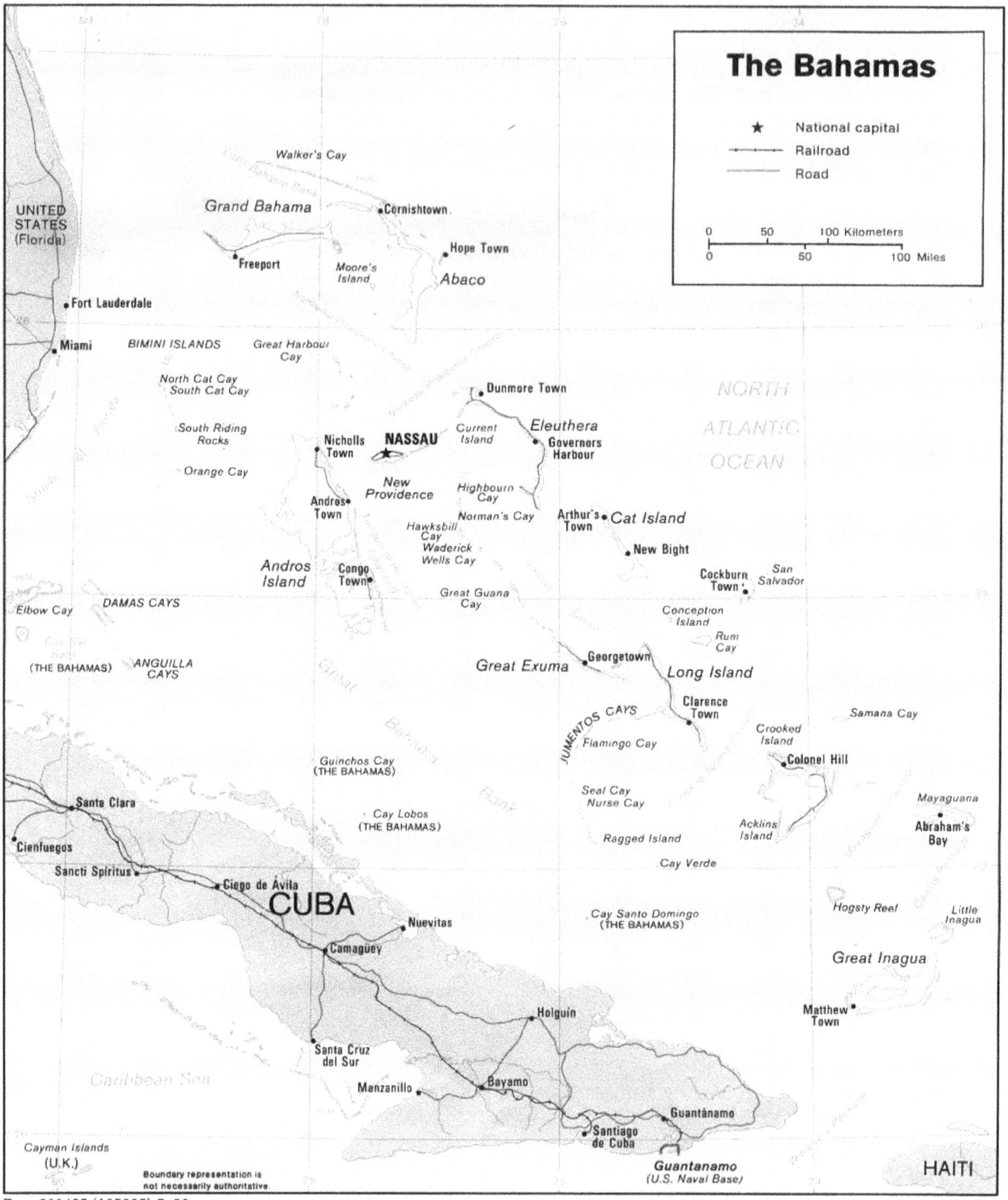

Base 800485 (A05607) 7-86

Terrain: long, flat coral formations with some low rounded hills
Elevation extremes:
lowest point: Atlantic Ocean 0 m
highest point: Mount Alvernia, on Cat Island 63 m
Natural resources: salt, aragonite, timber

Land use:
arable land: 1%
permanent crops: 0%
permanent pastures: 0%
forests and woodland: 32%
other: 67%
Irrigated land: NA sq km
Natural hazards: hurricanes and other tropical storms that cause extensive flood and wind damage
Environment—current issues: coral reef decay; solid waste disposal

Environment—international agreements:
party to: Biodiversity, Climate Change, Endangered Species, Hazardous Wastes, Law of the Sea, Nuclear Test Ban, Ozone Layer Protection, Ship Pollution, Wetlands
signed, but not ratified: none of the selected agreements

Geography—note: strategic location adjacent to US and Cuba; extensive island chain

PEOPLE

Population: 283,705

Age structure:
0-14 years: 27% (male 39,271; female 38,740)
15-64 years: 67% (male 92,830; female 96,814)
65 years and over: 6% (male 6,696; female 9,354)

Population growth rate: 1.36%
Birth rate: 20.58 births/1,000 population
Death rate: 5.43 deaths/1,000 population
Net migration rate: -1.55 migrant(s)/1,000 population
Sex ratio:
at birth: 1.02 male(s)/female
under 15 years: 1.01 male(s)/female
15-64 years: 0.96 male(s)/female
65 years and over: 0.72 male(s)/female
total population: 0.96 male(s)/female
Infant mortality rate: 18.38 deaths/1,000 live births

Life expectancy at birth:
total population: 74.25 years
male: 70.94 years
female: 77.64 years

Total fertility rate: 2.31 children born/woman
Nationality:
noun: Bahamian(s)
adjective: Bahamian
Ethnic groups: black 85%, white 15%

Religions: Baptist 32%, Anglican 20%, Roman Catholic 19%, Methodist 6%, Church of God 6%, other Protestant 12%, none or unknown 3%, other 2%

Languages: English, Creole (among Haitian immigrants)

Literacy:
definition: age 15 and over can read and write
total population: 98.2%
male: 98.5%
female: 98%

GOVERNMENT

Country name:
conventional long form: Commonwealth of The Bahamas
conventional short form: The Bahamas

Data code: BF
Government type: commonwealth
Capital: Nassau

Administrative divisions: 21 districts; Acklins and Crooked Islands, Bimini, Cat Island, Exuma, Freeport, Fresh Creek, Governor's Harbour, Green Turtle Cay, Harbour Island, High Rock, Inagua, Kemps Bay, Long Island, Marsh Harbour, Mayaguana, New Providence, Nicholls Town and Berry Islands, Ragged Island, Rock Sound, Sandy Point, San Salvador and Rum Cay

Independence: 10 July 1973 (from UK)

National holiday: National Day, 10 July (1973)
Constitution: 10 July 1973
Legal system: based on English common law
Suffrage: 18 years of age; universal

Executive branch:
chief of state: Queen ELIZABETH II (since 6 February 1952); represented by Governor General Dame Marguerite PINDLING (since 8 July 2014)
head of government: Prime Minister Hubert MINNIS (since 11 May 2017)
cabinet: Cabinet appointed by governor general on recommendation of prime minister
elections/appointments: the monarchy is hereditary; governor general appointed by the monarch; following legislative elections, the leader of the majority party or majority coalition usually appointed prime minister by the governor general; the prime minister recommends the deputy prime minister

Legislative branch:
description: bicameral Parliament consists of the Senate (16 seats; members appointed by the governor general upon the advice of the prime minister and the opposition leader to serve 5-year terms) and the House of Assembly (39 seats; members directly elected in single-seat constituencies by simple majority vote to serve 5-year terms); note - the government may dissolve the parliament and call elections at any time
elections: last held on 10 May 2017 (next to be held by May 2022)
election results: percent of vote by party - FNM 57%, PLP 37%; seats by party - FNM 35, PLP 4

Political parties and leaders: Progressive Liberal Party or PLP [Perry CHRISTIE]; Free National Movement or FNM [Hubert Alexander INGRAHAM]

International organization participation: ACP, C, Caricom, CCC, CDB, ECLAC, FAO, G-77, IADB, IBRD, ICAO, ICFTU, ICRM, IFC, IFRCS, ILO, IMF, IMO, Inmarsat, Intelsat, Interpol, IOC, ITU, NAM, OAS, OPANAL, OPCW, UN, UNCTAD, UNESCO, UNIDO, UPU, WHO, WIPO, WMO, WTrO (applicant)

Diplomatic representation in the US:
chief of mission: Ambassador Arlington Griffith BUTLER
chancery: 2220 Massachusetts Avenue NW, Washington, DC 20008
telephone: [1] (202) 319-2660
FAX: [1] (202) 319-2668
consulate(s) general: Miami and New York

Diplomatic representation from the US:
chief of mission: Ambassador Arthur SCHECHTER
embassy: Queen Street, Nassau
mailing address: local or express mail address: P.O. Box N-8197, Nassau; stateside address: American Embassy Nassau, P.O. Box 599009, Miami, FL 33159-9009; pouch address: Nassau, Department of State, Washington, DC 20521-3370
telephone: [1] (242) 322-1181
FAX: [1] (242) 356-0222

Flag description: three equal horizontal bands of aquamarine (top), gold, and aquamarine, with a black equilateral triangle based on the hoist side

ECONOMY

The Bahamas has the second highest per capital GDP in the English-speaking Caribbean with an economy heavily dependent on tourism and international banking. Tourism accounts for approximately 75-80% of GDP and directly or indirectly employs half of the archipelago's labor force. Financial services constitute the second-most important sector of the Bahamian economy, accounting for about 15% of GDP. Manufacturing and agriculture combined contribute less than 7% of GDP and show little growth, despite government incentives aimed at those sectors. On January 1, 2015, the Government introduced a 7.5% Value Added Tax (VAT) on most goods and services, a measure designed to strengthen the fiscal balance sheet. In August 2016, Moody's downgraded the Bahamas' bond and issue ratings to Baa3 from Baa2 with a stable outlook, maintaining that rating in its February 2017 review. In December 2016, S&P downgraded the country to BB+ (speculative grade) from BBB- (investment grade) with a stable outlook based on projections of slow economic growth and the pace of debt accumulation. The Bahamas is the only country in the Western Hemisphere that is not a member of the World Trade Organization

GDP (purchasing power parity):

$9.066 billion (2016 est.)
$9.042 billion (2015 est.)
$9.195 billion (2014 est.)
note: data are in 2016 dollars
country comparison to the world: 160

GDP (official exchange rate):
$9.047 billion (2016 est.)

GDP - real growth rate:
0.3% (2016 est.)
-1.7% (2015 est.)
-0.5% (2014 est.)
country comparison to the world: 191

GDP - per capita (PPP):
$24,600 (2016 est.)
$24,800 (2015 est.)
$25,500 (2014 est.)
note: data are in 2016 dollars
country comparison to the world: 77

Gross national saving:
14.1% of GDP (2016 est.)
11.2% of GDP (2015 est.)
9.2% of GDP (2014 est.)
country comparison to the world: 126

GDP - composition, by end use:
household consumption: 65.7%
government consumption: 16.3%
investment in fixed capital: 27.3%
investment in inventories: 1%
exports of goods and services: 36.9%
imports of goods and services: -47.2% (2016 est.)

GDP - composition, by sector of origin:
agriculture: 2.3%
industry: 7.6%
services: 90.1% (2016 est.)

Agriculture - products:
citrus, vegetables; poultry
Industries:
tourism, banking, oil bunkering, maritime industries, transshipment and logistics, salt, aragonite, pharmaceuticals

Industrial production growth rate:
1.5% (2016 est.)
country comparison to the world: 130

Labor force:
196,900 (2013 est.)
country comparison to the world: 170

Labor force - by occupation:
agriculture: 3%
industry: 11%
tourism: 49%
other services: 37% (2011 est.)

Unemployment rate:
15% (2014 est.)

15.8% (2013 est.)
country comparison to the world: 161

Population below poverty line:
9.3% (2010 est.)

Household income or consumption by percentage share:

lowest 10%: 1%
highest 10%: 22% (2007 est.)

Budget:
revenues: $1.9 billion
expenditures: $2.3 billion (2016 est.)

Taxes and other revenues:
21% of GDP (2016 est.)
country comparison to the world: 145

Budget surplus (+) or deficit (-):

-4.4% of GDP (2016 est.)
country comparison to the world: 147

Public debt:

64.4% of GDP (2016 est.)
64.4% of GDP (2015 est.)
country comparison to the world: 57

Fiscal year:
1 July - 30 June

Inflation rate (consumer prices):
1% (2016 est.)
1.9% (2015 est.)
country comparison to the world: 69

Central bank discount rate:

4.5% (1 January 2014)

4.5% (31 December 2012)
country comparison to the world: 83

Commercial bank prime lending rate:
6% (31 December 2016 est.)
4.8% (31 December 2015 est.)
country comparison to the world: 125

Stock of narrow money:
$2.061 billion (31 December 2016 est.)
$2.051 billion (31 December 2015 est.)
country comparison to the world: 130

Stock of broad money:
$6.952 billion (31 December 2016 est.)
$6.546 billion (31 December 2015 est.)
country comparison to the world: 121

Stock of domestic credit:
$9.5 million (31 December 2016 est.)
$8.922 million (31 December 2015 est.)
country comparison to the world: 188

Market value of publicly traded shares:
$2.78 billion (31 December 2012 est.)
country comparison to the world: 98

Current account balance:
-$1.019 billion (2016 est.)
-$1.415 billion (2015 est.)
country comparison to the world: 123

Exports:
$880 million (2016 est.)
$800 million (2015 est.)
country comparison to the world: 164

Exports - commodities:
Rock lobster, aragonite, crude salt, polystyrene products
Exports - partners:
Poland 25.9%, Cote dIvoire 20.6%, US 15.6%, Dominican Republic 14.1%

Imports:
$2.495 billion (2016 est.)
$2.585 billion (2015 est.)
country comparison to the world: 154

Imports - commodities:
machinery and transport equipment, manufactures, chemicals, mineral fuels; food and live animals

Imports - partners:
US 22.8%, China 15.2%, Japan 9.7%, Poland 7.8%, South Korea 7.4%, Colombia 6.9%, Brazil 5.7%, Singapore 5.6% (2015)

Reserves of foreign exchange and gold:
$1.02 billion (31 December 2016 est.)
$895.5 million (31 December 2015 est.)
country comparison to the world: 126

Debt - external:
$17.56 billion (31 December 2013 est.)
$16.35 billion (31 December 2012 est.)
country comparison to the world: 95

Exchange rates:
Bahamian dollars (BSD) per US dollar -
1 (2016 est.)
1 (2015 est.)
1 (2014 est.)
1 (2013 est.)
1 (2012 est.)

ENERGY

Electricity access:
electrification - total population: 100%

Electricity - production:
1.7 billion kWh (2014 est.)
country comparison to the world: 142

Electricity - consumption:
1.6 billion kWh (2014 est.)
country comparison to the world: 145

Electricity - exports:
0 kWh (2013 est.)
country comparison to the world: 110

Electricity - imports:
0 kWh (2013 est.)
country comparison to the world: 125

Electricity - installed generating capacity:
600,000 kW (2014 est.)
country comparison to the world: 140

Electricity - from fossil fuels:
100% of total installed capacity (2012 est.)
country comparison to the world: 5

Electricity - from nuclear fuels:
0% of total installed capacity (2012 est.)
country comparison to the world: 50

Electricity - from hydroelectric plants:
0% of total installed capacity (2012 est.)
country comparison to the world: 162

Electricity - from other renewable sources:
0% of total installed capacity (2012 est.)
country comparison to the world: 157

Crude oil - production:
0 bbl/day (2015 est.)
country comparison to the world: 109

Crude oil - exports:
0 bbl/day (2013 est.)
country comparison to the world: 99

Crude oil - imports:
0 bbl/day (2013 est.)
country comparison to the world: 164
Crude oil - proved reserves:
0 bbl (1 January 2016 est.)
country comparison to the world: 110

Refined petroleum products - production:
0 bbl/day (2013 est.)
country comparison to the world: 120

Refined petroleum products - consumption:
24,000 bbl/day (2014 est.)
country comparison to the world: 130

Refined petroleum products - exports:
923 bbl/day (2013 est.)
country comparison to the world: 111

Refined petroleum products - imports:
26,330 bbl/day (2013 est.)
country comparison to the world: 104

Natural gas - production:
0 cu m (2013 est.)
country comparison to the world: 159
Natural gas - consumption:
0 cu m (2013 est.)
country comparison to the world: 121

Natural gas - exports:
0 cu m (2013 est.)
country comparison to the world: 65

Natural gas - imports:
0 cu m (2013 est.)
country comparison to the world: 161

Natural gas - proved reserves:
0 cu m (1 January 2009 es)
country comparison to the world: 115

Carbon dioxide emissions from consumption of energy:
4.1 million Mt (2013 est.)
country comparison to the world: 132

COMMUNICATIONS

Telephones - fixed lines:
total subscriptions: 120,925
subscriptions per 100 inhabitants: 37 (July 2015 est.)
country comparison to the world: 140

Telephones - mobile cellular:
total: 311,000
subscriptions per 100 inhabitants: 96 (July 2015 est.)
country comparison to the world: 178

Telephone system:
general assessment: modern facilities
domestic: totally automatic system; highly developed; the Bahamas Domestic Submarine Network links all of the major islands; Bahamas Telecommunications Company (BTC) privatized in 2011, but the government reacquired 51% share in 2014
international: country code - 1-242; landing point for the Americas Region Caribbean Ring System (ARCOS-1) and two additional fiber-optic submarine cables that provide links to South and Central America, parts of the Caribbean, and the US; satellite earth stations - 2 (2017)

Broadcast media:
The Bahamas has 4 major TV providers that provide service to all major islands in the archipelago; 1 TV station is operated by government-owned, commercially run Broadcasting Corporation of the Bahamas (BCB) and competes freely with 3 privately owned TV stations; multi-channel cable TV subscription service is widely available; there are 31 licensed broadcast (radio) service providers, 28 are privately owned FM radio stations operating on New Providence, Grand Bahama Island, Abaco Island, and on smaller islands in the country; the BCB operates a multi-channel radio broadcasting network that has national coverage; the sector is regulated by the Utilities Regulation and Competition Authority (2017)

Internet country code:
.bs

Internet users:
total: 253,000
percent of population: 78% (July 2015 est.)
country comparison to the world: 151

TRANSPORTATION

National air transport system:
number of registered air carriers: 4
inventory of registered aircraft operated by air carriers: 16
annual passenger traffic on registered air carriers: 587,516
annual freight traffic on registered air carriers: 172,730 mt-km

Civil aircraft registration country code prefix:
C6 (2016)

Airports:
61 (2013)
country comparison to the world: 80

Airports - with paved runways:
total: 24
over 3,047 m: 2
2,438 to 3,047 m: 2
1,524 to 2,437 m: 13
914 to 1,523 m: 7

Airports - with unpaved runways:
total: 37
1,524 to 2,437 m: 4
914 to 1,523 m: 16
under 914 m: 17

Heliports:
1

Roadways:
total: 2,700 km
paved: 1,620 km
unpaved: 1,080 km
country comparison to the world: 170

Merchant marine:
total: 1,160
by type: barge carrier 1, bulk carrier 238, cargo 170, carrier 2, chemical tanker 87, combination ore/oil 8, container 57, liquefied gas 71, passenger 102, passenger/cargo 26, petroleum tanker 225, refrigerated cargo 97, roll on/roll off 13, specialized tanker 2, vehicle carrier 61

foreign-owned: 1,069 (Angola 6, Australia 1, Belgium 6, Bermuda 15, Brazil 1, Canada 96, Croatia 1, Cyprus 23, Denmark 69, Finland 8, France 15, Germany 30, Greece 225, Guernsey 6, Hong Kong 3, Indonesia 2, Ireland 3, Italy 1, Japan 88, Jordan 2, Kuwait 1, Malaysia 13, Monaco 8, Montenegro 2, Netherlands 23, Nigeria 2, Norway 186, Poland 34, Saudi Arabia 16, Singapore 7, South Korea 1, Spain 6, Sweden 11, Switzerland 1, Thailand 4, Turkey 3, UAE 23, UK 18, US 109)
registered in other countries: 6 (Panama 6) (2010)
country comparison to the world: 10

Ports and terminals:
major seaport(s): Freeport, Nassau, South Riding Point
container port(s) (TEUs): Freeport (1,116,272)

cruise port(s): Nassau

MILITARY

Military branches:
Royal Bahamas Defense Force: Land Force, Navy, Air Wing

Military service age and obligation:
18 years of age for voluntary male and female service; no conscription (2012)

TRANSNATIONAL ISSUES

Disputes - international:
disagrees with the US on the alignment of the northern axis of a potential maritime boundary

Refugees and internally displaced persons:
stateless persons: 11

Illicit drugs:
transshipment point for cocaine and marijuana bound for US and Europe; offshore financial center

IMPORTANT INFORMATION FOR UNDERSTANSING BAHAMAS

PROFILE

OFFICIAL NAME: Commonwealth of The Bahamas

Geography

Area: 13,939 sq. km. (5,382 sq. mi.); slightly larger than Connecticut and Rhode Island combined.
Cities: *Capital*--Nassau, New Providence. *Second-largest city*--Freeport, Grand Bahama.
Terrain: Low and flat.
Climate: Semitropical.

People

Nationality: *Noun and adjective*--Bahamian(s).
Population (2009 official est.): 342,400; (unofficial, including an estimated 30,000 undocumented Haitians): 370,000.
Annual growth rate (2009 est.): 1.24%.
Ethnic groups: African 85%, European 12%, Asian and Hispanic 3%.
Religions: Baptist (35%), Roman Catholic, Anglican, Evangelical Protestants, Methodist, Church of God, Rastafarian, traditional African.
Language: English (official); Creole.
Education (2003): *Years compulsory*--through age 16. *Attendance*--92%. *Literacy*--95.5%.
Health (2009 est.): *Infant mortality rate*--17.6/1,000. *Life expectancy*--73.15 years.
Work force (2008): 191,595; majority employed in the tourism, government, and financial services sectors.

Government

Type: Constitutional parliamentary democracy.
Independence: July 10, 1973.
Branches: *Executive*--British monarch (nominal head of state), governor general (representative of the British monarch), prime minister (head of government), and cabinet. *Legislative*--bicameral Parliament (41-member elected House of Assembly, 16-member appointed Senate). *Judicial*--Privy Council in U.K., Court of Appeal, Supreme Court, and magistrates' courts.
Political parties: Free National Movement (FNM), Progressive Liberal Party (PLP), Bahamas Democratic Movement (BDM).
Suffrage (2007): Universal over 18; 150,689 registered voters.

Economy

Natural resources: Salt, aragonite, timber, arable land.
Tourism (2004, including tourism-driven construction and manufacturing): 48% of GDP.
Government spending (current expenditure only 2008): 17.0% of GDP.
Financial services: 11.3% of GDP.
Business services and real estate: 17.7% of GDP.
Construction (2008; 11.4% of GDP): Products--largely tourism-related.
Manufacturing (2008; 3.3% of GDP): Products--plastics, pharmaceuticals, rum.
Agriculture and fisheries (2008; 1.2% of GDP): Products--fruits, vegetables, lobster, fish.
Trade (2007): *Exports* ($670 million)--mineral products and salt, rum, animal products, chemicals, fruits, and vegetables. *Export partners* (2007)--U.S. (71%), Canada (5.7%),

Netherlands (5.6%), France (4.9%), Germany (2.4%), U.K. (1.5%), South Africa (1.5%), China (1.5%). *Imports* ($3.104 billion)--foodstuffs and animals, machinery and transport equipment, manufactures, chemicals, mineral fuels. *Import partners* (2007)--U.S. (87.0%), Curacao (2.8%), Venezuela (2.1%), Puerto Rico (1.4%), Japan (1.1%).

PEOPLE

Eighty-five percent of the Bahamian population is of African heritage. About two-thirds of the population resides on New Providence Island (the location of Nassau). Many ancestors arrived in The Bahamas when the islands served as a staging area for the slave trade in the early 1800s. Others accompanied thousands of British loyalists who fled the American colonies during the Revolutionary War.

Haitians form the largest immigrant community in The Bahamas. 30,000-50,000 are estimated to be resident legally or illegally, concentrated on New Providence, Abaco and Eleuthera islands.

School attendance is compulsory between the ages of 5 and 16. The government fully operates 158 of the 210 primary and secondary schools in The Bahamas. The other 52 schools are privately operated. Enrollment for state primary and secondary schools is 50,332, with more than 16,000 students attending private schools. The College of The Bahamas, established in Nassau in 1974, provides programs leading to bachelors and associates degrees. Several non-Bahamian colleges also offer higher education programs in The Bahamas.

HISTORY

In 1492, Christopher Columbus made his first landfall in the Western Hemisphere in The Bahamas. Spanish slave traders later captured native Lucayan Indians to work in gold mines in Hispaniola, and within 25 years, all Lucayans perished. In 1647, a group of English and Bermudan religious refugees, the Eleutheran Adventurers, founded the first permanent European settlement in The Bahamas and gave Eleuthera Island its name. Similar groups of settlers formed governments in The Bahamas until the islands became a British Crown Colony in 1717.

The late 1600s to the early 1700s were the golden age for pirates and privateers. Many famous pirates and privateers--including Sir Francis Drake and Blackbeard--used the islands of The Bahamas as a base. The numerous islands and islets with their complex shoals and channels provided excellent hiding places for the plundering ships near well-traveled shipping lanes. The first Royal Governor, Woodes Rogers, brought law and order to The Bahamas in 1718 when he expelled the buccaneers.

During the American Revolution, American colonists loyal to the British flag settled in The Bahamas. These Loyalists and new settlers from Britain brought Colonial building skills and agricultural expertise. Until 1834, when Britain abolished slavery, they also brought slaves, importing the ancestors of many modern Bahamians from Western Africa.

Proximity to the U.S. continued to provide opportunity for illegal shipping activity. In the course of the American Civil War, The Bahamas prospered as a center of Confederate blockade-running. During Prohibition, the islands served as a base for American rumrunners. Today, The Bahamas is a major transshipment point for narcotics on the way to the U.S.

Bahamians achieved self-government through a series of constitutional and political steps, attaining internal self-government in 1964 and full independence within the Commonwealth on

July 10, 1973. Since independence, The Bahamas has continued to develop into a major tourist and financial services center.

GOVERNMENT AND POLITICAL CONDITIONS

The Bahamas is an independent member of the Commonwealth of Nations. It is a parliamentary democracy with regular elections. As a Commonwealth country, its political and legal traditions closely follow those of the United Kingdom. The Bahamas recognizes the British monarch as its formal head of state, while an appointed Governor General serves as the Queen's representative in The Bahamas. A bicameral legislature enacts laws under the 1973 constitution.

The House of Assembly consists of 41 members, elected from individual constituencies for 5-year terms. As under the Westminster system, the government may dissolve the Parliament and call elections at any time. The House of Assembly performs all major legislative functions. The leader of the majority party serves as prime minister and head of government. The Cabinet consists of at least nine members, including the prime minister and ministers of executive departments. They answer politically to the House of Assembly.

The Senate consists of 16 members appointed by the Governor General, including nine on the advice of the prime minister, four on the advice of the Leader of the Opposition, and three on the advice of the prime minister after consultation with the Leader of the Opposition.

The Governor General appoints the Chief Justice of the Supreme Court on the advice of the prime minister and the Leader of the Opposition. The Governor General appoints the other justices with the advice of a judicial commission. The Privy Council of the United Kingdom serves as the highest appellate court.

Local government districts elect councils for town planning, business licenses, traffic issues and maintaining government buildings. In some large districts, lower level town councils also have minor responsibilities.

For decades, the white-dominated United Bahamian Party (UBP) ruled The Bahamas, then a dependency of the United Kingdom, while a group of influential white merchants, known as the "Bay Street Boys," dominated the local economy. In 1953, Bahamians dissatisfied with UBP rule formed the opposition Progressive Liberal Party (PLP). Under the leadership of Lynden Pindling, the PLP won control of the government in 1967 and led The Bahamas to full independence in 1973.

A coalition of PLP dissidents and former UBP members formed the Free National Movement (FNM) in 1971. Former PLP cabinet minister and member of Parliament Hubert Ingraham became leader of the FNM in 1990, upon the death of Sir Cecil Wallace-Whitfield. Under the leadership of Ingraham, the FNM won control of the government from the PLP in the August 1992 general elections. The PLP regained power in 2002 under the leadership of Perry Christie, but the FNM, again led by Ingraham, returned to government by capturing 23 of the 41 seats in the House of Assembly during the May 2007 election. The next election must be held no later than May 2012.

In July 2008 Prime Minister Hubert Ingraham announced changes to ministerial portfolios and the creation of two additional ministries--the Ministry of Youth, Sports, and Culture and the Ministry of the Environment.

Principal Government Officials

Governor Gen., **Arthur FOULKES**
Prime Min., **Perry CHRISTIE**
Dep. Prime Min., **Philip DAVIS**
Min. of Agriculture, Marine Resources, & Local Govt., **Alfred GRAY**
Min. of Education, Science, & Technology, **Jerome FITZGERALD**
Min. of the Environment & Housing, **Kendred DORSETT**
Min. of Finance, **Perry CHRISTIE**
Min. of Financial Services, **Ryan PINDER**
Min. of Foreign Affairs & Immigration, **Frederick MITCHELL**
Min. for Grand Bahama, **Michael DARVILLE**
Min. of Health, **Perry GOMEZ**
Min. of Labor & National Insurance, **Shane GIBSON**
Min. of Legal Affairs, **Allyson MAYNARD GIBSON**
Min. of National Security, **Bernard NOTTAGE**
Min. of Social Services, **Melanie GRIFFIN**
Min. of Tourism, **Obediah WILCHCOMBE**
Min. of Transport & Aviation, **Glenys Hanna MARTIN**
Min. of Works & Urban Development, **Philip DAVIS**
Min. of Youth, Sports, & Culture, **Daniel JOHNSON**
Attorney Gen., **Allyson MAYNARD GIBSON**
Governor, Central Bank, **Wendy CRAIGG**
Ambassador to the US, **Cornelius SMITH**
Permanent Representative to the UN, New York, **Paulette A. BETHEL**

The Bahamas maintains an embassy in the United States at 2220 Massachusetts Ave., NW, Washington, DC 20008 (tel: 202-319-2660) and Consulates General in New York at 231 East 46th Street, New York, NY 10017 (tel: 212-421-6420); in Miami at Suite 818, Ingraham Building, 25 SE Second Ave., Miami, FL 33131 (tel: 305-373-6295); and in Atlanta at 2970 Clairmont Road, Atlanta, GA 30329 (tel: 404-636-3911).

ECONOMY

Currency	Bahamian dollar (BSD)
Fiscal year	1 July - 30 June
Trade organisations	WTO, CARICOM
	Statistics
GDP	$11.04 billion (2012 est. PPP)
GDP rank	140th (nominal) / 153rd (PPP)
GDP growth	2.5%
GDP per capita	$31,300
GDP by sector	agriculture: 2.1%, industry: 7.1%, services: 90.8% (2012 est.)
Inflation (CPI)	2.5%
Population below poverty line	9.3%
Labour force	184,000
Labour force by occupation	agriculture 5%, industry 5%, tourism 50%, other services 40%
Unemployment	14.2%
Main industries	tourism, banking, cement, oil transshipment, salt, rum, aragonite, pharmaceuticals, spiral-welded steel pipe
Ease-of-doing-business rank	121st (2017)
	External
Exports	$790 million

Export goods	mineral products and salt, animal products, rum, chemicals, fruit and vegetables
Main export partners	United States 24.1% Singapore 18.1% Colombia 13.4% Panama 9.8% Taiwan 5.7% Malaysia 4.8% (2013 est.)[2]
Imports	$2.882 billion (2012 est.)
Import goods	machinery and transport equipment, manufactures, chemicals, mineral fuels; food and live animals
Main import partners	United States 29.9% Mexico 20.1% Singapore 8.7% South Korea 6.7% China 5.0% Venezuela 4.3% Canada 4.2%
	Public finances
Public debt	$342.6 million
Revenues	$1.5 billion
Expenses	$1.8 billion
Economic aid	recipient: $5 million
Credit rating	BBB+ (Domestic) BBB+ (Foreign) A- (T&C Assessment) (Standard & Poor's)

The Bahamas is driven by tourism and financial services. Tourism and tourism-driven construction and manufacturing provide an estimated 60% of the gross domestic product (GDP). Tourism employs about half the Bahamian work force. In 2008, 4.6 million tourists visited The Bahamas, 85% from the United States. This was a 4.5% decrease in overall visitors when compared to 2007. There are about 110 U.S.-affiliated businesses operating in The Bahamas, and most are associated with tourism and banking. With few domestic resources and little industry, The Bahamas imports nearly all its food and manufactured goods from the United States. American goods and services tend to be favored by Bahamians due to cultural similarities and heavy exposure to American advertising. The Bahamian economy, due to its heavy dependence on U.S. tourism and trade, is deeply affected by U.S. economic performance.

The Bahamas is currently experiencing an economic downturn as a result of the worldwide economic recession. Tourism numbers dropped significantly during the last quarter of 2008, and approximately 1,000 tourism sector employees have been laid off since September 2008. The Bahamas is focusing on construction and other infrastructure projects in an effort to boost the economy and create employment. Future goals include continued development of tourism properties through large-scale private sector investment, including increased Bahamian ownership, redevelopment of the Grand Bahama economy following major hurricane losses in 2004, and the expansion of the robust Bahamian financial sector.
In addition to the decrease in tourism, other economic challenges facing The Bahamas include meeting continued employment demands, jumpstarting a lagging privatization process, and monitoring increasing levels of government debt. Another major challenge for Bahamians will be to prepare for hemispheric free trade. Currently, Bahamians do not pay income or sales

taxes. Most government revenue is derived from high tariffs and import fees. Reduction of trade barriers will probably require some form of taxation to replace revenues when the country becomes a part of the Free Trade Area of the Americas (FTAA). As evident by domestic opposition to the Caribbean Single Market Economy (CSME), the advantages of free trade have been hard for the government to sell. Despite some domestic opposition, the Bahamian Government signed an Economic Partnership Agreement (EPA) with the European Union (EU) in December 2008.

A number of planned hotel projects have promised to increase economic growth and create short- and long-term employment. The Atlantis Resort and Casino on Paradise Island remains a major tourist draw and an engine of the economy. The future of the Baha Mar hotel project was called into question after casino operator Harrah's pulled out of the deal in March 2008. However, in March 2009 the ExIm Bank of China formally agreed to finance the stalled project, estimated at $3.2 billion in funding. The government promises to expand Nassau International Airport and has turned over management to private operators. The Bahamian Government also has adopted a proactive approach to courting foreign investors and has conducted major investment missions to the Far East, Europe, Latin America, India, and Canada. The government continues to pay particular attention to China to encourage tourism and investment. The Chinese are funding the construction of a new $30 million sports stadium in New Providence and may provide an addition $100 million in road construction projects. While the FNM government has expressed a desire to increase Bahamian ownership interests in developments, The Bahamas' dependence on foreign investment is unlikely to change.

Financial services constitute the second-most important sector of the Bahamian economy, accounting for up to 15% of GDP, due to the country's status as a tax haven and offshore banking center. The Stop Tax Haven Abuse bill, which has been proposed in the U.S. Congress and which names The Bahamas as one of 34 secrecy jurisdictions, has generated considerable discussion in local media and amongst politicians. Many Bahamians feel the inclusion of The Bahamas in such a bill would result in significant job losses in the financial services sector. As of 2005, the government had licensed 262 banks and trust companies in The Bahamas. The Bahamas promulgated the International Business Companies (IBC) Act in January 1990 to enhance the country's status as a leading financial center. The act served to simplify and reduce the cost of incorporating offshore companies in The Bahamas. Within 9 years, more than 84,000 IBC-type companies had been established. In February 1991, the government also legalized the establishment of Asset Protection Trusts in The Bahamas. In 2000, in response to multilateral organizations' concerns, the government passed a legislative package of stronger measures to better regulate the financial sector and prevent money laundering in the country's banking sector, including creation of a Financial Intelligence Unit and enforcement of "know-your-customer" rules. Some of these measures have been challenged in Bahamian courts, and the number of offshore banks registered in The Bahamas has declined substantially since 2002. As many as half of the IBCs have also closed shop. As a result, the government is considering additional legislation to keep the industry competitive while complying with international standards, including possible reform of the regulatory structure and the signing of more Tax Information Exchange Agreements.

Agriculture and fisheries together account for about 1% of GDP. The Bahamas exports lobster and some fish but does not raise these items commercially. There is no large-scale agriculture, and most agricultural products are consumed domestically. Following an outbreak of citrus canker on Abaco in 2005, The Bahamas lost a main agricultural export, and the Ministry of Agriculture banned the export of plant materials from Abaco. The Bahamas imports more than $250 million in foodstuffs per year, representing about 80% of its food consumption.

The Bahamian Government maintains the value of the Bahamian dollar on a par with the U.S. dollar. The Bahamas is a beneficiary of the U.S.-Caribbean Basin Trade Partnership Act (CBTPA), Canada's CARIBCAN program, and the EU's Economic Partnership Agreement. Although The Bahamas participates in the political aspects of the Caribbean Community (CARICOM), it has not entered into joint economic initiatives, like the CSME, with other Caribbean states.

The Bahamas has a few notable industrial firms: the pharmaceutical firm PFC Bahamas (formerly Syntex); the BORCO oil facility, doing business as Vooak Terminal Bahamas; Sands Beer; and the Grand Bahama Brewery, all in Freeport; and the Commonwealth Brewery in Nassau, which produces Heineken, Guinness, and Kalik beers. Other industries include sun-dried sea salt in Great Inagua, a wet dock facility in Freeport for repair of cruise ships, and mining of aragonite--a type of limestone with several industrial uses--from the sea floor at Ocean Cay.

The Hawksbill Creek Agreement established a duty-free zone in Freeport, The Bahamas' second-largest city, with a nearby industrial park to encourage foreign industrial investment. The Hong Kong-based firm Hutchison Whampoa operates the container port in Freeport. The Bahamian Parliament approved legislation in 1993 that extended most Freeport tax and duty exemptions through 2054.

Business Environment

The Bahamas offers attractive features to the potential investor: a stable democratic environment, relief from personal and corporate income taxes, timely repatriation of corporate profits, proximity to the United States with extensive air and telecommunications links, and a good pool of skilled professional workers. The Government of The Bahamas welcomes foreign investment in tourism and banking and has declared an interest in agricultural and industrial investments to generate local employment, particularly in white-collar or skilled jobs. Despite its interest in foreign investment to diversify the economy, the Bahamian Government responds to local concerns about foreign competition and tends to protect Bahamian business and labor interests. As a result of domestic resistance to foreign investment and high labor costs, growth can stagnate in sectors which the government wishes to diversify.

The country's infrastructure is best developed in the principal cities of Nassau and Freeport, where there are relatively good paved roads and international airports. Electricity is generally reliable, although many businesses have their own backup generators. In Nassau, there are three daily newspapers, several weeklies, and international newspapers available for sale. There also are six radio stations. Both Nassau and Freeport have a television station. Cable TV and satellite also are available locally and provide most American programs with some Canadian and European channels.

Areas of Opportunity

The best U.S. export opportunities remain in the traditional areas of foodstuffs and manufactured goods: vehicles and automobile parts; hotel, restaurant, and medical supplies; and computers and electronics. Bahamian tastes in consumer products roughly parallel those in the United States. Merchants in southern Florida have found it profitable to advertise in Bahamian publications. Most imports are subject to high but nondiscriminatory tariffs.

FOREIGN RELATIONS

The Bahamas has strong bilateral relationships with the United States and the United Kingdom, represented by an ambassador in Washington and High Commissioner in London. The Bahamas also associates closely with other nations of the Caribbean Community

(CARICOM). The Bahamas has an ambassador to Haiti and works closely with the United States and CARICOM on political and migration issues related to Haiti. The Bahamas has diplomatic relations with Cuba, including embassies in each other's capitals. A repatriation agreement was signed with Cuba in 1996, and there are commercial and cultural contacts between the two countries. The Bahamas also enjoys a strengthening relationship with China. The Commonwealth of The Bahamas became a member of the United Nations in 1973 and the Organization of American States in 1982.

The Bahamas holds membership in a number of international organizations: the UN and some specialized and related agencies, including Food and Agriculture Organization (FAO), International Civil Aviation Organization (ICAO), and the International Labor Organization (ILO); International Monetary Fund (IMF); International Telecommunication Union (ITU); World Bank; World Meteorological Organization (WMO); World Health Organization (WHO); OAS and related agencies, including Inter-American Development Bank (IDB), Caribbean Development Bank (CDB), and Pan-American Health Organization (PAHO); the Caribbean Community (CARICOM), excluding its Common Market; the International Criminal Police Organization (INTERPOL); Universal Postal Union (UPU); International Maritime Organization (IMO); World Intellectual Property Organization (WIPO); and obtained observer status in the World Trade Organization (WTO) in 2001.

U.S.-BAHAMIAN RELATIONS

The United States historically has had close economic and commercial relations with The Bahamas. The countries share ethnic and cultural ties, especially in education, and The Bahamas is home to approximately 30,000 American residents. In addition, there are about 110 U.S.-related businesses in The Bahamas and, in 2008, 85% of the 4.6 million tourists visiting the country were American.

As a neighbor, The Bahamas and its political stability are especially important to the United States. The U.S. and the Bahamian Government have worked together on reducing crime and addressing migration issues. With the closest island only 45 miles from the coast of Florida, The Bahamas often is used as a gateway for drugs and illegal aliens bound for the United States. The United States and The Bahamas cooperate closely to handle these threats. U.S. assistance and resources have been essential to Bahamian efforts to mitigate the persistent flow of illegal narcotics and migrants through the archipelago. The United States and The Bahamas also actively cooperate on law enforcement, civil aviation, marine research, meteorology, and agricultural issues. The U.S. Navy operates an underwater research facility on Andros Island.

The Department of Homeland Security's Bureau of Customs and Border Protection maintains "preclearance" facilities at the airports in Nassau and Freeport. Travelers to the U.S. are interviewed and inspected before departure, allowing faster connection times in the U.S.

Principal U.S. Officials
Ambassador--vacant
Chargé d' Affaires, a.i.--Timothy Zuniga-Brown
Management Officer--David Elmo
Consular Section Chief--Robin Haase
Political-Economic Section Chief--Jefferson Dubel
Public Affairs Officer--Jefferson Dubel

The U.S. Embassy is located at 42 Queen Street, Nassau (tel. 242-322-1181; telex 20-138); the local postal address is P.O. Box N-8197, Nassau, The Bahamas.

Other Contact Information
U.S. Department of Commerce
International Trade Administration
Office of Latin America and the Caribbean
14th and Constitution, NW
Washington, DC 20230
Tel: 202-482-0704; 800-USA-TRADE
Fax: 202-482-0464

Caribbean/Latin American Action
1818 N Street, NW, Suite 310
Washington, DC 20036
Tel: 202-466-7464
Fax: 202-822-0075

TRAVEL AND BUSINESS INFORMATION

The U.S. Department of State's Consular Information Program advises Americans traveling and residing abroad through Country Specific Information, Travel Alerts, and Travel Warnings. **Country Specific Information** exists for all countries and includes information on entry and exit requirements, currency regulations, health conditions, safety and security, crime, political disturbances, and the addresses of the U.S. embassies and consulates abroad. **Travel Alerts** are issued to disseminate information quickly about terrorist threats and other relatively short-term conditions overseas that pose significant risks to the security of American travelers. **Travel Warnings** are issued when the State Department recommends that Americans avoid travel to a certain country because the situation is dangerous or unstable.

For the latest security information, Americans living and traveling abroad should regularly monitor the Department's Bureau of Consular Affairs Internet web site at http://www.travel.state.gov, where the current Worldwide Caution, Travel Alerts, and Travel Warnings can be found. Consular Affairs Publications, which contain information on obtaining passports and planning a safe trip abroad, are also available at http://www.travel.state.gov. For additional information on international travel, see http://www.usa.gov/Citizen/Topics/Travel/International.shtml.

The Department of State encourages all U.S. citizens traveling or residing abroad to register via the State Department's travel registration website or at the nearest U.S. embassy or consulate abroad. Registration will make your presence and whereabouts known in case it is necessary to contact you in an emergency and will enable you to receive up-to-date information on security conditions.

Emergency information concerning Americans traveling abroad may be obtained by calling 1-888-407-4747 toll free in the U.S. and Canada or the regular toll line 1-202-501-4444 for callers outside the U.S. and Canada.

The National Passport Information Center (NPIC) is the U.S. Department of State's single, centralized public contact center for U.S. passport information. Telephone: 1-877-4-USA-PPT (1-877-487-2778); TDD/TTY: 1-888-874-7793. Passport information is available 24 hours, 7 days a week. You may speak with a representative Monday-Friday, 8 a.m. to 10 p.m., Eastern Time, excluding federal holidays.

Travelers can check the latest health information with the U.S. Centers for Disease Control and Prevention in Atlanta, Georgia. A hotline at 800-CDC-INFO (800-232-4636) and a web site at http://wwwn.cdc.gov/travel/default.aspx give the most recent health advisories, immunization recommendations or requirements, and advice on food and drinking water safety for regions and countries. The CDC publication "Health Information for International Travel" can be found at http://wwwn.cdc.gov/travel/contentYellowBook.aspx.

THE CAPITAL MARKETS IN THE CARIBBEAN[1]

Accordingly, the CARICOM Secretariat has been mandated to develop and implement a Public Education and Awareness Programme across the Region. These booklets which were done for the programme are designed to enhance investors' knowledge of the functioning of the regional stock exchange/ market and carry the following titles: Volume 1: The Capital Market in the Caribbean; Volume 2: Buying and Selling Securities; Volume 3: The Importance of the Regional Stock Exchange; and, Volume 4: Cross Border Operations. These four volumes are also intended to provide an appreciation of:

- the role of investment in economic growth and development,
- the benefits of a diversified investment portfolio; and,
- the rationale of regional policy makers in encouraging the development of a regional capital market.

INTRODUCTION

Investing in stocks is a relatively new area for a number of Caribbean people. For a number of people, investment means buying a house or putting money in the bank. This view however, is slowly changing as more and more people are putting money in other areas of investment. As part of the mandate to the CARICOM Secretariat to educate the regional public, a monograph series has been developed , aimed at sensitizing the public on common issues in the area of regional investment. The series answer many questions about investing across the Region and provide some insight into the operations of the Regional Stock Exchange and investment in general. Caribbean people are realizing that they can no longer rely on the domestic economy for maximizing their financial goals and are seeking other avenues for that wealth creation. By this is meant getting the most out of a limited amount of income available to the average household.

Whenever an individual is thinking of making a new investment, one of the first thing to do is to get some basic research about the company, its principals and the investment. This is even more important when undertaking investment outside your domestic market. It is important that you read as much about the company as you can in order to know exactly what you are investing your money in. Knowing that information is hard to come by, The CARICOM Secretariat is producing this monograph series in an effort to keep the regional public informed about investment.

THE CAPITAL MARKET AND CARICOM[2]

To really understand the capital market it is important to understand the concept of a market. A market is a place where people meet to buy and sell goods. Most Caribbean people are familiar with the markets where ground provisions and other items are sold. At these markets which have a fixed location there are a number of buyers and sellers. These buyers can compare prices and then make their selection after they are satisfied that they are getting the best value for their money. In these markets the sellers of the goods have the benefit of reaching a number of buyers

[1] Prepared by: **Ms. Enid E. Bissember** Economic Intelligence & Policy Unit Eddy Grant Annexe CARICOM Secretariat 54 High Street Kingston Georgetown **GUYANA**. **for The Regional Capital Market Committee Educational and Awareness Program**

[2] Carebbean Community and Common Market

in one place and this saves time and money. If there are a number of buyers wanting a particular item then naturally the seller will be able to get more for it than if there were only a few people who want the item. The seller would then set the price based on the demand for the commodity.

The capital market operates in the much the same way. It is where business people and investors are brought together some want to raise capital and others want a return on their funds.

There are a number of institutions that make up the capital market. These include but are not limited to:-

- merchant banks/ investment banks
- insurance companies
- finance companies
- unit trusts
- stock exchanges

THE PRIMARY MARKET

An investor who purchases newly issued securities by a public company is participating in the primary market. When such securities are purchased the net proceeds go directly to the issuing company. This is the only time when the funds go to the company. The primary market directs funds from investors to companies and governments where it is put to use to help in the overall growth and development of the firm and economies. The primary market can provide the funds that are needed by firms to add new product lines, improve the services offered to customers, and create new jobs. Investors who participate in the primary market have the opportunity to purchase securities(stocks/ shares, bonds, and debentures) directly from the company. In any economy the primary market is one of the engines of growth.

THE SECONDARY MARKET

An investor who resells existing securities is participating in the secondary market. These are markets where investors buy and sell securities among themselves and the money generated here goes from the buying investor to the selling investor. If there were no secondary markets investors who bought securities from a company would have to hang on to them or wait on the right opportunity to sell. They would not be able recover their investment as easily as with the existence of a secondary market. If investors can't make money by selling the securities they bought in the primary market then it would be very difficult for companies wanting to offer shares to do so .The secondary market is very useful and important to investors. It provides them with an avenue to buy and sell their securities at any time that they desire. Being able to buy and sell at any time adds liquidity to the market. An active secondary markets gives support to the primary market.

THE STOCK MARKET

A stock market is an important part of modern economies and a vital link between companies needing capital and investors with money to invest. Through investment in securities such as common stocks/ shares investors become part owners of the companies of their choice and are able to participate in the companies' growth and development. In turn , companies which raise capital from the sale of common stocks are able to do the things that they would not have been able to do if they had to rely on another source of funds. This source might require regular payment of interest and principal at times when the company might not be in a position to do so perhaps because it is expanding its product line or modernizing its plant. Obtaining funds in the stock market allows the company to do all that and at the end of specified intervals declare a dividend for its shareholders.

THE STOCK EXCHANGE

Most people have heard of stock exchanges. They are a key element in the capital markets . A stock exchange is the place where buyers and sellers of securities (e.g. stocks, bonds,) trade with each other and where prices of the securities are established based on supply and demand. The more securities that are available for sale the lower the price at which the buyer can obtain those securities and the less that are available for sale the more the prospective buyer would be expected to pay . Companies can use the stock exchange to raise new capital , but most of the trading that is often talked about is trading among investors which is called secondary trading. The seller is no longer the company which issued the security, but someone who bought the security earlier, either as a new issue from the company or from another investor , and now would like to sell. The buyer of the security is another investor. The stock exchange is better known as a place where stocks, which have already, been issued can be traded among investors.

THE REGIONAL STOCK EXCHANGE

The idea for the development of a Regional stock exchange/ market emerged in 1989 on the initiative of the Government of Jamaica. In 1991 the three existing stock exchanges in the Region; the Barbados Securities Exchange, the Jamaica Stock Exchange and the Trinidad and Tobago Stock Exchange entered into an arrangement for cross border trading in equity. A Regional stock exchange/market was seen as an integral part of the deepening and widening of the integration process in CARICOM.

The objectives of the regional stock exchange have been identified as:

- to promote the movement of capital across the Region;
- to increase investment opportunities;
- to encourage optimum financing for CARICOM firms irrespective of where the entity resides; and,
- to increase the attractiveness of the region as an area for investment, both by regional and non-regional investors.

The Grand Anse Declaration agreed to a scheme for the movement of capital across the region; starting at first with the three existing exchanges (Barbados, Jamaica, Trinidad and Tobago). An arrangement was worked out and implemented in April 1991 under which those stock exchanges

(Barbados, Jamaica and Trinidad and Tobago) undertook to cross list and cross trade stocks.

MEMBERS OF THE REGIONAL STOCK EXCHANGE

The members of the Regional Stock Exchange are the stock exchanges of Barbados, Jamaica and Trinidad and Tobago.

THE REGIONAL STOCK EXCHANGE

The regional stock exchange is not a physical entity but an agreement of cooperation to facilitate the purchase and sale of shares cross border. There is no building called the Regional stock exchange. Instead the regional stock exchange is an arrangement entered into by the existing stock exchanges to facilitate the purchase and sale of securities cross border. The stock exchanges of Barbados, Jamaica and Trinidad and Tobago are part of this arrangement. In this market information is exchanged regarding prices and amounts so that the investors' representative who wants to buy or sell a securities can find it at the best price.

The telephone is very important in the Regional Capital Market arrangements.

ADDRESS AND CONTACT NUMBERS FOR MEMBERS OF THE REGIONAL STOCK EXCHANGE

1. SECURITIES EXCHANGE OF BARBADOS

5th Floor Central Bank
Church Village
Bridgetown
St. Michael
BARBADOS

Tel: 246 436 9871/2
Fax: 246 429 8942
E-Mail: sebd@caribsurf.com

2. JAMAICA STOCK EXCHANGE

40 Harbour Street
Kingston
JAMAICA

Tel: 876 967 3271/4
Fax: 876 922-6966
E-Mail: jse@infochan.com

3. TRINIDAD & TOBAGO SECURITIES EXCHANGE

1 Ajax Street
Port-of-Spain
TRINIDAD AND TOBAGO

Tel: 868 627 1704 or 625 7148
Fax: 868 625 0089
E-Mail: tsttstockx@tstt.net.tt

OTHER IMPORTANT ADDRESS

CARIBBEAN COMMUNITY SECRETARIAT (CARICOM)
Bank of Guyana Building
P.O. Box 10827
Georgetown
GUYANA. SOUTH AMERICA

Tel: 592 2 52981; 69261-9
Fax: 592 2 57341, 592-2-67816
E-Mail: webmaster@caricom.org

THE CARIBBEAN COMMUNITY AND COMMON MARKET

In the late 1980s, the members of the Caribbean Community and Common Market (Caricom) consisted of Antigua and Barbuda, the Bahamas, Barbados, Belize, Dominica, Grenada, Guyana, Jamaica, Montserrat, St. Christopher (hereafter, St. Kitts) and Nevis, St. Lucia, St. Vincent and the Grenadines, and Trinidad and Tobago. The members faced problems typical of many developing societies: high birth rates, unemployment and an unskilled labor force, inadequate infrastructure, balance of payments constraints, and insufficient domestic savings to achieve development goals. In addition, Caricom members lacked diversified economies and were incapable of producing most capital goods and some basic consumer goods necessary for productive expansion. The Caricom members, therefore, were forced to rely heavily on imports of essential goods. As a result, development goals were subordinated because of the need to raise foreign exchange to pay for the imports.

Since 1981 the ability of Caricom members to raise the needed capital via export expansion has been severely limited by the lack of export diversification and the reliance on primary products and tourism services, which are extremely vulnerable to changing forces of demand, supply, and price in the international political economy. In the late 1980s, intraregional cooperation was urgently needed to create an atmosphere conducive to overcoming the handicaps of small market size, economic fragmentation, and external dependence.

Caricom's goal of regional integration was designed to serve as a catalyst for sustained growth in the short or medium term by allowing for market expansion, harmonization of production strategies, and development of economies of scale. Integration was also expected to promote industrial growth by eliminating excess capacity in the manufacturing sector and to stimulate investment in new sectors of the expanded market. The long-term hope was for balanced growth, minimal unemployment, a higher standard of living, and optimal use of available human and natural resources.

BACKGROUND AND OBJECTIVES

Following the example of the European Economic Community (EEC), many nations have organized themselves into regional integration organizations, such as Latin America's Central American Common Market, the Latin America Integration Association, and the Andean Pact. The Commonwealth Caribbean made a serious move toward establishing a unit of integration by creating the West Indies Federation in 1958. The federation, formed under the auspices of the British, was doomed from the start by nationalistic tendencies and the lack of taxation privileges, and it failed when Jamaica and Trinidad and Tobago attained independence and withdrew in 1962. Nevertheless, a few institutions, such as the University of the West Indies (UWI) and the Regional Shipping Council, were established under the short-lived federation and continue today. After the demise of the West Indies Federation, economist W. Arthur Lewis attempted to organize a smaller organization among the so-called Little Eight islands (Antigua and Barbuda, Barbados, Dominica, Grenada, Montserrat, St. Kitts-Nevis-Anguilla, St. Lucia, and St. Vincent and the Grenadines); however, his efforts yielded little success.

The first call for a regional Caribbean community was made in a January 1962 speech by Eric Williams, former prime minister and first head of state of independent Trinidad and Tobago. However, it was not until the late 1960s that advocates of a new federation focused their attention on the issue of regional integration. In July 1965, Antigua and Barbuda, Barbados, and Guyana signed the Treaty of Dickenson Bay, which established the Caribbean Free Trade Association (Carifta). Under the terms of the 1968 Treaty of St. John's, Carifta was widened to include Anguilla, Dominica, Grenada, Jamaica, St. Kitts and Nevis, St. Lucia, Montserrat, St. Vincent and the Grenadines, and Trinidad and Tobago. Although a free-trade area was established, Carifta did not provide for the free movement of labor and capital or the coordination of agricultural, industrial, defense, and foreign policies. Thus, over the next five years, little progress was made toward creating a regionally integrated unit. In 1970 the prospect of Britain's joining the EEC alerted the islands to their vulnerability to any disruption in their preferential trading ties with Britain. In the same year, economists at the UWI issued a report contending that the creation of a free-trade area alone was not sufficient to procure full gains from regional integration. These events led to the development of the present Caricom structure.

In 1973 the Carifta members signed the Treaty of Chaguaramas, replacing the ineffective Carifta structure with Caricom. Caricom has three essential components: economic integration based on a regional common market; functional cooperation in such areas as culture, education, health, labor relations, tourism, and transportation; and coordination of foreign and defense policies. Although the regional common market is an integral part of the broader based community arrangements, it has a completely separate identity juridically. Thus, it was possible for the Bahamas to become a member of the community in 1983 without joining the Common Market. In 1981 the Eastern Caribbean islands of Antigua and Barbuda, Dominica, Grenada, Montserrat, St. Kitts and Nevis, St. Lucia, and St. Vincent and the Grenadines established an associate entity, the Organisation of Eastern Caribbean States (OECS--see Glossary), which replaced the West Indies States Association (WISA) as the islands' administrative body. The OECS coordinates development strategies among its members and provides for cooperation in economic, foreign policy, and defense matters. The OECS was created after studies indicated that most of the benefits derived from integration were flowing to the larger islands (especially Jamaica and Trinidad and Tobago) at the expense of the smaller.

INSTITUTIONAL STRUCTURE

The institutional structure of Caricom consists of the Heads of Government Conference, the Common Market Council of Ministers, the Caribbean Community Secretariat, and other special bodies (see fig. A, this appendix). Unlike in the EEC, each member has a right of veto. Decision making in Caricom, although centralized at some levels, is quite decentralized at others.

The Heads of Government Conference is the supreme decision making body. Each member of Caricom has one vote, and a unanimous vote is required to legislate decisions or to make policy recommendations. The conference determines the policies to be pursued by Caricom's related institutions. This conference also is responsible for concluding all treaties, making financial disbursements, and maintaining relations with other international organizations.

The Common Market Council of Ministers is the second principal body of Caricom and the principal body of the regional Common Market. The Common Market Council consists of one ministerial representative from each member. Decisions are made by unanimous vote, with minor exceptions. The council resolves problems and makes proposals to the Heads of Government Conference to achieve efficient development and operation of the Common Market.

The Caribbean Community Secretariat is Caricom's principal administrative component. The Secretariat operates to serve the interests of the region rather than those of each government. Although the Secretariat has no decision making-power, its discussions, studies, and projects have made it a dynamic element in the integration process.

Other offices responsible for specific sectoral aspects of regional integration are the nine Standing Committees of Ministers (health, education, labor, foreign affairs and defense policy, finance, agriculture, mines, industry, and transport). In addition, independent associate institutions include the Caribbean Development Bank (CDB), the Caribbean Examinations Council, the Council of Legal Education, the University of Guyana, the UWI, the Caribbean Meteorological Council, the Caribbean Food Corporation, the Regional Shipping Council, and the

Caribbean Marketing Enterprise. Finally, the Joint Consultative Group, comprising business, consumer, and trade groups, meets to review the integration process and ensure interest group participation in Caricom activities.

MARKET INTEGRATION MECHANISMS

Caricom seeks to achieve economic integration through market forces. The Common Market was established to promote intraregional trade. It achieves this through trade liberalization by removing duties, licensing arrangements, quotas, and other tariff and nontariff barriers to trade; the Rules of Origin; the Common External Tariff (CET) and the Common Protective Policy (CPP); and trade arrangements such as the Agricultural Marketing Protocol and the Oils and Fats Agreement.

The Common Market contains a number of important mechanisms for liberalizing trade. These include eliminating extraregional export duties, removing quantitative restrictions on regional exports, permitting free transit for products of members, and eliminating quantitative restrictions on imported goods. Article 28 of the Treaty of Chaguaramas permits the application of quantitative restrictions if the member has severe balance of payments problems. However, because of the invocation of this clause in 1977 by both Guyana and Jamaica and the continuing economic problems confronting the Caricom members, removal of this provision was being considered in 1987.

The Rules of Origin establish the conditions of eligibility of regional products so that they may be considered of Common Market origin and thus qualified for preferential treatment. In 1986 a new set of Rules of Origin was adopted to increase the use of regional products and promote employment, investment, and savings of foreign exchange. Given the scarcity of products within Caricom in the late 1980s, observers believed that achieving high levels of regional value-added worth even with the new Rules of Origin would be difficult.

The Treaty of Chaguaramas mandates gradually implementing the CET and CPP. The CET stimulates production by imposing low tariffs on capital goods and industrial raw materials and higher tariffs on finished products. The CPP standardizes quantitative restrictions to protect specific regional industrial sectors. Together, the CET and CPP, coupled with intraregional trade liberalization, were expected to stimulate reciprocal investment and trade among members. In reality, these had not been achieved by the late 1980s because of problems in implementing the CPP and excluding goods from the CET.

The final market integration mechanism aims at providing guaranteed markets and prices for Caricom exports to overcome the volatile trade in primary commodities. The Agricultural Marketing Protocol and the Oils and Fats Agreement regulate intraregional trade via certain buy-and-sell accords at fixed prices resulting from shortages or surpluses within Caricom. Caricom also has the Guaranteed Market Scheme, whereby in certain circumstances Jamaica, Barbados, and Trinidad and Tobago will purchase fixed quantities of agricultural products from the other members.

MECHANISMS OF COOPERATION IN MARKETING AND PRODUCTION

Joint regional action in production and marketing activities is viewed by Caricom as a means of coordinating and controlling each member's output to avoid injury to other members or to the entire region. Coordinating policies is also intended to encourage specialization and complementary production. One important mechanism in this regard is regional industrial programming aimed at promoting specialization and economic diversification and avoiding duplication of investment. Although regional industrial programming was first considered in 1973, concrete actions did not begin until 1985 with the completion of the first phase of regional industrial programming. Of the thirty-five projects originally considered, only twenty-three have been identified as feasible. Only sixteen had been implemented by 1986. The most cited example of industrial cooperation and integration was a regional alumina (see Glossary) refinery that was to use bauxite (see Glossary) from Jamaica and Guyana and oil from Trinidad and Tobago. Although the project was thoroughly discussed during the 1970s, it remained doubtful in the late 1980s that such a project would ever be realized. In addition, related agricultural programs offered joint efforts to provide extension, marketing, and research and development services to reduce unit costs, increase quality and yield, and slash imports of basic foodstuffs.

The Regional Food and Nutrition Strategy is the main instrument for Caricom's agricultural development. The strategy establishes a framework and identifies priorities for a regional approach to agricultural self- sufficiency. The Caribbean Food Corporation, founded in 1976, is the main mechanism for planning and implementing the strategy's objectives. Also, the Caribbean Food and Nutrition Institute was established by Caricom at the UWI in Mona, Jamaica.

Transportation is indispensable for effective trade, export promotion, and other integration objectives. Cooperation in maritime transportation is envisioned through the West Indies Shipping Corporation (WISCO), which was established in 1961 and restructured in 1975. WISCO theoretically provides services to all Caricom nations. In early 1987, however, Belize, Dominica, and St. Vincent and the Grenadines withdrew from WISCO, claiming they had received few benefits from the service. In the late 1980s, air transportation remained inadequate because of the lack of coordination among the existing airlines. Standardizing air transport by coordinating and planning routes and fares, as well as mergers, was necessary to improve service and reduce costs.

Tourism is important to the region by providing foreign exchange, increasing employment, encouraging the production of tourist-oriented products and services, and stimulating the construction of basic infrastructure. Some regional cooperation in tourism has been carried out by the Caribbean Tourism Association, the Caribbean Tourism Research and Development Centre (located in Barbados), and the Hotel Training School at the UWI in the Bahamas. Nevertheless, in the late 1980s further cooperation was needed to link the tourism sector to the rest of the economy and to establish regional tourism enterprises.

MECHANISMS OF FINANCIAL COOPERATION

Financial cooperation tries to fulfill the objectives of economic integration by facilitating payments for intraregional trade and by mobilizing investment funds to productive sectors of the economy. The principal vehicle for financial cooperation is Caricom's Multilateral Clearing Facility (CMCF). It was established in 1977 by the central banks and other financial entities of Caricom's members. The facility's objectives are to reduce the use of foreign exchange and expedite intraregional payments through credit and other financial arrangements. Other related mechanisms include harmonizing exchange rates by pegging the six existing currencies to the United States dollar and by issuing regional traveler's checks through the Central Bank of Trinidad and Tobago. Finally, the CDB contributes to the equitable development of the region by providing low-interest loans for projects and related integration plans.

FUNCTIONAL COOPERATION

The Treaty of Chaguaramas also envisioned coordinating efforts in many noneconomic areas. The Caricom structure has formalized and expanded this kind of cooperation to include meteorological services and hurricane insurance; health and nutrition services; technical assistance; public utilities; education and job training; broadcasts, printed media, and information; culture and language; social security, labor, and industrial relations; science and technology; and harmonizing the laws and legal systems within Caricom. This cooperation has been successful in improving services to the members (especially the smaller ones) and lowering costs of activities through joint ventures. The regional university and health and nutrition systems are examples of successful functional cooperation.

COORDINATION OF DEFENSE AND FOREIGN POLICIES

The Heads of Government Conference and the Standing Committee of Ministers of Foreign Affairs and Defence Policy are responsible for coordinating the defense and foreign policies of members to increase their international bargaining power. Caricom has been able to present a regional foreign policy position in defense of the principles of regional security and nonintervention; support of the territorial integrity of Guyana and Belize in their border disputes; and various negotiations for the Lomé Convention (see Glossary), by which many Third World nations have gained preferential access to EEC markets and economic assistance.

A BRIEF EVALUATION OF THE INTEGRATION EFFORT

One method of evaluating Caricom's integration efforts is to look at three of its principal goals: defense and foreign policy coordination, functional cooperation, and economic and trade cooperation. In the late 1980s, some positive results had been achieved in defense and foreign policy coordination. Caribbean expressions of solidarity on issues of regional security and territorial integrity focused international attention on the region and strengthened Caricom's bargaining position in negotiations with regional and extraregional nations and in international forums. Ultimately, however, parochial concerns have always overshadowed regional interests. The ideological pluralism of the region and the often drastic changes in government orientation have hurt the coordination process through bilateralism and polarization of interests.

Functional cooperation had improved by the late 1980s, as reflected in the successful regional air transport, education, and health systems. However, Caricom had not expanded beyond these programs to develop common cultural and political linkages. Although a Caribbean parliament could potentially be an important force, in the late 1980s none appeared likely to materialize. Many observers argued that Caricom had spread itself too thin and should concentrate on solving problems rather than expanding.

Economic and trade cooperation had also improved. Examples of such improvements are Caricom's collective ability to mobilize large volumes of external capital, to gain greater access to third-country markets, to facilitate significant financial transfers to its members (especially to those not producing or refining oil), and to achieve a fair degree of access to internal markets. Nevertheless, two outstanding shortcomings remained: the failure to achieve significant benefits from the complementary use of the region's human and natural resources and the inability to formulate a common policy vis-à-vis foreign investment. Both of these issues have immense significance for the long-term development objectives of greater self-reliance and reduced external dependence.

Although the increase in intraregional trade in the 1973-81 period consisted largely of manufactured consumer products not previously traded, such an increase indicated neither diversification nor specialization of production as envisioned by Caricom's designers. On the contrary, duplication of production was evident. When coupled with the foreign exchange crisis and the weak extraregional trade performance since 1981, the nations have been forced to borrow from abroad; this has caused increased foreign debt and reduced imports of consumer goods, which comprise much intraregional trade. The Caribbean Community Secretariat reported that the decline in intraregional trade was approximately 33 percent in 1986, following declines of 3.3 percent in 1985, 10.9 percent in 1984, and 12.2 percent in 1983. Finally, many observers have noted the polarized development patterns and disproportionate gains from Caricom's integration mechanisms. Nevertheless, this polarization may not be an inherent fault of Caricom, but rather the result of a political economy that many argue continues to be biased toward the more developed nations. Thus, simple changes in trade patterns could not modify the situation without substantial structural change.

Since its inception, Caricom has experienced continuous crises. These have occurred to such a degree that many observers have come to regard the situation as a natural condition associated with developing nations, especially in light of external debt and trade constriction. However, in 1987 a group of Caribbean experts expressed cautious optimism because the institutional framework of the community remained intact, intraregional dialogue was maintained, and trade and functional cooperation continued to show resilience.

EVENTS AFFECTING THE COMMUNITY IN THE 1980S

A purposeful and cooperative spirit characterized Caricom's seventh summit conference, which was held in Guyana in July 1986. The highlights of this conference included establishing a regional Export Credit Facility (ECF) by July 1987 and implementing the regional industrial programming by late 1986.

In a declaration published at the end of the summit, Caricom leaders decided to implement the articles dealing with external trade, industrial policy, and joint development of resources. The creation of the ECF (ratified in May 1987) was aimed at providing pre- and post-shipment credit for Caricom manufacturers exporting goods both inside and outside Caricom, excluding such traditional products as bananas, bauxite, oil, and sugar. The industrial policy was intended to encourage regional joint ventures and investment initiatives geared toward improving the production structure of the Caricom members.

Approximately 25 percent of the funding for the ECF--around US$75 million--will be subscribed by the Caricom nations. The remainder will be raised through loans from the CDB, the World Bank (see Glossary), and other sources. Colombia has offered to provide technical assistance and will help to coordinate the ECF program. At the seventh summit conference, talks continued on reactivating the CMCF, whose activities were suspended in 1983 after reaching its credit ceiling via emergency loans to Jamaica and Guyana. Related to this, Barbados and Guyana discussed a US$100 million joint venture in lumber production and marketing that should help Guyana finance its debt to the CMCF. (In 1987 Jamaica was several years in arrears on its debt to the CMCF.)

Much of the discussion at the seventh summit conference focused on the 1984 Nassau Agreement. This agreement, aimed at reducing trade barriers and harmonizing external tariffs, recommended the use of the CET, not quantitative restrictions, to protect industrial development. The agreement also advocated removing price controls, developing incentives for industrial production, and improving training programs for displaced workers. A proposal for creating a common monetary unit was rejected on the grounds that the frequent fluctuation in Caricom's exchange rates would undermine such efforts. Nevertheless, summit participants decided that the members should consult Caricom's financial institutions if planning devaluations or pegging exchange rates.

In addition to the collective decisions reached at this summit, certain bilateral accords and negotiations were announced. One principal accord involved air transport between Jamaica and Trinidad and Tobago. Air Jamaica was granted landing rights in Port-of-Spain (with intermediate locations), whereas Trinidad and Tobago's carrier, British West Indian Airways, was authorized to service Kingston with intermediate stops. Barbados and Trinidad and Tobago announced talks aimed at a similar accord.

* * *

In the years since Caricom was established in 1973, a considerable amount of material has been published on the structure, positive and negative aspects, and future of the organization. The Inter-American Development Bank's *Ten Years of Caricom* and Economic and Social Progress in Latin America&1 and the Caribbean Community Secretariat's yearly publication, *Report to the Secretary General of Caricom,* are recommended. A concise overview of Caricom may be found in Eduardo Margain's *Development Challenges and Cooperation in the Commonwealth Caribbean;* detailed essays on Caricom and the Commonwealth Caribbean may be found in Anthony Payne and Paul Sutton's *Dependency under Challenge.*

BAHAMAS BANKING AND FINANCIAL MARKET

CENTRAL BANK OF THE BAHAMAS / INSPECTOR OF BANKS & TRUST COMPANIES

As a sovereign country, with strong regulatory oversight and sensitivity to the requirements of a global market, The Bahamas is committed to the financial services industry. Aspects of the Bahamas environment that have supported the development of this industry over the last 60 years include:

- Independent judicial system, based on English Common Law;
- Long history of constitutional democracy, dating back to 1729;
- Large, diverse and highly-skilled professional community;
- Easy access, located at the crossroads of the Americas, with many direct flights each day from America and Europe;
- Absence of exchange control for non-residents;
- Modern and accommodating legislative framework;
- No personal or corporate income, capital gains, estate, gift or inheritance taxes;
- Regulatory environment that is conducive to investment opportunity, while maintaining the highest international standards of operation and conduct
- Public/private sector cooperation

The Central Bank of The Bahamas has the duty to promote and maintain monetary stability and credit and balance of payments conditions conducive to the orderly development of the economy. In collaboration with the financial institutions, the Central Bank has the further duty to promote and maintain adequate banking services and high standards of conduct and management. The Bank advises the Minister of Finance on matters of financial or monetary nature.

The Governor of the Central Bank is empowered to licence banks and trust companies pursuant to enhanced and specific licensing criteria included within the Banks and Trust Companies Regulation Act, 2000.

Supervision

The Banks and Trust Companies Regulation Act, 2000 provided enhanced supervisory powers for the Central Bank, through an Inspector of Banks and Trust Companies.

Included amongst the enhancements are the powers to conduct on-site examinations and off-site supervision to ensure compliance with the Banks and Trust Companies Regulations Act and the Financial Transactions Reporting Act.

The Central Bank of the Bahamas Act 2000 allows the Central Bank, subject to certain conditions and controls, to share supervisory information with overseas regulatory authorities, in order to enable those authorities to exercise regulatory functions.

Additionally, the new provisions of the Act facilitate consolidated supervision by the Central Bank.

Contact: Inspector of Banks and Trust Companies Tel: (242) 302-2615 Fax: (242) 356-4324
Email: bsd@centralbankbahamas.com

There have been no new licences granted for "managed banks" over the last 2 years, and it is the Government plan to phase out this category of bank licence in due course. Banks will be able to operate under "management agent" arrangements, but subject to strict conditions relative to management contracts and senior officer staffing, records being maintained in The Bahamas, and physical presence requirements.

Since 1965 (introduction of banking regulations), The Bahamas has had uninterrupted growth and development, underpinned by the commitment of long-term partners. Economic stability and a strong partnership between the government and the constituents of the financial services sector have contributed to this success. The presence of the many international corporate partners in The Bahamas has been credited by the Prime Minister as giving encouragement of a bright and prosperous future for The Bahamas, particularly as a thriving international financial center.

CONTACT

Wendy Craigg, Governor
Phone: (242) 322-2193
Fax: (242) 356-4307
E-mail: banking@centralbankbahamas.com
Web: http://www.centralbankbahamas.com

ADDRESS

P.O. Box N-4868
Nassau, Bahamas

RESTRICTED AND NON-RESTRICTED BANKING LICENCE

Banks with restricted licenses may carry on business solely with, or for persons specified in the license. Unrestricted licensees are free to do business with the public and some of them are clearing agents. The major banks of North America and Europe have a presence in The Bahamas, which is not a brass plate financial centre.

Numbered among the public institutions are those designated by the Exchange Control Department to deal in Bahamian and foreign currencies and gold; Trust Companies designated as authorised agents to deal in foreign securities, or authorised dealers in gold, foreign currency and Bahamian dollars, or Authorised Agents/Dealers operating in Bahamian and foreign currency and securities and in gold and foreign currencies. Also included in the public institutions are Eurocurrency branches of banks based in the U.S., U.K., South America, Asia and Europe. The remaining are subsidiaries of banks or other institutions based outside The Bahamas, and Bahamian-based banks and/or trust companies.

These two new Acts provide for:

- improved supervision of banks and trust companies
- on-site inspection of banks and trust companies
- full cooperation on cross-border supervision of banks and trust companies
- enhanced cooperation between the Central Bank and overseas regulatory authorities
- extensive information gathering powers for the Central Bank
- enhanced supervisory powers for the Inspector of Banks and Trust Companies
- enhanced role of the Central Bank Governor
- expansion of the licensing criteria for banks and trust companies

THE BAHAMIAN FINANCIAL INDUSTRY

The Bahamas is an archipelago of 700 islands extending over 500 miles into the Atlantic Ocean from a point 50 miles off the east coast of Florida. The Bahamas' English-speaking population of just over 330,000, concentrated mainly on the major islands of New Providence (where Nassau, the capital city, is located) and Grand Bahama (where Freeport, the largest free trade zone in the hemisphere, is located), has an adult literacy rate of 95% and an average per capita income of more than $20,000, one of the highest in the region. A parliamentary democracy for more than two-and-a-half centuries, The Bahamas has continued to enjoy political and social stability since its independence from Britain in 1973.

The Bahamas' well-developed economy is driven largely by tourism, which accounts for approximately 60% of the nation's $7 billion gross domestic product, and a rapidly expanding financial services industry. The balance of economic output comes from retail and wholesale trade, fishing, light manufacturing and agriculture.

An independent nation since 1973 and one of the oldest, vibrant democracies in the Western Hemisphere, the Commonwealth of The Bahamas is a member of the Commonwealth of Nations, the United Nations and has observer status to the World Trade Organization.

FINANCIAL SERVICES

Long-established as one of the foremost international financial centres and a key operational base for many of world's most recognised and respected banking and financial organisations, The Bahamas has preserved its crucial tax neutrality advantage in the new financial architecture that has emerged in the country. In the process, it has become an even more attractive jurisdiction in which to do business.

With more than 6000+ professionals covering every aspect of financial services, The Bahamas is one of the most developed financial centres in the world. Products and services comprise banking, private banking and trust services, investment fund administration, capital markets, investment advisory services, accounting and legal services, e-commerce, insurance, and corporate and shipping registries.

The Bahamas has been providing banking and trust services to the international financial community since the 1930s. Over 250 banks and trust companies are licensed by the Central Bank of the Bahamas, with most maintaining a physical presence.

STRATEGIC INFORMATION AND OPERATIONS

FINANCIAL SERVICES SECTOR

By standards of developing countries, the financial sector of The Bahamas is highly developed and dynamic, providing a wide array of services by several types of intermediaries. Apart from the Central Bank of The Bahamas, and the Financial Intelligence Unit (FIU, December 2000), the sector consists of commercial banks, savings banks, trust companies, offshore banks, insurance companies, a development bank, a publicly controlled pension fund, a housing corporation, a public savings bank, private pension funds, cooperative societies and credit unions.

Although financial intermediation is dominated by commercial banks, the insurance industry and the numerous private pension schemes, which constitute the institutional investor base, mobilize a sizeable pool of long-term investment resources for economic growth. Credit unions are also gaining in importance and statutory bodies, such as The Bahamas Mortgage Corporation, The Bahamas Development Bank and the National Insurance Board, perform an integral role in the mobilization and intermediation of funds in The Bahamas. Capital and money market activities received a significant boost in 2000, with the introduction of The Bahamas International Securities Exchange (BISX), which operates alongside the informal over-the-counter exchange of public sector bonds and bills, which is administered through the Central Bank.

As a mature and sophisticated financial centre, the array of financial services in The Bahamas also includes international business companies (IBC), mutual funds, and insurances services. The IBC is a flexible form of corporate vehicle governed by the International Business Companies Act, 2000, which superseded the existing 1989 IBC Act and made significant changes to the operation of the vehicle. IBCs can only be incorporated by a bank or trust company - which is regulated by the Central Bank - or a person licensed under the Financial and Corporate Services Providers Act, 2000. Mutual Funds operating in The Bahamas take the form of either managed investment companies with shares, or trusts with units representing ownership. Mutual Funds are regulated by the Mutual Funds Act, 1995 and the Mutual Funds Regulations, 1995 with oversight and supervision by the Securities Commission of The Bahamas.

A significant number of insurance companies are also registered to operate in or from within The Bahamas. While many of these insurance companies service the domestic risk needs of The Bahamas, a number were also established to insure risks situated elsewhere in the world. The current legislative regime governing the insurance sector includes the Insurance Act, 1969, as amended; the Insurance (Registration) Regulations 1970, as amended; the Non-Resident Insurer (Exemption) Regulations 1978; the External Insurance Act, 1983 and the External Insurance Regulation 1984. Oversight and supervision is exercised by the Registrar of Insurance.
By mandate, the Central Bank of The Bahamas assumed a critical role in economic management, particularly balance of payments stability and the preservation of the value of the Bahamian currency. Over time, monetary policy tools have been fine-tuned, in keeping with changes in the domestic sector, focusing in this regard on credit controls and liquidity management.

OBJECTIVES OF MONETARY POLICY

The fundamental objective of monetary policy in The Bahamas has always been to maintain stable credit and other conditions to support the fixed parity between the Bahamian and U.S. dollars that has prevailed since 1973, while simultaneously allowing the economic development objective to be pursued. Indeed, upon establishment, the Bank was given a statutory mandate to ensure that external reserves are maintained at 50% of the value of total notes and coins and demand liabilities of the Bank.

The stability objective includes maintaining the domestic as well as the external value of the currency, while the development objective requires promoting and supporting a high level of domestic production, employment and growth. In formulating its monetary policy, the Central Bank takes into consideration the prevailing and prospective domestic economic situation, fiscal operations and emerging external sector developments. In particular, credit and liquidity conditions are continuously monitored by the Central Bank.

The main instruments of monetary policy in The Bahamas are reserve requirements, changes in the Bank discount rate and selective credit controls, supplemented by moral suasion. Over the years, the Central Bank has relied extensively on interest rate controls in combination with moral suasion and other policies to manage financial sector liquidity. The Central Bank affects interest rates by varying the Bank discount rate, which is used mainly to signal changes in monetary policy. For the most part, interest rate policy reflects changing responses to bank liquidity and domestic credit conditions.

The use of market operations in the conduct of monetary policy is limited in The Bahamas——the scope of which includes the authority of the Central Bank to issue treasury bills and bonds on behalf of the Government, and which permits the Bank to buy, hold and sell stock issued to the

public and maturing within 20 years from the date of acquisition. This facility though is subject to the provision that the Bank's holdings of government bonds (Registered Stock) at any point in time, does not exceed 20% of the Bank's own demand liabilities.
As recent illustrations of the Bank's conduct of monetary policy, policy-tightening initiatives were implemented in July 2001, when it became evident that the slowing US economy was exerting a drag on The Bahamas. Initially, moral suasion was used to encourage a more conservative posture in private sector lending, including more rigorous application of collateral requirements and scrutiny of credit worthiness.

Given that consumer lending played less significantly in the overall credit trends, the Bank also directed its attention more generally at overall private sector credit, and subsequently, imposed a direct freeze on the outstanding level of credit, rolled back to the first week of September 2001. Banks were allowed to grant new loans only to the extent of resources obtained from ongoing repayments, and were at liberty to determine how these resources would be allocated within their portfolios. The credit restrictions were lifted in August 2004, following the improvement in economic and monetary conditions.

THE MONETARY POLICY COMMITTEE

The Monetary Policy Committee (MPC) was established in June 1980 by then Governor, Sir William C. Allen. Its purpose is to track and review monetary and financial trends and developments within the banking sector, with a view to defining policies to effect a stable monetary environment. The composition of the Committee is determined by the Governor, and currently includes the Deputy Governor, Economic Advisor and various department heads. The MPC has no statutory basis or authority, although its deliberations have formed the basis of all policy actions taken by the Central Bank since 1980. In this regard, decisions and policy measures originate from the Governor, relying on recommendations formulated by the Committee

OPEN MARKET OPERATIONS

Open Market Operations involve the purchase or sale of securities, such as Treasury Bills or Government bonds, by the Central Bank in order to influence the money supply. When the Bank sells (purchases) these securities to (from) a bank or an individual, money is withdrawn from (added to) the flow of money in the economy.

The Central Bank is the current Official Registrar and Transfer Agent of securities for the Government, the Bahamas Mortgage Corporation, the Bridge Authority and the Clifton Heritage Authority. The Bank maintains both a primary and secondary market for the Government's local currency securities, which at present includes Treasury Bills and Registered Stock. Treasury Bills, sold through a tender for periods of 91 or 182 days in increments of B$100, provide short-term financing to the Government. Registered Stocks, which are issued under The Bahamas Registered Stock Act, 1973, are long-term securities with maturities of up to 25 years. With a minimum investment of B$100, they are issued at par, in multiples of 100, and carry varying interest rates, usually tied to the Bahamian prime lending rate.

The amount issued in any fiscal year is based on budgeted financing provisions authorized by resolution of the House of Assembly. The ceiling for Treasury bills outstanding is limited by law to 25% of the Government's average ordinary revenue in the three preceding years.

In the absence of an active secondary market in Treasury bills and Registered Stock, the Central Bank provides liquidity to the market by standing ready to discount these securities before maturity, although there is no legal requirement to do so. Treasury bills are rediscounted at a rate of 0.5 percentage points above the average discount rate, and sold, after the tender, at a rate of 0.1 percentage points below the average discount rate. The Bank may also extend loans against the collateral of Government paper, with the interest rate on these loans rising in line with the duration of the loan.

Primary and secondary operations have also been accommodated for the Bridge Authority's bonds. In the case of the Bahamas Mortgage Corporation, only primary activities have been undertaken although by virtue of the registrar functions, the Bank is also able to track secondary trading. Open market operations are facilitated through the Bank's **Banking Department**.

THE BAHAMAS MORTGAGE CORPORATION BONDS

Established by an Act of Parliament, the Bahamas Mortgage Corporation commenced operations in 1983 and during its tenure has averaged approximately 272 loan approvals per annum. Its asset portfolio includes loans to individuals for the construction of new homes, the purchase of new or existing dwellings and financing for housing rehabilitation and structural enlargement. The Corporation, which currently falls under the responsibility of the Minister of Housing and National Insurance, places particular emphasis on Government initiated projects, which comprises the largest share of its total outstanding loans.

By its Act, the Corporation has the authority to issue bonds, and has received from Parliament, Government's guarantee for the issuance of up to $120 million in bonds. Bahamas Mortgage Corporation's Bonds are issued in denominations of $100,000 and usually attract interest rates that are tied to the Bahamian prime lending rate. Bond-holders include The National Insurance Board, the clearing banks and insurance companies. As of June 2007, total bonds outstanding were $99.8 million.
The Central Bank of The Bahamas is the official Registrar of Securities for the Bahamas Mortgage Corporation.

THE BRIDGE AUTHORITY

The Bridge Authority is a body corporate established by an Act of Parliament on 26 June 1998, as a continuation of the former Paradise Island Bridge Authority -- established in 1988. The Bridge Authority incorporates all of the powers of the Paradise Island Bridge Authority, with extended powers and responsibilities, which allow it to construct, own, manage, and operate any bridge in The Bahamas.

In October 1997, following a competitive bidding process, the Government of The Commonwealth of The Bahamas, entered into a contract with Interbeton BV, a company based in The Netherlands, to design and construct a second bridge, from New Providence to Paradise Island, over the Nassau Harbour, including bridge approaches and toll collection facility, at a cost of $21.6 million. This second bridge was intended to supplement the original (eastern) Paradise Island Bridge, which following its commission in 1967 offered one access lane to Paradise Island and one exit lane to New Providence. The parties also agreed to a $4.9 million, restoration of the original (eastern) bridge. In March 1999, the Bridge Authority issued a $28.0 million bond to cover these costs, along with additional financing and pre-opening costs.

The terms and conditions of the offering, included the following:

Issuer:	The Bridge Authority
Guarantor:	The Government of the Commonwealth of The Bahamas
Amount:	B$28,000,000
Maturity Dates:	B$5,000,000 due on March 24, 2014 B$7,000,000 due on March 24, 2019 B$8,000,000 due on March 24, 2024 B$8,000,000 due on March 24, 2029
Interest Rates:	Maturity 24/03/2014 - Prime Rate + 1% p.a. Maturity 24/03/2019 - Prime Rate + 1 ¼% p.a.

Maturity 24/03/2024 - Prime Rate + 1½% p.a.
Maturity 24/03/2029 - Prime Rate + 15/8% p.a.

The new (western) bridge was commissioned on December 11, 1998. It serves traffic entering Paradise Island, while the two-lane original (eastern) bridge serves traffic leaving the Island. The Central Bank of Bahamas is the Registrar and Transfer Agent of The Bridge Authority

EXCHANGE CONTROL ADMINISTRATION

In 1974, the Central Bank was appointed the Controller of Exchange. The Regulations provide that all investments by non-Bahamians in the domestic economy be approved and the resultant currency flows recorded; that all Bahamian companies (except International Business Companies) in which non-Bahamians hold an interest be designated resident or non-resident, depending on where they will operate; that all settlements and trusts be designated for Exchange Control purposes; that, in general, appropriate residential status for individuals, firms, organizations, etc. vis-a-vis Exchange Control be conferred. They also provide for specific guidelines affecting residents who emigrate.

As an Article VIII member of the International Monetary Fund, The Bahamas agrees not to place restrictions on current transactions, such as payments for imports. In its administration of Exchange Control, although the Central Bank has set certain limits for various types of current payments (Current Payments under Delegated Authority), it does not withhold approval for legitimate foreign exchange purchases for current transactions. In fact, in its efforts to better facilitate the needs of the general public, the Bank has delegated certain powers to some of the major banks and trust companies to act on its behalf.

Within certain limits, banks with 'Authorised Dealer' status are empowered to conduct foreign currency transactions with residents of The Bahamas; while banks and trust companies designated as 'Authorised Agents' are permitted to act as depositories for foreign securities of residents and to conduct certain transactions in securities in respect of non-resident companies under their management. As at September, 2007, there were 8 Authorised Dealers and 15 Authorised Agents.

Foreign exchange transactions that fall outside the authority of the Authorised Dealers and Agents must be referred to the Central Bank, and can be dealt with either at the Exchange Control Counter by the completion and approval of forms, or through correspondence. These applications include loans, dividends, profits, capital repatriation, foreign currency accounts (Guidelines for Opening and Classification of Accounts), Exchange Control designations, emigration facilities, issue and transfer of shares, travel, import and sundry payment facilities exceeding the Authorised Dealer limits, gift remittances, and investment currency transactions (e.g. purchase of real estate abroad, or purchase of shares of a foreign entity). Personal Allowance Cards used for gifts and credit card payments are dealt with at the Exchange Control Counter of the Central Bank, the area of the Bank with which the public is most familiar.

BANK SUPERVISION DEPARTMENT

Bank Supervision's underlying philosophy revolves around the concept that banks and trust companies should be free to allocate credit according to market forces and should be entitled to set terms and conditions for their operations in an environment of competition. However, strict supervisory rules should be set for bank behaviour in order to protect depositors and other creditors and the financial system as a whole. Pursuant to this, the objective of bank supervision in The Bahamas is to promote and maintain the safety, soundness, and integrity of the Bahamian banking and financial system and of each institution within the system; while promoting confidence in the financial system through the implementation of policies and standards that are in keeping with international best practices for supervision and regulation.

The **Bank Supervision Department** spearheads the licensing and supervisory functions of the Central Bank. Since the enactment of policy revisions in 2000, one of the Department's primary focuses has been on strengthening this new regulatory framework. This process has involved ongoing consultations with the industry and other interested public parties; and has led to the development and adoption of new supervisory regulations and prudential guidelines, along with revisions to existing ones. Moreover, the strengthening of domestic and international cooperative mechanisms continue to be a high priority.

The work of the Department is co-ordinated over three units: the **Supervision Unit**, **Policy Unit** and the **Administration and Operations Unit**. The **Supervision Unit** is responsible for all aspects of the onsite and offsite examinations relative to legal and regulatory compliance including, governance structures and prudential indicators. Almost two thirds of the Department's staff is dedicated to these activities. The latest thrust of supervisory activities included the programme to discontinue "managed" banking institutions, or "shell" banks.
Established in 2002, the **Policy Unit** is charged with the research, development and implementation of supervisory policies which are consistent with international best practices, and which effectively address the supervisory issues of the Bahamian banking and trust industry. Supervisory policies and guidelines are developed in a consultative framework, where industry participants and the wider public are allowed to comment on policy documents before they are finalised. Among the initiatives in the Unit's work programme, is industry preparation for the eventual adoption of the new capital framework (Basel II).

The primary functions of the **Administration and Operations Unit** are to provide back office support for supervisory activities, with direct responsibility for ensuring that licensees satisfy reporting requirements; to maintain databases of information relating to licensees; and to monitor and analyse balance sheets in order to assess capital adequacy and liquidity trends of licensees. The Unit also coordinates the human resources and training needs of the Department and provides administrative support for the operations of the Deposit Insurance Corporation and the Agricultural Credit Guarantee Fund.

BANK SUPERVISION INITIATIVES

CORPORATE GOVERNANCE

Following industry-wide consultation, in December 2001, the Central Bank adopted comprehensive **Guidelines for the Corporate Governance of Banks and Trust Companies Licensed to Do Business within or from within The Bahamas**, to which licensees were required to be fully compliant by December 2003. The Guidelines articulate the Central Bank's expectations for the corporate governance of all licensees, and establishes international best practices related to their management and operations. Commencing in 2003, the Boards of Directors of all banks and trust companies licensed by the Central Bank were required to certify that an assessment of their organization's corporate governance and risk management framework was carried out during the year, and accordingly report any material deficiencies in these structures and where appropriate, submit an action plan for addressing them.
Central Bank Expectations & Corporate Governance
The Role of the Regulator in Corporate Governance
Corporate Governance: Central Bank's Expectations

AML-CFT INITIATIVES

Money laundering describes the process to conceal or move assets which would have been obtained or generated by illegal means, with the end of obscuring the link between those assets and the crime. While the development and promotion of policies to combat money laundering has been a long held priority of the international community, in the aftermath of the terrorist attacks of September 11, 2001, such efforts have gained impetus. Particularly as proceeds derived from such activities have on occasion been linked to the financing of terrorist activity. Money launderers generally seek out jurisdictions with the weakest and least effective anti-money laundering systems, and as such, the international focus has been on strengthening national laws and international mechanisms, as they relate to **Anti-Money Laundering and Combating the Financing of Terrorism (AML/CFT)**.

In collaboration with financial institutions, the Central Bank has the duty to promote and maintain high standards of conduct and management in the provision of banking and trust services. Moreover, the Banks and Trust Companies Regulation Act, 2000 directs the Inspector of Banks and Trust Companies to ensure that institutions have in place strict Know-Your-Customer (KYC) rules that promote high ethical and professional standards, and so prevent the use of the institution for criminal purposes. The methodology for Assessing Compliance with AML/CFT Standards as agreed between the IMF, the World Bank and the Financial Action Task Force (FATF), is currently under review by The Bahamas Government.

BASEL II

With the new Basel Capital Accord (Basel II) scheduled for an end-2006 implementation date, developments related to this new capital adequacy framework are being closely monitored by the Policy Unit of the Bank Supervision Department. In 1992, standards established by the 1988 Basel Capital Accord (Basel I), were implemented in The Bahamas and, to date, compliance is monitored by the Central Bank on a quarterly basis, as part of the review of the financial condition. The Central Bank is optimistic about the implementation of Basel II, which comprises three primary pillars: **Minimum Capital Adequacy, Supervision Review** and **Market Discipline**. The Bahamas, along with other Caribbean banking supervisors, will be undertaking a quantitative impact study to determine the effects of Basel II on our banking systems.

KEY INDUSTRY LEGISLATION

In 2000, the Government embarked on an ambitious overhaul of financial sector legislation enacting nine new laws on the 29th of December. Together, these new laws provide for more comprehensive and enhanced supervision of financial institutions, corporate service providers and international business companies; while establishing a more coordinated system of deterrence against money laundering and other criminal abuses within the financial sector; in the context of a framework that allows for greater international cooperation in the oversight of the financial system. The new laws included:

- The Banks and Trust Companies Regulation Act, 2000
- The Central Bank of The Bahamas Act, 2000
- The Financial Intelligence Unit Act, 2000
- The Proceeds of Crime Act, 2000
- The Financial and Corporate Service Providers Act, 2000
- The Financial Transactions Reporting Act, 2000
- The International Business Companies Act, 2000
- The Evidence (Proceedings in other Jurisdictions) Act, 2000 and
- Criminal Justice (International Cooperation) Act, 2000
- The Anti-Terrorism Act, 2004

(N.B. The hyperlinks above will take you to The Government of The Bahamasâ€™ site, which contains downloadable versions of the referenced legislation. The Central Bank of The Bahamas (the Bank) provides these links merely for your convenience. The Bank accepts no responsibility or liability for any information on that site or, for any damages arising from your access to that site.)
Key features of the new enactments included: enhanced powers of the Governor of the Central Bank to issue and revoke licences to carry on banking and/or trust business from within the Commonwealth of The Bahamas; operational independence of the Central Bank in supervision

and regulation of banks and trust companies; increased provision for information sharing with other regulators for supervisory purposes; provisions upgrading banking supervision, including, but not limited to, on-site examination of banks and trust companies, as well as examinations by appropriate overseas supervisory authorities; the upgrade and broadening of KYC requirements and suspicious and unusual transactions reporting; establishment of a Financial Intelligence Unit (FIU); introduction of licensing of financial and corporate service providers, such as lawyers, accountants and management companies; the removal of bearer shares from International Business Companies (IBCs) shareholding structures, and the granting of permission for Bahamians to own IBCs.

In more recent developments, at the end of December, 2003, the Government enacted amendments to the Financial Transactions Reporting Act (FRTA) and the Financial Transactions Reporting Regulations (FTRR), which provided the basis for financial institutions to implement a risk based approach to customer due diligence and anti-money laundering procedure. The amendments realign The Bahamas' KYC regime with the Financial Action Task Force's (FATF) Revised 40 Recommendations issued in June 2003, with specific regard to the implementation of a risk rating framework for assessing the money laundering risks that client relationships pose to licensees.

Additionally, in 2004 Parliament enacted the Anti-Terrorism Act, 2004, which addressed several of the FATF's Special Recommendations. In addition to defining the offence of terrorism and criminalizing the financing of terrorism, the law provides for the seizure and confiscation of terrorist assets; reporting of suspicious transactions related to terrorist financing; and strengthening of existing mechanisms for cooperation in this regard between The Bahamas and other countries.

OFFSHORE FINANCIAL AND BUSINESS CLIMATE

FREEDOM FROM TAXATION

One of the most attractive elements about investing in The Bahamas is the tax free status accorded income. There are no taxes levied on capital gains, corporate earnings, personal income, sales, inheritance, or dividends. This tax freedom is available to all resident corporations, partnerships, individuals and trusts.

ECONOMIC AND MONETARY STABILITY

Investors are also attracted to the stability of the economy which is steadied by the solid value of the Bahamian dollar. This currency is pegged to the US dollar on a 1:1 ratio. US dollars and Bahamian dollars are used interchangeably throughout the island chain.

INVESTMENT INCENTIVES IN THE BAHAMAS

The Bahamas levies no taxes on capital gains, corporate earnings, personal income, sales, inheritance,or dividends. This tax freedom is available to all resident corporations partnerships, individuals and trusts.

The Bahamas has become a particularly favorable target for international investment. It has established generous legal incentives to attract foreign investors and has streamlined government bureaucracy for expeditious project approval. The Bahamas possesses an outstanding infrastructure for commercial and industrial activity, and offers a highly-skilled workforce. The professional community of accountants, international bankers, trustees, and investment specialists is large, diverse and highly skilled. There is also a full complement of respected and experienced law firms. The climate for foreign investment is particularly favorable to the finance industry, insurance, manufacturing, shipping, import & export trade, and of course, tourism development.

FREEDOM FROM TAXATION

One of the most attractive elements of investing in The Bahamas is the tax-free status accorded to income. There are no taxes levied on capital gains, corporate earnings, personal income, sales, inheritance, or dividends. This tax freedom is available to all resident corporations, partnerships, individuals and trusts.

ECONOMIC AND MONETARY STABILITY

Investors are also attracted to the stability of the economy, which is steadied by the solid value of the Bahamian dollar. This currency is pegged to the US dollar on a 1:1 ratio. US dollars and Bahamian dollars are used interchangeably throughout the island chain.

A WEALTH OF INVESTMENT INCENTIVES

The inducement of a tax-free environment and a stable currency are enhanced by a series of investment incentives that provide relief from customs duties on approved raw materials, equipment, and building supplies, as well as allowing exemptions from business licenses and real property taxes for up to 20 years.

The Hotels Encouragement Act exempts hotel developers from customs duties on raw materials and equipment. Exemptions from real property tax and licensing fees are also available.

The Industries Encouragement Act exempts exporters from import duties on raw materials and equipment and business license fees. This act is of particular benefit for manufacturers.

The Export Manufacturing Industries Encouragement Act provides an approved manufacturer who intends to export or annually exports at least 95% of the total approved products produced by the manufacturer is afforded duty-free import of raw materials, equipment and building supplies used in the manufacture of the product or facilities for the same and duty-free export of those products.

The Bahamas Free Trade Zone Act

The Agricultural Manufactories Act provides subsidies to agricultural businesses in the form of interest-free loans for the purchase of supplies and exemption from duties on a wide range of products, including building suppliers, processing materials and farm trucks. It also provides exemption from export taxes.

Freeport on Grand Bahama Island gives businesses in the free trade zone exemption from taxes on profits, capital gains, inheritance, income, earnings, distributions, gifts, or on imported and exported goods. In addition, import duties and taxes on real estate have been waived through August 3, 2015.

The **Tariff Act** provides exemptions to approved manufacturers for the import of capital equipment and raw material for garment manufacturing, food processing, the production of handicraft and souvenir items, and cottage industries.

The Spirit and Beer Manufacture Act provides duty-free import of raw material and equipment for spirits and beer manufacturers.

NO EXCHANGE CONTROLS/FREE REPATRIATION OF PROFITS

In accordance with terms of the *International Monetary Fund Agreement*, The Bahamas has no restriction on current account transactions. Additionally, there are no restrictions on the free repatriation of profits. Exchange control is administered by *The Central Bank*. The Bank, however, delegates to its authorized dealers the power to approve allocations of foreign exchange for certain payments.

ACCESSIBLE INTERNATIONAL FINANCING

The Bahamas is associated with several organizations that ease access to financing and provide important safeguards for investors. The US Government's *Overseas Private Investment Corporation (OPIC)*, for example, makes direct financing and loan guarantees available to foreign investors. The *Multilateral Investment Guarantee Agency* is a *World Bank* unit and parent of the *Multilateral Investment Guarantee Convention*, which provides protections similar to those of OPIC. The Bahamas also recently agreed to become a party to the convention on the settlement of investment disputes.

FACILITATED INCORPORATION AND REGISTRATION

The International Business Companies Act of 1989 and the Companies Act of 1992 have made it easier than ever before to establish a commercial presence in The Bahamas.

FLEXIBLE IMMIGRATION POLICY

Necessary work permits for key personnel are readily granted. Businesses requiring work permits for other than key personnel are encouraged to advise The Bahamas Investment Authority of their needs at an early stage in their discussions.

Accelerated consideration for annual or permanent residence is given to major investors and to owners of residences valued in excess of $250,000. All international persons owning residences in The Bahamas are eligible to receive, upon application to the Director of Immigration, a "Home Owners Card." The card does not provide residency status for tax purposes; however, it facilitates entry into The Bahamas and entitled the owner, his/her spouse and minor children to enter and remain in The Bahamas for the duration of the validity of the card.

BAHAMAS INVESTMENT AUTHORITY

The Bahamas Investment Authority (BIA) was established to "cut red tape and lay out the red carpet" for investors.

The proactive economic growth and development policies of the government of the Bahamas are guided by **The Bahamas Investment Authority (BIA)**, established to "cut red tape and lay out the red carpet" for investors. Operating from the Office of the Prime Minister, the BIA has been designated as a "one-stop shop" designed to simplify investing in The Bahamas. The agency has a four-fold mandate to:

Develop investment policies;

- Promote investment;
- Evaluate project proposals;
- Monitor projects and provide support.

PROJECT PROPOSALS

Proposals to establish a business should be submitted to the BIA, which coordinates investment matters with other arms of government, and grants approvals. All proposals should include the following information:

Name

Address ***(include telephone/fax)***

Description of Proposal ***(an executive summary of project)***

Type of Business ***(state whether entity is a share company, partnership, individual, or joint venture)***

Principals ***(persons investing in the venture/major beneficial shareholders)***

Proposed Location

Land or Factory Space Requirements

Proposed Start-Up Date

Management/Personnel Requirement *(years of experience, training, success of similar, previous, or current activity; work permits required for key personnel)*

Employment Projection *(number of bahamian and non-Bahamian employees)*

Environmental Impact *(toxic waste, disposal procedures, toxic input)*

Concessions Sought *(Customs duty exemptions)*

Local Representative *(attorney, account, or agent)*

NB: All information supplied shall be held in the strictest confidence.

For further information, contact:
Bahamas Investment Authority
(Financial Services Secretariat)
Office of the Prime Minister
P.O. Box CB 10980
Nassau, N.P., The Bahamas
Tel: (242) 327-5970-4
Fax: (242) 327-5907

TRUST FORMATION IN THE BAHAMAS

The Bahamian trust is considered a private agreement between the parties concerned, therefore, registration with a government agency is not required. No business license fees, filing fees, or registered office fees are payable. Professional service fees depend on the complexity of establishing the trust.

FORMING A BAHAMIAN TRUST

There are several ways to form a Bahamian Trust. The trust document can vary in size, depending on its requirements and the complexity of the dispositive provisions. Any lawyer or competent individual can write up a trust document, However, to ensure compliance with Bahamian Trust law, and avoiding the document being ruled invalid by a court, the document should be reviewed and approved by a Bahamian attorney. Some institutions have standard trust documents in which certain items, such as dispositive provisions, are included in one of the schedules. Such standard documents should also be approved by a Bahamian attorney.

To establish a Bahamian Trust, it is necessary for the attorney or trustee to know:

- who the beneficiaries are going to be;
- how and when the beneficiaries are going to receive their share of the trust's assets;
- if there is going to be a protector named in the trust document, who that person is;
- what powers the protector is going to have and how to appoint his/her successor.

(Note: A protector is not subject to the same degree of responsibility as the trustee, under law. There can be a "letter of wishes," in which the settlor states in detail what is to happen to the trust's assets during and after his/her lifetime.)

A Bahamian Trust is not exclusive to Bahamian beneficiaries. Upon establishment, the trust must be designated "resident" or "non-resident" for Exchange Control purposes.

Under normal circumstances, in order to establish a trust, the trustee will charge between US$1,000 and US$3,000. The trust law in The Bahamas implies that all the trustee's powers must be stated in the trust document. There is no section in the Trust Act which specifies general powers of the trustee and which can be referred to in the trust document. Thus, if the trust document does not allow for the compensation of the trustee, then the trustee cannot take a fee. In some cases, broad discretionary powers may be given to the trustee, or very strict rules may be laid down. Once the trust is set up, the annual trustee fee can either be based on a flat fee or on a percentage of the assets. If the former, the fee will range from US$1,000 to US$5,000 a year; if the latter, the fee will range from 0.25% to 1%. The range depends on the complexity of administration and the risks involved to the trust company.

TRUST LAWS

The laws governing trusts in The Bahamas are similar to those of Great Britain and other common law jurisdictions. The concept of the Trust is an integral part of Bahamian Law. The principal statutory instrument is the *Trustee Act, 1893*, which sets out the court's powers as to the administration of a trust and the regulation of trustees. Bahamian law allows for the establishment of three types of trusts:

Standard Trust, also an asset protection trust. It can be either "revocable" or "irrevocable," "discretionary" or "non-discretionary."

Testamentary Trust, which becomes active upon the death of the settlor and the assets are turned over to the estate.

Charity Trust has the advantage of having no perpetuity period, which in The Bahamas is approximately 80 years. To qualify, beneficiaries have to be genuine charities as defined in law.

There are several new pieces of legislation specifically enacted to make the Bahamian Trust a more effective instrument for today's global financial market. They include:

THE TRUST (CHOICE OF GOVERNING LAW) ACT, 1989

This Act permits a settlor to expressly declare that Bahamian Law will be the governing law of the Trust, and such a declaration will be recognized by the Bahamian courts as valid and conclusive regardless of any other circumstances. The Act also recognizes provisions in a trust deed for the changing of the governing law to or from the laws of The Bahamas. The legislation addresses several other areas concerned with the administration validity and capacity of a settlor to a Bahamian Trust and is intended to eliminate many of the jurisdictions that may be at issue, such as concepts of forced heirship or community property.

THE FRAUDULENT DISPOSITION ACT, 1991

This Act is known in many jurisdictions as "Asset Protection Trust" legislation. It provides that every disposition of property made with an intent to defraud and at an undervalue will be voidable and can be set aside by professional business persons who wish to insulate some of their assets from future claims not in existence at the date of the gift. The burden of establishing fraudulent intent falls on the claimant seeking to challenge the disposition, with the Statue of Limitations set at two years from the date of the disposition.

The Bahamian trust is considered a private agreement between the parties concerned, therefore, registration with a government agency is not required. No business license fees, filing fees, or registered office fees are payable. Professional service fees depend on the complexity of establishing the trust.

ESTABLISHING A FINANCIAL INSTITUTION IN THE BAHAMAS

The financial sector, with over 40 years of steady growth and experience in the offshore banking and trust industry, is the second leading contributor to the economy of The Bahamas, employing more than 10% of the country's labour force and comprisiong 12% of GDP ($340 million).

The Bahamas, one of the most mature offshore financial centres, owes its development to a number of enduring features. These features, while encouraging the general development of the nation of islands, have spurred the development of the financial services sector in particular. This sector, with over 40 years of steady growth and experience in the offshore banking and trust industry, is the second leading contributor to the economy of The Bahamas, employing more than 10% of the country's labour force and comprising 12% of GDP ($340 million).

The financial centre of The Bahamas has consistently attracted well-established, internationally-recognised financial institutions and substantial investors. The centre, which manages assets of about $200 billion, offers the following benefits:

A convenient location, just 50 miles from the mainland United States, coupled with an inviting climate.

- A commitment to zero taxation, offering freedom from taxes on income, capital gains, profits, gifts, inheritance and estates, as well as no withholding taxes on dividends, interest or royalties, and no payroll taxes.
- Strict enforcement of the complete confidentiality of banker-customer relations, through both common law and statue.
- A progressive, state of the art telecommunications system.
- A stable economic and political environment.
- Readily available professional services: legal, accounting, insurance, and management.

The Bahamas' Financial Centre offers a variety of services to the international community. These services are being strengthened continuously through the Government's partnership with the private sector. Represented by The Bahamas Investment Authority, incorporating the Financial Services Secretariat, the Government has reaffirmed its commitment to maintaining and improving The Bahamas' role as a sophisticated offshore finance centre, through the introduction of new and innovative legislation and the strengthening of existing legislation.

The Bahamas is poised to offer opportunities to innovative, progressive investors. The financial services sector is a haven to such investors.

UP-TO-DATE LEGISLATION

The legislative framework governing the activities of the financial services industry is modern and accommodating. Representatives of the private sector are regularly consulted in a continuous effort to keep financial services legislation abreast of changing investor requirements.

Non-residents who do business in The Bahamas enjoy considerable freedom from exchange controls. The repatriation of foreign investment funds, foreign assets and dividends, and profits arising from foreign investment is allowed and facilitated.

- Bahamian law strongly protects the right to confidentiality and privacy of bank clients and further protects the security and good name of investments in The Bahamas. Legislation criminalising money laundering in The Bahamas has strengthened the jurisdiction's reputation for being clean, reputable, and worthy of the full confidence of discerning international investors and business persons.
- Recent changes in legislation include passage of the Mutual Funds Act, governing the establishment of mutual funds, and a new Trustee Act was recently introduced in Parliament. The International Business Companies (IBCs) Act 1989 provides the offshore financial sector with a corporate vehicle that is flexible and cost-effective. More than 36,000 IBC's have registered since 1990, many in the areas of mutual funds and portfolio management services.

Currently under development is a stock market that will allow closed-end mutual funds to register in The Bahamas. .

NO TAXATION

With no personal or corporate income, capital gains, estate, gift, or inheritance taxes, the Bahamas offers an ideal tax environment.

A STRONG WORK FORCE

One of the greatest assets of the Bahamian economy is its large, skilled workforce. The nation enjoys an adult literacy rate of 95%, and **The Bahamas Institute of Bankers** sponsors academic programs in conjunction with **The College of The Bahamas** that are designed to keep the nation's workforce competitive with any in the world.

The professional community of accountants, international bankers, trustees, and investment specialists is large, diverse and highly skilled. There is also a full complement of respected and experienced law firms.

TYPES OF LICENSES ISSUED

As stipulated by The Banks and Trust Companies Regulation Act, banks and trust companies are issued licenses to operate in The Bahamas under the following designations:

BAHAMAS OFFSHORE SECTOR FOR FINANCIAL AND INVESTMENT ACTIVITY

OFFSHORE ACTIVITIES AND REGULATIONS

The Bahamas was one of the first offshore jurisdictions to offer trust services, its growth as a significant offshore financial center has been relatively recent, with most of the key legislative initiatives dating from the last ten years. The Bahamas' 1989 International Business Company legislation was updated in 1994 and has been very successful, although not on the same scale as the British Virgin Islands.

There is a substantial banking sector, second only to the Cayman Islands among offshore jurisdictions. The Government has particularly targeted mutual funds and trust business, and in 1999 set legislation in place covering stock and securities exchanges, which it plans to open shortly. The captive insurance sector is small, and new legislation is in the pipeline to reanimate it. The Bahamian Government has paid great attention to financial regulation, and has created a world-standard regulatory structure to avoid money-laundering and other criminal activity. The islands also offer a shipping registry.

BASIC OFFSHORE OPERATIONS

FINANCIAL HOLDING AND INVESTMENT

More than 80,000 International Business Companies have been formed in the Bahamas, many of them as holding companies for investment or trading activity in other countries. Since there are no corporation or income taxes in the Bahamas, it is a very effective financial base, although like all low- or no-tax financial centres, it is vulnerable to 'Controlled Foreign Corporation' legislation if the Bahamian company is majority-owned by a mother company in a high-tax country.

The very rapid recent growth in IBC incorporations has been fed by political instability in Latin and Central America, and more recently the handover of Hong Kong to mainland China. Many of these newer IBCs have been formed as asset protection vehicles, sometimes in association with trusts, either to hold shares or other types of asset. The Bahamas are one of the most popular jurisdictions for these markets, because of the flexible IBC legislation, good secrecy, good reputation, and high-quality professional services.

INVESTMENT FUND MANAGEMENT

It is estimated that there are more than $70bn of funds under management in the Bahamas, making it one of the leading jurisdictions in this respect. The mutual fund sector is regulated under the Mutual Funds Act 1995 and the Securities Board Act 1995, which established a Securities Board operating on self-regulatory principles: mutual funds can be directly regulated, but more commonly are regulated through licensed administrators who can grant licenses directly to funds. In 1999 the Securities Board is converting into a Securities Commission under the Securities Industry Act 1999, which lays the foundations for a stock and securities exchange. Mutual fund administrators will continue to be licensed under the Mutual Funds Act 1995, and regulated by the Commission directly or indirectly.

The Mutual Funds Act divides investment funds into a number of classes:

- Exempt Funds (ie exempt from licensing), being funds with no more than 15 investors, a majority of whom can appoint or remove the fund manager;
- Authorised funds, being funds with a minimum subscription level of $50,000, or which are listed on a recognised stock exchange - such funds need only to register with the Securities Board; and
- Other funds, which are required to be licensed.

Licenses are normally obtained from a Mutual Fund Administrator, who is in turn licensed by the Securities Board. Investment funds in the Bahamas normally take one of four corporate forms: the International Business Company (IBC); the Limited Duration Company (LDC); the Unit Trust; or the Exempted Limited Partnership All of these forms are exempt from taxes and stamp duty.

BANKING

Banks in the Bahamas must be licensed under the Banks and Trust Companies Act 1965. The Central Bank of the Bahamas applies stiff criteria to incoming banks in order to exclude money laundering and criminal activity. Banks cannot use the Bahamian International Business Company form, and operate either as branches (usually representative offices) or subsidiaries, necessitating the formation of a Bahamian company under the Companies Act. The minimum capital requirement for a full, public banking license is $2m; there are various categories of restricted license with lower requirements. For further details of licensing requirements and procedures and fees payable

The Bahamas is one of the world's top ten international banking centers, with 400 licensed banks from more than 30 countries, and a total asset base around $200bn. Capital ratios average over 10%. The country's improved legislation and regulatory structure, its highly-skilled workforce, and its stable government have attracted some of the most prestigious financial institutions from around the globe. About half of licensed banks are incorporated locally, and more than half offer trust services alongside banking activity.

Evidently, private banking is a major component of the Bahamian banking industry: asset protection rather than tax avoidance as such is the driving force, so that the stability of the Bahamas alongside stringent banking secrecy and its sophisticated investment environment are very attractive to wealthy individuals, particularly those from the US where the Bahamas have a very good reputation.

TRUST MANAGEMENT

Trust Management has been a major activity in the Bahamas for 50 years or more. Originally the trust was used primarily by wealthy individuals from the major common law countries, but it is now accepted as a major technique of asset protection in all parts of the world. In the last 10 years the Bahamas have extended and adapted their trust laws, most recently with a new Trustee Act 1998, to accommodate this wider market, which is not necessarily interested so much just in tax avoidance, but also in the efficient management of wealth in a more general sense. See Law of Offshore for a fuller treatment of trust law in the Bahamas.

There is a large and sophisticated community of professional advisers on trust matters in the Bahamas. Individuals can provide trust services without registration, but companies offering trust services must be licensed under the Banks and Trust Companies Act 1965. Foreign or Bahamian companies may obtain licenses. These are issued by the Central Bank of the Bahamas, following a stringent application procedure.

A licensed trust company may be 'public' or 'restricted'. 'Restricted' companies require less capital, but are more strictly controlled.

Bahamian trusts (other than those holding Bahamian property) do not have to be registered, and the 1998 Act disapplies Exchange Control Regulations to non-resident settlors, donors, beneficiaries and trustees - therefore it is no longer necessary for trusts to be registered with the Central Bank as non-resident. This applies to existing trusts as well as to new ones.

The 1998 Act provides for the appointment of a 'protector of trust', effectively a supervisor of the trustee(s), and also managing and custodian trustees.

INSURANCE

The insurance sector in the Bahamas is regulated under the Insurance Act 1969 as amended and the External Insurance Act 1983. The Government is targetting insurance as a sector for expansion, and more modern legislation is in the pipeline.

The domestic insurance sector is very active, with more than 50 licensed insurers; but the international (captive) sector, although growing, is not yet very well developed compared with the leading offshore captive jurisdictions such as Bermuda.

Insurance companies cannot use the Bahamian International Business Company form, necessitating the formation of a Bahamian company under the Companies Act (see Forms of Company), or the use of Foreign Company status, which has the same effect.

Insurance licenses are issued by the Minister of Finance, following recommendations by the Registrar of Insurance Companies. There are statutory minimum capitalisation and solvency ratios, and initial capitalisation is normally in cash.

SHIP MANAGEMENT AND MARITIME OPERATIONS

The Bahamas established themselves as a shipping registry with the Merchant Shipping Act 1976, and due to a combination of geographical, financial and operational factors have been very successful, building the fifth largest world fleet. More than 1,500 vessels are registered in the Bahamas, totalling over 25m gross tonnes.

The Bahamas operate a 'flag of convenience' registry, which does not impose minimum wage or nationality standards on its ships. However, the Bahamas registry belongs to the International Maritime Organisation and adheres to its principal safety conventions. The Bahamas Maritime Organisation, headquartered in London, administers the registry, supervises initial and subsequent ship surveys through a world-wide network of authorised inspectors,and ensures adequate training and skill levels among the crews of Bahamian vessels.

Registration fees are as follows:

- US$1.20 per net registered ton for vessels up to 5,000 tons;
- US$1.10 per net registered ton for vessels over 5,000 tons with a maximum of $27,500;
- Annual tonnage dues are 10% of the initial fee plus $1,500 for vessels up to 25,000, and $0.11 per ton for vessels over 25,000 tons, plus $1,500.

OFFSHORE LAWS AND REGULATIONS

This is a non-exhaustive list of the main Bahamas statutes affecting offshore and non-resident business. The statutes are listed in alphabetical order – click on the statute for a fuller description of the statute or the legal regime it forms part of.

Bahamas Free Trade Zone Act
Banks and Trust Companies Act 1965
Business Licenses Act 1980
Companies Act 1992
Exchange Control Act 1952
Exchange Control Regulations 1956
Exempted Limited Partnership Act 1995
External Insurance Act 1983
Fraudulent Dispositions Act 1991
Hotels Encouragement Act
Industries Encouragement Act
Insurance Act 1969
International Business Companies Act 1989
International Business Companies (Amendment) Act 1994
International Persons Landholding Act 1993
Merchant Shipping Act 1976
Mutual Funds Act 1995
Registration of Business Names Act 1989
Securities Board Act 1995
Trust (Choice of Governing Law) Act 1989
Trustee Act 1893
Trustee Act 1998

In the effort to bring The Bahamas' financial services sector into compliance with international standards and practices, there is much legislation that has been amended but the government has some way to go before it fully complies with the rules of the international community. Laws currently under review are the:

- new Financial Intelligence Unit Act 2000
- new Criminal Justice (International Cooperation) Act 2000
- Central Bank of the Bahamas (Amendment) Act 2000
- Banks and Trust Companies Regulation (Amendment) Act 2000
- Banks (Amendment) Act 2000
- new Proceeds of Crime Act 2000
- new International Business Companies Act 2000
- new Financial Service Providers Act 2000
- Mutual Legal Assistance (Amendment) Act 2000

The new laws will be introduced to the Bahamas' Parliament during October-November 2000. Already the government has created a Finance Intelligent Unit which will have the authority to request a bank to hold the money of an account holder suspected of criminal activity for up to 72 hours while it goes to court for an order to confiscate money or block transactions.'

TRUST LAW

Bahamian trust law is based on English common law, and the Bahamian Trustee Act 1893. Later legislation includes The Trust (Choice of Governing Law) Act 1989, the Fraudulent Dispositions Act 1991 and the Trustee Act 1998, which repeals the Trustee Act 1983 and the Variation of Trusts Act 1983.

The Trust (Choice of Governing Law) Act 1989 gives protection to Bahamian trusts and their settlors in civil law countries against forced inheritance claims. The Act makes Bahamian law the proper law of a trust if the deed so declares, and makes the trust immune to foreign judgements.

The Fraudulent Dispositions Act 1991 establishes a 2-year limitation period for creditors' attacks on asset protection trusts; the attacker has to prove fraud against the settlor.

The Trustee Act 1998 is an important piece of legislation which updates Bahamian trust law on many fronts. Some of the more important provisions are as follows:

- A settlor can retain a wide range of powers without falling foul of 'sham' trust legislation;
- Trustees are given wide statutory investment and management powers unless the trust deed negates them;
- Trustees' indemnities are recited in the statute;
- A wide range of trust purposes are encompassed, including accumulation trusts;
- The role of Protector is recognised;
- There are extensive disclosure provisions;
- Exemption from all taxes and from stamp duty (an initial $50 stamp is required on all trust deeds);
- Exemption from registration except where an interest in Bahamian property is to be protected;
- Exemption from exchange control regulations for non-resident beneficiaries.

The Act was to have included legislation covering purpose trusts; this will now be enacted separately.

Much trust work in the Bahamas is handled by Public or Restricted Trust Administration companies, which are often affiliated to or owned by banks. Trust Administrators are licensed by the Central Bank under the Banks and Trust Companies Regulation Act 1965. The application process is lengthy and thorough, particularly for Public Trust Administrators. A foreign company can apply for a license as a branch, or with a subsidiary, which is necessarily a Bahamian-incorporated company (not an International Business Company). The license when issued specifies that a Trust Administrator is either resident (subject to exchange controls) or non-resident (exempt from exchange controls).

The minimum capital requirement for Trust Administrators is $1m for Public and $100,000 for Restricted Administrators (the clients of a Restricted Administrator are specified in the license and cannot be changed without approval). Capital is then expected to keep pace with the growth of the business, not falling below 5% of total assets. Public Trust Administrators must also post a fidelity bond of $1m.

BANKING LAW

The Bahamian banking is regulated by the Central Bank of the Bahamas under the Banks and Trust Companies Regulation Act 1965. Banking licenses are restricted or unrestricted (public); restricted licenses permit banking services to be provided only to a named list of clients which cannot be changed without approval. Restricted licenses are suited to group treasury operations.

The Central Bank prefers that applications for unrestricted banking licenses should come from reputable financial institutions; if this is not the case then the Central Bank requires ownership to be spread among five or more independent shareholders, and will examine antecedents and net worth very carefully.

The application process demands extensive information, and includes an interview at the Central Bank, a 5-year business plan including pro-forma financial statements, and a description of proposed operational control structures. Once licensed, full financial statements must be filed annually. See Offshore Legal and Tax Regimes for details of registration fees payable.

The minimum paid-up capital required for a public bank is $2m, and capital must keep pace with growth of the business, at a minimum 5% of assets, or 8% of risk assets. No more than 15% of total assets may be loaned to or invested in any one business or group. Minimum paid-up capital for a restricted-license bank is $100,000.

A foreign bank can operate either as a branch or through a subsidiary. The licensing process is the same in both cases. A subsidiary will have to be a Companies Act company (see Forms of Company) rather than an International Business Company (they are not permitted to engage in banking services), which is not ideal. It is quite normal for the Bahamian operations of foreign banks to be managed by local professional firms, thus avoiding local business licensing requirements (a banking license is still required).

Banking licenses specify the exchange control status of the bank concerned: a resident license means that the bank can operate freely in Bahamian dollars, but will need to pay a premium to buy other currencies; a non-resident license means that the bank is free to operate in foreign currencies, but requires permission for Bahamian dollar transactions.

As part of the Bahamas' response to its inclusion in June 2000 on the FATF list of 15 jurisdictions having inadequate defences against money laundering, the Bahamas amended its Bank and Trust Company Regulations to require all licensees to be physically present in the Bahamas. Companies are to maintain their banking records locally, and existing offshore companies will be required to conform to these regulations within 3 years. The Government expects that the adoption of the amendments to the Central Bank Act and the Banks and Trust Companies Regulation Act and the implementation of the new regulatory and supervisory regime by The Central Bank will result in improved supervision, including an appropriate level of on-site inspection of banks, full cooperation on cross-border supervision of banks, and enhanced cooperation between the Central Bank and overseas regulatory authorities.

INSURANCE LAW

Bahamian captive insurers are regulated by Office of the Registrar of Insurance, part of the Finance Ministry, under the External Insurance Act 1983. Licenses are issued by the Finance Minister on the Registrar's recommendation after a thorough application process; the Registrar will want to meet applicants and needs to know the identity and to establish the bona fides and substance of the key parties involved.

Insurance companies need to use Companies Act incorporation since the International Business Company is not permitted to engage in insurance activity.

The External Insurance Act lays down minimum net worth figures, but the Registrar will normally expect to see at least $250,000 provided in cash for an external insurer. There is no legal requirement for these funds to be held locally, but the Registrar may in some cases insist on it. A net premium to capital and surplus ratio of not wider than 3:1 is expected. To qualify for a license under the External Insurance Act, an insurer is normally expected to take in at least $500,000 of premiums annually; smaller companies will be licensed under the domestic Insurance Act, qualified as non-resident.

The Government knows that Bahamian insurance law needs to be updated, and legislation can be expected soon. See Offshore Legal and Tax Regimes for details of registration and license fees payable.

MUTUAL FUND LAW

The mutual fund sector is regulated under the Mutual Funds Act 1995 and the Securities Board Act 1995, which established a Securities Board operating on self-regulatory principles: mutual funds can be directly regulated, but more commonly are regulated through licensed administrators who can grant licenses directly to funds. In 1999 the Securities Board is converting into a Securities Commission under the Securities Industry Act 1999, which lays the foundations for a stock and securities exchange. Mutual fund administrators will continue to be licensed under the Mutual Funds Act 1995, and regulated by the Commission directly or indirectly.

The Mutual Funds Act divides investment funds into a number of classes:

- Exempt Funds (ie exempt from licensing), being funds with no more than 15 investors, a majority of whom can appoint or remove the fund manager;
- Authorised funds, being funds with a minimum subscription level of $50,000, or which are listed on a recognised stock exchange - such funds need only to register with the Securities Board; and
- Other funds, which are required to be licensed.

Licenses are normally obtained from a Mutual Fund Administrator, who is in turn licensed by the Securities Board. Mutual Fund Administrators licenses are unrestricted or restricted. Restricted licenses limit the administrator to a specified list of clients which cannot be changed without approval. Unrestricted licensees must have minimum capital of $500,000 (or $150,000 plus liability insurance coverage of $350,000), must have a physical office in the Bahamas, and at least two resident agents.

Licensed Administrators are subject to numerous regulations, and need to apply 'know your customer' rules to their clients. They are audited annually by approved auditors and must submit audited accounts within 4 months of the end of a year (the same rule applies to the mutual funds themselves).

Bahamian mutual funds have investment freedom, except as regards Bahamian real estate. Most funds choose International Business Company, Limited Duration Company, Exempted Limited Partnership or Unit Trust form, all of which have taxation and exchange control advantages - see Forms of Company and Offshore Legal and Tax Regimes). Funds of funds and umbrella funds are permitted. Units can be offered in bearer form, although many institutions won't deal in them.

The Commission has sweeping powers to control mutual funds and mutual fund administrators, if it chooses to use them.

NB: This is an abbreviated statement of some of the main features of the Bahamas Mutual Funds Act and should not be used as the basis for making investment decisions, which require appropriate professional guidance.

BASIC LEGAL BUSINESS ENTITIES FOR OFFSHORE ACTIVITIES

The majority of companies formed in the BVI for offshore purposes are incorporated under the International Business Companies Act 1989 (see below). However this law did not supersede the existing companies law, most recently re-stated in the Companies Act 1992, which is based on English law and is used to form various types of company used by businesses trading in the Bahamas, and also for certain other special purposes.

Companies formed under the Companies Act 1992 can be private companies limited by shares or by guarantee, or can be public companies. For all these types of company, Memorandum and Articles of Association must be filed at the Companies Registry, there need to be a minimum of two members, and there must be a registered office in the Bahamas. If a company is going to trade locally, it will need an appropriate business license.

DOMESTIC LIMITED COMPANY

A domestic resident company limited by shares is usually formed for the purposes of carrying on local business.

There must be at least two directors. The company's annual return includes a list of the members, and is kept on the public register. An annual audit can be dispensed with, if all shareholders agree. There is no requirement to file financial statements.

Shares need not have a par value, and when paid up, need not have distinguishing numbers. Bearer shares can be issued with exchange control permission.

COMPANY LIMITED BY GUARANTEE

Under the Companies Act, a company limited by guarantee must have a minimum of two members; the Memorandum of Association contains a statement of the amount up to which the members guarantee the company's debts. The Articles can provide for the members to have differing 'shares' of the assets and liabilities.

The Company Limited by Guarantee has certain advantages, including that there is no list of members on the annual return, and that control over assets can be achieved without the use of shares; in some jurisdictions, profits realised from such companies are classified as capital gains rather than as income. Specialist advice is required by anyone considering the use of a company limited by guarantee.

PUBLIC COMPANY

A public company formed under the Companies Act is similar to a private company limited by shares except that there is a compulsory annual audit, and there must be at least three directors. A list of all officers, directors and managers of the company must be kept at the registered office and sent to the Registrar-General along with the annual return.

INTERNATIONAL BUSINESS COMPANY

The International Business Company is the most widely used vehicle for offshore operations in the Bahamas; it normally takes the form of a private company limited by shares. The governing legislation is the International Business Companies Act 1989, updated by the International Business Companies (Amendment) Act 1994. Statutory requirements are minimal, and flexible:

- Only one director, who may be corporate, and two shareholders are required;
- Shareholders, directors and officers need not be resident in the Bahamas and there is no stipulation as to their nationality;
- There is no minimum capital requirement; shares may be either registered or bearer and may be issued in any currency;
- Accounts need not be kept; however, if they are kept there is no requirement for an audit.
- A share register needs to be kept, but shareholders may be nominees or 'bearer'; no returns are needed of shareholders, directors or officers;
- Shareholders and directors meetings need not be held in the Bahamas and can be held by telephone;
- The Memorandum and Articles of Association are the only documents to be held on the public record;
- The legislation contains asset protection clauses against actions emanating from without the Bahamas; it also contains provisions for the protection of minority shareholders;
- An IBC is exempt from Bahamian Exchange Control, from stamp duty and from other taxes and estate duties for 20 years from the date of incorporation;
- an IBC can be managed, controlled and operated from the Bahamas.

A company incorporated or (if foreign) registered under the Companies Act 1992 can switch to IBC status if it qualifies under the legislation.

IBC status is granted subject to certain conditions:

- No business may be transacted with residents in the Bahamas;
- No ownership interest in real property in the Bahamas is permitted; property may be leased for office use only;
- Banking, insurance or re-insurance business is not permitted;
- Engaging in the business of company management or providing registered facilities for Bahamian incorporated companies is not permitted.

IBCs are permitted to own shares in other Bahamian companies, maintain bank accounts in the jurisdiction and employ the services of local professionals.

It is usual to use a registered agent in the Bahamas to incorporate an IBC (eventually it is obligatory to appoint one anyway). Fees for incorporation of an IBC are based on the company's authorised share capital. Normally, the incorporation process takes no more than one day.

Statutory incorporation and annual registration fees are as follows:

Authorised Capital	Incorporation Fee	Annual Fee
Up to $5,000	$900	$100
$5,001 to $50,000	$1,100	$300
Over $50,000	$1,500	$1,000

LIMITED DURATION COMPANY

The International Business Company (Amendment) Act 1994 introduced the Limited Duration Company, which is essentially the same as the IBC but with a life limited to 30 years. This form is directed towards a certain class of US investors - when suitably structured the LDC has the characteristics of a partnership and is treated as such in the US, where it is known as a Limited Liability Company.

FOREIGN COMPANY

A foreign company can operate a branch in the Bahamas with minimal formality and no registration requirements, but once the branch is recognised as an 'undertaking' under the Companies Act 1992, or as a 'trading' branch, it has to register with the Registrar-General. The following amount to having 'undertaking' status:

- the keeping of a place of business;
- the holding of a licence (or the requirement to hold one) for specified business;
- the holding of a licence (or the requirement to hold one) for selling securities; or
- having a local telephone listing.

Registration involves filing a notarised and legalised copy of the company's Memorandum and Articles of Association (or its Statutes) and details of the directors and officers. A Certificate of Registration is issued, and the company (the branch) then has the same position as a Bahamian incorporated company, ie it must maintain a local registered office, etc etc as above.

Fees payable on registration are $50 plus stamp duty of $600, then $1,000 annual registration fee.

If the foreign company (branch) intends to trade within the Bahamas or to employ more than two Bahamians, it needs to apply to the Bahamas Investment Authority for clearance from the National Economic Council, and it needs to obtain the relevant business licence as does a Bahamian company.

It is open to a qualifying foreign company, once registered, to become an International Business Company (see above).

LIMITED PARTNERSHIP

Bahamian law relating to partnerships is essentially similar to English law. General or limited partnerships are allowed.

Iin a limited partnership there must be at least one general partner with unlimited liability, and the limited partners may not take part in management of the partnership. There must be a written partnership agreement which must be registered, and one of the general partners must file a notarised declaration of the sum contributed by the limited partners.

Partnerships which trade in the Bahamas need the appropriate business license, as for limited companies.

EXEMPTED LIMITED PARTNERSHIP

The Exempted Limited Partnership Act (1995) created a partnership form (ELP) equivalent to the International Business Company, and has the same limitations on local activity as the IBC (see above). The structure is the same as for a limited partnership (see above); a general partner can also be a limited partner, and one of the general partners must be either a Bahamian resident or a company incorporated under the Companies Act 1992 or the International Business Companies Act 1989.

An ELP must be registered, and the names and addresses of all general partners must be filed. On issue of the registration certificate, the ELP becomes exempt for 50 years from exchange controls, from all forms of taxation, from stamp duty, and from business license fees. (However, if one of the general partners is a Bahamian resident, then there may be some exchange control implications).

The initial registration fee for an ELP is $850, and the continuing annual fee is $450. An annual declaration must be filed confirming adherence to the local trading prohibition.

TRUSTS

The trust law of the Bahamas is based on English trust law, and was codified in the Trustee Act 1893, but there have been a number of recent statutes which update and extend Bahamas trust law, particularly the Trustee Act 1998 which repeals the Trustee Act 1983 and the Variation of Trusts Act Cap 166. The Trust (Choice of Governing Law) Act 1989 protects against forced heirship provisions; the Fraudulent Dispositions Act 1991 strengthened the position of asset protection trusts; and legislation dealing with purpose trusts is being drafted. See Law of Offshore for a fuller description of the legal regime for Trusts in the Bahamas.

Bahamian trusts (other than those holding Bahamian property) do not have to be registered, and the 1998 Act disapplies Exchange Control Regulations to non-resident settlors, donors, beneficiaries and trustees - therefore it is no longer necessary for trusts to be registered with the Central Bank as non-resident. This applies to existing trusts as well as to new ones.

Trusts (other than those holding Bahamian real estate) with non-resident beneficiaries are exempt from all taxes, including stamp duty on transfers into trust.

Under the 1998 Act, new trusts need to be stamped with a $50 Bahamas revenue stamp, which can be bought for cash and does not involve any disclosures. See Offshore Legal and Tax Regimes for further details of the tax position of Bahamian trusts.

The 1998 Act provides for the appointment of a 'protector of trust', effectively a supervisor of the trustee(s), and also managing and custodian trustees.

A company offering trust services must obtain a licence under the Banks and Trust Companies Act 1965 and conform to various conditions.

OFFSHORE TAX REGULATIONS FOR BAHAMAS

The term 'offshore' is not used in Bahamian legislation or in describing company forms. Abstaining from local trading activity is the key factor which allows use of the various 'offshore' corporate forms, and ensures long term exemption from taxation and some or all of stamp duty, exchange controls and business licensing requirements. Since there are no general corporate taxes other than stamp duty, there is no separate 'offshore' sector as such in taxation terms.

FORMS OF OFFSHORE OPERATION

Offshore (external) operations take place mostly within the following forms:

- Domestic Limited Company
- International Business Company
- Limited Duration Company
- Exempted Limited Partnership
- Foreign Company
- Trust

TAX TREATMENT OF OFFSHORE OPERATIONS

In the Bahamas there is no income or corporation tax, no capital gains tax, no VAT or sales tax, and no withholding tax. Companies and partnerships pay annual fees to the Government depending on their nature and capitalisation. There is stamp duty and there are some property taxes. Exempted Limited Partnerships are exempt from both, as are Trusts provided that their beneficiaries are non-resident.

Banks and Trust Companies (ie administrators of trusts) are also exempt provided that they have non-resident licenses (this is a matter of practice - a license is issued as resident or non-resident depending on circumstances). All of the offshore entities, and non-resident domestic companies, are exempt from exchange controls.

Mutual Funds are exempt from taxes and exchange controls if they have an appropriate corporate form; in practice therefore they are exempt.

FEES PAYABLE BY FINANCIAL INSTITUTIONS

Financial institutions licensed under the Banks and Trust Companies Law 1965 pay fees on registration and annual fees as follows:

Authorised Agents and Authorised Dealers	$160,000
Authorised Dealers	$100,000
Authorised Agents	$60,000
Other Public Institutions	$25,000
Restricted Bank and Trust	$5,000
Restricted Bank	$5,000
Restricted Trust	$3,000
Non-Active Bank and Trust	$1,800

'Other Public Institutions' includes banks and trust administration companies; 'Restricted' banks and trusts are those that deal only with a list of customers included in their license and which cannot be altered without permission.

Captives are licensed under the External Insurance Act 1983, and pay a fee of $2,500 on registration and annually thereafter. In addition, $650 is paid annually for each underwriting manager employed by a captive insurer.

On registration, a captive insurer gains exemption from taxes for 15 years.

Resident insurance companies pay a registration fee of $1,000 and the same annually thereafter, plus 2% of gross premiums collected each quarter.

Insurance companies are not permitted to use the International Business Coimpany or LDC corporate forms, but must establish a Bahamian domestic limited company or must register as foreign companies. Captives registered under the External Insurance Act are exempt from exchange controls.

New insurance legislation is in the pipeline which will update the somewhat outdated Bahamian insurance acts.

Mutual funds and their administrators are licensed under the Mutual Fund Law 1995 and pay fees on registrationn and annually thereafter as follows:

- Unrestricted mutual fund administrator: $5,000;
- Restricted mutual fund administrator: $2,000;
- Self-administered or single-fund administrator: $500;
- Unlicensed mutual fund: $200.

NB: Fees charged by administration or registration agents are a separate matter; the above fees are simply set annual dues.

TAXATION OF FOREIGN EMPLOYEES OF OFFSHORE OPERATIONS

This section refers to the taxation of foreign employees in the Bahamas. See Domestic Personal Taxes for the general principles of individual taxation in the Bahamas, which also apply to the resident employees of non-resident entities. There are in fact no personal taxes as such in the Bahamas, and there is no distinction between the employees of resident or non-resident operations.

EXCHANGE CONTROL

The Bahamas have exchange controls, under the Exchange Control Act and Regulations 1956, applying to resident individuals and companies, who need consent from the Central Bank to conduct operations in foreign currencies. Likewise, non-resident or offshore companies, who are free to deal in foreign currencies, require Central Bank consent to deal in Bahamian dollars.

Residents comprise: Bahamian nationals, companies beneficially owned in the Bahamas, and companies whether Bahamanian or foreign-owned operating within the Bahamas. Foreign nationals with work permits who live in the Bahamas are also normally considered to be resident.

Non-residents comprise: foreign nationals living abroad, or, if living in the Bahamas, without the right to work there; and foreign companies and foreign-owned Bahamian companies trading exclusively outside the Bahamas.

Residents who want to make external investments in foreign currencies will usually be allowed to do so, but have to buy the foreign currency at a premium; non-residents who want to invest into the Bahamas may do so, but the opportunities for portfolio investment are very limited.

OFFSHORE ACTIVITIES IN THE BAHAMAS

The International Business Company and its cousin, the Limited Duration Company, are not allowed to do business with Bahamian residents, but are allowed the following activities in the Bahamas:

- To maintain bank accounts;
- To make and maintain contact with professional firms;
- To maintain books and records;
- To hold meetings of directors or members;
- To lease real estate for use as an office.

It is possible to obtain a license from the Minister of Finance to carry out other types of business activity on the island, if he considers it is in the interests of Bermuda.

Other offshore and non-resident entities operate under broadly similar regimes to the International Business Company.

THE BAHAMAS INCLUSION ON FATF BLACKLIST

In June 2000, the Bahamas was identified by the FATF as a non-cooperative and harmful tax haven. The result of this is that the Bahamas is one of fifteen tax jurisdictions placed on an FATF blacklist. Each 'harmful' tax haven has a year in which to correct its tax regulations and legislation, once it has done so the tax haven will be removed from the list.

The FATF released its next annual report in June 2001, in which the organisation revised its list of countries and territories deemed non-cooperative. Only four were removed from the list, including the Bahamas (the other three being the Cayman Islands, Liechtenstein and Panama). The Bahamas was praised by the FATF for its substantial efforts to conform to forty recommendations set out by the FATF in a code of good practice governing money laundering.

EMPLOYMENT AND RESIDENCE

Work permits are necessary for non-Bahamians to be employed: key (senior or specially-skilled) people are issued permits; in other cases it is wise to discuss the possibility of a permit with the Bahamas Investment Authority in advance.

Anyone wishing to reside in the Bahamas must obtain a residence permit from the Immigration Department. Home-owners can obtain an annually-renewable Home Owner's Residence Card which acts as a visa for entry and residence during its validity. Major international investors and existing owners of properties worth more than $500,000 benefit from accelerated treatment of residence applications

The International Persons Landholding Act 1993 reversed a previously deterrent stance and actively encourages the purchase of local residential property by foreigners. Acquisition of a single family dwelling or up to 5 acres of vacant land for construction of a dwelling no longer needs an advance permit, but can be registered after purchase. Rule for inheritors of Bahamian properties have been similarly relaxed. Fees for the (compulsory) registration of real estate and residence permits are as follows:

- Application for registration: $25
- Application for permit: $25
- On issue of certificate of registration or issue of permit:

Value of property, $	Fee, $
Up to 50,000	50
Under 101,000	75
101,000 and over	100

Homeowner resident card: $500

CORPORATE TAXATION

In the Bahamas there are no taxes on profits, dividends or income; there is no capital gains tax, no withholding tax and no sales tax. The taxes impinging on companies are business license fees, stamp duty, property taxes and import duty. Most offshore or non-resident entities are exempt from business license fees and many are exempt from stamp duty. Corporate entities pay incorporation or registration fees to the Government:

BUSINESS LICENSE FEES

Under the Business Licenses Act 1980 (as amended) enterprises operating in the Bahamas are liable to pay annual license fees. Non-resident entities, International Business Companies, Limited Duration Companies and Exempted Limited Partnerships are not liable for these fees; nor are banks, trust companies, insurance companies, mutual funds or ship holding companies, all of which have their own separate fee regimes

Business License Fees depend on annual turnover and gross profit percentage; the rules are complicated and professional advice is necessary. Some illustrative situations are as follows:

- Businesses with turnover below $50,000 are exempt;
- Businesses with turnover between $50,000 and $100,000 pay between $250 and $800 depending on the level of gross profit;
- Larger businesses pay gradually increasing amounts; a business with turnover of $30m and a high gross profit percentage might pay as much as $500,000 or 1% of turnover.

PAYROLL TAXES

Under the National Insurance Act 1972 as amended, Bahamian employers, employees and the self-employed pay social security contributions.

Employees pay 3.4% of earnings (up to maximum earnings of $13,000 pa); employers pay 5.4% of earnings to the same maximum; self-employed persons pay 8.8% of earnings to the same maximum.

Although all employers and employees pay these contributions, whether or not they are resident, benefits can generally be claimed only by resident Bahamians. Even in Paradise, it seems, there are thorns on the roses. Expatriates returning home to die at 60 after a lifetime of service in the Bahamas may be able to get a refund of contributions, or can elect to receive a pension.

STAMP DUTIES

Stamp duties are payable in a number of situations in the Bahamas. The most important of these are company incorporation, real estate transactions and overseas remittances of Bahamian currency.

Stamp duty on the capital (initially and on subsequent increases) of a domestic limited company runs at $64 on the first $5,000 and $3 on each additional $1,000.

Stamp duty on real estate transactions ranges from 2% on small amounts to 8% on sales over $100,000. It is normally shared between the parties. There is a 1% stamp duty on mortgages paid by the borrower.

Bahamian currency exported from the jurisdiction is stamped at 0.25%.

REAL ESTATE TAX

Real estate tax is levied on the following types of land and real property:

- Developed real estate on the island of New Providence;
- Developed real estate on other islands if owned by non-Bahamian persons;
- Undeveloped real estate on New Providence owned by (you guessed it) non-Bahamian persons.

Real estate holdings must be declared annually to the Chief Valuation Officer.

The rates of tax are as follows:

- Owner-occupied property:

Value, $	Rate of tax, %
Up to 100,000	Nil
100,001 - 500,000	1.0
Over 500,000	1.5

- Other property:

Value, $	Rate of tax, %
Up to 500,000	1.0
Over 500,000	2.0

Unimproved property in New Providence	3.0

DOUBLE TAX TREATIES

Since the Bahamas do not levy direct taxes, there are no double tax treaties between the Bahamas and other countries.

OTHER INTERNATIONAL AGREEMENTS

Mutual Assistance Treaties: There are mutual assistance treaties with the US, Canada and the UK which include exchange of information provisions; but fiscal information is excluded. Disclosure is limited to criminal matters, and tax evasion is not a crime in the Bahamas. The Bahamian statute Reciprocal Enforcement of Judgements Act 1924 allows Commonwealth judgements to be enforced in the Bahamas, but revenue matters are excluded.

In June 2000 the Bahamas was placed on the FATF blacklist of 15 jurisdictions having inadequate defences against money-laundering, and the US State Dept issued an 'Advisory' against the jurisdiction. The Bahamas also figures on the OECD's list of 35 offshore jurisdictions offering 'unfair' tax competition.

Jurisdictions which do not conform to OECD 'requirements' by May 2001 face possible sanctions from the US and other OECD countries. As part of its endeavours to avoid sanctions and to have the 'Advisory' lifted, the Bahams has taken a number of steps, including the establishment of a Financial Intelligence Unit. In August 2000 an amendment was made to the Evidence (Proceedings In Other Jurisdictions) Act. This now allows international investigators to obtain details of local or foreign bank account holders in The Bahamas under a considerably wider range of circumstances than before.

BILATERAL INVESTMENT AGREEMENTS

The Bahamas is in the process of negotiating an investment protection agreement with the United Kingdom. There is no Bilateral Investment Treaty (BIT) between The Bahamas and the United States.

Bahamas 'Caribbean Basin Initiative (CBI): The Bahamas was designated a beneficiary of the Caribbean Basin Initiative (CBI) in 1985. As a result, with certain restrictions, products manufactured in the Bahamas qualify for duty-free entry into the United States. High wage rates, however, combined with the country's small manufacturing and agricultural sectors, have hindered The Bahamas' ability to exploit these benefits. In addition, The Bahamas' failure to enter negotiations with the United States for a bilateral Tax Information Exchange Agreement (TIEA) precluded the use of 936 (QPS II) credits for projects in The Bahamas or the use of the convention tax benefit for business conventions held in The Bahamas.

OPIC AND OTHER INVESTMENT INSURANCE PROGRAMS

In 1992, OPIC approved two investment projects in The Bahamas. It guaranteed up to $10.8 million in loans to the UNIROYAL Chemical Company, Ltd. to assist in the purchase and refurbishment of a plant in Freeport formerly owned by Gist-Brocades, Ltd. UNIROYAL currently uses the plant to produce high performance antioxidants used in the manufacture of plastics for export to North America, Europe, and Asia. In addition, OPIC committed itself to loan up to $1.6

million to LANDQUEST, ltd. for the development of the Princess Cays cruise ship facility on Eleuthera island near Bannerman Town.

CAPITAL OUTFLOW POLICY

Foreign investors in The Bahamas enjoy complete freedom of repatriation on their investments and profits. The Bahamian government does not offer any incentives for investment in other developing countries.

Net inflows associated with transportation services were reduced by $14.4 million to $34.3 million and government's net overseas expenses for services rendered were up by $6.7 million to $23.8 million. Other miscellaneous services net outflows grew by an estimated $12.6 million to $214.8 million.

MAJOR FOREIGN INVESTORS

Major current foreign investments in The Bahamas include:

--Atlantis, a hotel, resort, and casino complex on Paradise Island near Nassau recently purchased by the South African firm Sun Hotels International;
--Ruffin's Crystal Palace Resort, Casino, And Convention Center, operated by Host Marriott Corporation;
--Coral Island Underwater Observatory, Marine Park, and Hotel formerly owner by an Israeli firm and recently sold to the Ruffin Group owners of the Marriott Crystal Palace Hotel and Casino which also recently bought the Fort Nassau Beach Hotel;
--A container port facility opened in Freeport by Hong Kong investors, Hutchison Whampoa;
--Ambassador Beach Hotel recently purchased from the Bahamian government by the Jamaican company, Superclubs, under the trade name Breezes;
--Royal Bahamian Hotel recently purchased by Sandals company of Jamaica from the Bahamian government;
--The Winding Bay Hotel in Eleuthera owned by Venta, an Italian group;
--PFC Bahamas in Freeport, formerly known as Syntex is now owned by the Swiss pharmaceutical firm Roche;
--Uniroyal Chemical plant manufacturing high performance antioxidants in Freeport;
--Walt Disney World, Orlando recently purchased Gorda Cay, a private island;
--Bahama Star, a large citrus farm being developed on Abaco island by the B.G. Harmon Fruit Company of Florida;
--Grand Bahama Beach and Lucayan Beach Hotels sold to German owned Sun and Sea Estates Limited;
--Cotton Bay Club, Eleuthera recently purchased by Colombian Carlos Sarmiento;
--A large shrimp farm on Long Island operated by the American firm Maritek;
--A tropical fish farm operated on Walker's Cay by Aqua Life, Ltd.;
--Princess Cays, a cruise ship landing facility on Eleuthera Island owned by Landquest;
--Club Med resorts on Paradise Island, Eleuthera, and San Salvador;
--Comfort Suites on Paradise Island;
--Freeport/Lucaya Marina Village developed recently by European investors;
-- Cable Bahamas, Ltd. recently established by a Canadian group
--Island Outpost Resort at Compass Point recently built by a Jamaican music magnate.

TRADE AND PROJECT FINANCING

Bahamian banks tend to be far more conservative than their American counterparts in making business loans, often asking for high levels of collateral. At the end of 1996, the prime lending rate in The Bahamas was unchanged at 6.75%. Commercial bank rates for residential and commercial mortgages ranged from 10.06 - 10.87%, respectively. Consumer loan rates were 14.69%.

The Bahamas Development Bank (BD) was created to assist Bahamians in establishing new businesses or expanding existing concerns through the provision of concessionary funding and technical assistance, for projects which generate jobs and which contribute to the economic growth and development of The Bahamas. Joint ventures between international investors and Bahamians are eligible to access funding from BDB or from the domestic capital market. Bahamians may, however, borrow a percentage of their contributions from BDB or the domestic capital market. An established joint-venture is not debarred from accessing BDB funds.

Recently, there has been talk in the financial sector about eliminating exchange controls. The government has already allowed commercial banks limited exchange control powers. Local financiers believe that eliminating exchange controls will increase investor confidence, facilitate the free flow of currency in and out of the economy, and enable the government to measure the performance of the economy accurately.

The Bahamas is a beneficiary of the Caribbean Basin Initiative (CBI) and the Overseas Private Investment Corporation (OPIC), and EXIMBANK financing is available.

U.S. commercial banks operating in The Bahamas include:

BRITISH-AMERICAN BANK
P. O. Box N-7502
Nassau, Bahamas
Tel: (242) 327-5170
Fax: (242) 327-5166

CITIBANK BAHAMAS
P. O. Box N-8158
Nassau, Bahamas
Tel: (242) 322-4240
Fax: (242) 323-3088

THE CAPITAL MARKETS IN THE CARIBBEAN[3]

Accordingly, the CARICOM Secretariat has been mandated to develop and implement a Public Education and Awareness Programme across the Region. These booklets which were done for the programme are designed to enhance investors' knowledge of the functioning of the regional stock exchange/ market and carry the following titles: Volume 1: The Capital Market in the Caribbean; Volume 2: Buying and Selling Securities; Volume 3: The Importance of the Regional Stock Exchange; and, Volume 4: Cross Border Operations. These four volumes are also intended to provide an appreciation of:

- the role of investment in economic growth and development,
- the benefits of a diversified investment portfolio; and,
- the rationale of regional policy makers in encouraging the development of a regional capital market.

Investing in stocks is a relatively new area for a number of Caribbean people. For a number of people, investment means buying a house or putting money in the bank. This view however, is slowly changing as more and more people are putting money in other areas of investment. As part of the mandate to the CARICOM Secretariat to educate the regional public, a monograph series has been developed , aimed at sensitizing the public on common issues in the area of regional investment. The series answer many questions about investing across the Region and provide some insight into the operations of the Regional Stock Exchange and investment in general. Caribbean people are realizing that they can no longer rely on the domestic economy for maximizing their financial goals and are seeking other avenues for that wealth creation. By this is meant getting the most out of a limited amount of income available to the average household.

Whenever an individual is thinking of making a new investment, one of the first thing to do is to get some basic research about the company, its principals and the investment. This is even more important when undertaking investment outside your domestic market. It is important that you read as much about the company as you can in order to know exactly what you are investing your money in. Knowing that information is hard to come by, The CARICOM Secretariat is producing this monograph series in an effort to keep the regional public informed about investment.

THE CAPITAL MARKET ANS CARICOM[4]

To really understand the capital market it is important to understand the concept of a market. A market is a place where people meet to buy and sell goods. Most Caribbean people are familiar with the markets where ground provisions and other items are sold. At these markets which have a fixed location there are a number of buyers and sellers. These buyers can compare prices and then make their selection after they are satisfied that they are getting the best value for their money. In these markets the sellers of the goods have the benefit of reaching a number of buyers in one place and this saves time and money. If there are a number of buyers wanting a particular item then naturally the seller will be able to get more for it than if there were only a few people who want the item. The seller would then set the price based on the demand for the commodity.

[3] Prepared by: **Ms. Enid E. Bissember** Economic Intelligence & Policy Unit Eddy Grant Annexe CARICOM Secretariat 54 High Street Kingston Georgetown **GUYANA**. **for The Regional Capital Market Committee Educational and Awareness Program**
[4] Carebbean Community and Common Market

The capital market operates in the much the same way. It is where business people and investors are brought together some want to raise capital and others want a return on their funds.

There are a number of institutions that make up the capital market. These include but are not limited to:-

- merchant banks/ investment banks
- insurance companies
- finance companies
- unit trusts
- stock exchanges

THE PRIMARY MARKET

An investor who purchases newly issued securities by a public company is participating in the primary market. When such securities are purchased the net proceeds go directly to the issuing company. This is the only time when the funds go to the company. The primary market directs funds from investors to companies and governments where it is put to use to help in the overall growth and development of the firm and economies. The primary market can provide the funds that are needed by firms to add new product lines, improve the services offered to customers, and create new jobs. Investors who participate in the primary market have the opportunity to purchase securities(stocks/ shares, bonds, and debentures) directly from the company. In any economy the primary market is one of the engines of growth.

THE SECONDARY MARKET

An investor who resells existing securities is participating in the secondary market. These are markets where investors buy and sell securities among themselves and the money generated here goes from the buying investor to the selling investor. If there were no secondary markets investors who bought securities from a company would have to hang on to them or wait on the right opportunity to sell. They would not be able recover their investment as easily as with the existence of a secondary market. If investors can't make money by selling the securities they bought in the primary market then it would be very difficult for companies wanting to offer shares to do so .The secondary market is very useful and important to investors. It provides them with an avenue to buy and sell their securities at any time that they desire. Being able to buy and sell at any time adds liquidity to the market. An active secondary markets gives support to the primary market.

THE STOCK MARKET

A stock market is an important part of modern economies and a vital link between companies needing capital and investors with money to invest. Through investment in securities such as common stocks/ shares investors become part owners of the companies of their choice and are able to participate in the companies' growth and development. In turn , companies which raise capital from the sale of common stocks are able to do the things that they would not have been able to do if they had to rely on another source of funds. This source might require regular payment of interest and principal at times when the company might not be in a position to do so perhaps because it is expanding its product line or modernizing its plant. Obtaining funds in the stock market allows the company to do all that and at the end of specified intervals declare a dividend for its shareholders.

THE STOCK EXCHANGE

Most people have heard of stock exchanges. They are a key element in the capital markets . A stock exchange is the place where buyers and sellers of securities (e.g. stocks, bonds,) trade with each other and where prices of the securities are established based on supply and demand. The more securities that are available for sale the lower the price at which the buyer can obtain those securities and the less that are available for sale the more the prospective buyer would be expected to pay . Companies can use the stock exchange to raise new capital , but most of the trading that is often talked about is trading among investors which is called secondary trading. The seller is no longer the company which issued the security, but someone who bought the security earlier, either as a new issue from the company or from another investor , and now would like to sell. The buyer of the security is another investor. The stock exchange is better known as a place where stocks, which have already, been issued can be traded among investors.

THE REGIONAL STOCK EXCHANGE

The idea for the development of a Regional stock exchange/ market emerged in 1989 on the initiative of the Government of Jamaica. In 1991 the three existing stock exchanges in the Region; the Barbados Securities Exchange, the Jamaica Stock Exchange and the Trinidad and Tobago Stock Exchange entered into an arrangement for cross border trading in equity. A Regional stock exchange/market was seen as an integral part of the deepening and widening of the integration process in CARICOM.

The objectives of the regional stock exchange have been identified as:

- to promote the movement of capital across the Region;
- to increase investment opportunities;
- to encourage optimum financing for CARICOM firms irrespective of where the entity resides; and,
- to increase the attractiveness of the region as an area for investment, both by regional and non-regional investors.

The Grand Anse Declaration agreed to a scheme for the movement of capital across the region; starting at first with the three existing exchanges (Barbados, Jamaica, Trinidad and Tobago). An arrangement was worked out and implemented in April 1991 under which those stock exchanges (Barbados, Jamaica and Trinidad and Tobago) undertook to cross list and cross trade stocks.

MEMBERS OF THE REGIONAL STOCK EXCHANGE

The members of the Regional Stock Exchange are the stock exchanges of Barbados, Jamaica and Trinidad and Tobago.

IS THE REGIONAL STOCK EXCHANGE AN ACTUAL PLACE?

The regional stock exchange is not a physical entity but an agreement of cooperation to facilitate the purchase and sale of shares cross border. There is no building called the Regional stock exchange. Instead the regional stock exchange is an arrangement entered into by the existing stock exchanges to facilitate the purchase and sale of securities cross border. The stock exchanges of Barbados, Jamaica and Trinidad and Tobago are part of this arrangement. In this market information is exchanged regarding prices and amounts so that the investors' representative who wants to buy or sell a securities can find it at the best price.

The telephone is very important in the Regional Capital Market arrangements.

ADDRESS AND CONTACT NUMBERS FOR MEMBERS OF THE REGIONAL STOCK EXCHANGE

1. SECURITIES EXCHANGE OF BARBADOS

5th Floor Central Bank
Church Village
Bridgetown
St. Michael
BARBADOS

Tel: 246 436 9871/2
Fax: 246 429 8942
E-Mail: sebd@caribsurf.com

2. JAMAICA STOCK EXCHANGE

40 Harbour Street
Kingston
JAMAICA

Tel: 876 967 3271/4
Fax: 876 922-6966
E-Mail: jse@infochan.com

3. TRINIDAD & TOBAGO SECURITIES EXCHANGE

1 Ajax Street
Port-of-Spain
TRINIDAD AND TOBAGO

Tel: 868 627 1704 or 625 7148
Fax: 868 625 0089
E-Mail: tsttstockx@tstt.net.tt

OTHER IMPORTANT ADDRESS

CARIBBEAN COMMUNITY SECRETARIAT (CARICOM)
Bank of Guyana Building
P.O. Box 10827
Georgetown
GUYANA. SOUTH AMERICA

Tel: 592 2 52981; 69261-9
Fax: 592 2 57341, 592-2-67816
E-Mail: webmaster@caricom.org

OFFSHORE BUSINESS SECTOR

OFFSHORE ACTIVITIES

Barbados is well-developed as an international financial centre, although this has come about in an unspectacular way. For 25 years the Government has welcomed offshore business, and has consistently re-invented its legislative apparatus to stay abreast of the competition, while preserving its defences against money-laundering and other criminal activity. Barbados can't claim to have any of the world's largest offshore business sectors, but has growing and successful communities in banking, insurance, 'foreign sales corporations' and shipping, as well as IBC and trust business; mutual funds are a very recent addition to the Barbados product range, and there is a stock exchange, which by the end of 1999 had listings from 18 local companies and a number of international companies including 7 banks.

In July 2000, Barbados pledged to make changes to its financial supervisory regime in order to have its name removed from an OECD blacklist.

This section of the lowtax.net site describes the most important types of offshore business activity carried out from Barbados.

Trade, Marketing and Distribution

Barbados has encouraged commercial activity and manufacturing, especially in high technology. It has taken advantage of its physical location alongside the US to attract a considerable number of Foreign Sales Corporations.

The Government offers either direct or through the Barbados Investment and Development Corporation a wide range of investment incentives applying broadly to manufacturing industry under the Fiscal Incentives Act 1974 and other legislation, giving tax holidays up to 10 years, duty-free importation of materials, assistance with construction of factories, etc.

As well as the US-aimed Foreign Sales Corporation, there is a wide variety of offshore company formats to choose from to suit all purposes.

Along with other offshore jurisdictions, Barbados is a suitable place in which to base e-commerce services for retail or wholesale distribution of material or non-material goods. Barbados has developed a strong computer facilities industry, and can probably give better support to e-commerce than many other jurisdictions.

Banking

Barbados established an offshore banking sector under the Offshore Banking Act 1979 as amended. The Act provides for the licensing of offshore banks, and contains a precise description of offshore banking (see Law of Offshore for details) as the obtaining of funds as deposits or through the sale of financial instruments, the use of such funds to give advances or finance investment, and the use of trusts to hold money or property.

Offshore banking licenses are made available to 'eligible companies' and 'qualified foreign banks'. An eligible company:

- is a limited liability company incorporated under the Companies Act 1982;

- restricts its objects or activities to offshore banking from Barbados;
- has at least one resident Barbadian citizen among its directors;
- meets minimum capital requirements.

Under the Act, the minimum capital is BDS$1m authorised and BDS$0.5m issued if controlled by residents, but BDS$2m authorised and BDS$1m issued if controlled by non-residents. These figures are due to be increased, and the Central Bank is already applying higher limits.

A qualified foreign bank is one that was already licensed under the Offshore Banking Act when it came into effect in 1980, a foreign bank with minimum assets as above, or a subsidiary of a foreign bank approved by the Central Bank.

There are 40 licensed offshore banks in Barbados. The Central Bank has recently strengthened its vetting procedures over applicant banks in response to international money laundering and criminal concerns. Subsidiaries of foreign banks have to provide written authorisation from the parent supervisory authority, and the activities of in-house corporate treasury operations must be consolidated into published group accounts.

Trust Management

Trust Management has been a considerable activity in Barbados for 30 years or more, much of it conducted by the trust departments of banks. Originally the trust was used primarily by wealthy individuals from the major common law countries, but it is now accepted as a major technique of asset protection in all parts of the world. The International Trusts Act 1995 gave Barbados a modern, comprehensive, business-oriented trust regime which has proven attractive, particularly to corporate users. This new, wider market-place for trusts is not necessarily interested so much just in tax avoidance, but also in the efficient management of wealth in a more general sense. There is a sophisticated community of professional advisers on trust matters in Barbados. Individuals can provide trust services without registration, but companies offering trust services must be licensed by the Central Bank under the Offshore Banking Act 1979. Foreign or Barbados-resident companies may obtain licenses.

Real Estate Holding

Barbadian International Business Companies have been put to a variety of uses, but one of the most popular has been as holding vehicles for US real estate, taking advantage of the terms of the US/Barbados double tax convention.

The US tax convention has anti-treaty-shopping clauses, but they are more favourable than is the case in many other double tax treaties. Essentially, a non-Barbadian person can use a Barbados International Business Company to hold the shares of a US real estate company (which should be income-producing); this structure can take advantage of the treaty provisions to escape US estate duty, among other tax benefits.

Insurance

The Barbados insurance sector is regulated under the Exempt Insurance Act 1983. The Ministry of Finance and Economic Affairs is responsible for the insurance sector, and day-to-day supervision is in the hands of the Supervisor of Insurance. Entities involved in insurance are licensed by the Minister under the Act.

More than 300 insurers are licensed under the Act, with annual premiums of approximately US$2bn and assets of US$10bn. A majority of these insurers originate from the US, and are taking advantage of the provisions of the Barbados/US Double Tax Convention, which are not available to insurers located in the other main Caribbean jurisdictions. The Convention allows captives and other insurers in Barbados to write business in the US while avoiding the creation of a permanent establishment, and thus to escape much US taxation.

The Act defines exempt insurance as the business of insuring risks outside Barbados by a company which is not owned by persons resident in Caricom. An applicant for a license under the Act must:

- be incorporated under the Companies Act 1982 as a limited liability company or as a mutual insurance company
- carry on only exempt insurance business;
- have at least one resident Barbadian citizen as a director;
- have only shareholders who are resident outside Caricom;
- must have minimum issued capital (or reserves, in the case of a mutual insurer) of BDS$250,000.

Rent-a-captives are permitted, but there is no provision for protected cell companies.

Solvency rules are as follows:

Premium income
Solvency Requirement
First year
Net assets BDS$250,000
Below BDS$1.5m in previous year
Net assets BDS$250,000
Between BDS$1.5m and $10m in previous year
Net assets 20% of income
Above BDS$10m in previous year
Net assets BDS$2m plus 10% of income over $10m

Licenses are issued to insurers as such; holding companies and management companies involved in offhsore insurance business must register with the Supervisor of Insurance. Licensees and registrants pay an application fee of BDS$500, and initial and ongoing annual license/registration fees of BDS$5,000..

Ship Management and Maritime Operations

The Shipping Act 1994 established a Barbados Ships Registry. Barbados had been a member of the International Maritime Orgaisation since 1969, and subscribes to all the main maritime safety and environmental conventions. There are about 100 vessels in the Barbados registry.

The Principal Registrar is based in London, with a subsidiary Registrar in Bridgetown, and there are provisional registration offices with inspectorates in a number of international maritime centres. Eleven of the major Classification Societies act on behalf of the Barbados Registry. The Registry has obtained ISO 9002 status. Applications for registration require a fairly standard package of title, survey and registration documentation.

The Shipping Act provides for registration of all types of vessel, however owned, but the new Registry is particularly aimed at 'foreign-going' vessels, meaning those which ply to and from Caricom states (but not within Caricom) or outside Caricom altogether. 'Foreign-going' vessels less than 20 years old may join the Registry if they are 'foreign-owned', which means not exclusively owned by Barbados persons; older vessels may join at the Registrar's discretion. There are tax benefits for 'foreign' vessels

The Shipping Corporations Act 1996, which mirrors the provisions of the Companies Act 1982, provides a stand-alone basis for incorporation of a ship ownership or management company, whether the ships concerned are registered in Barbados or elsewhere. Shipping Corporations are non-residential and are exempt from taxes.

As is the case with some other offshore sectors in Barbados, the Barbados/US Tax Convention provides particularly favourable opportunities to US shipping owners and operators, who can obtain domestic tax benefits by operating through a Barbados resident. 'Resident' is so defined that it includes an International Business Company managed and controlled from Barbados.

Registration fees for the Barbados Registry are:

- For ships up to 5,000 tonnes, the greater of BDS$2.40 per tonne or BDS$4,800;
- For ships between 5,000 and 25,000 tonnes, BDS$2.20 per tonne;
- For ships over 25,000 tonnes, BDS$55,000.

SELECTED BUSINESS CONTACTS

OFFSHORE COMPANY FORMATION AND SHIP REGISTRATION

Alpha & Omega Law Group

Top Floor, Atlantis Building, Shallow Draught, Bridgetown, Barbados, West Indies	Telephone +1 246 431 0978	Fax +1 246 431 0797

Barclays Bank Plc (Offshore Banking Centre)

P O Box 180, Barclays House, 1st Floor, Rendezvous, Christ Church, Barbados, West Indies	Telephone +1 246 431 5262	Fax +1 246 429 4785

Carrington & Sealy

P O Box 36, Belmont House, Belmont Road, St Michael, Barbados, West Indies	Telephone +1 246 436 6700	Fax +1 246 228 9548

Citco Barbados Limited

Whitepark House, White Park Road, P.O. Box 806E, Bridgetown, Barbados	Telephone +1 246 427 8716	Fax +1 246 426 8913

BANKING, ASSET MANAGEMENT AND FINANCIAL SERVICES

Barclays Bank Plc (Offshore Banking Centre)

P O Box 180, Barclays House, 1st Floor, Rendezvous, Christ Church, Barbados, West Indies	Telephone +1 246 431 5262	Fax +1 246 429 4785

Citco Barbados Limited		
Whitepark House, White Park Road, P.O. Box 806E, Bridgetown, Barbados	Telephone +1 246 427 8716	Fax +1 246 426 8913
Excelsior Bank		
Central Bank Building, Bridgetown, Barbados, West Indies	Telephone +1 246 435 3155	Fax +1 246 435 3157
Rothscarmon Corporation		
Newstead Chambers, Pinfold Street, Bridgetown, Barbados, West Indies	Telephone +1 246 426 3406	Fax +
RBC Dominion Securities (Caribbean) Ltd		
Building 2, Chelston Park, Collymore Rock St Michael, Barbados, West Indies	Telephone + 1 246 228 6130	Fax +1 246 228 6135
Royal Bank of Canada (Caribbean) Corporation		
2nd Floor, Building 2, Chelston Park, Collymore Rock St Michael, Barbados, West Indies	Telephone + 1 246 429 4923	Fax +1 246 429 4948

TRUST MANAGEMENT

Alpha & Omega Law Group		
Top Floor, Atlantis Building, Shallow Draught, Bridgetown, Barbados, West Indies	Telephone +1 246 431 0978	Fax +1 246 431 0797
Barclays Bank Plc (Offshore Banking Centre)		
P O Box 180, Barclays House, 1st Floor, Rendezvous, Christ Church, Barbados, West Indies	Telephone +1 246 431 5262	Fax +1 246 429 4785

TAXES, ACCOUNTING AND AUDITING

Deloitte and Touche		
P O Box 806E, Whitepark House, White Park Road, Bridgetown, Barbados, West Indies	Telephone +1 246 429 5257	Fax +1 246 436 7887
Ernst & Young Trust Corporation		
P O Box 261, Bush Hill, Bay Street, St Michael, Barbados, West Indies	Telephone +1 246 430 3900	Fax +1 246 429 6446
PricewaterhouseCoopers		
Collymore Rock, St Michael, P O Box 634C Barbados, West Indies	Telephone +1 246 436 7000	Fax +1 246 436 7057

Cottle Catford & Co		
17 High Street, P O Box 63, Bridgetown, Barbados, West Indies	Telephone +1 246 426 3298	Fax +1 246 426 3726
Ernst & Young Trust Corporation		
P O Box 261, Bush Hill, Bay Street, St Michael,Barbados, West Indies	Telephone +1 246 430 3900	Fax +1 246 429 6446
Global Overseas Ltd.		
Atlantis Building, Shallow Draught, Bridgetown, Barbados, West Indies	Telephone +1 246 431 8826	Fax +1 246 431 0894
PricewaterhouseCoopers		
Collymore Rock, St Michael, P O Box 634C Barbados, West Indies	Telephone +1 246 436 7000	Fax +1 246 436 7057
Trident Corporate Services (Barbados) Limited		
Whitepark House, White Park Road, P O Box 836E, Bridgetown, Barbados, West Indies	Telephone + 1 246 431 0760	Fax +1 246 431 0591

IMPORTANT FINANCIAL OPERATIONS LAWS AND REGULATIONS

PRINCIPAL LAWS AND REGULATIONS AFFECTING BANKING ANS FINANCIAL OPERATION[5]

BANKING & TRUSTS

REGULATORY

- The Banks Act, 1909
- The Banks & Trust Companies Regulations Act, 1965
- The Banks & Trust Companies Regulation (Amendment) Act, 1989
- The Banks & Trust Companies Regulation (Amendment) Act, 2007
- The Banks & Trust Companies Regulation Act, 2000
- The Central Bank of The Bahamas Act, 2000
- The Central Bank of The Bahamas (Amendment) Act, 2007

PRIVATE TRUST COMPANIES

- The Banks & Trust Companies Regulations (Amendment) Act, 2006
- The Central Bank of the Bahamas (Amendment) Act, 2006
- The Banks & Trust Companies (Private Trust Companies) Regulations, 2007
- Guidance Notice BTCRA 6 (1)
- Guidance Notice BTCRA (7)
- Central Bank Guidelines

PURPOSE TRUST

- The Purpose Trust Act, 2004
- The Purpose Trust (Amendment) Act, 2005
- The Purpose Trust (Amendment) Act, 2007

ORDINARY TRUST

- The Trustee Act, 1998
- The Trustee (Amendment) Act, 2004

OTHER RELEVANT LEGISLATION

- The Trusts (Choice of Governing Law) Act, 1989
- The Trusts (Choice of Governing Law)(Amendment) Act, 1996
- The Fraudulent Disposition Act, 1991 (Asset Protection Trust)
- The Perpetuities Act, 1995
- The Perpetuities (Amendment) Act, 2004

[5] For complete texts of the listed below and other laws and regulations, please contact Global Investment and Business center, USA at ibpusa@comcast.net

COMPANIES

- The Companies Act, 1992
- The Exempted Limited Partnership Act, 1995
- The Exempted Limited Partnership (Amendment) Act, 1999
- The Financial and Corporate Service Providers Act, 2000
- The Financial and Corporate Service Providers (Amendment) Act, 2007
- The Financial and Corporate Service Providers (Amendment) Act, 2008
- The Financial & Corporate Service Providers (General) Regulations, 2001
- The Financial & Corporate Service Providers (Licence) (Amendment) Order 2009
- The International Business Companies Act, 2000
- The International Business Companies (Amendment) Act 2004
- The International Business Companies (Amendment to Fee Schedule) Order, 2004
- International Business Companies (Amendment) Act 2008
- The Segregated Accounts Companies Act, 2004

E-COMMERCE

- Computer Misuse Act 2003
- Data Protection Act 2003
- Electronic Communications and Transactions 2003

FOUNDATIONS

- The Foundations Act, 2004
- The Foundations (Amendment) Act, 2005
- The Foundations (Amendment) Act, 2007
- The Foundations Regulations, 2004

IMMIGRATION

- The Bahamas Nationality Act, 1973

INSURANCE

- The External Insurance Act, 1983
- The External Insurance (Amendment) Act, 2007
- The Insurance Act 1969
- The Insurance (Amendment) Act 2001
- The Insurance (Amendment) Act 2007

INTERNATIONAL CO-OPERATION, ANTI MONEY LAUNDERING & ANTI-TERRORISM

- The Anti-Terrorism Act, 2004
- The Criminal Justice (International Co-operation) Act, 2000
- The Criminal Justice (International Co-operation) Regulations, 2000
- The Evidence (Proceedings in Other Jurisdictions) Act, 2000
- The Evidence (Proceedings in Other Jurisdictions) (Amendment) Act, 2000
- The Financial Intelligence Unit Act, 2000
- The Financial Intelligence Unit (Amendment) Act, 2008

- The Financial Intelligence (Transactions Reporting) Regulations 2001
- The Financial Intelligence (Transactions Reporting) (Amendment) Regulations 2009
- The Financial Transactions Reporting Act, 2000
- The Financial Transactions Reporting (Amendment) Regulations, 2003
- The Financial Transactions Reporting (Amendment) Act, 2007
- The Financial Transactions Reporting (Amendment) Act, 2008
- The Financial Transactions Reporting Regulations, 2000
- The Financial Transactions Reporting (Amendment) Act 2003
- The Financial Transactions Reporting (Amendment) Regulations, 2009
- The Financial Transactions Reporting (Wire Transfer) Regulations 2009
- The Money Laundering (Proceeds of Crime) Act 1996
- The Money Laundering (Proceeds of Crime) Regulations 1996
- The Money Laundering (Proceeds of Crime) Amendment Act 1999
- The Mutual Legal Assistance (Criminal Matters) Act 1988
- The Proceeds of Crime Act 2000
- The Proceeds of Crime (Amendment) Act 2007
- The Proceeds of Crime (Designated Countries & Territories) Order, 2001

MISCELLANEOUS

- The Business License Act, 1980
- The Business Licence (Amendment) Act, 1999
- The Business Names Act 1989 (Registration of)
- The Exchange Control Regulations Act, 1952
- The Exchange Control Regulations, 1956
- The Bahamas-US TIEA Act, 2003
- The Stamp Act, 1925

SECURITIES INDUSTRY

- The Investment Funds Act 2003
- The Investment Funds (Amendment) Act 2007
- The Investment Funds Regulations 2003
- The Investment Funds (SMART Fund) Rules 2003
- The Investment Funds (SMART Fund) Rules 2005
- The Investment Funds (SMART Fund) Rules 2009
- The Securities Industry Act, 1999
- The Securities Industry (Amendment) Act 2001
- The Securities Industry (Amendment) Act 2007
- The Securities Industry (Amendment) Act 2008
- The Securities Industry Regulations, 2000
- The Securities Industry (Amendment) Regulations 2009

SHIPPING

- The Bahamas Maritime Authority Act, 1995
- The Merchant Shipping Act, 1976
- The Merchant Shipping (Amendment) Act, 1979
- The Merchant Shipping (Amendment) Act, 1982
- The Merchant Shipping (Amendment) Act, 1995

REAL ESTATE

- The International Persons Landholding Act, 1993
- The International Persons Landholding Act Guidelines, 1993
- The International Persons Landholding (Amendment) Act, 1995 (May)
- The International Persons Landholding (Amendment) Act, 1995 (Nov)

BANKS AND TRUST COMPANIES REGULATION

An Act to make fresh provisions to regulate banks and trust companies within The Bahamas; and for connected purposes.

38 of 2000
S.I. 128/2001

[Commencement 29th December, 2000]

Short title.

1. This Act may be cited as the Banks and Trust Companies Regulation Act, 2000.

Interpretation.

2. In this Act-

"authorised agent" means a person designated by a bank or trust company under the provisions of section 4;

"bank" means any person carrying on banking business;

"banking business" means the business of accepting deposits of money which may be withdrawn or repaid on demand or after a fixed period or after notice and employing those deposits in whole or in part by lending or otherwise investing them for the account and at the risk of the person accepting them; and "banker" shall be construed accordingly;

"Board of Directors" means the Board of Directors of the Central Bank provided for by subsection (4) of section 3 of the Central Bank of the Bahamas Act;

"Central Bank" means the Central Bank of The Bahamas established pursuant to section 3 of the Central Bank of The Bahamas Act;

"company" means a company incorporated either under the laws of The Bahamas or under the laws of any other country or place;

"Governor" means the person appointed as Governor under paragraph 1 of the Schedule to the Central Bank of The Bahamas Act;

"Inspector" means the office of Inspector of Banks and Trust Companies established under section 13;

"licence" means a licence granted under section 4 or deemed to be so granted in accordance with that section;

"licensee" means any person holding a licence under the provisions of this Act and for the purposes of this Act "licensee" includes the branches or subsidiaries of a licensee operating outside of The Bahamas;

"Minister" means the Minister of Finance;

"Supervisory Authority" in relation to a country or territory outside The Bahamas means a foreign entity charged with the responsibility of conducting consolidated supervision of banking and trust business by organisations licensed in its home country;

"trust business" means the business of acting as trustee, executor or administrator;

"trust company" means any company carrying on trust business.

3. (1) No banking business shall be carried on from within The Bahamas whether or not such business is carried on in The Bahamas except by a person who is in possession of a valid licence granted by the Governor authorising him to carry on such business.

Licence required to carry on banking business or trust business.

(2) No trust company shall carry on trust business from within The Bahamas whether or not such business is carried on in The Bahamas unless it is in possession of a valid licence granted by the Governor authorising it to carry on such business.

(3) Every person who contravenes the provisions of this section shall be guilty of an offence and shall be liable on summary conviction to a fine not exceeding one hundred thousand dollars or to imprisonment for a term not exceeding five years or to both such fine and imprisonment and in the case of a continuing offence to a fine not exceeding two thousand five hundred dollars for each day during which the offence continues.

4. (1) Any person desirous of carrying on banking business and any company desirous of carrying on trust business from within The Bahamas shall make application to the Governor for the grant of a licence.

Application shall be made to the Governor.

(2) Every application made pursuant to subsection (1) shall be in writing and shall contain such information and particulars and shall be accompanied by such references as may be prescribed and the Governor shall consider the following factors-

(a)
that the applicant is a fit and proper person or company to carry on banking business or trust business, as the case may be;

(b)
the nature and sufficiency of the financial resources of the applicant to provide continuing financial support for the bank or trust company, as the case may be;

(c)
the soundness and feasibility of the business plan;

(d)
the business record and experience of the applicant;

(e)
whether those who will operate the bank or trust company will do so responsibly and whether such persons have the character, competence and experience for operating a bank or trust company, as the case may be; and

(f)
the best interests of the financial system in The Bahamas,

and, if satisfied, may grant a licence to such person or company subject to such terms and conditions, if any, as the Governor may deem necessary:

Provided that the Governor shall in every case in which application is made pursuant to subsection (1) advise the Minister of his decision to either grant or refuse the grant of such licence.

(3) Whenever he considers it to be in the public interest, the Governor may refuse to grant a licence.

(4) A licence shall not be granted to any bank or trust company having its head office or its registered office outside The Bahamas unless-

(a)
such bank or trust company designates and notifies to the Governor-

(i)
a principal office in The Bahamas;

(ii)
by name one of its officers who is to be the bank's or trust company's authorised agent in The Bahamas; and

(iii)
by name another of its officers who in the absence or inability of the officer named under subparagraph (ii) is to be the bank's or trust company's authorised agent in The Bahamas;

(b)
the Governor is satisfied that the bank or trust company is subject to adequate consolidated supervision by the Supervisory Authority and that the Supervisory Authority makes no objection to the establishment of the branch or subsidiary in The Bahamas;

(c)
the Supervisory Authority is permitted to examine, wherever they are kept, the books of the bank or trust company;

(d)
there are no constraints on internal and external audits imposed by the Supervisory Authority;

(e)
the Supervisory Authority is informed where the bank or trust company will be managed;

(f)
the Supervisory Authority has agreed to inform the Governor as soon as reasonably possible of any circumstances that arise which may seriously jeopardise the interests of creditors of the bank or trust company.

(5) It shall be a condition of every licence granted to a bank or trust company to which subsection (4) applies, that the bank or trust company shall forthwith notify the Governor in writing of any change of-

(a)
its principal office in The Bahamas; or

(b)
either or both of the officers designated pursuant to paragraph (a)(ii) or (iii) of subsection (4).

(6) In respect of a licence granted under subsection (2), the Governor may at any time-

(a)
make the licence subject to such conditions or limitations that are consistent with this Act and that relate to the business of the bank or trust company as the Governor considers necessary;

(b)
amend or revoke any authorisation contained in the licence or any condition or limitation to which the licence is subject:

Provided that before taking any action under paragraph (a) or (b) the Governor shall provide the bank or trust company with an opportunity to make representation regarding any proposed action.

Approval of Governor.

5. A licensee incorporated or registered in The Bahamas shall not without the prior written approval of the Governor establish, outside of The Bahamas, a subsidiary, branch, agency or representative office.

6. (1) No shares in a company or certificates of deposit or any other securities of such company which is a licensee under this Act shall be issued and no issued shares shall be transferred or disposed of in any manner without the prior approval of the Governor:

Shares, etc., not to be issued or transferred without approval.

Provided that the Governor may exempt any licensee or group or class of licensees from the provision of this section subject to such terms and conditions if any as the Governor may deem necessary.

(2) All dividends of the shareholders of a bank or trust company shall be paid out of the profits and not out of the subscribed capital of the bank or trust company.

7. (1) Except with the approval of the Governor no person, other than a licensee acting under and in accordance with the terms of his licence, shall-

Use of the word "bank", etc.,

(a)
use or continue to use the words "bank", "trust", "trust company", "trust corporation","savings" or "savings and loan" or any of their derivatives either in English or in any other language, in the description or title under which such person is carrying on business from within The Bahamas whether or not such business is carried on in The Bahamas;

(b)
make, or continue to make, whether directly or indirectly, any representation in any bill-head, letter, letter-head, circular, paper, notice or advertisement or by any other means whatsoever, whether similar to the foregoing or not, that such person is carrying on banking business or trust business or is authorised by the law of The Bahamas to carry on such respective business;

(c)
in any manner whatsoever, solicit or receive deposits from the public.

(2) Except with the approval of the Governor-

(a)
the Registrar General shall not register a company; and

(b)
no company if already registered immediately before the twenty-fifth day of November, 1968, shall be entitled to remain registered on or after that date,

with a name which contains the words "bank", "trust", "trust company", "trust corporation", "savings" or "savings and loan" or any of their derivatives either in English or in any other language.

(3) Before giving his approval under subsection (1) or subsection (2) the Governor may require of any person such references and such other information and particulars as may be prescribed.

(4) Whenever he considers it to be in the public interest the Governor may withdraw any approval given under subsection (1).

(5) The Governor may refuse to grant a licence to a bank or a trust company, or if such bank or trust company is already in possession of a licence, he may revoke such licence, if in his opinion such bank or trust company is carrying on or intending to carry on banking or trust business, as the case may be, under a name which-

(a)
is identical with that of any company, firm or business house whether within The Bahamas or not or which so nearly resembles that name as to be calculated to deceive;

(b)
is calculated to suggest, falsely, the patronage of or connection with some person or authority whether within The Bahamas or not; or

(c)
is calculated to suggest, falsely, that such bank or trust company has a special status in relation to or derived from the Government of The Bahamas or has the official backing of or acts on behalf of the said Government or of any department or official thereof or is recognised in The Bahamas as a national or central bank or trust company.

(6) Every person who contravenes the provisions of this section shall be guilty of an offence and shall be liable on summary conviction to a fine not exceeding fifty thousand dollars or to a term of imprisonment not exceeding one year or to both such fine and imprisonment and in the case of a continuing offence to a fine not exceeding one thousand dollars for each day during which the offence continues.

(7) Where it appears to the Governor-

(a)
that a company has contravened any prohibition contained in subsection (1), and that no other effective means exists of dealing with the company in relation to the contravention; or

(b)
that a company is disentitled to remain registered by reason of being in breach of paragraph (b) of subsection (2),

then in either such case he may direct the Registrar General to give notice in writing to the company requiring it to show cause within thirty days why it should not be struck off the register of companies; and the Registrar General shall serve such notice accordingly, specifying the contravention or breach complained of, by causing the same to be delivered personally or sent by prepaid registered post to the secretary of the company at its registered office; and in the case of a notice sent by post it shall be deemed to have been served on the fifth day after the posting of the registered envelope or packet containing the same.

(8) If any company fails within thirty days of the service of a notice under the provisions of subsection (7) to show cause why it should not be struck off the register or to satisfy the Governor that the contravention or breach complained of has been discontinued and will not be repeated, then the Governor may in writing direct the Registrar General to strike the company off the register; and the Registrar General shall act accordingly and thereupon the company shall be dissolved.

(9) Upon the removal of a company pursuant to this section the provisions of section 271(4) to 274 (inclusive) of the Companies Act shall have effect in relation to such company as they have effect in relation to any company removed from the register pursuant to that Act.

Yearly statements to be published.

8. (1) Every licensee shall, within four months of the end of its financial year, publish in the *Gazette* a true and full yearly statement of its accounts and the auditor of the licensee shall certify that such statement is properly drawn up so as to exhibit a true and correct view of the state of the licensee's affairs as shown by the books of the licensee, and the auditor of the licensee shall have the right of access at all times to the books, accounts and vouchers of the licensee; provided that the Governor may, if he sees fit, exempt any licensee from the provisions of this section.

(2) Such statement shall be signed by the manager or by such other person or officer of the licensee as may from time to time be authorised by the licensee to sign such statement on behalf of the licensee; and the correctness thereof shall be declared to in such manner and by such persons as the Governor may direct.

(3) Such statements shall be in such form and contain such particulars as the Governor may from time to time direct.

Governor may call for further

9. A licensee shall from time to time, if required by the Governor, furnish to the Governor a special return and such further information as the Governor may reasonably see fit to call for. information.

Failure to comply with the requirements of section 8.

10. If any licensee-

(a)
fails to comply with the requirements of section 8 within a period of four months of the end of its financial year; or

(b)
fails to comply with the requirements of section 9 for forty-two days after the date appointed by the Governor under section 9 for so doing,

the licensee or person so in default shall be liable to a penalty of two hundred and fifty dollars for every day of such default:

Provided that the Governor may extend the time for sending such return for such further period not exceeding sixty days as he thinks expedient.

The Governor may require financial statement, etc., of licensee.

11. The Governor, in relation to a licensee which is or appears to become unable to meet its obligation or which in the opinion of the Governor is carrying on business in a manner detrimental to the public's interest or to the interest of creditors or depositors of such licensee, may by instrument in writing require the manager or authorised agent of such licensee to supply within such reasonable time as may be specified in the instrument-

(a)
the financial statement of that licensee as of a date determined by the Governor audited by an auditor who shall be a chartered accountant or a certified public accountant approved of by the Governor; and

(b)
such other information relating to the licensee as may be so specified,

and any person who contravenes the requirements of such an instrument or who in response to such an instrument knowingly or wilfully supplies false information to the Governor shall be guilty of an offence and shall be liable on summary conviction to a fine not exceeding one hundred thousand dollars or to imprisonment for a term not exceeding two years or to both such fine and imprisonment.

Appointment of auditor.

12. The appointment of the auditors of a licensee shall be subject to the approval of the Governor:

Provided that the Governor may at any time withdraw such approval and require the replacement of an auditor, by notice in writing delivered to the usual place of business of the auditor and licensee.

Power and duties of the Inspector.

13. (1) There is hereby established within the Central Bank of The Bahamas the Office of Inspector of Banks and Trust Companies and the functions of that office shall be performed by such person as the Governor considers suitable for the purpose of performing the powers and duties assigned to such Inspector under this Act.

(2) It shall be the duty of the Inspector-

(a)
to maintain a general review of bank and trust company practice in The Bahamas;

(b)
whenever he thinks fit and when required by the Governor to conduct on-site examinations and off-site supervision of the business of the licensee for the purpose of satisfying himself that the provisions of this Act or the Financial Transactions Reporting Act, 2000 are being complied with, that the licensee is in sound financial position and, after the conclusion of each examination or supervision, to report to the Governor, or in such cases where the Inspector is unable to conduct such examination or supervision, to appoint an auditor, at the expense of the licensee, to conduct such examination or supervision and to report thereon to the Governor; and the Governor may assess charges to recover the cost of such examination or supervision;

(c)
to examine and to report on the several returns delivered to the Governor pursuant to section 8 of this Act;

(d)
to examine and make recommendations to the Governor with respect to applications for licences;

(e)
to examine, by way of receipt of regular returns or in such other manner as he thinks necessary the affairs or business of any licensee carrying on business in or from within The Bahamas for the purpose of satisfying himself that the Act is being complied with and that the licensee is in sound financial position;

(f)
to inspect and supervise banks and trust companies in accordance with the Rules for Inspection and Supervision set out in the First Schedule.

(3) In the performance of his functions under this Act and subject to the provisions of section 19, the Inspector shall be entitled at all reasonable times-

(a)
to have access to such books, records, vouchers, documents, cash and securities of any licensee;

(b)
to call upon the manager or any officer designated by the manager of any licensee for such information or explanation;

(c)
to call upon the auditors of any licensee for such auditor's reports, working papers, information or explanation;

(d)
to require that the auditor of a bank report to the Inspector on the extent of the procedures of the auditor in the examination of the annual financial statements and may require that the auditors enlarge the scope of that examination or direct that any other particular procedure be performed in any particular case;

(e)
to require that the auditor make a particular examination relating to the adequacy of the procedures adopted by the bank for the safety of its creditors and shareholders, or any other examination as considered necessary by the Inspector,

as the Inspector may reasonably require for the purpose of enabling him to perform his functions under this Act.

(4) The Inspector with the approval of the Governor may in writing authorise any other person to assist the Inspector in the performance of his functions under this Act.

(5) No duty of confidentiality to which an auditor of a licensee may be subject shall be regarded as having been breached by reason of his communicating in good faith to the Inspector, pursuant to paragraphs (a), (b) and (c) of subsection (3), any information or opinion which is relevant to the Inspector's functions and responsibilities under this Act.

(6) Where any person-

(a)
fails to comply with any requirement made by the Inspector, pursuant to subsection (3), within the period determined by the Inspector or within such further period as the Inspector may determine, it shall be presumed, in the absence of satisfactory evidence being furnished by the licensee justifying such a failure to comply with such requirement, that the licensee concerned has been carrying on business in contravention of the terms of its licence with effect from the date of such failure;

(b)
knowingly or intentionally supplies false or misleading information to the Inspector or any person authorised to assist the Inspector;

(c)
as an auditor of a licensee in the performance of an audit, grossly violates the duties of such auditor as set out in subsection (1) of section 8; or makes untrue statements in an audit report or omits essential facts or fails to request pertinent information from the licensee or fails to report his findings to the Inspector; or

(d)
perpetrates a fraud or a crime which involves the making of misrepresentations in advertising or otherwise or using the domicile of The Bahamas for such purposes,

he shall be guilty of an offence and shall be liable on summary conviction to a fine not exceeding one hundred thousand dollars or to a term of imprisonment not exceeding five years or to both such fine and imprisonment and in the case of a continuing offence to a fine not exceeding two thousand dollars for each day during which the offence continues.

(7) No civil or criminal liability shall attach to the Inspector, or any person duly authorized by the Inspector under subsection (4), for an act done in good faith in the discharge or purported discharge of such person's functions under this Act.

(8) The Board of Directors may indemnify the Governor and the Governor may indemnify the Inspector or any person duly authorised by the Inspector under subsection (4), against the cost of defending their actions while so discharging their functions.

Inspection by foreign supervisory authority.

14. (1) A Supervisory Authority which is responsible for regulating a bank or trust company with a branch or subsidiary incorporated inside The Bahamas may upon written notification to and approval by the Inspector, conduct an inspection, under conditions of confidentiality, and subject to the conditions set out in subsection (2), solely for purposes of consolidated supervision, of the books and accounts of any branch or subsidiary of that bank or trust company in The Bahamas and may gather only such information as is necessary for the performance of consolidated supervision of any branch or subsidiary of that bank or trust company in The Bahamas, being information as to whether such branch or subsidiary of that bank or trust company as a constituent of the banking group-

(a)
is adequately organized;

(b)
has adequate risk management systems and appropriately identifies, limits and monitors risks inherent in that bank's business activities;

(c)
is managed by persons who are fit and proper for the conduct of business activities;

(d)
complies with capital-adequacy and risk-diversification requirements on a consolidated basis; and

(e)
correctly complies with its reporting duties to the Supervisory Authority.

(2) Any branch or subsidiary of a bank or trust company to which subsection (1) applies shall, subject to the conditions set out below, permit the Supervisory Authority at all reasonable times, to conduct its inspection under subsection (1) where-

(a)
the Supervisory Authority has obtained the prior written approval of the Inspector;

(b)
the Supervisory Authority is prohibited by its domestic laws from divulging information obtained in the course of the inspection to any other person or where the Supervisory authority has given such written undertaking, as the Inspector may require, as to the confidentiality of the information obtained;

(c)
the Supervisory Authority has given to the Inspector a written undertaking to comply with the provisions of this Act and any condition imposed by the Inspector under this section;

(d)
the Supervisory Authority has given to the Inspector a written undertaking to use the information obtained exclusively for the purpose of consolidated supervision;

(e)
the Supervisory Authority has given to the Inspector a written undertaking that it shall not transmit information obtained during the course of its inspection to any other authorities or bodies without the written consent of the Inspector;

(f)
the Supervisory Authority agrees to subsequently report to the Inspector on the general results of the inspection.

(3) Where information concerning criminal or penal matters comes to the attention of the Supervisory Authority in the course of an inspection, and the Supervisory Authority wishes to convey such information to any person or entity in the Supervisory Authority's home country, or elsewhere, the Supervisory Authority shall not, without first obtaining the consent in writing of the Inspector, divulge such information to any person or entity in the home country of the Supervisory Authority or elsewhere:

Provided that in all cases, the Supervisory Authority shall inform the Inspector of any information concerning criminal or penal matters which come to the Supervisory Authority's attention in the course of an inspection.

(4) The Supervisory Authority, in carrying out an inspection under subsection (1), shall not have access to information relating to the assets under management or deposit operations of individual customers of a licensee:

Provided however, that where the Supervisory Authority during an inspection within The Bahamas wishes to gain access to information, which directly or indirectly relates to assets under management or deposit operations of any individual customer for the purpose of assessing any risks and addressing any specific supervisory concerns, the Supervisory Authority shall inform the Inspector and the Inspector shall gather the information himself and shall, upon being satisfied that the information meets the requirements set out in this subsection, transmit it to the Supervisory Authority requesting it.

(5) The Inspector or any authorized agent of the Inspector may, whenever the Inspector thinks fit or upon the request of a licensee accompany a Supervisory Authority during its inspection within The Bahamas of a licensee, pursuant to this section.

15. (1) A Supervisory Authority may, with the prior written approval of the Inspector, appoint another body to conduct the inspection referred to in subsection (1) of section 14 and in such event the provisions of this section and subsections (1), (2), (3), (4) and (5) of section 14 shall apply to the appointed body in the same way as they apply to the Supervisory Authority.

Appointed body to conduct inspection.

(2) The Inspector may, at any time after granting approval for an inspection under this section require the Supervisory Authority to comply with such other conditions as the Inspector may determine.

16. (1) Any person who has, by any means, access to a report or other information or document produced by the Inspector or a Supervisory Authority upon examination or inspection of a licensee under section 13 or 14, by reason of his acting in any of the following capacities-

Confidentiality of reports of Inspector and Supervisory Authority.

(a)
director, officer, employee or agent of any licensee or former licensee;

(b)
counsel and attorney, consultant or auditor of The Central Bank or as an employee or agent of such counsel and attorney, consultant or auditor;

(c)
counsel and attorney, consultant, auditor, accountant, receiver or liquidator of any licensee or former licensee or as an employee or agent of such counsel and attorney, consultant, auditor, accountant, receiver or liquidator;

(d)
auditor of any customer of any licensee or former licensee or as an employee or agent of such auditor,

shall not communicate the report or other information or document or any part thereof to any person other than a director, officer, employee or agent of the licensee without the prior written permission of the Inspector.

(2) The Inspector may grant permission under subsection (1) subject to such conditions as may be determined by the Inspector.

(3) If any person receives a report or any part of a report or other information or document referred to in subsection (1), knowing or having reasonable grounds to believe, that such report or other information or document or part thereof was communicated to him in contravention of this section, that person shall be guilty of an offence unless he proves-

(a)
that the report or other information or document or part thereof, as the case may be, was communicated to him contrary to his intention; and

(b)
where the communication was effected in any written form, that he has conveyed or has taken reasonable steps to convey the report or other information or document or part thereof, as the case may be, to the Inspector.

(4) Any person guilty of an offence under this section shall be liable on summary conviction to a fine not exceeding twenty-five thousand dollars or to imprisonment for a term not exceeding two years or to both such fine and imprisonment.

17. The rules set out in the First Schedule shall be observed by the Inspector for the purpose of supervising banks and trust companies and their operations so as to ensure the preservation of the soundness and efficiency of the banking system.

Rules for inspection and supervision of banks.

18. (1) The Governor may-

Powers of the

Governor.

(a)
by order, revoke the licence of a licensee-

(i)
if, in the opinion of the Governor, the licensee is carrying on its business in a manner detrimental to the public interest or to the interests of its depositors or other creditors or is either in The Bahamas or elsewhere contravening the provisions of this or any other Act or of any order or regulations made under this Act, or any term or condition subject to which the licence was issued;

(ii)
if the licensee has ceased to carry on banking business or trust business; or

(iii)
if the licensee becomes bankrupt or goes into liquidation or is wound up or otherwise dissolved;

and he shall subsequently advise the Minister of his decision;

(b)
apply to the Supreme Court for an order compelling the licensee to comply with the direction, cease the contravention or to do anything required to be done where the licensee-

(i)
is contravening or has failed to comply with a direction of the Governor;

(ii)
is contravening the Act; or

(iii)
has omitted to do anything under the Act that is required to be done by the bank or trust company;

(c)
impose, amend or vary conditions upon the licence;

(d)
require the substitution of any director or officer of the licensee;

(e)
at the expense of the licensee, appoint a person to advise the licensee on the proper conduct of its affairs and to report to the Governor thereon within three months of the date of his appointment;

(f)
at the expense of the licensee, appoint a receiver to assume control of the licensee's affairs in the interest of creditors who will have all the powers of a receiver under the Companies Act; and

(g)
require such action to be taken by the licensee as the Governor considers necessary.

(2) Whenever the Governor is of the opinion that any action under subsection (1)(a)(i) and (b) should be taken against a licensee, he may forthwith suspend the licence of such licensee and before taking such action the Governor shall give that licensee notice in writing of his intention so to do setting out in such notice the grounds on which he proposes to act and shall afford the licensee within such time as may be specified therein, not being less than seven days, an opportunity of submitting to him a written statement of objection to such action, and thereafter the Governor shall advise the licensee of his decision.

(3) Whenever the Governor shall suspend a licence under subsection (2) he may cause notice of such suspension to be published in the *Gazette*.

(4) Any suspension of a licence under subsection (2) shall be for a period of ninety days, or until the Governor takes action under subsection (1) (a) (i) or (b) or until the Governor notifies the licensee that the suspension is removed, whichever period is the shorter.

(5) Where the Governor suspends or revokes a licence under this section, he may apply to the Supreme Court for an order that the licensee be forthwith wound up by the court in which case the provisions of the Companies Act relating to the winding up of a company by the court shall, *mutatis mutandis*, apply.

(6) The Governor may, in any case in which a licensee or person who has at any time been a licensee is being wound up voluntarily, apply to the Supreme Court if he considers that the winding up is not being conducted in the best interests of its depositors, the beneficiaries of any trust or other creditors, and the court shall make such order as it shall consider appropriate in the winding up of the licensee.

Preservation of confidentiality.

19. (1) No person who has acquired information in his capacity as-

(a)
director, officer, employee or agent of any licensee or former licensee;

(b)
counsel and attorney, consultant or auditor of the Central Bank or as an employee or agent of such counsel and attorney, consultant or auditor;

(c)
counsel and attorney, consultant, auditor, accountant, receiver or liquidator of any licensee or former licensee or as an employee or agent of such counsel and attorney, consultant, auditor, accountant, receiver or liquidator;

(d)
auditor of any customer of any licensee or former licensee or as an employee or agent of such auditor;

(e)
the Inspector under the provisions of this Act;

(f)
a Supervisory Authority or as a director, officer, employee or agent of a Supervisory Authority,

shall, without the express or implied consent of the customer concerned, disclose to any person any such information relating to the identity, assets, liabilities, transactions or accounts of a customer of a licensee or relating to any application by any person under the provisions of this Act, as the case may be, except-

(i)
for the purpose of the performance of his duties or the exercise of his functions under this Act, if any;

(ii)
for the purpose of the performance of his duties within the scope of his employment;

(iii)
when a licensee is lawfully required to make disclosure by any court of competent jurisdiction within The Bahamas, or under the provisions of any law of The Bahamas;

(iv)
for the purpose of enabling or assisting the Governor to exercise any functions conferred upon him by any written law;

(v)
to a person with a view to the institution of, or for the purpose of-

(A)
criminal proceedings;

(B)
disciplinary proceedings, whether within or outside The Bahamas, relating to the exercise by a counsel and attorney, auditor, accountant, valuer or actuary of his professional duties; or

(C)
disciplinary proceedings relating to the discharge by a public officer or a member or employee of the Central Bank of his duties.

(2) Subsection (1) shall not apply in any case where in accordance with such conditions as the Inspector may determine, information of such class or classes as the Inspector may from time to time approve, is transmitted from a licensee to the head office, a branch or subsidiary of that licensee outside of The Bahamas, solely for the purposes of carrying out collation, synthesis or processing of information on behalf of the licensee.

(3) In any civil proceedings where information is likely to be disclosed in relation to a customer's bank account, those proceedings may, if the court, of its own motion or on the application of a party to the proceedings, so orders, be held *in camera* and the information shall be confidential as between the court and the parties thereto.

(4) No person shall publish the name, address or photograph of any parties to those civil proceedings as are referred to in subsection (3) or any information likely to lead to the identification of the parties thereto either during the currency of the proceedings or after they have been terminated.

(5) The Governor may, subject to the provisions of section 14(2), provide information on the beneficial owners, directors, officers and operations of a licensee (including any report produced by the Inspector pursuant to any inspection or examination of the licensee) to the Supervisory Authority which is responsible for regulating the head office of the licensee for the purpose of consolidated supervision of the licensee by the Supervisory Authority.

(6) To facilitate regulatory co-operation within The Bahamas, the Governor may provide information on the beneficial owners, directors, officers and operations of a licensee and any of its affiliates to the domestic regulatory authorities specified in the Second Schedule.

(7) Nothing contained in this section shall-

(a)
prejudice or derogate from the rights and duties subsisting at common law between a licensee and its customer;

(b)
prevent a licensee from providing upon a legitimate business request in the normal course of business a general credit rating with respect to a customer; or

(c)
prevent the Inspector from sharing information relating to the identity, assets, liabilities, transactions or accounts of a customer of a licensee with the Financial Intelligence Unit where he believes that a suspicious transaction was not reported as required under the Financial Transactions Reporting Act.

(8) Every person who contravenes the provisions of subsection (1) shall be guilty of an offence and shall be liable on summary conviction to a fine not exceeding twenty-five thousand dollars or to a term of imprisonment not exceeding two years or to both such fine and imprisonment.

Transfer to Bank of unclaimed balances.

20. (1) Where a liability exists by reason of a deposit account at a bank in The Bahamas in respect of which no transaction has taken place, or no statement of account has been requested or no written acknowledgement has been received from the customer, during a period of seven years-

(a)
in the case of a deposit made for a fixed period, from the day on which the fixed period terminated; and

(b)
in the case of any other deposit, from the date on which the last customer initiated transaction occurred or a statement of account was requested or acknowledged by the customer, whichever is the later,

the bank shall pay to the Central Bank an amount equal to the amount owing by the bank in respect of the account and payment accordingly discharges the bank from all liability in respect of the account.

(2) Where a bank has paid to the Central Bank an amount in respect of an account, it shall keep all signature cards, signing authorities and records relating to the account or microfilm or electronically stored copies thereof until notified by the Central Bank that they are no longer required.

(3) In this section "deposit account" includes deposit accounts of gold and silver bullion.

Charges for account to be by agreement.

21. No bank shall directly or indirectly charge or receive any sum of money for the establishment, maintenance or service of an account unless such charge is made by express and specific agreement between the bank and the customer.

Power of search.

22. (1) If a Magistrate is satisfied by information on oath given by the Inspector or by a person authorised under section 13(4) to assist the Inspector either-

(a)
that a licence has been suspended; or

(b)
that there is reasonable ground for suspecting that an offence against this Act has been or is being committed and that evidence of the commission of the offence is to be found at any premises specified in the information or in any vehicle, vessel or aircraft so specified; or

(c)
that any books, records, vouchers, documents, cash or securities which ought to have been produced under section 13(3) and have not been produced are to be found at any such premises or in any such vehicle, vessel or aircraft,

he may grant a search warrant authorising the Inspector or such person authorised under section 13(4) or any police officer together with any other person named in the warrant and any other police officers, to enter the premises specified in the information or, as the case may be, any premises upon which the vehicle, vessel or aircraft so specified may be, at any time within one month from the date of the warrant, and to search the premises or, as the case may be, the vehicle, vessel or aircraft.

(2) The person authorised by any such warrant as aforesaid to search any premises or any vehicle, vessel or aircraft may search every person who is found in or whom he has reasonable ground to believe to have recently left or to be about to enter those premises or that vehicle, vessel or aircraft, as the case may be, and may seize any books, records, vouchers, documents, cash or securities found in the premises or in the vehicle, vessel or aircraft which he has reasonable ground for believing to be evidence of the commission of any offence against this Act or any such books, records, vouchers, documents, cash or securities found in the premises or in the vehicle, vessel or aircraft which he has reasonable ground for believing ought to have been produced under section 13(3):

Provided that no female shall, in pursuance of any warrant issued under this subsection, be searched except by a female.

(3) Where by virtue of this section a person has any power to enter any premises he may use such force as is reasonably necessary for the purpose of exercising that power.

(4) Every person who shall obstruct the Inspector or any other person in the exercise of any powers conferred on him by virtue of this section shall be guilty of an offence and shall be liable on summary conviction to a fine not exceeding one thousand dollars or to imprisonment for a term not exceeding three months or to both such fine and imprisonment.

23. (1) No prosecution in respect of any offence committed under this Act shall be instituted except by or with consent of the Attorney-General. Attorney-General's fiat.

(2) Any penalty incurred under this Act shall be paid to the Central Bank.

24. The Governor may make regulations for all or any of the following purposes- Regulations.

(a)
to prescribe the information, particulars and references which may be prescribed under section 4(2) and section 7(3);

(b)
to establish fines not exceeding five thousand dollars for failure to comply with any regulation;

(c)
generally for carrying out the purposes or provisions of this Act into effect.

25. (1) The provisions of this Act shall have effect in addition to and not in derogation of any other provisions having the force of law in the Bahamas. No derogation.

(2) This Act shall not apply to the Post Office Savings Bank.

26. (1) An appeal shall lie to the Supreme Court from any decision of the Governor- Appeal.

(a)
revoking a licence under section 4(6), section 7(5) or section 18;

(b)
withdrawing any approval under section 7(4);

(c)
requiring a licensee to take certain steps which the Governor may specify under section 18.

(2) An appeal against the decision of the Governor shall be on motion and the appellant within twenty-one days after the day on which the Governor has given his decision shall serve on the Attorney-General a notice in writing signed by the appellant or his counsel and attorney of his intention to appeal and of the general ground for his appeal:

Provided that any person aggrieved by the decision of the Governor may upon notice to the Attorney-General apply to the Supreme Court for leave to extend the time within which the notice of appeal prescribed by this section may be served, and the Supreme Court upon the hearing of such application may extend the time prescribed in this section as it deems fit.

(3) The Attorney-General shall upon receiving the notice of appeal transmit to the Registrar of the Supreme Court without delay a copy of the Governor's decision and all papers relating to the appeal:

Provided that the Attorney-General shall not be compelled to disclose any information if he considers that the public interest would suffer by such disclosure.

(4) The Registrar shall set the appeal down for hearing on such day, and shall cause notice of the same to be published in such manner, as the Supreme Court may direct.

(5) At the hearing of the appeal the appellant shall, before going into the case, state all the grounds of appeal on which he intends to rely and shall not, unless by leave of the Supreme Court, go into any matters not raised by such statement.

(6) The Supreme Court may adjourn the hearing of the appeal and may upon hearing thereof confirm, reverse, vary or modify the decision of the Governor or remit the matter with the opinion of the Supreme Court thereon to the Governor.

(7) An appeal against a decision of the Governor shall not have the effect of suspending the execution of such decision.

Fees.

27. (1) The provisions of the Third Schedule shall have effect for the payment of fees in respect of the matters mentioned in that Schedule, and all such fees shall be payable to the Treasurer.

(2) All fees paid pursuant to subsection (1) and the Third Schedule shall be placed in the Consolidated Fund.

(3) The Minister may by regulations vary the fees prescribed in the Third Schedule, so, however, that any such regulations which increase the amount of any fees payable under this Act shall be exempt from the provisions of section 32 of the Interpretation and General Clauses Act but instead be subject to affirmative resolution of both Chambers of Parliament.

(4) In subsection (3) the expression "affirmative resolution of both Chambers of Parliament" in relation to regulations means that the regulations are not to come into operation unless and until affirmed by a resolution of each of those Chambers.

(5) If any person fails to comply with any requirement of subsection (1) and the Third Schedule, he, or, where such person is a company, the company and every director, manager, secretary or other officer of the company who knowingly and wilfully authorises or permits the default, shall on summary conviction be liable, for every day during which the default continues, to a fine not exceeding one thousand dollars.

Repeal.

28. The Banks and Trust Companies Regulation Act and the Banks Act are hereby repealed.

Savings.

29. Any licence, authority, approval or exemption granted under the repealed Act which is in force immediately before the coming into force of this Act-

(a)
shall continue to have effect after the coming into force of this Act as if granted under this Act;

(b)
in the case of a grant for a specific period, shall remain in force for so much of that period as falls after the coming into force of this Act.

FIRST SCHEDULE (Section 17)

RULES OF INSPECTION AND SUPERVISION OF BANKS

1. The Inspector shall-

(a)
regularly evaluate the condition, solvency and liquidity of all licensees;

(b)
establish appropriate and prudent standards for conducting safe and sound banking

and trust business;

(c)
set prudent and appropriate capital adequacy requirements not less than those established in the Basel Capital Accord and its Amendments;

(d)
evaluate banks' policies, practices and procedures related to the granting of loans and making of investments and the on-going management of the loan and investment portfolios;

(e)
ensure that banks have management information systems that enable management to identify portfolio concentration in line with established limits;

(f)
ensure that banks have in place and use systems that accurately measure, monitor and adequately control market and other risks;

(g)
ensure that banks establish and adhere to adequate policies, practices and procedures for evaluating the quality of assets and the adequacy of loan-loss provisions and loan-loss reserves;

(h)
ensure that banks have in place internal controls adequate to the nature and scale of their operations, and adequate policies, practices and procedures, including strict know-your-customer rules that promote high ethical and professional standards, and so prevent the use of the bank for criminal purposes;

(i)
co-operate with inspectors and supervisors in other jurisdictions to the extent necessary for the purposes of cross-border supervision consistent with the policy established by the Basel Committee for cross-border supervision.

2. In this Part-

"Basel Capital Accord" or "Basel Committee" means the committee of banking supervisory authorities established by central-bank Governors of the Group of Ten countries in 1975 and its report.

SECOND SCHEDULE (Section 19 (6))

DOMESTIC REGULATORY AUTHORITIES

1. Financial Intelligence Unit.
2. Registrar of Insurance.
3. Registrar of Companies.
4. Securities Commission of The Bahamas.

THIRD SCHEDULE (Section 27)

FEES

1. Subject to the following paragraphs of this Schedule, the following shall be the fees under this Act, that is to say-

Matters in respect of which fee is payable	Amount of fee $
(a) Appointment of a licensee by the Controller of Exchange as an authorised dealer as defined in paragraph (1) of regulation 44 of	250,000
(b)	100,000

Continuance in being on the first day of January in any year as a person appointed as mentioned in subparagraph (a) of this paragraph	
(c) Appointment of a licensee as authorised agent for a beneficial owner of investment currency or foreign currency securities pursuant to the Exchange Control Regulations	60,000
(d) Continuance in being on the first day of January in any year as a person appointed as mentioned in subparagraph (c) of this paragraph	60,000
(e) Grant of licence to carry on banking business or trust business or to carry on both banking business and trust business without any limitation on the persons with or for whom such respective business may be carried on, where the licensee-	
(i) has been declared by the Controller of Exchange pursuant to the Exchange Control Regulations to be resident in The Bahamas; and	
(ii) has not been appointed as mentioned in subparagraph (a) or (c) of this paragraph	25,000
(f) Continuance in being on the first day of January in any year as a person licensed as mentioned in subparagraph (e) of this paragraph	25,000
(g) Grant of licence to carry on banking business or trust business or to carry on both banking business and trust business without any limitation on the persons with or for whom such respective business may be carried on where the licensee-	
(i) has been declared by the Controller of Exchange pursuant to the Exchange Control Regulations not to be resident in The Bahamas; and	
(ii) has not been appointed as mentioned in subparagraph (a) or (c) of this paragraph	25,000
(h) Continuance in being on the first day of January in any year as a person licensed as mentioned in subparagraph (g) of this paragraph	25,000
(i) Grant of licence to carry on banking business solely with person specified in the licence	5,000
(j) Continuance in being on the first day of January in any year as a person licensed as mentioned in subparagraph (i) of this paragraph	5,000
(k) Grant of licence to carry on banking business and trust business solely with or for persons specified in the licence	5,000
(l) Continuance in being on the first day of January in any year as a	5,000

person licensed as mentioned in subparagraph (k) of this paragraph

(m) Grant of licence solely to carry on the trust business specified in the licence	2,500
(n) Continuance in being on the first day of January in any year as a person licensed as mentioned in subparagraph (m) of this paragraph	2,500
(o) Grant of any licence not mentioned in subparagraph (e), (g), (i), (k) or (m) of this paragraph	1,000
(p) Continuance in being on the first day of January in any year as a person licensed as mentioned in subparagraph (o) of this paragraph	1,000

2. Where any person by reason of falling within a class mentioned in subparagraphs (a) to (p) of paragraph 1 of this Schedule has paid a fee therein prescribed in respect of that class for any year and would, but for provisions of this paragraph of this Schedule, be required to pay in that year a further fee or further fees by reason of such person during that year coming additionally within another such class as aforesaid, such person shall not be required to pay in respect of fees under this Act for that year more in total than the highest fee prescribed in respect of any of the classes within which such person falls:

Provided that any person in any year falling within a class mentioned at subparagraph (a) or (b) and at the same time within a class mentioned at subparagraph (c) or (d) of the said paragraph 1 of this Schedule shall, subject to paragraphs 3 and 4 of this Schedule, be required to pay the fee prescribed in respect of both such classes for that year.

3. As respects the fees specified at subparagraph (b), (d), (f), (h), (j), (l), (n) and (p) of paragraph 1 of this Schedule-

(a)
not more than sixty days grace, to be calculated from the first day of January in each year, may be allowed by the Treasurer for the payment of the fees payable in any year; and

(b)
no such fees shall be payable in any year where the original appointment or licence to which such fee relates was made or granted on or after the first day of September in the preceding year.

4. Any fee paid by any person in any year pursuant to subsection (1) of section 300, and paragraph 3 of the Third Schedule to, the Companies Act shall be deducted from any fees payable by such person in that year under this Act.

CENTRAL BANK OF THE BAHAMAS ACT

An Act to repeal the Central Bank of The Bahamas Act and to make fresh provisions for the establishment of a Central Bank, its functions and duties; and for connected purposes.

37 of 2000
S.I. 128/2001

[Commencement 29th December, 2000]

PART IPRELIMINARY

1. This Act may be cited as the Central Bank of The Bahamas Act, 2000.

Short title.

2. In this Act-

Interpretation.

"Bank" means the Central Bank of The Bahamas established by section 3;

"bank" means a financial institution lawfully carrying on banking business including the accepting of deposits of money withdrawable by cheque;

"banking business" means the business of accepting deposits of money which may be withdrawn or repaid on demand or after a fixed period or after notice, and employing those deposits in whole or in part by lending or otherwise investing them for the account and at the risk of the person accepting them; and "banker" shall be construed accordingly;

"Board" means the Board of Directors of the Bank provided for by subsection (4) of section 3;

"civil and administrative investigations and proceedings" means proceedings in any court of law in the jurisdiction of an overseas regulatory authority and investigations undertaken by the overseas regulatory authority preliminary to bringing such proceedings;

"coins" means coins of the currency of The Bahamas;

"commercial bank" means a bank licensed to carry on banking business in The Bahamas;

"company" means a company incorporated under any law in force whether in The Bahamas or elsewhere;

"director" means a member of the Board;

"financial institution" means an institution carrying on banking business;

"Governor" means the person appointed as such under paragraph 1 of the Schedule;

"Minister" means the Minister of Finance;

"notes" means notes of the currency of The Bahamas;

"overseas regulatory authority" means an authority [i]* which, in a country or territory outside The Bahamas, exercises functions corresponding to-

(a)
any functions of the Bank; or

(b)
any additional regulatory functions in relation to companies or financial services as the Bank may specify by order including the conduct of civil and administrative investigations and proceedings to enforce laws, regulations and rules administered by that authority;

"public corporation" means a body corporate established directly by statute for public purposes;

"regulatory functions" means functions of the Bank, or functions corresponding to such functions, and any other similar functions relating to companies or financial services as may be specified by the Bank;

"regulatory laws" means the Banks and Trust Companies Regulation Act, 2000;

"securities" means shares, stocks, bonds, debentures or debenture stock;

"trust business" means the business of acting as trustee or executor and administrator;

"trust company" means a company carrying on trust business;

"year" means financial year of the Bank.

PART II ESTABLISHMENT AND FUNCTIONS OF THE BANK

3. (1) There shall continue to be a bank, to be called "the Central Bank of The Bahamas" having the functions assigned to it by the following provisions of this Act.

The Central Bank of The Bahamas.

(2) The Bank shall be a body corporate having perpetual succession and a common seal and, subject to the provisions of this Act, with power to acquire, hold and dispose of movable and immovable property of whatever kind and to enter into contracts and to do all things necessary for the purpose of its functions.

(3) The Bank may sue and be sued in its corporate name and may for all purposes be described by that name.

(4) There shall be a Board of Directors of the Bank, who, subject to the provisions of this Act, shall be responsible for the policy of the Bank and shall manage its affairs and business.

(5) The provisions of the Schedule shall have effect as to the Board of Directors and otherwise in relation to the Bank.

4. The Bank shall have its principal place of business in the City of Nassau and may in The Bahamas or elsewhere-

Places of business, etc.

(a)
establish and maintain such branch offices; and

(b)
appoint such agents and correspondents,

as the Bank thinks fit.

5. (1) It shall be the duty of the Bank, subject to the provisions of this Act-

The Bank's functions.

(a)
to promote and maintain monetary stability and credit and balance of payments conditions conducive to the orderly development of the economy;

(b)
in collaboration with the financial institutions, to promote and maintain adequate banking services and high standards of conduct and management therein;

(c)
to advise the Minister on any matter of a financial or monetary nature referred to by him to the Bank for its advice.

(2) The Bank shall, subject to provisions of subsections (4), (5) and (7) of section 38, have the power to assist and co-operate with overseas regulatory authorities.

(3) The bank shall, subject as aforesaid, have power to do anything, whether in The Bahamas or elsewhere, which is calculated to facilitate, or is incidental or conducive to the discharge of its duty under this section.

PART III CAPITAL AND RESERVES

Capital of the Bank.

6. (1) The authorised capital of the Bank shall be three million dollars.

(2) Any capital required to make up the authorised capital of the Bank shall be paid from the Consolidated Fund at such times and in such amounts as the Board, with the approval of the Minister, may determine.

General Reserve.

7. (1) The Bank shall establish and maintain a General Reserve, to which, subject to the provisions of this section, at the end of each year the net profit of the Bank shall be credited (after the making of such deductions and allowances for other reserves and contingencies as the Bank may think fit) or the net loss incurred by the Bank debited, as the case may require.

(2) Whenever at the end of any year the amount in the General Reserve exceeds-

(a)
twice the authorised capital of the Bank;

(b)
fifteen per centum of the demand liabilities of the Bank,

whichever is greater, then the amount of any such excess shall be paid over to the Consolidated Fund, unless the Minister otherwise determines.

PART IV CURRENCY

Currency of The Bahamas.

8. (1) The currency of The Bahamas shall be the notes and coins issued by the Bank under the provisions of this Act.

(2) The unit of the said currency shall be the dollar, which shall be divided into one hundred cents.

Parity of the dollar.

9. The parity of the dollar shall be equivalent to 0.736662 grams of fine gold, so, however, that the Minister may, after consultation with the Bank, by order alter the said parity whether in terms of gold or any other standard.

Contracts, etc., deemed to be in Bahamian currency.

10. Every contract, sale, payment, bill, note or security for money and every transaction, dealing, proceeding, matter or thing whatever relating to money or involving the payment of, or the liability to pay, money shall be deemed to be made, executed or entered into in or in relation to the currency of The Bahamas unless it is expressly made executed or entered into in or in relation to the currency of some other country.

11. (1) The Bank shall have the sole right and authority to issue notes and coins throughout The Bahamas.

Sole right of Bank to issue notes and coins.

(2) No person other than the Bank shall issue in The Bahamas notes or coins or any documents or tokens having the appearance of notes or coins.

(3) Any person who contravenes the provisions of subsection (2) shall be guilty of an offence and shall be liable on conviction thereof to a fine not exceeding one hundred thousand dollars or to imprisonment for a term not exceeding five years or to both such fine and imprisonment.

12. The Bank shall from time to time as circumstances may require-

Issue, etc., of notes and coins.

(a)
arrange for the printing of notes and the minting of coins; and

(b)
issue, re-issue and redeem notes and coins.

13. The Minister may, after consultation with the Bank, by order prescribe-

Denominations and form of notes and coins.

(a)
the denominations (being multiples or fractions of a dollar), forms and designs of the notes and coins; and

(b)
the standard weight and composition of such coins, and the amount of tolerance and the variation which shall be allowed therein.

14. (1) Subject to the provisions of this section-

Legal tender.

(a)
notes issued by the Bank shall be legal tender in The Bahamas at their face value for the payment of any amount;

(b)
coins issued by the Bank shall be legal tender in The Bahamas at their face value up to an amount not exceeding one hundred dollars in the case of coins of a denomination of not less than one dollar, and up to an amount not exceeding five dollars in the case of coins of a lesser denomination.

(2) All notes and coins lawfully in circulation immediately before commencement of this section shall be deemed for all purposes to be notes and coins issued by the Bank under this Act and to be legal tender until withdrawn from circulation under the provisions of subsection (3).

(3) The Bank may, on giving not less than one month's notice in the *Gazette*, call in any notes or coins on payment of the face value thereof, and any such notes or coins shall, on the expiration of the notice, cease to be legal tender but, subject to the provisions of section 15, shall be redeemable by the Bank on demand.

(4) A coin which has been impaired, diminished in size or lightened otherwise than by fair wear and tear, or which has been defaced by stamping, engraving or piercing shall not be legal tender.

15. No person shall be entitled as of right to recover from the Bank the value of any lost, stolen, mutilated or imperfect note or coin; but the Bank may in its discretion as an act of grace refund to any person the value of any mutilated or imperfect note or coin.

Damaged currency, etc.

16. Notes and coins issued by the Bank shall be exempt from the payment of stamp duty.

Exemption from stamp duty.

PART V GOLD, FOREIGN EXCHANGE, EXTERNAL RESERVE, ETC.

17. Subject to the provisions of this Act, the Bank may-

Power of Bank in relation to foreign exchange, etc.

(a)
buy and sell gold, foreign exchange, foreign bills of exchange and securities of foreign governments;

(b)
maintain deposits in any foreign financial institution and utilise any such deposit in such manner as the Bank may think expedient for the due performance of the functions of the Bank;

(c)
make arrangements with any foreign financial institution to borrow, on such terms and conditions as the Bank may think fit, any foreign currency.

18. (1) The Bank shall at all times maintain a reserve of external assets consisting of all or any of the following-

External reserve.

(a)
gold (whether coins or bullion);

(b)
notes and coins (other than gold coins);

(c)
balances payable an demand held with financial institutions or agents;

(d)
money at call;

(e)
bills in the nature of Treasury Bills maturing within one hundred and eighty-four days issued by any foreign government;

(f)
marketable securities issued or guaranteed by any foreign government;

(g)
any reserve asset deemed by the Board to be an internationally recognised reserve asset:

Provided that at no time shall any securities held by the Bank pursuant to paragraph (f) which mature beyond five years constitute more than thirty per centum in value of the whole of the assets in the reserve of external assets.

(2) The value of the said reserve shall not at any time be less than fifty per centum of the value of the aggregate of notes and coins in circulation and the demand liabilities of the Bank.

PART VI
RELATIONS WITH THE COMMERCIAL BANKS

19. (1) Subject to the provisions of this section, every commercial bank shall establish and maintain a reserve to be called "the Statutory Reserve" of not less than that percentage of the amount of its deposit liabilities in Bahamian dollars that is at any time fixed by the Bank under this section.

Statutory Reserve.

(2) The Bank may by order fix and from time to time vary the percentage required by subsection (1):

Provided that-

(a)
the percentage fixed as aforesaid shall not at any time be less than five nor more than twenty per centum;

(b)
different percentages may be so fixed for different classes of commercial banks;

(c)
any such order may require a proportion of the said reserve (which shall be specified in the order) to be lodged with the Bank; and

(d)
no such order shall be made increasing any percentage at the time in force by more than five per centum in any period of thirty days.

(3) If any bank contravenes or fails to comply with any provision of an order made under this section, it shall be guilty of an offence, and shall be liable on conviction thereof to a fine based on the amount of the deficiency of twice the annual discount rate prevailing at the time of the contravention or failure to comply for every day during which the contravention or failure continues.

Liquid assets.

20. (1) Every commercial bank shall so conduct its business as to ensure, taking one month with another, that its liquid assets are on average not less than that percentage of the amount of its deposit liabilities in Bahamian dollars that is at any time fixed by the Bank under this section.

(2) The Bank may by order fix and from time to time vary the percentage required by subsection (1):

Provided that-

(a)
the percentage fixed as aforesaid shall not at any time be less than ten nor more than thirty per centum;

(b)
different percentages may be so fixed for different classes of commercial banks; and

(c)
no such order shall be made increasing any percentage at the time in force by more than five per centum in any period of thirty days.

(3) In this section "liquid assets" means-

(a)
notes and coins;

(b)
any cash balance held at the Bank;

(c)
money at call and demand balances at any financial institution carrying on business in The Bahamas;

(d)
Treasury Bills;

(e)
stock of the Government;

(f)
any instrument or security of a kind referred to in subsection (1)(f)(ii) of section 29;

(g)
any freely convertible foreign currency;

(h)
money at call and demand balances at any financial institution abroad being money at call or demand balances held in freely convertible foreign currency;

(i)
any other asset designated for the purposes of this subsection by the Bank.

(4) In subsection (3)-

"freely convertible foreign currency" means any foreign currency which at the time in question is in the opinion of the Bank a currency that is freely negotiable and transferable in international exchange markets at exchange rate margins consistent with the Articles of Agreement of the International Monetary Fund;

"money at call and demand balances at any financial institution" means money at call and demand balances held by any commercial bank at any financial institution less money at call and demand balances held at that bank by any financial institution.

(5) If any bank contravenes or fails to comply with any provision of an order made under this section, it shall be guilty of an offence and shall be liable on conviction thereof to a fine based on the amount of the deficiency of twice the annual discount rate prevailing at the time of the contravention or failure to comply for every day during which the contravention or failure continues.

Power of Governor to fine.

21. (1) Notwithstanding section 39, the Governor may where he is satisfied that a bank has committed an offence under section 19 or section 20 order the bank to pay a fine based on the amount of the deficiency of twice the annual discount rate prevailing at the time of the contravention or failure to comply for every day during which the contravention or failure continues.

(2) Where the Governor makes an order under this section-

(a)
the order shall be put in writing;

(b)
the order shall specify the offence which the bank committed and the penalty imposed by the Governor;

(c)
a copy of the order shall be given to the bank;

(d)
once the bank pays the fine as ordered, the bank shall not be liable to any further prosecution in respect of the offence and where any such prosecution is brought it shall be a good defence for the bank to prove that the offence with which it is charged has been dealt with under this section; and

(e)
the order may be enforced in the same manner as an order of the court.

Credit

22. (1) Subject to subsection (2), the Bank may by regulations prescribe-

controls.

(a)
the maximum amounts of loans or advances which commercial banks may have outstanding at any time or during such period or periods as may be specified in the regulations;

(b)
the purposes for which, the maturities for which and the security on which loans or advances may or may not be made by commercial banks;

(c)
the methods of computation, the minimum and maximum amounts of interests payable in respect to loans, advances and deposits or classes thereof.

(2) Any such regulations-

(a)
may be made applicable to all the loans and advances of any specified commercial bank or to any specified class or classes of loans or advances of any specified class or classes of such banks;

(b)
shall not have effect so as to impose in respect of any loan or advance any limit or restriction that is more rigorous than applies to that loan or advance at the date of the coming into force of the regulations;

(c)
shall fix a date for the coming into force of the regulations, which shall not be earlier than thirty days after the date of the receipt of written notice by the relevant bank at its principal place of business in The Bahamas.

Bank as banker to commercial banks.

23. The Bank may act as banker to any commercial bank in The Bahamas and as banker, agent or correspondent to any bank abroad.

Transfer of money.

24. The Bank may accept deposits that are required to be transferred to it in accordance with the Banks and Trust Companies Regulation Act, pay interest on money so deposited and pay out money to any person entitled thereto.

Clearing house.

25. The Bank may promote the establishment of a bank clearing system and provide facilities therefor.

PART VII RELATIONS WITH THE GOVERNMENT

Bank as banker to Government.

26. The Bank may act as banker to the Government or any public corporation.

Bank as agent for Government.

27. The Bank may act generally as agent for the Government on such terms and conditions as may be agreed between the Government and the Bank where the Bank can so act consistently with its functions under this Act and, in particular, the Bank may act as the agent of the Government in the management of the public debt.

Advances to the Government.

28. (1) Subject to the provisions of this section, the Bank may make temporary advances to the Government on such terms and conditions as may be agreed between the Minister and the Bank.

(2) Every such advance made by the Bank to the Government shall be repaid by the Government as soon as possible.

(3) The amount of any such advances by the Bank to the Government which may be outstanding at any one time shall not exceed ten per centum of the average ordinary revenue of the Government or ten per centum of the estimated ordinary revenue of the Government, whichever is the less.

(4) In subsection (3)-

"ordinary revenue" means all income or contributions to Government revenue not being loans, capital grants or other receipts of a capital nature;

"average ordinary revenue" means the annual average of the ordinary revenue of the Government over the three years (for which accounts have been laid before Parliament) next before the year in which any question under the subsection is raised;

"estimated ordinary revenue" means the ordinary revenue, as estimated in the estimates of the Government as laid before Parliament, for that year.

PART VIII GENERAL POWERS OF THE BANK

29. (1) Subject to the provisions of this Act, the Bank may, in the discharge of its functions- Powers of the Bank.

(a)
open accounts for, accept deposits from, and collect money for or on account of, the Government or any commercial bank or any public corporation;

(b)
buy, hold, sell, discount or re-discount-

(i)
bills of exchange, promissory notes or other credit instruments maturing within one hundred and eighty days from the date of their acquisition by the Bank;

(ii)
Treasury Bills;

(c)
buy, hold and sell securities issued or guaranteed by the Government, being securities issued to the public and maturing within twenty years from the date of their acquisition by the Bank, but so that the total amount of any such securities at any time held by the Bank which mature beyond five years after their date of issue (including any such securities held by the Bank as security for any loans or advances) shall not exceed twenty per centum of the demand liabilities of the Bank;

(d)
for the purpose of promoting the development of a securities market, buy, hold and sell fixed term and fixed interest securities of any company, but so that the total amount of any such securities at any time held by the Bank (including any such securities held by the Bank as security for any loans or advances) shall not exceed five per centum of the total liabilities of the Bank;

(e)
with the approval of the Minister, buy, hold and sell securities of any public corporation or any company, being a public corporation or company established for the purpose of developing a securities market, or financing economic development, in The Bahamas;

(f)
make to any commercial bank or any public corporation, on such terms and conditions as may be determined by the Bank, loans or advances on the security of any of the following, that is to say-

(i)
gold coins or gold bullion;

(ii)
bills of exchange, promissory notes, other credit instruments, Treasury Bills or securities, being bills of exchange, promissory notes, credit instruments, Treasury Bills or securities of any kind mentioned in paragraph (b) or (c);

(iii)
warehouse warrants or other documents to goods duly insured and secured by a letter of hypothecation from the owner; or

(iv)
securities of any kind mentioned in paragraph (d) or (e).

(2) Where any loan or advance is made on the security of any instrument mentioned in subsection (1)(f)(ii)-

(a)
the loan or advance shall not extend beyond the maturity date of the instrument itself or ninety-three days, whichever is the longer; and

(b)
the amount of any such loan or advance shall not exceed eighty-five per centum of the market value of the instrument at the date of its acquisition by the Bank.

(3) Subject to the provisions of this Act, the Bank may in the discharge of its functions do any other banking business incidental to or consequential upon the functions of the Bank.

Prohibited activities.

30. Except as expressly authorised by this Act, the Bank shall not-

(a)
engage in trade or otherwise have a direct interest in any business undertaking, except such as the Bank may acquire in the course of the satisfaction of debts due to the Bank, but so that it shall be the duty of the Bank to dispose as soon as may be of any such interest so acquired;

(b)
grant unsecured loans or advances to any person; or

(c)
acquire any interest in real property except in so far as the Bank may consider necessary or expedient for the provision, or the future provision, of premises for the conduct of its business or for any purpose (including use of, or residence in, any such premises by directors, officers or servants of the Bank) incidental to the performance of its functions.

PART IX ACCOUNTS, STATEMENTS AND AUDIT

Financial year.

31. The financial year of the Bank shall end on the thirty-first day of December.

Publication of accounts.

32. (1) The Bank shall, within four months after the end of each financial year, cause to be made and transmit to the Minister-

(a)
a report of the operations of the Bank during that year; and

(b)
a statement of the accounts of the Bank in respect of that year certified by the auditors appointed under subsection (1) of section 34.

(2) The Bank-

(a)
shall, in the preparation of the said accounts, exclude from its calculations any profit or loss arising from any revaluation of any assets or liabilities of the Bank occasioned by any change in the value of the currency of The Bahamas or any foreign currency;

(b)
shall credit or debit, as the case may require, any such profit or loss to an account (to be established and maintained by the Bank and called "the Exchange Equalisation Account"), and

(c)
may from time to time transfer to the General Reserve provided for by section 7 any balance at any time in the said Account, or any part thereof, as the Bank thinks fit.

(3) The Minister shall as soon as possible after their receipt-

(a)
cause a copy of the said report and statement of accounts to be laid before each House of Parliament; and

(b)
cause a copy of the said statement of accounts to be published in the *Gazette*.

Publication of statements.

33. The Bank shall on or before the end of every month prepare and transmit to the Minister and publish in the *Gazette* a statement of the assets and liabilities of the Bank as at the last working day of the preceding month.

Audit.

34. (1) The accounts of the Bank shall be audited annually by auditors appointed by the Board with approval of the Minister.

(2) Without prejudice to the provisions of subsection (1), the Minister may at any time require the Auditor-General to examine and report on the accounts of the Bank as a whole or any aspect of the operations of the Bank, and the Bank shall provide the Auditor-General with all necessary and proper facilities for such an examination.

PART X MISCELLANEOUS

Information may be required from financial institutions.

35. (1) The Bank may require any financial institution or trust company, or any director, officer or servant of such an institution or company, to supply to the Bank in such form and within such time as the Bank may determine such information as the Bank considers necessary to enable the Bank to carry out it functions under this Act.

(2) The Bank may at all reasonable times by notice in writing given-

(a)
to a person regulated under the regulatory laws;

(b)
to a connected person; or

(c)
to a person reasonably believed to have information relevant to an enquiry by the Bank,

require him-

(i)
to provide specified information or information of a specified description, or

(ii)
to produce specified documents or documents of a specified description,

as it may reasonably require in connection with the exercise by the Bank of functions conferred on it by or under this Act or the regulatory laws.

(3) Where, in accordance with section 38, the Bank is satisfied that assistance should be provided in response to a request by an overseas regulatory authority it may in writing direct-

(a)
a person regulated under the regulatory laws;

(b)
a connected person;

(c)
a person that is engaging in an activity that is subject to regulation under the regulatory laws; or

(d)
a person reasonably believed to have information relevant to enquiries to which the request relates,

within a stated time, to-

(i)
provide the Bank with specified information or information of a specified description with respect to any matter relevant to the inquiries to which the request relates,

(ii)
produce specified documents or documents of a specified description relevant to those inquiries; or

(iii)
give to the Bank such assistance in connection with those inquiries as the Bank may specify in writing.

(4) Where a person fails to comply with a requirement under subsection (2) or a direction given under subsection (3) within three days from the date of the requirement or direction or such longer period as the Bank may permit, the Bank may apply to a Stipendiary and Circuit Magistrate for an order requiring the person to comply with the requirement or direction.

(5) Where, in connection with a requirement under subsection (2) or a direction given under subsection (3), the Bank considers it necessary to examine a person on oath, the Bank may apply to a Stipendiary and Circuit Magistrate to have that person examined by the court and to have the results of that examination sent to the Bank.

(6) The court shall process an application under subsection (5) within seven days of its receipt and shall send the result of the examination to the Bank within fourteen days of the examination.

(7) Where documents are produced pursuant to subsection (2) or (3) the Bank may take copies of them or extracts from them.

(8) A person shall not be required under this section to disclose information or to produce a document which he would be entitled to refuse to disclose or to produce on the grounds of legal professional privilege in court proceedings.

(9) Where a person claims a lien on a document, its production under this section is without prejudice to his lien.

(10) In this section "document" includes information recorded in any form and, in relation to information recorded otherwise than in legible form, the power to require its production includes power to require the production of a copy of it in legible and intelligible form.

(11) For the purposes of this section, any information or other matter comes to a professional legal adviser in privileged circumstances if it is communicated or given to him-

(a)
by, or by a representative of, a client of his in connection with the giving by the adviser of legal advice to the client;

(b)
by, or by a representative of, a person seeking legal advice from the adviser; or

(c)
by any person-

(i)
in contemplation of, or in connection with, legal proceedings; and

(ii)
for the purpose of those proceedings.

(12) No information or other matter shall be treated as coming to a professional legal adviser in privileged circumstances if it is communicated or given with a view to furthering any criminal purpose.

(13) For the purposes of subsections (2) and (3) a person is connected with a person regulated under the regulatory laws (the "regulated person") if he is or has at any relevant time been-

(i)
a member of the regulated person's group;

(ii)
a controller of the regulated person;

(iii)
any other member of a partnership of which the regulated person is a member; or

(iv)
a member, officer, manager, employee or agent of the regulated person.

(14) A person who without reasonable cause-

(a)
fails to comply with a requirement of the Bank under subsection (2) or a direction of the Bank under subsection (3);

(b)
with intent to avoid the provisions of subsections (2) or (3) destroys, mutilates, defaces, hides or removes a document; or

(c)
wilfully obstructs an inquiry by the Bank made in accordance with the provisions of subsection (2) or (3),

shall be guilty of an offence and shall be liable on conviction thereof to a fine not exceeding one hundred thousand dollars and if the offence of which he is convicted is continued after conviction he commits a further offence and shall be liable to a fine of ten thousand dollars for every day on which the offence is continued.

(15) Where-

(a)
an offence under this section, which has been committed by a body corporate, is proved to have been committed with the consent or connivance of, or to be attributable to any neglect on the part of, any director, manager, secretary or other similar officer of the body corporate, or any person who was purporting to act in any such capacity, he, as well as the body corporate, shall be guilty of that offence and be liable to be proceeded against and punished accordingly;

(b)
the affairs of a body corporate are managed by its members, paragraph (a) shall apply in relation to the acts and defaults of a member in connection with his functions of management as if he were a director of the body corporate.

Assistance in obtaining information.

36. (1) The Bank may-

(a)
seek the assistance of the Commissioner of Police in the exercise of its powers under this law; and

(b)
authorise a competent person to exercise any of those powers.

(2) No such assistance shall be sought or authority granted under subsection (1) except for the purpose of investigating-

(a)
the affairs, or any aspect of the affairs, of a person specified by the Bank; or

(b)
a subject matter specified by the Bank, being a person who, or a subject matter which, is the subject of the inquiries being carried out by or on behalf of an overseas regulatory authority or the Bank.

(3) No person shall be bound to comply with a requirement imposed by a person exercising powers by virtue of an authority granted under this section unless he has, if required, produced evidence of his authority.

(4) Where the Bank seeks assistance or grants an authority under subsection (1), the assistance or authority shall be provided or executed in such manner as the Bank may determine; and where the Bank grants such an authority to a person, he shall make a report to the Bank in such manner as the Bank may require, on the exercise of that authority and the results of exercising it.

Supplying false statement.

37. Any person who supplies or is concerned in supplying to the Minister or the Bank or any other person any statement, account, report or other information pursuant to this Act or any purpose for which any such statement, account, report or information is lawfully required thereunder, knowing the same to be false in a material particular, shall be guilty of an offence and shall be liable on conviction thereof to a fine not exceeding one hundred thousand dollars or to imprisonment for a term not exceeding five years and in the case of a continuing offence to a fine not exceeding two thousand dollars for each day during which the offence continues.

Confidentiality.

38. (1) Subject to subsections (2) and (3), whoever is a director, officer, employee, agent or adviser of the Bank and who discloses any information relating to-

(a)
the affairs of the Bank;

(b)
any application made to the Bank or the Government under the regulatory laws;

(c)
the affairs of a bank or trust company; or

(d)
the affairs of a customer, client or policyholder of, or a company or mutual fund managed by, a bank or trust company,

that he has acquired in the course of his duties or in the exercise of the Bank's functions under this or any other law, is guilty of an offence and shall be liable on conviction to a fine not exceeding fifty thousand dollars or to imprisonment for three years.

(2) Subsection (1) shall not apply to a disclosure-

(a)
lawfully required or permitted by any court of competent jurisdiction within The Bahamas;

(b)
for the purpose of assisting the Bank to exercise any functions conferred on it by this Act, by any other Act or by regulations made thereunder;

(c)
in respect of the affairs of a bank or trust company or of a customer, client, policyholder of, or a company or mutual fund managed by a bank or trust company, with the authority of the bank or trust company, customer, client, policyholder, company or mutual fund, as the case may be which consent has been voluntarily given;

(d)
if the information disclosed is or has been available to the public from any other source;

(e)
where the information disclosed is in a manner that does not enable the identity of any bank or trust company or of any customer, client, or policyholder of, or company or mutual fund managed by, a bank or trust company to which the information relates to be ascertained;

(f)
to a person with a view to the institution of, or for the purpose of-

(i)
criminal proceedings;

(ii)
disciplinary proceedings, whether within or outside The Bahamas, relating to the exercise by a counsel and attorney, auditor, accountant, value or actuary of his professional duties; or

(iii)
disciplinary proceedings relating to the discharge by a public officer, or a member or employee of the Bank of his duties; or

(g)
for the purposes of any legal proceedings in connection with-

(i)
the winding-up or dissolution of a bank or trust company; or

(ii)
the appointment or duties of a receiver of a bank or trust company.

(3) Subject to subsection (7), the Bank may disclose to an overseas regulatory authority information necessary to enable that authority to exercise regulatory functions including the conduct of civil or administrative investigations and proceedings to enforce laws, regulations and rules administered by that authority.

(4) In deciding whether or not to exercise its power under subsection (3), the Bank may take into account-

(a)
whether the inquiries relate to the possible breach of a law or other requirement which has no close parallel in The Bahamas or involve the assertion of a jurisdiction not recognised by The Bahamas; and

(b)
the seriousness of the matter to which the inquiries relate, the importance to the inquiries of the information sought in The Bahamas.

(5) The Bank may decline to exercise its powers under subsection (3) unless the overseas regulatory authority undertakes to make such contribution towards the costs of the exercise as the Bank considers appropriate.

(6) In subsection (4)(a) "relevant country or territory" means the country or territory from which the request for assistance is made.

(7) Nothing in subsection (3) authorises a disclosure by the Bank unless-

(a)
the Bank has satisfied itself that the intended recipient authority is subject to adequate legal restrictions on further disclosures which shall include the provision of an undertaking of confidentiality; or

(b)
the Bank has been given an undertaking by the recipient authority not to disclose the information provided without the consent of the Bank; and

(c)
the Bank is satisfied that the assistance requested by the overseas regulatory authority is required for the purposes of the overseas regulatory authority's regulatory functions including the conduct of civil or administrative investigations or proceedings to enforce laws administered by that authority; and

(d)
the Bank is satisfied that information provided following the exercise of its powers under subsection (3) will not be used in criminal proceedings against the person providing the information.

(8) Where in the opinion of the Bank it appears necessary in relation to any request for assistance received from an overseas regulatory authority to invoke the jurisdiction of a Stipendiary and Circuit Magistrate in the manner contemplated by subsections (4) and (5) of section 35, the Bank shall immediately notify the Attorney-General with particulars of the request, and shall send him copies of all documents relating to the request, and the Attorney-General shall be entitled, in a manner analogous to *amicus curiae*, to appear or take part in any proceedings in The Bahamas, or in any appeal from such proceedings, arising directly or indirectly from any such request.

Offences.

39. Every offence against this Act shall be tried summarily.

Offences by corporations.

40. Where an offence under this Act which has been committed by a body corporate is proved to have been committed with the consent or connivance of, or to be attributable to any neglect on the part of, a director, manager, secretary or other similar officer of the body corporate, or any person who was purporting to act in any such capacity, he, as well as the body corporate, shall be guilty of that offence and be liable to be proceeded against accordingly.

Exemption.

41. The Bank shall be exempt from tax under the Real Property Tax Act.

PART XI REPEAL, TRANSITIONAL, ETC.

Repeal.

42. The Central Bank of The Bahamas Act is hereby repealed.

Transitional provisions.

43. (1) Upon the day of the coming into operation of this Act-

(a)
every person who immediately before that day was appointed a director to the Board of Directors shall be deemed to have been appointed under this Act and shall continue to serve in that office for the unexpired portion of the term remaining to be served;

(b)
all real and personal property and every right and interest in property that immediately before that day was vested in the Bank under the repealed Act, shall, by force of this section, continue to be vested in the Bank for the purposes of this Act subject to any debts, trusts and liabilities affecting them;

(c)
all rights accruing or accrued to the Bank in respect of any property vested in the Bank by virtue of this section are vested in the Bank and may be enforced against the Bank;

(d)
all contracts, agreements, leases and undertakings made by the Bank and all securities lawfully given to or by the Bank and in force immediately before that day shall have effect as contracts, agreements, leases and undertakings by and with the Bank and may be enforced by and against the Bank accordingly;

(e)
all debts due and moneys payable by the Bank and all claims, liquidated or unliquidated, recoverable against the Bank shall be debts due and moneys payable by and claims recoverable against the Bank;

(f)
any legal or other proceedings that might, but for this section, have been continued or commenced by or against the Bank may be continued or commenced by or against the Bank.

(2) A reference-

(a)
in a law of The Bahamas; and

(b)
in any document,

in force immediately before the date of the coming into operation of this Act to the Bank shall be read, deemed and taken to refer to the Bank.

(3) The persons who immediately before the coming into operation of this Act were appointed the Governor and Deputy Governor under the repealed Act shall continue under the title of Governor and Deputy Governor respectively under this Act as if those persons had been appointed under this Act on the same terms and conditions for a term expiring on the day on which the appointment under the repealed Act would expire.

(4) Any officer or servant appointed or employed by the Bank shall continue in office or employment with the Bank on the same terms and conditions as existed before the coming into operation of this Act.

Savings.

44. Any licence, authority, approval or exemption granted by the Bank which is in force immediately before the coming into force of this Act-

(a)
shall continue to have effect after the coming into force of this Act as if granted by the Bank;

(b)
in the case of a grant for a specific period, shall remain in force for so much of that period as falls after the coming into force of this Act.

SCHEDULE (Section 3(5))

THE BANK

The Board of Directors

1. (1) The Board of Directors shall consist of the following persons to be appointed by the Governor-General, that is to say-

(a)
a Governor, who shall be a person of recognised experience in financial matters and shall be appointed by the Minister by instrument in writing for a period not exceeding five years and shall be eligible for re-appointment; he shall be appointed on such terms and conditions as may be set out in his instrument of appointment, and such terms and conditions may not be altered to his disadvantage during his tenure of office;

(b)
two Deputy Governors, who shall perform the functions conferred on them by this Act and, under the supervision of the Governor such other functions as may be conferred on them by the Board;

(c)
two other directors, being persons appearing to the Governor-General to have wide experience in, and to have shown capacity in, financial or commercial matters, industry, law or administration.

(2) The Board may make bye-laws regulating the conduct of the Bank's business and may make regulations and issue orders for the purpose of giving effect to the provisions of this Act.

(3) Paragraphs 2 to 10 shall have effect in relation to the Board.

2. (1) Each director shall, subject to the provisions of this paragraph, hold and vacate his office in accordance with the terms of his appointment and shall, on ceasing to hold office, be eligible for re-appointment.

(2) The Deputy Governors shall not be appointed or re-appointed for a period exceeding five years.

(3) A director other than the Governor or the Deputy Governors shall not be appointed or re-appointed for a period exceeding four years.

3. (1) The Governor and the Deputy Governors shall not while holding office as such hold any other office or employment, whether remunerated or not, without the prior approval of the Governor-General.

(2) Subject to subparagraph (1), a person may not be appointed or remain a director who-

(a)
is a member of either House of Parliament; or

(b)
is a director, officer or servant of, or is a shareholder of, or has a controlling interest in, any financial institution.

4. The Governor-General may appoint any person eligible to be appointed a director to act temporarily in the place of any director who is absent or unable to act.

5. Any director may at any time by notice in writing to the Governor-General resign his office.

6. If the Governor-General is satisfied that a director-

(a)
has been absent from meetings longer than three consecutive months without the permission of the Board;

(b)
has become bankrupt or made arrangements with his creditors;

(c)
is incapacitated by physical or mental illness; or

(d)
is otherwise unable or unfit to discharge the functions of a director,

the Governor-General may declare his office as director to be vacant and shall notify that fact in such manner as the Governor-General thinks fit, and thereupon that office shall become vacant.

7. The names of all the directors and every change therein shall be published in the *Gazette*.

8. The Bank shall pay to the directors such remuneration (if any), whether by way of

salary, honorarium or fees, as the Governor-General may determine and, if a person ceases to be a director and it appears to the Governor-General that there are special circumstances which may make it right that the person should receive compensation, the Governor-General may require the Bank to pay to that person a sum of such amount as the Governor-General may determine.

9. (1) The Governor, or in case of his absence or disability, a Deputy Governor, shall-

(a)
preside as chairman at the meetings of the Board;

(b)
serve as chief executive officer of the Bank responsible to the Board for the execution of its policy and the management of the Bank;

(c)
except as may otherwise be provided in this Act, the bye-laws of the Bank or the resolutions of the Board, have the power to act, contract, and sign instruments and documents on behalf of the Bank and, pursuant to the resolutions of the Board, delegate such power to other officers of the Bank.

(2) The Deputy Governors may attend all meetings of the Board but shall not have the right to vote at those meetings.

(3) Notwithstanding subparagraph (2), where a Deputy Governor presides as chairman under subparagraph (1)(a) he shall have the right to vote.

(4) The Governor and the Deputy Governors shall devote the whole of their professional services to the Bank and while holding office shall not without the approval of the Minister-

(a)
receive any salary or supplementation thereto from any source other than the Bank;

(b)
occupy any other office or employment, whether remunerated or not.

(5) Notwithstanding subparagraph (4), the Governor may-

(a)
act as a member of any board, committee or commission established by the Government;

(b)
become a Governor, director or member of the board, by whatever name called, of any international bank or international financial institution of which The Bahamas is a member;

(c)
become a director of any corporation in The Bahamas in which the Government is a participant.

10. (1) The Board shall meet as often as may be required for the due performance of its functions, and in any case at least once in every month.

(2) A meeting of the Board-

(a)
may be convened by the Governor or, in his absence, a Deputy Governor; or

(b)
shall be convened on the written requisition of two directors specifying the reasons for which the meeting is required.

(3) Meetings of the Board shall be presided over by the Governor or, in the event of his inability to act, by a Deputy Governor.

(4) Three directors (of whom one shall be either the Governor or a Deputy Governor)

shall form a quorum at any meeting.

(5) A decision shall be adopted by a simple majority of the directors present and in the case of an equality of votes the person presiding at the meeting shall have and exercise a casting vote.

(6) A director who is directly or indirectly interested otherwise than as a director or in common with other directors in a contract or other transaction made or proposed to be made by the Bank, shall disclose the nature of his interest at the first meeting of the Board at which he is present after the relevant fact have come to his knowledge and any such disclosure shall be recorded in the minutes of the Board and after the disclosure that director shall not take part in any deliberation or decision of the Board with respect to that contract or transaction.

(7) Minutes of each meeting of the Board shall be kept in such form as the Board may determine.

(8) No act or proceeding of the Board shall be invalidated merely by reason of any vacancy in the Board or of any defect in the appointment of a director.

(9) No action, suit, prosecution or other proceedings shall be brought or instituted personally against any director in respect of any act done *bona fide* in pursuance of the execution or intended execution of this Act.

(10) Where any director is exempt from liability by reason only of the provisions of subparagraph (9) the Bank shall be liable to the extent that it would be if that member were an employee or agent of the Bank.

Staff

11. The Bank may appoint and employ at such remuneration and on such terms and conditions as it thinks fit, such officers, servants and agents as the Board considers necessary for the due discharge of the functions of the Bank.

12. The Bank shall have power-

(a)
to pay to or in respect of officers or servants of the Bank such pensions or gratuities;

(b)
to make such payments towards the provisions for them of pensions or gratuities; or

(c)
to maintain for them such pension schemes (whether contributor or not),

as the Bank may determine.

Authentication of Documents

13. (1) The seal of the Bank shall be kept under the control of the Governor or the Deputy Governor and the affixing thereof shall be authenticated by the signature of the Governor or the Deputy Governor and one other director authorised by the Board to act in that behalf.

(2) Any document purporting to be a document duly executed under the seal of the Bank shall be received in evidence and shall, unless the contrary is proved, be deemed to be a document so executed.

[i]Section 2 of S.I. 49/2001 provides as follows:

"For the purposes of section 2 of the Act, an overseas regulatory authority also includes an authority, which in a country or territory outside The Bahamas, regulates securities markets, securities exchanges and trading in securities.".

FINANCIAL INTELLIGENCE UNIT ACT

An Act to provide for the establishment of a body to be known as the Financial Intelligence Unit; the functions and powers of that body; and for connected purposes.

39 of 2000
20 of 2001
S.I. 128/2001

[Commencement 29th December, 2000]

Short title.

1. This Act may be cited as the Financial Intelligence Unit Act, 2000.

Interpretation.

2. In this Act-

"Director" means the Director of the Financial Intelligence Unit, appointed pursuant to section 3;

"Financial Intelligence Unit" means the Financial Intelligence Unit established pursuant to section 3;

"Foreign Financial Intelligence Unit" means such body or bodies in another jurisdiction which performs functions similar to those of the Financial Intelligence Unit;

"Minister" means the Minister responsible for the administration of this Act.

Establishment of Financial Intelligence Unit.

3. (1) There is hereby established a body to be known as the Financial Intelligence Unit having perpetual succession and a common seal with power to enter into contracts and to do all such things necessary for the purpose of its functions.

(2) The Financial Intelligence Unit shall consist of-

(a)
a Director appointed in writing by the Minister who shall be the chief executive officer of the Financial Intelligence Unit;

(b)
a counsel and attorney appointed in writing by the Minister;

(c)
a public accountant appointed in writing by the Minister;

(d)
such number of consultants, having suitable qualifications and experience to provide services to the Financial Intelligence Unit, appointed in writing by the Minister;

(e)
such number of police officers appointed by the Commissioner of Police on the recommendation of the Director;

(f)
such other personnel as the Director considers necessary.

(3) The First Schedule shall have effect with respect to the Director and otherwise in relation to the Financial Intelligence Unit.

Functions of the Financial Intelligence Unit.

4. (1) In the exercise of its functions under subsection (2), the Financial Intelligence Unit shall act as the agency responsible for receiving, analysing, obtaining and disseminating information which relates to or may relate to the proceeds of the offences specified in the Second Schedule.

(2) Without limiting the foregoing and not withstanding any other law to the contrary the Financial Intelligence unit-

(a)
shall receive all disclosures of information such as are required to be made pursuant to the Proceeds of Crime Act, 2000 which are relevant to its functions, including information from any Foreign Financial Intelligence Unit;

(b)
may upon receipt of such disclosures as are referred to in paragraph (a), order in writing any person to refrain from completing any transaction for a period not exceeding seventy-two hours;

(c)
may upon receipt of a request from a Foreign Financial Intelligence Unit or law enforcement authority including the Commissioner of Police of The Bahamas order any person to freeze a person's bank account for a period not exceeding five days if satisfied that the request relates to the proceeds of any of the offences specified in the Second Schedule:

> Provided that an aggrieved person may apply to a judge in chambers to discharge the order of the Financial Intelligence Unit and shall servenotice on the Financial Intelligence Unit to join in the proceedings but such order shall remain in full force and effect until the judge determines otherwise;

(d)
may require the production of such information excluding information subject to legal professional privilege that the Financial Intelligence Unit considers relevant to fulfil its functions;

(e)
shall retain a record of all information that it receives for a minimum of five years after the information is received;

(f)
shall provide information, subject to such conditions as may be determined by the Director, to the Commissioner of Police where the information may relate to the commission of an offence specified in the Second Schedule;

(g)
may provide information relating to the commission of an offence specified in the Second Schedule to any Foreign Financial Intelligence Unit, subject to any conditions as may be considered appropriate by the Director;

(h)
may enter into any agreement or arrangement, in writing, with a Foreign Financial Intelligence Unit which the Director considers necessary or desirable for the discharge or performance of the functions of the Financial Intelligence Unit;

(i)
shall inform the public and financial and business entities of their obligations under measures that have been or might be taken to detect, prevent and deter the commission of the offences specified in the Second Schedule.

(3) Any person failing or refusing to provide such information as is required by paragraph (d) of subsection (2) is guilty of an offence and shall be liable on summary conviction to a fine not exceeding fifty thousand dollars or to imprisonment for a term not exceeding two years or to both such fine and imprisonment.

Directions of the Minister.

5. The Minister may give to the Financial Intelligence Unit directions in writing of a general nature as to the policy to be followed by the Financial Intelligence Unit in the performance of its functions as appear to the Minister to be requisite in the public interest and the Financial Intelligence Unit shall give effect to those directions.

No order.

6. Notwithstanding the provisions of any other Act, no order for the provision of information, documents or evidence may be issued in respect of the Financial Intelligence Unit or against the Minister, Director, officers or personnel of the Financial

Intelligence Unit or any person engaged pursuant to this Act.

No liability.

7. No action shall lie against the Minister, Director, officers or personnel of the Financial Intelligence Unit or any person acting under the direction of the Director for anything done or omitted to be done in good faith and in the administration or discharge of any functions, duties or powers under this Act.

No criminal or civil liability for information.

8. (1) No proceedings for breach of banking or professional confidentiality may be instituted against any person or against directors or employees of a financial or business entity who in good faith transmit information or submit reports in accordance with the Proceeds of Crime Act, 2000 or under this Act.

(2) No civil or criminal liability action may be brought nor any professional sanction may be taken against any person or against directors or employees of a financial or business entity who in good faith transmit information or submit reports to the Financial Intelligence Unit.

Confidentiality.

9. (1) Any person who obtains information in any form as a result of his connection with the Financial Intelligence Unit shall not disclose that information to any person except so far as it is required or permitted under this Act or any written law.

(2) Any person who communicates any information in breach of subsection (1) commits an offence and shall be liable on summary conviction to a fine not exceeding ten thousand dollars or to a term of imprisonment not exceeding one year or to both such fine and imprisonment.

Annual Report.

10. (1) The Director shall-

(a)
from time to time advise the Minister on the work of the Financial Intelligence Unit and in particular on matters that could affect public policy or the priorities to be set by the Financial Intelligence Unit;

(b)
prepare and submit to the Minister on or before June 30 in each year an annual report reviewing the work of the Financial Intelligence Unit.

(2) The Minister shall lay or cause to be laid a copy of every annual report on the table of both Houses of Parliament.

Funds and Resources.

11. The funds and resources of the Financial Intelligence Unit shall consist of any moneys as may from time to time be provided by Parliament.

Annual budget.

12. The Financial Intelligence Unit shall prepare for each new financial year an annual budget of revenue and expenditure which shall be submitted to the Minister at least two months prior to the commencement of the financial year.

Accounts and audit.

13. (1) The Financial Intelligence Unit shall keep proper accounts and other recordsin relation thereto, and shall prepare in respect of each financial year a statement of accounts.

(2) The accounts of the Financial Intelligence Unit for each financial year shall be audited by an auditor to be appointed by the Director with the approval of the Minister.

(3) As soon as the accounts have been audited the Financial Intelligence Unit shall submit a copy thereof to the Minister together with a copy of any report made by the auditor.

(4) The Minister shall lay a copy of every such audited accounts before each House of Parliament, together with a copy of any report made by the auditor on the accounts.

Regulations.

14. (1) The Minister, after consultation with the Financial Intelligence Unit, may make such regulations as he thinks necessary or convenient for carrying out or giving effect to this Act.

(2) Without prejudice to the generality of subsection (1), such regulations may in particular-

(a)
require financial and other institutions as may be prescribed to establish and maintain procedures relating to the identification of clients, the keeping of records, the making of reports and training;

(b)
create criminal offences and penalties triable summarily for failing to comply with the regulations;

(c)
provide that in determining whether a person has complied with the regulations the trial court shall take account of any relevant guidelines issued by the Financial Intelligence Unit;

(d)
prescribe all matters required or permitted by this Act to be prescribed.

Financial Intelligence Unit to issue guidelines.

15. (1) Subject to section 16, the Financial Intelligence Unit shall from time to time issue, in respect of each kind of financial institution to which the Financial Transactions Reporting Act, 2000 applies, guidelines-

(a)
setting out any features of a transaction that may give rise to a suspicion that the transaction is or may be relevant to the enforcement of the Proceeds of Crime Act, 2000;

(b)
setting out any circumstances in which a suspicious transaction report relating to such a transaction may be made orally in accordance with section 14(3) of the Financial Transactions Reporting Act, 2000 and the procedures for making such an oral report.

(2) Suspicious transaction guidelines shall be issued in such manner as the Financial Intelligence Unit shall from time to time determine.

(3) The Financial Intelligence Unit may from time to time issue an amendment or revocation of any suspicious transaction guidelines.

(4) Without limiting subsection (1), suspicious transaction guidelines issued under this section may relate to one or more kinds of financial institution; and such guidelines may make different provisions for different kinds of financial institutions and different kinds of transactions.

Consultation on proposed guidelines.

16. (1) The Financial Intelligence Unit shall, before issuing any suspicious transaction guidelines-

(a)
consult with, and invite representations from the Central Bank of The Bahamas, the Securities Commission, the Compliance Commission, the Registrar of Insurance, the Gaming Board and such other agencies and/or entities as the Minister may by order designate and shall have regard to any such representations;

(b)
give public notice of the Financial Intelligence Unit's intention to issue the guidelines, which notice shall contain a statement-

(i)
indicating the Financial Intelligence Unit's intention to issue the guidelines; and

(ii)
inviting financial institutions that are likely to be affected by the proposed guidelines, and industry organisations that are representative of those financial institutions, to express to the Financial Intelligence Unit, within such reasonable period as is specified in the notice, their interest in being consulted in the course of the development of the guidelines; and

(c)
consult with, and invite representations from, those financial institutions and industry organisations which express such an interest, and shall have regard to any such representations.

(2) Nothing in subsection (1) prevents the Financial Intelligence Unit from adopting any additional means of publicising the proposal to issue any suspicious transaction guidelines or of consulting with interested parties in relation to such a proposal.

(3) This section shall apply in respect of any amendment or revocation of any suspicious transaction guidelines.

17. On request by any financial institution in respect of which any suspicious transaction guidelines are for the time being in force, or by any industry organisation that represents any such financial institution, the Financial Intelligence Unit shall, without charge- Financial Intelligence Unit to make guidelines available.

(a)
make those guidelines, and all amendments to those guidelines, available for inspection, by that financial institution or, as the case requires, that industry organisation, at its offices; and

(b)
provide copies of those guidelines, and all amendments to those guidelines, to that financial institution, or, as the case requires, that industry organisation.

18. (1) The Financial Intelligence Unit shall from time to time review any suspicious transaction guidelines for the time being in force. Review of guidelines.

(2) Section 16 shall apply, with all necessary modifications, in relation to any such review as if the review were a proposal to issue suspicious transaction guidelines.

FIRST SCHEDULE (Section 3(3))

THE DIRECTOR OF THE FINANCIAL INTELLIGENCE UNIT

1. (1) The Director shall, subject to the provisions of this paragraph, hold and vacate his office in accordance with the terms of his appointment and shall, on ceasing to hold office, be eligible for re-appointment.

(2) The Director shall not be appointed or re-appointed for a period exceeding five years.

2. (1) The Director shall not while holding office as such hold any other office or employment, whether remunerated or not, without the prior approval of the Minister.

(2) Subject to subparagraph (1) of this paragraph, a person may not be appointed or remain Director who-

(a)
is a member of either House of Parliament;

(b)
is a public officer; or

(c)
is a director, officer or servant of, or has a controlling interest in, any financial institution.

3. The Minister may appoint any person eligible to be appointed to act temporarily in the place of the Director who is absent or unable to act.

4. The Director may at any time by notice in writing to the Minister resign his office.

5. If the Minister is satisfied that the Director-

(a)
has become bankrupt or made arrangements with his creditors; or

(b)
is incapacitated by physical or mental illness; or

(c)
is otherwise unable or unfit to discharge the functions of a director,

the Minister may declare the office of Director vacant and shall notify the fact in such manner as the Minister thinks fit, and thereupon that office shall become vacant.

6. The Director shall receive such remuneration whether by way of salary, honoraria or fees, as the Minister may determine and, if a person ceases to be the Director and it appears to the Minister that there are special circumstances which make it right that the person should receive compensation, the Minister may direct to pay to that person a sum of such amount as the Minister may determine.

7. The Director shall have charge of the day-to-day management and operation of the Financial Intelligence Unit.

FINANCIAL AND CORPORATE SERVICE PROVIDERS ACT

An Act to provide for the licensing and regulation of financial and corporate service providers and for connected purposes.

41 of 2000
18 of 2001
S.I. 128/2001

[Commencement 29th December, 2000]

PART I PRELIMINARY

Short title.

1. This Act may be cited as the Financial and Corporate Service Providers Act, 2000.

Interpretation.

2. In this Act-

"auditor" means a public accountant licensed under the provisions of the Public Accountants Act;

"financial and corporate services" means the provision of financial and corporate services for profit or reward in or from within The Bahamas and includes-

(a)
the conduct or the carrying on of financial services in or from The Bahamas, including on-line financial services;

(b)
the registration or management and administration of international business companies incorporated or existing under the International Business Companies Act;

(c)
the provision of registered agent services and registered office services for companies mentioned in paragraph (b);

(d)
the provision of directors or officers for companies mentioned in paragraph (b);

(e)
the provision of nominee shareholders for companies mentioned in paragraph (b);

(f)
the provision of partners for partnerships registered and existing under the Exempted Limited Partnership Act, 1995; and

(g)
the provision of registered agent services and registered office services for partnerships registered and existing under the Exempted Limited Partnership Act, 1995;

"Inspector" means the Inspector of Financial and Corporate Services appointed under section 12;

"licence" means a licence granted under subsection (4) of section 4;

"licensee" means a person holding a licence under this Act;

"Minister" means the Minister responsible for Companies.

PART II LICENCES

Requirement for licence.

3. Subject to section 20 and notwithstanding any other law or practice, no person shall carry on the business of financial and corporate services in or from within The Bahamas unless that person has obtained a licence under this Act for those purposes.

Application for licence.

4. (1) An application for a licence under this Act shall be made to the Inspector in the form specified in the Schedule.

(2) The Minister may by order prescribe different types of licences subject to such terms and conditions as is deemed necessary.

(3) The Inspector shall in granting a licence take into account the following-

(a)
whether the applicant is a fit and proper person;

(b)
whether the applicant is qualified to carry out the business of a financial and corporate service provider;

(c)
the professional reputation and experience of the applicant;

(d)
whether each officer, director or manager of the applicant is a fit and proper person to act as such;

(e)
in the case of an application by a partnership, whether each partner is a fit and proper person to act as such; and

(f)
whether the applicant, if an individual, is resident in The Bahamas or, if a company, is registered under the Companies Act.

(4) An appeal against a decision to refuse to grant a licence shall be made to the Supreme Court.

(5) The Inspector shall cause notice of the grant of a licence under this Act to be published in the *Gazette*.

Fees.

5. (1) An application under section 4 shall be accompanied by such fee as the Minister may by regulations prescribe.

(2) The issue of a licence under section 4 shall be subject to the payment of such fee as the Minister may by regulations prescribe.

Duration of licence.

6. (1) A licence issued under this Act is valid until the 31st December of the year in which it is issued but is renewable as of the 1st January in each year thereafter for a further period of one year upon payment of such fee as the Minister may by regulations prescribe.

(2) The Inspector before renewing a licence under this Act shall take into consideration those matters referred to in section 4(3).

Notification of change in particulars of licensee.

7. Where a change occurs in the particulars of a licensee as set out in the application for the licence, the licensee shall within thirty days, inform the Inspector of the change.

Display of licence.

8. A licence issued under this Act shall be prominently displayed on the premises where the business of financial and corporate services is carried on.

Register of management companies.

9. (1) The Inspector shall maintain a register in which shall be entered the following particulars-

(a)
the name of the licensee:

(b)
the address of the licensee;

(c)
the location of the registered office; and

(d)
the date the licence was issued.

(2) The register shall be open to inspection by the public.

PART III TRANSFERABILITY OF SHARES AND CHANGES IN DIRECTORS

Shares, etc. not to be issued or transferred

10. (1) No shares in a company or partnership licensed under this Act shall be issued, transferred or otherwise disposed of without the prior written approval of the Inspector.

(2) No appointment of directors of a company licensed under this Act shall be made without the prior written approval of the Inspector. without approval.

(3) Any change of officers of a company shall be notified to the Inspector.

PART IV ADMINISTRATION

Inspector of Financial and Corporate Services.

11. (1) The Minister shall appoint an Inspector of Financial and Corporate Services for the purposes of ensuring the proper administration of this Act.

(2) The Inspector shall be a body corporate with perpetual succession and a common seal with power to acquire hold and dispose of land and other property of whatever kind and to sue and be sued.

(3) The functions of the Inspector are-

(a)
to maintain a general review of financial and corporate services in The Bahamas;

(b)
on an annual basis and when required by the Minister, at the expense of the licensee, to conduct on-site and off-site examinations of the business of the licensee for the purpose of satisfying himself that the provisions of this Act, the Financial Transactions Reporting Act, the International Business Companies Act and any other law are being complied with and in such cases where the Inspector is unable to conduct such examination, to appoint an auditor, at the expense of the licensee, to conduct such examination and to report thereon to the Inspector.

(4) In the performance of his duties under this Act the Inspector may at all reasonable times-

(a)
require a licensee to produce for examination such of his books, records and other documents that the licensee is required to maintain pursuant to section 15; and

(b)
require a licensee to supply such information or explanation,

as the Inspector may reasonably require for the purpose of enabling him to perform his functions under this Act.

(5) The Inspector may, with the approval of the Minister authorise in writing any person or persons to assist him in the performance of his functions under this Act.

Confidentiality.

12. (1) Subject to subsections (2) and (3), the Inspector or any officer, employee, agent or adviser of the Inspector who discloses any information relating to-

(a)
the affairs of the Inspector;

(b)
any application made to the Inspector;

(c)
the affairs of a licensee; or

(d)
the affairs of the client of a licensee,

that he has acquired in the course of his duties or in the exercise of the Inspector's functions under this or any other law is guilty of an offence and shall be liable on summary conviction to a fine not exceeding fifty thousand dollars or to imprisonment for a term not exceeding three years.

(2) Subsection (1) shall not apply to a disclosure-

(a)
lawfully required or permitted by any court of competent jurisdiction within The Bahamas;

(b)
for the purpose of assisting the Inspector to exercise any functions conferred on him by this Act, by any other Act or by regulations made thereunder;

(c)
in respect of the affairs of a licensee or of a client of a licensee, with the consent of the licensee or client, as the case may be, which consent has been voluntarily given,

(d)
where the information disclosed is or has been available to the public fro any other source;

(e)
where the information disclosed is in a manner that does not enable the identity of any licensee or of any client of a licensee to which the information relates to be ascertained;

(f)
to a person with a view to the institution of, or for the purpose of-

(i)
criminal proceedings,

(ii)
disciplinary proceedings, whether within or outside The Bahamas, relating to the exercise by a counsel and attorney, auditor, accountant, valuer or actuary of his professional duties,

(iii)
disciplinary proceedings relating to the discharge by a public officer, or a member or employee of the Inspector of his duties; or

(g)
in any legal proceedings in connection with-

(i)
the winding-up or dissolution of a licensee, or

(ii)
the appointment or duties of a receiver of a licensee.

(3) Subject to subsection (6), the Inspector may disclose to an overseas regulatory authority information necessary to enable that authority to exercise regulatory functions including the conduct of civil or administrative investigations and proceedings to enforce laws, regulations and rules administered by that authority.

(4) In deciding whether or not to exercise its power under subsection (3), the Inspector may take into account-

(a)
whether the inquiries relate to the possible breach of a law or other requirement which has no closer parallel in The Bahamas or involve the assertion of a jurisdiction not recognised by The Bahamas; and

(b)
the seriousness of the matter to which the inquiries of the information sought in The Bahamas.

(5) The Inspector may decline to exercise his power under subsection (3) unless the overseas regulatory authority undertakes to make such contribution towards the cost of the exercise as the Inspector considers appropriate.

(6) Nothing in subsection (3) authorises a disclosure by the Inspector unless-

(a)
the Inspector has satisfied himself that the intended recipient authority is subject to adequate legal restrictions on further disclosures which shall include the provision of an undertaking of confidentiality; or

(b)
the Inspector has been given an undertaking by the recipient authority not to disclose the information provided without the consent of the Inspector; and

(c)
the Inspector is satisfied that the assistance requested by the overseas regulatory authority is required for the purposes of the overseas regulatory authority's regulatory functions including the conduct of civil or administrative investigations or proceedings to enforce laws, regulations and rules administered by that authority; and

(d)
the Inspector is satisfied that information provided following the exercise of his power under subsection (3) will not be used in criminal proceedings against the person providing the information.

(7) Where in the opinion of the Inspector it appears necessary in relation to any request for assistance received from an overseas regulatory authority to invoke the jurisdiction of a Stipendiary and Circuit Magistrate in obtaining information requested by the overseas regulatory authority, the Inspector shall immediately notify the Attorney-General with particulars of the request, and shall send him copies of all documents relating to the request, and the Attorney-General shall be entitled, in a manner analogous to *amicus curiae*, to appear or take part in any proceedings in The Bahamas, or in any appeal from such proceedings, arising directly or indirectly from any such request.

(8) The Inspector may provide information that it has acquired in the course of its duties or in the exercise of its functions under this or any other law to any other regulatory authority in The Bahamas where it considers such information may be relevant to the functions of such other regulatory authority.

(9) In this section-

"overseas regulatory authority" means an authority which in a country or territory outside The Bahamas exercises functions corresponding to any functions of the Inspector.

PART V COMPLIANCE MEASURES FOR LICENSEES

Duty to maintain professional conduct.

13. (1) Every licensee shall-

(a)
maintain a high standard of professional conduct in the performance of his duties as a licensee; and

(b)
refrain from engaging himself or any of his employees in any illegal or improper conduct.

(2) No licensee shall indulge in any activity, whether within or outside The Bahamas, that may reflect adversely on other service managers or the reputation of The Bahamas as an international financial centre.

Obligation of a licensee to clients.

14. (1) Where any request is made to a licensee by a client to provide financial or corporate services, the licensee shall verify the identity of the client.

(2) A licensee shall obtain from each client who instructs him-

(a)
details of the client's principal place of business, business address, telephone, facsimile, telex numbers and electronic address of the principals or professionals concerned with the client;

(b)
two sources of reference to provide adequate indication on the reputation and standing of the client.

(3) A licensee shall keep a record in respect of each client, including the name and address of the beneficial owners of all international business companies incorporated and or existing under the International Business Companies Act, and the name and address of all partners registered under the Exempted Limited Partnership Act on behalf of the client and any information obtained under subsection (1).

(4) The following shall be exempt from the provisions of subsections (2)(b) and (3)-

(a)
any financial institution regulated by the Central Bank of The Bahamas, The Securities Commission of The Bahamas, The Registrar of Insurance, or the Gaming Board, only where the financial institution is instructing a licensee on behalf of its client;

(b)
a financial institution located in a jurisdiction specified in the First Schedule to the Financial Transactions Reporting Act which is regulated by a body having equivalent regulatory and supervisory responsibilities as the Central Bank of The Bahamas, the Securities Commission of The Bahamas, The Registrar of Insurance, or the Gaming Board, only where the financial institution is instructing a licensee on behalf of its client;

(c)
a publicly traded company or mutual fund listed on The Bahamas International Stock Exchange or any other Stock Exchange prescribed by Regulations made under the Financial Transactions Reporting Act and approved by the Securities Commission of The Bahamas;

(d)
a regulated mutual fund as defined in section 2(1) of the Mutual Funds Act or a regulated mutual fund located in a country specified in the First Schedule to the Financial Transactions Reporting Act and regulated by a body having equivalent regulatory and supervisory responsibilities to the Securities Commission of The Bahamas.

(5) Where the service provided to a client is for any reason discontinued, the record kept in his case pursuant to subsection (2) shall continue to be maintained for a period of not less than six years from the date of discontinuation.

Keeping record of clients.

15. In addition to the requirement of section 13(2), a licensee shall maintain adequate information on a file about each client so as to enable the licensee to fulfil the obligations under the Act and any rules and regulations made thereunder and any other law.

Suspension of licence.

16. (1) Where the Inspector is of the opinion that a licensee is-

(a)
acting contrary to section 10 or fails to provide access to any document under section 11(4) or fails to obtain any information for the purposes of section 14; or

(b)
in contravention of this Act or any other law,

the Inspector may require him forthwith to take such steps as may be necessary to rectify the matter, and may forthwith suspend the licence.

(2) A suspension shall not exceed a period of thirty days unless extended from time to time by an order of the court on application of the Inspector on the grounds that it is in the public interest that the suspension continue and specifying the duration of such period of further suspension, which shall not itself exceed sixty days each at any one time.

Revocation of licence.

17. (1) The Inspector may by order, revoke the licence of a licensee-

(a)
if the Inspector is of the opinion that the licensee is carrying on his business in a manner detrimental to the public interest, the interest of the companies managed by him or to the reputation of The Bahamas;

(b)
if the licensee has ceased to carry on financial and corporate services; or

(c)
if the licensee becomes bankrupt or goes into liquidation or is wound up or otherwise dissolved.

(2) An appeal under this section shall not operate as a suspension of the revocation.

Offences.

18. (1) Any person who carries on the business of financial and corporate services in or from within The Bahamas without obtaining a licence under this Act commits an offence and is liable on summary conviction to a fine of seventy-five thousand dollars and where the offence continues subsequent to conviction that person is liable to a fine of one thousand dollars for each day the offence continues.

(2) Subject to subsection (1), a person who with intent to deceive, by any act or omission contravenes any provision or requirement of this Act, commits an offence and is liable on summary conviction to a fine of one hundred thousand dollars.

(3) Any licensee who advertises inviting either directly or indirectly other parties to commit breaches of the law of the country in which such advertisement appears or to which such advertisement is directed, commits an offence and is liable on summary conviction to a fine of fifty thousand dollars.

(4) Any person who with intent to deceive, for any purposes of this Act makes any representation that he knows to be false or does not believe to be true, commits an offence and is liable on summary conviction to a fine of one hundred thousand dollars.

(5) Where a limited liability company is convicted of an offence under subsection (3), every director and every officer concerned with the management of the company is also liable to be convicted for that offence unless he satisfies the court that the offence was committed without his knowledge or consent or that he took all reasonable steps to prevent the commission of the offence.

(6) Any person who-

(a)
assaults or obstructs the Inspector or other person in the performance of his functions under this section;

(b)
contravenes any provision of this Act for which no punishment is specially provided,

commits an offence and is liable on summary conviction to a fine of ten thousand dollars.

(7) Any licensee who fails to comply with section 14(3) commits an offence and is liable on summary conviction to a fine of fifty thousand dollars.

Appeals.

19. (1) An appeal lies to the Supreme Court from any decision of the Inspector-

(a)
revoking a licence under subsection (1) of section 17; or

(b)
suspending a licence under subsection (1) of section 16.

(2) An appeal against the decision of the Inspector shall be by motion.

(3) The following procedure applies to appeals from the Inspector-

(a)
the appellant within twenty-one days after the day on which the Inspector has given his decision shall serve a notice in writing, signed by the appellant or his attorney, on the Attorney-General of his intention to appeal and of the general grounds of his appeal, except that any person aggrieved by a decision of the Inspector may upon serving notice on the Attorney-General apply to the court within fourteen days after the day on which the Inspector has given his decision for leave to extend the time within which notice of appeal prescribed by this section may be served, and the court upon hearing the application may extend the time prescribed by this section as it deems fit;

(b)
the Attorney-General shall within twenty-one days of receiving the notice of appeal obtain a copy of the Inspector's decision and transmit to the Registrar of the Supreme Court without delay a copy thereof together with all papers relating to the appeal, except that the Inspector is not compelled to disclose any information if he considers that the public interest would suffer by such disclosure and a certificate given by the Inspector under the Public Seal is conclusive that disclosure is not in the public interest;

(c)
the Registrar of the Supreme Court shall set down the appeal for hearing on such day as is convenient, and shall cause notice of the hearing to be published, in such manner as, the court may direct; and

(d)
the court may adjourn the hearing of any appeal and may, upon the hearing thereof, confirm, reverse, vary or modify the decision of the Inspector or remit the matter with the opinion of the court thereon to the Inspector.

(4) An appeal against a decision of the Inspector shall not operate as a suspension of the decision of the Inspector.

Act not applicable to Banks and Trust Companies Regulation Act.

20. This Act does not apply to a company licensed under the Banks and Trust Companies Regulation Act.

Regulations.

21. The Minister may make regulations generally for carrying out the purpose and provisions of this Act into effect, and specifically-

(a)
prescribing anything by this Act authorized or required to be prescribed; and

(b)
exempting any person or business, or class of persons or business, from any provision of this Act.

Minister may give directions.

22. The Minister may give to the Inspector directions of a general or of a specific nature as to the policy to be followed by the Inspector in the carrying out or pursuit of his functions as appear to the Minister requisite in the public interest and the Inspector shall give effect to any such directions.

23. Without limiting or affecting section 21, the Minister may, from time to time, issue by publication in the *Gazette*, directions in relation to the inspection and such matters as he may think fit and appropriate and failure by any licensee to comply with the directions shall be taken into consideration when any action is proposed to be taken under section 16 or 17. Directions.

24. A person who at the date of the commencement of this Act is lawfully permitted to carry on the business of financial and corporate services including registered agents shall make an application within three months from the coming into force of this Act for a licence under this Act. Transitional.

SCHEDULE (Section 4(1))

APPLICATION FOR A FINANCIAL AND CORPORATE SERVICES LICENCE

1. Name of applicant
2. Address of principal office of applicant and, in the case of a company, its registered

____
____
____
____

3. In the case of a company, the names, addresses and nationalities of all directors

____
____
____
____
____
____

4. In the case of a company, the names, addresses and nationalities of all shareholders

____
____
____
____
____
____

5. In the case of a company, the names, addresses and nationalities of the beneficial

____
____
____
____
____

6. In the case of a partnership, the names and addresses of all partners

____
____
____
____
____

7. In the case of a company, the names and addresses of all officers and managers

____
____
____

8. Names and addresses of attorneys, if any, for the applicant, together with a letter from the attorneys confirming that they act for the applicant

9. In the case of a company, the name and address of the registered office in The Bahamas upon which any required notices may be served

10. In the case of a company-

(a) a certified copy of a certificate of incorporation;

(b) a certified copy of Memorandum and Articles of Association; and

(c) a certificate of good standing.

11. A detailed resumé, two character references in writing, one financial reference from a bank or trust company registered under the Banks and Trust Companies Regulation Act, or registered in a country specified in the First Schedule to the Financial Transactions Reporting Act, a police certificate for the previous five years in respect of each shareholder, beneficial owner, officer and director.

12. Status for the purposes of the Exchange Control Regulations Act and any regulations made thereunder and in force at the date of the application.

13. A detailed overview/summary of internal control procedures to be put in place.

FINANCIAL TRANSACTIONS REPORTING ACT

PART I PRELIMINARY PROVISIONS

Short title.

1. This Act may be cited as the Financial Transactions Reporting Act, 2000.

Interpretation.

2. (1) In this Act-

"accountant" means a person registered and licensed under the Public Accountants Act, 1991;

"cash" means any coin or paper money that is designated as legal tender in the country of issue and includes bearer bonds, travellers cheques, postal orders and money orders;

"Commission" means the Compliance Commission established under section 39;

"Comptroller" has the same meaning as in section 2 of the Customs Management Act;

"counsel and attorney" means a counsel and attorney admitted to practice under the Legal Profession Act, 1992;

"document" has the same meaning as in section 2 of the Evidence Act, 1996;

"facility" subject to any regulations made under this Act-

(a)
means any account or arrangement-

(i)
that is provided by a financial institution to a facility holder; and

(ii)
by, through or with which a facility holder may conduct two or more transactions whether or not they are so used; and

(b)
without limiting the generality of the foregoing, includes-

(i)
a life assurance policy;

(ii)
membership of a superannuation scheme;

(iii)
the provision, by a financial institution, of facilities for safe custody, including (without limitation) a safety deposit box;

"facility holder", in relation to a facility-

(a)
means the person in whose name the facility is established;

(b)
without limiting the generality of the foregoing, includes-

(i)
any person to whom the facility is assigned; and

(ii)
any person who is authorised to conduct transactions through the facility;

(c)
in relation to a facility that is a life assurance policy, means any person who for the time being is the legal holder of that policy;

"Financial Intelligence Unit" means the Financial Intelligence Unit established under section 3 of the Financial Intelligence Unit Act, 2000;

"financial institution" has the meaning given to it by section 3;

"foreign financial institution" means a financial institution which, in a country specified in the First Schedule, exercises functions equivalent to the corresponding financial institution in The Bahamas and referred to in section 2(3);

"funds" means cash, securities, cheques, drafts, bank deposits, payment orders and other negotiable instruments which are readily convertible into cash;

"industry organisation" means any organisation the purpose of which, or one or the purposes of which, is to represent the interests of any class or classes of financial institution;

"Inspector" means the Inspector of Banks and Trust Companies established under section 9 of the Banks and Trust Companies Regulation Act;

"life assurance policy" means a policy within the meaning of section 2 of the Insurance Act;

"Minister" means the Minister responsible for the administration of this Act;

"money laundering offence" has the same meaning as in the Proceeds of Crime Act, 2000;

"occasional transaction" subject to any regulations made under this Act, means any transaction-

(a)
that involves the payment, deposit, withdrawal, debit, repayment, encashment, exchange, or transfer of cash; and

(b)
that is conducted by any person otherwise than through a facility in respect of which that person is a facility holder;

"prescribed amount" in relation to Part II, means such amount as is for the time being prescribed for the purposes of that Part by regulations made under section 51;

"principal facility holder" in relation to a facility provided by a financial institution, means the facility holder or facility holders whom that financial institution reasonably regards, for the time being, as principally responsible for the operation, use or administration of that facility;

"real estate broker" has the same meaning as in section 2 of the Real Estate (Brokers and Salesmen) Act, 1995;

"real estate transaction" means any matter that involves any work that may be done only-

(a)
by or under the supervision of a counsel and attorney by virtue of section 22 of the Legal Profession Act, 1992; or

(b)
by a real estate broker who holds a licence in force under the Real Estate (Brokers and Salesmen) Act, 1995;

"superannuation scheme" means a superannuation scheme within the meaning of the Superannuation and other Trust Funds (Validation) Act; but does not include-

(a)
any superannuation scheme established principally for the purpose of providing retirement benefits to employees where-

(i)
contributions to the scheme by employees are made only by way of deduction from the salary or wages of those employees; and

(ii)
the trust deed governing the scheme (or, as the case requires, the statute under which the scheme is constituted) does not permit a member to assign his or her interest in the scheme to any other person; or

(b)
any superannuation scheme in respect of which no advertisement has been published inviting the public or any section of the public to become contributors to the scheme;

"suspicious transaction guidelines" means any guidelines for the time being in force;

"suspicious transaction report" means a report made pursuant to section 14(1);

"transaction"-

(a)
means any deposit, withdrawal, exchange or transfer of funds (in whatever currency denominated), whether-

(i)
in cash;

(ii)
by cheque, payment order or other instrument; or

(iii)
by electronic or other non-physical means; and

(b)
without limiting the generality of the foregoing, includes any payment made in satisfaction, in whole or in part, of any contractual or other legal obligation;

but does not include any of the following-

(c)
the placing of any bet;

(d)
participation in any game of chance defined in the Lotteries and Gaming Act;

(e)
any transaction that is exempted from the provisions of this Act by or under regulations made under section 51.

(2) For the purposes of this Act, a person becomes a facility holder in relation to a facility when that person is first able to use the facility to conduct transactions.

(3) For the purposes of sections 7(2)(b), 8(6)(c), 9(6)(c), 11(3)(b)(iii) and 11(4)(b)(iii) "financial institution" means those financial institutions mentioned in paragraphs (a), (b), (e), (f), and (i) of section 3 and the Minister may by order add to, or delete from, the list of such institutions.

Definition of "financial institution".

3. (1) Subject to any regulations made under this Act, the term "financial institution" means any of the following-

(a)
a bank or trust company, being a bank or trust company licensed under the Banks and Trust Companies Regulation Act;

(b)
a company carrying on life assurance business as defined in section 2 of the Insurance Act or insurance business as defined in section 2 of the External Insurance Act;

(c)
a co-operative society registered under the Co-operative Societies Act;

(d)
a friendly society enrolled under the Friendly Societies Act;

(e)
a licensed casino operator within the meaning of the Lotteries and Gaming Act;

(f)
a broker-dealer within the meaning of section 2 of the Securities Industry Act;

(g)
a real estate broker, but only to the extent that the real estate broker receives funds in the course of the person's business for the purpose of settling real estate transactions;

(h)
a trustee or administration manager or investment manager of a superannuation scheme;

(i)
a mutual fund administrator or operator of a mutual fund within the meaning of the Mutual Funds Act, 1995;

(j)
any person whose business or a principal part of whose business consists of any of the following-

(i)
borrowing or lending or investing money;

(ii)
administering or managing funds on behalf of other persons;

(iii)
acting as trustee in respect of funds of other persons;

(iv)
dealing in life assurance policies;

(v)
providing financial services that involve the transfer or exchange of funds, including (without limitation) services relating to financial leasing, money transmissions, credit cards, debit cards, treasury certificates, bankers draft and other means of payment, financial guarantees, trading for account of others (in money market instruments, foreign exchange, interest and index instruments, transferable securities and futures), participation in securities issues, portfolio management, safekeeping of cash and liquid securities, investment related insurance and money changing; but not including the provision of financial services that consist solely of the provision of financial advice;

(k)
a counsel and attorney, but only to the extent that the counsel and attorney receives funds in the course of that person's business-

(i)
for the purposes of deposit or investment;

(ii)
for the purpose of settling real estate transactions; or

(iii)
to be held in a client account;

(l)
an accountant, but only to the extent that the accountant receives funds in the course of that person's business for the purposes of deposit or investment.

(2) A person shall not be regarded as a financial institution for the purposes of this Act merely because that person carries on business as a security guard within the meaning of section 2 of the Inquiry Agents and Security Guards Act.

Amounts not in Bahamian currency.

4. (1) Where, for the purposes of any provision of this Act, it is necessary to determine whether or not the amount of any cash (whether alone or together with any other amount of cash) exceeds the prescribed amount, and the cash is denominated in a currency other than Bahamian currency, the amount of the cash shall be taken to be the equivalent in Bahamian currency, calculated at the rate of exchange on the date of the determination, or, if there is more than one rate of exchange on that date, at the average of those rates.

(2) For the purposes of subsection (1), a written certificate purporting to be signed by an officer of any bank in The Bahamas that a specified rate of exchange prevailed between currencies on a specified day and that at such rate a specified sum in one currency is equivalent to a specified sum in terms of the currency of The Bahamas shall be sufficient evidence of the rate of exchange so prevailing and of the equivalent sums in terms of the respective currencies.

Act to bind the

5. This Act binds the Crown.

Crown.

PART II
OBLIGATIONS ON FINANCIAL INSTITUTIONS TO VERIFY IDENTITY

Financial institutions to verify identity of facility holders.

6. (1) Subject to subsection (5), where any request is made to a financial institution for a person to become a facility holder (whether in relation to an existing facility provided by that financial institution or by means of the establishment, by that financial institution, of a new facility), that financial institution shall verify the identity of that person.

(2) Where subsection (1) applies in respect of any request for a person to become a facility holder in relation to a facility (whether existing or new), the financial institution shall verify the identity of that person before that person becomes a facility holder in relation to that facility.

(3) Notwithstanding anything in subsection (1) where in relation to a facility provided by a financial institution there are two or more facility holders, it shall be necessary for that financial institution to have verified the identity of every such facility holder.

(4) Where, during the course of a business relationship, a financial institution has reason to doubt the identity of an existing facility holder, the financial institution shall seek to verify the identity of such facility holder.

(5) Notwithstanding anything in subsection (1), nothing in that subsection requires a trustee or administration manager or investment manager of a superannuation scheme to verify the identity of any person-

(a)
who becomes a member of that superannuation scheme by virtue of the transfer, to that scheme, of all the members of another superannuation scheme; or

(b)
who becomes a member of a section of that superannuation scheme by virtue of the transfer, to one section of that scheme, of all the members of another section of the same scheme.

(6) In the case of an existing facility-

(a)
the financial institution shall verify the identity of the facility holder within twelve months from the date of commencement of this Act; [i]*

(b)
the Minister may, if he thinks it expedient, by order extend the period of twelve months for a further period of up to twelve months;

(c)
where at the end of the said period of twelve months or further period of up to twelve months, as the case may be, the financial institution is unable to verify the identity of the facility holder, the financial institution shall transfer or assign the facility to the Central Bank of The Bahamas in accordance with section 16 of the Banks and Trust Companies Regulation Act.

Financial institutions to verify identity of persons conducting certain occasional transactions.

7. (1) Subject to subsection (2), where any person conducts an occasional transaction by, through or with a financial institution, that financial institution shall verify the identity of that person in any case where-

(a)
the amount of cash involved in the transaction exceeds the prescribed amount; or

(b)
the following conditions apply, namely-

(i)
that person, or any other person, has also conducted or is conducting one or more other occasional transactions through that financial institution;

(ii)
the circumstances in which those transactions have been or are being, conducted provide reasonable grounds to believe that the transactions have been, or are being, structured to avoid the application of paragraph (a); and

(iii)
the total amount of cash involved in those transactions exceeds the prescribed amount.

(2) Notwithstanding anything in subsection (1), nothing in that subsection requires a financial institution to verify the identity of a person who conducts an occasional transaction (in this subsection referred to as "the transactor") through that financial institution in any case where-

(a)
that financial institution is unable to readily determine whether or not the transaction involves cash because the funds involved in the transaction are deposited by the transactor into a facility (being a facility in relation to which that financial institution is a facility holder) provided by another financial institution;

(b)
the financial institution has obtained in writing confirmation that the other financial institution has verified the identity of the person:

Provided that such confirmation may be accepted from a foreign financial institution.

(3) Without limiting any other factors that a financial institution may consider for the purpose of determining whether or not any transactions are or have been structured to avoid the application of subsection (1)(a), a financial institution shall consider, for that purpose, the following factors-

(a)
the time frame within which the transactions are conducted;

(b)
whether or not the parties to the transactions are the same person, or are associated in any way.

(4) Where subsection (1) applies in respect of any transaction, the financial institution shall verify the identity of the person conducting the transaction-

(a)
where paragraph (a) of subsection (1) applies, before the transaction is conducted;

(b)
where paragraph (b) of subsection (1) applies, as soon as practicable after the conditions specified in the paragraph are satisfied in respect of that transaction.

(5) Where subsection (1) applies in respect of any transaction, the financial institution shall also ask the person who is conducting or, as the case may be, conducted the transaction whether or not the transaction is being conducted or was conducted on behalf of any other person.

(6) Nothing in subsection (5) limits section 8.

Verification where persons acting on behalf of others in

8. (1) Subject to subsection (6) and without limiting section 7, where-

(a)
a person conducts an occasional transaction by, through or with a financial institution;

(b)
the amount of cash involved in the transaction exceeds the prescribed amount; and

respect of occasional transactions.

(c)
the financial institution has reasonable grounds to believe that the person is conducting the transaction on behalf of any other person or persons,

then in addition to complying with the requirements of section 7, the financial institution shall verify the identity of the other person or persons:

Provided that where a financial institution has reasonable grounds to believe, after an occasional transaction has been conducted, that the person who conducted the transaction was acting on behalf of another person or persons, the financial institution shall verify the identity of the other person or persons.

(2) Without limiting section 7, where a person conducts an occasional transaction through a financial institution and the following conditions apply, namely-

(a)
that person, or any other person, has also conducted or is conducting one or mere other occasional transactions through that financial institution; and

(b)
the circumstances in which those transactions have been, or are being, conducted provide reasonable grounds to believe-

(i)
that the person is conducting the transactions on behalf of any other person or persons; and

(ii)
that the transactions have been, or are being, structured to avoid the application of subsection (1); and

(c)
the total amount of cash involved in those transactions exceeds the prescribed amount,

then in addition to complying with the requirements of section 7, the financial institution shall verify the identity of the person or persons on whose behalf it is believed the transactions are being conducted.

(3) Without limiting any other factors that a financial institution may consider for the purpose of determining whether of not any transactions have been structured to avoid the application of subsection (1), a financial institution shall consider, for that purpose, the following factors-

(a)
the time frame within which the transactions are conducted;

(b)
whether or not the parties to the transactions are the same persons, or are associated in any way.

(4) Where subsection (1) applies in respect of any transaction, the financial institution shall verify the identity of the relevant person or persons before the transaction is conducted.

(5) Where subsection (2) applies in respect of any transaction, the financial institution shall verify the identity of the relevant person or persons as soon as practicable after the conditions specified in that subsection are satisfied.

(6) Nothing in subsection (1) requires a financial institution to verify the identity of any person in any case where-

(a)
the person who is conducting the transaction is a financial institution;

(b)
the identity of the other person is required, by any provision of this Part, to be verified by that other financial institution; and

(c)
the financial institution has obtained in writing confirmation that the other financial institution has verified the identity of the person:

Provided that such confirmation may be accepted from a foreign financial institution.

9. (1) Subject to subsections (6) and (7), where-

Verification where facility holders acting on behalf of others.

(a)
a person who is a facility holder in relation to a facility provided by a financial institution conducts a transaction through that facility;

(b)
the amount of cash involved in the transaction exceeds the prescribed amount; and

(c)
the financial institution has reasonable grounds to believe that the person is conducting the transaction on behalf of any other person or persons,

the financial institution shall verify the identity of the other person or persons.

(2) Where a person who is a facility holder in relation to a facility provided by a financial institution conducts a transaction through that facility, and the following conditions apply, namely-

(a)
that person, or any other person, has also conducted or is conducting one or more other transactions through that facility;

(b)
the circumstances in which those transactions have been, or are being, conducted provide reasonable grounds to believe-

(i)
that the person is conducting the transaction on behalf of any other person or persons;

(ii)
that the transactions have been, or are being, structured to avoid the application of subsection (1); and

(c)
the total amount of cash involved in those transactions exceeds the prescribed amount,

the financial institution shall verify the identity of the other person or persons.

(3) Without limiting any other factors that a financial institution may consider for the purpose of determining whether or not any transactions are or have been structured to avoid the application of subsection (1), a financial institution shall consider, for that purpose, the following factors-

(a)
the time frame within which the transactions are conducted;

(b)
whether or not the parties to the transactions are the same persons, or are associated in any way.

(4) Where subsection (1) applies in respect of any transaction, the financial institution shall verify the identity of the relevant person or persons before the transaction is conducted.

(5) Where subsection (2) applies in respect of any transaction, the financial institution shall verify the identity of the relevant person or persons as soon as practicable after the conditions specified in that subsection are satisfied.

(6) Nothing in subsection (1) requires a financial institution to verify the identity of any person in any case where-

(a)
the person who is conducting the transaction is a financial institution;

(b)
the identity of the other person is required, by any provision of this Part, to be verified by the other financial institution; and

(c)
the financial institution has obtained in writing confirmation that the other financial institution has verified the identity of the person:

Provided that such confirmation may be accepted from a foreign financial institution.

(7) Nothing in subsection (1) requires a financial institution to verify the identity of any person (in this subsection referred to as the "other person") where-

(a)
the transaction is conducted by any person in his or her capacity as an employee of the other person, or as a director or principal or partner of the other person; and

(b)
the financial institution has already verified the identity of the other person pursuant to this Part.

Application of sections 8 and 9 in relation to beneficiaries under a trust.

10. Nothing in sections 8 and 9 requires the verification of the identity of any person, in any case where on reasonable grounds it is believed-

(a)
that a transaction is being, or has been, conducted on that person's behalf in his or her capacity as the beneficiary under a trust; and

(b)
that the person does not have a vested interest under the trust.

Procedures for verifying identity.

11. (1) Subject to subsections (3) to (5), where, by virtue of any provision of this Part, a financial institution is required to verify the identity of any person, that verification shall be done by means of such documentary or other evidence as is reasonably capable of establishing the identity of that person, including official documents and structural information in the case of corporate entities.

(2) Without limiting the generality of subsection (1), in verifying the identity of any person, a financial institution may rely (in whole or in part) on evidence used by that financial institution on an earlier occasion to verify that person's identity, if the financial institution has reasonable grounds to believe that the evidence is still reasonably capable of establishing the identity of that person:

Provided that such verification may be accepted from a foreign financial institution.

(3) Where-

(a)
by virtue of any provision of this Part, a financial institution is required to verify the identity of any person in relation to any facility; and

(b)
transactions may be conducted through that facility by means of an existing facility-

(i)
that is provided by another financial institution;

(ii)
in relation to which that person is a facility holder; and

(iii)
the financial institution has obtained in writing confirmation that the other financial institution has verified the identity of the person:

Provided that such confirmation may be accepted from a foreign financial institution,

the first-mentioned financial institution shall be deemed to have complied with the requirement to verify the identity of that person if that financial institution takes all such steps as are reasonably necessary to confirm the existence of the other facility.

(4) Where-

(a)
by virtue of any provision of this Part, a financial institution is required to verify the identity of any person in relation to an occasional transaction; and

(b)
that occasional transaction is conducted by means of an existing facility-

(i)
that is provided by another financial institution;

(ii)
in relation to which that person is a facility holder; and

(iii)
the financial institution has obtained in writing confirmation that the other financial institution has verified the identity of the person:

Provided that such confirmation may be accepted from a foreign financial institution,

the first-mentioned financial institution shall be deemed to have complied with the requirement to verify the identity of that person if the financial institution takes all such steps as are reasonably necessary to confirm the existence of the facility.

(5) Where-

(a)
by virtue of any provision of this Part, a trustee or administration manager or investment manager of a superannuation scheme is required to verify the identity of any person by reason that the person has become, or is seeking to become, a member of that scheme; and

(b)
the superannuation scheme is established principally for the purpose of providing retirement benefits to employees,

that trustee or manager shall be deemed to have complied with the requirement to verify the identity of that person if that person's identity has been verified by his or her employer.

12. [ii]* (1) Every financial institution commits an offence against this section which- Offences.

(a)
in contravention of section 6(2), permits a person to become a facility holder in relation to any facility (being a facility provided by that institution) without first having verified the identity of that person;

(b)
in contravention of section 7(4)(a), permits any person to conduct an occasional transaction through that financial institution, without first having verified the identity of that person, in any case where the amount of funds involved in the transaction exceeds the prescribed amount;

(c)
where an occasional transaction is conducted by any person through that financial institution, fails, in contravention of section 7(4)(b), to verify the identity of that person as soon as practicable after the conditions specified in section 7(1)(b) are satisfied in respect of that transaction;

(d)
where-

(i)
an occasional transaction is conducted by any person through that financial institution;

(ii)
the amount of funds involved in the transaction exceeds the prescribed amount; and

(iii)
the financial institution has reasonable grounds to believe that the person is conducting the transaction on behalf of any other person or persons,

fails, in contravention of section 8(4), to verify the identity of that other person or, as the case requires, those other persons before the transaction is conducted, or as soon as practicable after the financial institution has reasonable grounds to believe that the transaction is being, or has been, so conducted;

(e)
where-

(i)
an occasional transaction is conducted by any person through that financial institution; and

(ii)
the conditions specified in paragraphs (a) to (c) of section 8(2) apply in respect of that transaction,

fails, in contravention of section 8(5), to undertake the verification required by section 8(2) as soon as practicable after the conditions specified in section 8(2) are satisfied in respect of that transaction;

(f)
where-

(i)
a person who is a facility holder in relation to a facility provided by that financial institution conducts a transaction through that facility;

(ii)
the amount of funds involved in the transaction exceeds the prescribed amount;

(iii)
the financial institution has reasonable grounds to believe that the person is conducting the transaction on behalf of any other person or persons,

fails, in contravention of section 9(4), to verify the identity of that other person or, as the case requires, those other persons before the transaction is conducted; or as soon as practicable after the financial institution has reasonable grounds to believe that the transaction is being, or has been, so conducted; or

(g)
where-

(i)
a person who is a facility holder in relation to a facility provided by that financial institution conducts a transaction through that facility; and

(ii)
the conditions specified in paragraphs (a) to (c) of section 9(2) apply in respect of that transaction,

fails, in contravention of section 9(5), to undertake the verification required by section 9(2) as soon as practicable after the conditions specified in section 9(2) are satisfied in respect of that transaction.

(2) Every financial institution which commits an offence against this section is liable on summary conviction to a fine not exceeding-

(a)
in the case of an individual, twenty thousand dollars;

(b)
in the case of a body corporate, one hundred thousand dollars.

Defence.

13. (1) It is a defence to a charge against a person in relation to a contravention of, or a failure to comply with, any provision of this Part if the defendant proves-

(a)
that he took all reasonable steps to ensure that he complied with that provision; or

(b)
that, in the circumstances of the particular case, he could not reasonably have been expected to ensure that he complied with the provision.

(2) In determining, for the purposes of subsection (1)(a), whether or not a financial institution took all reasonable steps to comply with a provision of this Part, the court shall have regard to-

(a)
the nature of the financial institution and the activities in which it engages;

(b)
the existence and adequacy of any procedures established by the financial institution to ensure compliance with the provision, including (without limitation)-

(i)
staff training; and

(ii)
audits to test the effectiveness of any such procedures; and

(c)
any relevant guidelines issued by the Financial Intelligence Unit.

(3) Except as provided in subsection (4), subsection (1) shall not apply unless, within twenty-one days after the service of the summons, or within such further time as the court may allow, the defendant has delivered to the prosecutor a written notice-

(a)
stating that the defendant intends to rely on subsection (1); and

(b)
specifying the reasonable steps that the defendant will claim to have taken.

(4) In any such prosecution, evidence that the defendant took a step not specified in the written notice required by subsection (3) shall not, except with the leave of the court, be admissible for the purpose of supporting a defence under subsection (1).

PART III
OBLIGATION TO REPORT SUSPICIOUS TRANSACTIONS

Financial institutions to report suspicious transactions.

14. (1) Notwithstanding any other written law or any rule of law, but subject to section 17, where-

(a)
any person conducts or seeks to conduct any transaction by, through or with a financial institution (whether or not the transaction or proposed transaction involves funds); and

(b)
the financial institution knows, suspects or has reasonable grounds to suspect that the transaction or proposed transaction involves proceeds of criminal conduct as defined in the Proceeds of Crime Act, 2000, or any offence under the Proceeds of Crime Act, 2000 or an attempt to avoid the enforcement of any provision of the Proceeds of Crime Act, 2000,

the financial institution shall, as soon as practicable after forming that suspicion, report that transaction or proposed transaction to the Financial Intelligence Unit.

(2) Subject to subsection (3), every suspicious transaction report shall-

(a)
be in the prescribed form (if any);

(b)
contain the details specified in the Second Schedule;

(c)
contain a statement of the grounds on which the financial institution holds the suspicion referred to in subsection (1)(b); and

(d)
be forwarded, in writing, to the Financial Intelligence Unit-

(i)
by way of facsimile transaction; or

(ii)
by such other means (including, without limitation, electronic mail or other similar means of communication) as may be agreed from time to time between the Financial Intelligence Unit an the financial institution concerned.

(3) Notwithstanding paragraph (a) or paragraph (d) of subsection (2), where the urgency of the situation requires, a suspicious transaction report may be made orally to the Financial Intelligence Unit, but in any such case the financial institution shall, as soon as practicable, forward to the Financial Intelligence Unit a suspicious transaction report that complies with the requirements of subsection (2).

Auditors to report suspicious transactions.

15. Notwithstanding any other written law or any rule of law, any person who, in the course of carrying out the duties of that person's occupation as an auditor, has reasonable grounds to suspect, in relation to any transaction that the transaction is or may be relevant to the enforcement of the Proceeds of Crime Act, 2000, shall report that transaction to any member of the Police.

Protection of persons reporting suspicious transactions.

16. (1) Where any information is disclosed or supplied in any suspicious transaction report made, pursuant to section 14, by any person, no civil, criminal or disciplinary proceedings shall lie against that person-

(a)
in respect of the disclosure or supply, or the manner of the disclosure or supply, of that information by that person; or

(b)
for any consequences that follow from the disclosure or supply of that information.

(2) Where any information is disclosed or supplied, pursuant to section 15, to any member of the Police by any person, no civil, criminal or disciplinary proceedings shall lie against that person-

(a)
in respect to the disclosure or supply, or the manner of the disclosure or supply, of that information by that person; or

(b)
for any consequences that follow from the disclosure or supply of that information,

unless the information was disclosed or supplied in bad faith.

(3) Nothing in subsection (1) or subsection (2) applies in respect of proceedings for an offence against section 20.

Legal professional privilege.

17. (1) Nothing in section 14 requires any counsel and attorney to disclose any privileged communication.

(2) For the purposes of this section, a communication is a privileged communication only if-

(a)
it is a confidential communication, whether oral or written, passing between-

(i)
a counsel and attorney in his or her professional capacity and another counsel and attorney in such capacity; or

(ii)
a counsel and attorney in his or her professional capacity and his or her client,

whether made directly or indirectly through an agent of either;

(b)
it is communicated or given to a counsel and attorney by, or by a representative of, a client of his or her in connection with the giving by the counsel and attorney of legal advice to the client;

(c)
it is made or brought into existence for the purpose of obtaining or giving legal advice or assistance; and

(d)
it is not made or brought into existence for the purpose of committing or furthering the commission of some illegal or wrongful act.

(3) Where the information consists wholly or partly of, or relates wholly or partly to, the receipts, payments, income, expenditure or financial transactions of a specified person (whether a counsel and attorney, his or her client or any other person), it shall not be a privileged communication if it is contained in, or comprises the whole or part of, any book, account, statement or other record prepared or kept by the counsel and attorney in connection with a client's account of the counsel and attorney.

(4) For the purposes of this section, references to a counsel and attorney include a firm in which he or she is a partner or an associate or is held out to be a partner or an associate.

Suspicious transaction reports not to be

18. (1) A financial institution that has made, or is contemplating making, a suspicious transaction report shall not disclose the existence of that report or, as the case requires, that the making of such a report is contemplated to any person except-

disclosed.

(a)
the financial institution's Supervisory Authority;

(b)
the Financial Intelligence Unit;

(c)
the Commissioner of Police or a member of the Police who is authorised by the Commissioner to receive the information;

(d)
an officer or employee or agent of the financial institution, for any purpose connected with the performance of that person's duties;

(e)
a counsel and attorney, for the purpose of obtaining legal advice or representation in relation to the matter;

(f)
the Central Bank of The Bahamas, for the purpose of assisting the Central Bank to carry out its functions under the Central Bank of The Bahamas Act, 2000.

(2) No person referred to in paragraph (b) of subsection (1) to whom disclosure of any information to which that subsection applies has been made shall disclose that information except to another person of the kind referred to in that subsection, for the purpose of-

(a)
the performance of the first-mentioned person's duties; or

(b)
obtaining legal advice or representation in relation to the matter.

(3) No person referred to in paragraph (e) of subsection (1) to whom disclosure of any information to which that subsection applies has been made shall disclose that information except to a person of the kind referred to in that subsection for the purpose of giving legal advice or making representations in relation to the matter.

(4) Subject to section 19, nothing in subsections (1) to (3) shall prevent the disclosure of any information in connection with, or in the course of, proceedings before a court.

Protection of identity of persons making suspicious transaction reports.

19. (1) This section applies in respect of the following information-

(a)
any suspicious transaction report;

(b)
any information the disclosure of which will identify, or is reasonably likely to identify, any person-

(i)
as a person who, in his or her capacity as an officer, employee or agent of a financial institution, has handled a transaction in respect of which a suspicious transaction report was made;

(ii)
as a person who has prepared a suspicious transaction report; or

(iii)
as a person who has made a suspicious transaction report.

(2) No member of the Police shall disclose any information to which this section applies except for one or more of the following purposes-

(a)
the enforcement of the Proceeds of Crime Act, 2000;

(b)
the detection, investigation and prosecution of any relevant offence (within the meaning of the Proceeds of Crime Act, 2000), in any case where that offence may reasonably give rise to, or form the basis of, any proceedings under that Act;

(c)
the administration of the Mutual Legal Assistance (Criminal Matters) Act, 1988;

(d)
to assist the Financial Intelligence Unit and Foreign Intelligence Units to carry out their functions.

(3) No person shall be required to disclose, in any judicial proceeding any information to which this section applies, unless the Judge or, as the case requires, the person presiding at the proceeding is satisfied that the disclosure of the information is necessary in the interests of justice.

(4) Nothing in this section prohibits the disclosure of any information for the purposes of the prosecution of any offence against any of subsections (3) to (5) of section 20.

Offences.

20. [iii]* (1) Every financial institution commits an offence against this section which, in any case where-

(a)
a transaction is conducted or is sought to be conducted through that financial institution; and

(b)
that financial institution has reasonable grounds to suspect that the transaction or, as the case requires, the proposed transaction is or may be relevant to the enforcement of the Proceeds of Crime Act, 2000,

fails, in contravention of section 14(1), to report that transaction or, as the case requires, that proposed transaction to the Financial Intelligence Unit as soon as practicable after forming that suspicion.

(2) Every financial institution which commits an offence against subsection (1) is liable on summary conviction to a fine not exceeding-

(a)
in the case of an individual, twenty thousand dollars;

(b)
in the case of a body corporate, one hundred thousand dollars.

(3) Every person commits an offence and is liable on summary conviction to a fine not exceeding ten thousand dollars who, in making a suspicious transaction report-

(a)
makes any statement that the person knows is false or misleading in a material particular;

(b)
omits from any statement any matter or thing without which the person knows that the statement is false or misleading in a material particular.

(4) Every person commits an offence who-

(a)
for the purpose of obtaining, directly or indirectly, an advantage or a pecuniary gain for that person or any other person; or

(b)
with intent to prejudice any investigation into the commission or possible commission of a money laundering offence,

contravenes any of subsections (1) to (3) of section 18.

(5) Every person commits an offence who-

(a)
being an officer or employee or agent of a financial institution;

(b)
having become aware, in the course of that person's duties as such an officer or employee or agent, that any investigation into any transaction or proposed transaction that is the subject of a suspicious transaction report is being, or may be, conducted by the Police;

(c)
knowing that he or she is not legally authorised to disclose the information; and

(d)
either-

(i)
for the purpose of obtaining, directly or indirectly, an advantage or a pecuniary gain for that person or any other person; or

(ii)
with intent to prejudice any investigation into the commission or possible commission of a money laundering offence,

discloses that information to any other person.

(6) Every person who commits an offence against subsection (4) or subsection (5) is liable on summary conviction to imprisonment for a term not exceeding two years.

(7) Every person who knowingly contravenes any of subsections (1) to (3) of section 18 commits an offence and is liable on summary conviction-

(a)
in the case of an individual, to a fine not exceeding five thousand dollars or to imprisonment for a term not exceeding six months;

(b)
in the case of body corporate, to fine not exceeding twenty thousand dollars.

Defence.

21. (1) It is a defence to a charge against a person in relation to a contravention of, or a failure to comply with, section 14(1) if the defendant proves-

(a)
that he took all reasonable steps to ensure that he complied with that provision; or

(b)
that, in the circumstances of the particular case, he could not reasonably have been expected to ensure that he complied with the provision.

(2) In determining, for the purposes of subsection (1)(a), whether or not a defendant took all reasonable steps to comply with section 14(1), the court shall have regard to-

(a)
the nature of the financial institution and the activities in which it engages;

(b)
the existence and adequacy of any procedures established by the financial institution to ensure compliance with that provision, including (without limitation)-

(i)
staff training; and

(ii)
audits to test the effectiveness of any such procedures;

(c)
any relevant guidelines issued by the Financial Intelligence Unit.

(3) Except as provided in subsection (4), subsection (1) shall not apply unless, within twenty-one days after the service of the summons, or within such further time as the court may allow, the defendant has delivered to the prosecutor a written notice-

(a)
stating that the defendant intends to rely on subsection (1); and

(b)
specifying the reasonable steps that the defendant will claim to have taken.

(4) In any such prosecution, evidence that the defendant took a step not specified in the written notice required by subsection (3) shall not, except with the leave of the court, be admissible for the purpose of supporting a defence under subsection (1).

Application of information.

22. Any information contained in a suspicious transaction report shall be deemed to be obtained only for the following purposes-

(a)
the detection, investigation, and prosecution of offences against this Act;

(b)
the enforcement of the Proceeds of Crime Act, 2000;

(c)
the detection, investigation, and prosecution of any relevant offence (within the meaning of the Proceeds of Crime Act, 2000), in any case where that offence may reasonably give rise to, or form the basis of, any proceedings under that Act;

(d)
the administration of-

(i)
the Mutual Legal Assistance (Criminal Matters) Act, 1988;

(ii)
the Financial Intelligence Unit Act, 2000;

(iii)
the Criminal Justice (International Co-operation) Act, 2000.

PART IV
RETENTION ON RECORDS

Obligation to keep transaction records.

23. (1) In relation to every transaction that is conducted through a financial institution, that financial institution shall keep such records as are reasonably necessary to enable that transaction to be readily reconstructed by the Financial Intelligence Unit.

(2) Without limiting the generality of subsection (1), such records shall contain the following information-

(a)
the nature of the transaction;

(b)
the amount of the transaction, and the currency in which it was denominated;

(c)
the date on which the transaction was conducted;

(d)
the parties to the transaction;

(e)
where applicable, the facility through which the transaction was conducted, and any other facilities (whether or not provided by the financial institution) directly involved in the transaction.

(3) Every financial institution shall retain the records kept by that financial institution, in accordance with this section, in relation to a transaction for a period of not less than five years after the completion of that transaction.

Obligation to keep verification records.

24. (1) In respect of each case in which a financial institution is required by section 6, 7, 8, 9 or 11 to verify the identity of any person, that financial institution shall keep such records as are reasonably necessary to enable the nature of the evidence used for the purposes of that verification to be readily identified by the Financial Intelligence Unit.

(2) Without limiting the generality of subsection (1), such records may comprise-

(a)
a copy of the evidence so used; or

(b)
where it is not practicable to retain that evidence, such information as is reasonably necessary to enable that evidence to be obtained.

(3) Notwithstanding anything in subsections (1) and (2), in respect of each case in which a financial institution, in reliance on the provisions of subsection (3) or (4) of section 11, verifies the identity of any person by confirming the existence of a facility provided by another financial institution, the first-mentioned financial institution shall keep such records as are reasonably necessary to enable-

(a)
the identity of the other financial institution;

(b)
the identity of that facility; and

(c)
the identity confirmation of the person,

to be readily identified at any time by the Financial Intelligence Unit.

(4) Every financial institution shall retain the records kept by that financial institution, in accordance with this section, for the following periods-

(a)
in the case of records relating to the verification of the identity of any person in relation to any facility, where the verification is carried out for the purposes of section 6, for a period of not less than five years after that person ceases to be a facility holder in relation to that facility;

(b)
in the case of records relating to the verification of the identity of any person in relation to any facility, where-

(i)
that person is not a facility holder in relation to that facility, and

(ii)
the verification is carried out, for the purposes of section 9, with respect to a person who is such a facility holder,

for a period of not less than five years after that facility holder ceases to be a facility holder in relation to that facility;

(c)
in the case of any other records relating to the verification of the identity of any person, for a period of not less than five years after the verification is carried out.

Obligation to keep prescribed records.

25. Every financial institution shall keep such records as may be prescribed by regulations made under section 51 and shall retain them for such period as may be prescribed by such regulations.

How records to be kept.

26. Records required by section 23, 24 or 25 to be kept by any financial institution shall be kept either in written form in the English language, or so as to enable the records to be readily accessible and readily convertible into written form in the English language.

When records need not be kept.

27. Nothing in section 23, 24 or 25 requires the retention of any records kept by a financial institution (being a company) in any case where the company has been liquidated and finally dissolved or (being a partnership) in any case where the partnership has been dissolved.

Destruction of records.

28. (1) Subject to subsection (2) every financial institution shall ensure that-

(a)
every record retained by that financial institution pursuant to any provision of this Part; and

(b)
every copy of any such record,

is destroyed as soon as practicable after the expiry of the period for which the financial institution is required, by any provision of this Part, to retain that record.

(2) Nothing in this section requires the destruction of any record, or any copy of any record, in any case where there is a lawful reason for retaining that record.

(3) Without limiting the generality of subsection (2), there is a lawful reason for retaining a record if the retention of that record is necessary-

(a)
in order to comply with the requirements of any other written law;

(b)
to enable any financial institution to carry on its business; or

(c)
for the purposes of the detection, investigation or prosecution of any offence.

Other laws not affected.

29. Nothing in this Part limits or affects any other written law that requires any financial institution to keep or retain any record.

Offences.

30. [iv]* (1) Every financial institution commits an offence against this section which in contravention of section 23, 24 or 25 fails, without reasonable excuse, to retain or to properly keep records sufficient to satisfy the requirements of the section.

(2) Every financial institution which commits an offence against this section is liable on summary conviction to a fine not exceeding-

(a)
in the case of any individual, twenty thousand dollars;

(b)
in the case of a body corporate, one hundred thousand dollars.

PART V
SEARCH WARRANTS

Search warrants.

31. Any Magistrate who, on an application in writing made on oath, is satisfied that there are reasonable grounds for believing that there is in or on any place or thing-

(a)
any thing upon or in respect of which any offence against this Act or any regulations made under this Act has been, or is suspected of having been, committed;

(b)
any thing which there are reasonable grounds for believing will be evidence as to the commission of any such offence; or

(c)
any thing which there are reasonable grounds for believing is intended to be used for the purpose of committing any such offence,

may issue a search warrant in respect of that thing.

Form and content of search warrant.

32. (1) Every search warrant shall be in the prescribed form.

(2) Every search warrant shall be directed to any member of the Police by name, or to any class of members of the Police specified in the warrant, or generally to every member of the Police.

(3) Every search warrant shall be subject to such special conditions (if any) as the person issuing the warrant may specify in the warrant.

(4) Every search warrant shall contain the following particulars-

(a)
the place of thing that may be searched pursuant to the warrant;

(b)
the offence or offences in respect of which the warrant is issued;

(c)
a description of the articles or things that are authorised to be seized;

(d)
the period during which the warrant may be executed, being a period not exceeding fourteen days from the date of issue;

(e)
any conditions specified pursuant to subsection (3).

Powers conferred by warrant.

33. (1) Subject to any special conditions specified in a warrant pursuant to section 32(3) every search warrant shall authorise the member of the Police executing the warrant-

(a)
to enter and search the place or thing specified in the warrant at any time by day or night during the currency of the warrant;

(b)
to use such assistance as may be reasonable in the circumstances for the purpose of the entry and search;

(c)
to use such force as is reasonable in the circumstances for the purposes of effecting entry, and for breaking open anything in or on the place searched;

(d)
to search for and seize any thing referred to in any of paragraphs (a) to (c) of section 31; and

(e)
in any case where any thing referred to in any of those paragraphs is a document-

(i)
to take copies of the document, or extracts from the documents;

(ii)
to require any person who has the document in his or her possession or under his or her control to reproduce, or to assist the person executing the warrant to reproduce, in usable form, any information recorded or stored in the document.

(2) Every person called upon to assist any member of the Police executing a search warrant shall have the powers described in paragraphs (c) and (d) of subsection (1).

Person executing warrant to produce evidence of authority.

34. Every member of the Police executing any search warrant-

(a)
shall have that warrant with him or her;

(b)
shall produce it on initial entry and, if requested, at any subsequent time; and

(c)
shall, if requested at the time of the execution of the warrant or at any subsequent time, provide a copy of the warrant within seven days after the request is made.

Notice of execution of warrant.

35. Every member of the Police who executes a search warrant shall, not later than seven days after the seizure of any thing pursuant to that warrant, give to the owner or occupier of the place or thing searched, and to every other person whom the member of the Police has reason to believe may have an interest in the thing seized, a written notice specifying-

(a)
the date and time of the execution of the warrant;

(b)
the identity of the person who executed the warrant;

(c)
the thing seized under the warrant.

Custody of property seized.

36. Where property is seized pursuant to a search warrant, the property shall be kept in the custody of a member of the Police, except while it is being used in evidence or is in the custody of any court, until it is dealt with in accordance with another provision of this Act.

Procedure where certain documents seized.

37. Section 70 of the Criminal Procedure Code, so far as applicable and with all necessary modifications, shall apply in respect of the seizure of any documents under any search warrant as if the search warrant had been issued under section 70 of that Act.

Disposal of things seized.

38. (1) This section shall apply with respect to anything seized under a search warrant.

(2) In any proceedings for an offence relating to anything seized under a search warrant, the court may order, either at the trial or hearing or on an application, that the thing be delivered to the person appearing to the court to be entitled to it, or that it be otherwise disposed of in such manner as the court thinks fit.

(3) Any member of the Police may at any time, unless an order has been made under subsection (2), return the thing to the person from whom it was seized, or apply to a Magistrate for an order as to its disposal; on any such application, the Magistrate may make any order that a court may make under subsection (2).

(4) If proceedings for an offence relating to the thing are not brought within a period of three months of seizure, any person claiming to be entitled to the thing may, after the expiration of that period, apply to a Magistrate for an order that it be delivered to him or her; on any such application, the Magistrate may adjourn the application, on such terms as he or she thinks fit, for proceedings to be brought, or may make any order that a court may make under subsection (2).

(5) Where any person is convicted in any proceedings for an offence relating to anything in respect of which a search warrant has been issued enabling seizure, and any order is made under this section, the operation of the order shall be suspended-

(a)
in any case until the expiration of the twenty-one days for the filing of notice of appeal or an application for leave to appeal;

(b)
where notice of appeal is filed within the time so prescribed, until the determination of the appeal; and

(c)
where application for leave to appeal is filed within the time so prescribed, until the application is determined and, where leave to appeal is granted, until the determination of the appeal.

(6) Where the operation of any such order is suspended until the determination of the appeal, the court determining the appeal may, by order, cancel or vary the order.

PART VI
COMPLIANCE COMMISSION

Establishment of Commission.

39. (1) There is hereby established a body to be known as the Compliance Commission for the purpose of ensuring compliance with the provisions of this Act.

(2) The Commission shall be a body corporate having perpetual succession and a common seal with power to enter into contracts and do all such things necessary for the purpose of its functions.

Membership of Commission.

40. The Commission shall consist of three members, appointed by the Governor-General in writing, being persons appearing to the Governor-General to have wide experience in, and to have shown capacity in, financial and commercial matters, industry, law or law enforcement.

Term of appointment.

41. The members of the Commission may be appointed for a term of three years and be eligible for reappointment.

Exclusion from membership.

42. A person may not be appointed a member or remain a member of the Commission who-

(a)
is a member of either House of Parliament;

(b)
is a director, officer or servant of, or has a controlling interest in, any financial institution.

Functions of the Commission.

43. The functions of the Commission are-

(a)
to maintain a general review of financial institutions in relation to the conduct of financial transactions and to ensure compliance with the provisions of this Act;

(b)
on an annual basis and when deemed necessary by the Commission, at the expense of the financial institution, to conduct on-site examinations of the business of the financial institution for the purpose of ensuring compliance with the provisions of this Act, and in such cases where the Commission is unable to conduct such examination, to appoint an auditor at the expense of the financial institution to conduct such examination and to report thereon to the Commission.

Production of records.

44. (1) In the performance of its duties under this Act the Commission may at all reasonable times-

(a)
require the financial institution to produce for examination such records that are required to be kept pursuant to sections 23, 24 and 25; and

(b)
require a financial institution to supply such information or explanation, as the Commission may reasonably require for the purpose of enabling the Commission to perform its functions under this Act.

(2) Any person failing or refusing to produce any record or to supply any information or explanation as is required by subsection (1) is guilty of an offence and shall be liable on summary conviction to a fine not exceeding fifty thousand dollars or to imprisonment for a term not exceeding three years or to both such fine and imprisonment.

Confidentiality.

45. (1) Subject to subsections (2) and (3), the Commission or any officer, employee, agent or adviser of the Commission who discloses any information relating to-

(a)
the affairs of the Commission;

(b)
the affairs of a financial institution; or

(c)
the affairs of a customer or client of a financial institution,

that it or he has acquired in the course of its or his duties or in the exercise of the Commission's functions under this or any other law, is guilty of an offence and shall be liable on summary conviction to a fine not exceeding fifty thousand dollars or to imprisonment for a term not exceeding three years.

(2) Subsection (1) shall not apply to a disclosure-

(a)
lawfully required or permitted by any court of competent jurisdiction within The Bahamas;

(b)
for the purpose of assisting the Commission to exercise any functions conferred on it by this Act, by any other Act or by regulations made thereunder;

(c)
in respect of the affairs of a financial institution or of a customer or client of a financial institution, with the consent of the financial institution, customer or client, as the case may be, which consent has been voluntarily given;

(d)
where the information disclosed is or has been available to the public from any other source;

(e)
where the information disclosed is in a manner that does not enable the identity of any financial institution or of any customer or client of a financial institution to which the information relates to be ascertained;

(f)
to a person with a view to the institution of, or for the purpose of-

(i)
criminal proceedings;

(ii)
disciplinary proceedings, whether within or outside The Bahamas, relating to the exercise by a counsel and attorney, auditor, accountant, valuer or actuary of his professional duties;

(iii)
disciplinary proceedings relating to the discharge by a public officer, or a member or employee of the Commission of his duties; or

(g)
in any legal proceedings in connection with-

(i)
the winding-up or dissolution of a financial institution; or

(ii)
the appointment or duties of a receiver of a financial institution.

(3) Subject to subsection (6), the Commission may disclose to an overseas regulatory authority information necessary to enable that authority to exercise regulatory functions including the conduct of civil or administrative investigations and proceedings to enforce laws, regulations and rules administered by that authority.

(4) In deciding whether or not to exercise its power under subsection (3), the Commission may take into account-

(a)
whether the inquiries relate to the possible breach of a law or other requirement which has no close parallel in The Bahamas or involve the assertion of a jurisdiction not recognised by The Bahamas; and

(b)
the seriousness of the matter to which the inquiries relate and the importance to the inquiries of the information sought in The Bahamas.

(5) The Commission may decline to exercise its power under subsection (3) unless the overseas regulatory authority undertakes to make such contribution towards the cost of the exercise as the Commission considers appropriate.

(6) Nothing in subsection (3) authorises a disclosure by the Commission unless-

(a)
the Commission has satisfied itself that the intended recipient authority is subject to adequate legal restrictions on further disclosures which shall include the provision of an undertaking of confidentiality; or

(b)
the Commission has been given an undertaking by the recipient authority not to disclose the information provided without the consent of the Commission; and

(c)
the Commission is satisfied that the assistance requested by the overseas regulatory authority is required for the purposes of the overseas regulatory authority's regulatory functions including the conduct of civil or administrative investigations or proceedings to enforce laws, regulations and rules administered by that authority; and

(d)
the Commission is satisfied that information provided following the exercise of its power under subsection (3) will not be used in criminal proceedings against the person providing the information.

(7) Where in the opinion of the Commission it appears necessary in relation to any request for assistance received from an overseas regulatory authority to invoke the jurisdiction of a Stipendiary and Circuit Magistrate in obtaining information requested by the overseas regulatory authority, the Commission shall immediately notify the Attorney-General with particulars of the request, and shall send him copies of all documents relating to the request, and the Attorney-General shall be entitled, in a manner analogous to *amicus curiae*, to appear or take part in any proceedings in The Bahamas, or in any appeal from such proceedings, arising directly or indirectly from any such request.

(8) The Commission may provide information that it has acquired in the course of its duties or in the exercise of its functions under this or any other law to any other regulatory authority in The Bahamas where it considers such information may be relevant to the functions of such other regulatory authority.

(9) In this section-

"overseas regulatory authority" means an authority which in a country or territory outside The Bahamas exercises functions corresponding to any functions of the Commission.

Meaning of financial institution.

46. For the purposes of this Part "financial institution" means those institutions specified in paragraphs (c), (d), (g), (h), (j), (k) and (l) of section 3.

Codes of practice.

47. The Commission may from time to time after consultation with the Inspector, The Bahamas Bar Council, The Bahamas Institute of Chartered Accountants, the Financial Intelligence Unit and such other bodies and organisations representative of such financial institutions as are required to be regulated under this Act, issue such codes of practice as the Commission thinks necessary-

(a)
for the purpose of providing guidance as to the duties, requirements and standards to be complied with and the procedures (whether as to verification, record-keeping, reporting of suspicious transactions or otherwise) and best practices to be observed by financial institutions;

(b)
generally for the purposes of this Act.

PART VII MISCELLANEOUS PROVISIONS

Liability of employers and principals.

48. (1) Subject to subsection (3), anything done or omitted by a person as the employee of another person shall, for the purposes of this Act, be treated as done or omitted by that other person as well as by the first-mentioned person, whether or not it was done with that other person's knowledge or approval.

(2) Anything done or omitted by a person as the agent of another person shall, for the purposes of this Act, be treated as done or omitted by that other person as well as by the first-mentioned person, unless it is done or omitted without that other person's express or implied authority, precedent or subsequent.

(3) In any proceedings under this Act against any person in respect of anything alleged to have been done or omitted to be done by an employee or agent of that person, it shall be a defence for that person to prove that he or she or it took such steps as were reasonably practicable to prevent the employee or agent, as the case may be, from doing or omitting to do such thing.

Directors and officers of bodies corporate.

49. Where any body corporate is convicted of an offence against this Act or any regulations made under this Act, every director and every officer concerned in the management of the body corporate shall be guilty of the offence where it is proved that the act or omission that constituted the offence took place with that person's knowledge, authority, permission or consent.

Non-compliance not excused by contractual obligations.

50. (1) The provisions of this Act shall have effect notwithstanding anything to the contrary in any contract or agreement.

(2) No person shall be excused from compliance with any requirement of this Act by reason only that compliance with that requirement would constitute breach of any contract or agreement.

Regulations.

51. The Minister may from time to time make regulations for all or any of the following purposes-

(a)
prescribing the forms of application, reports and other documents required under this Act;

(b)
prescribing amounts that are required be prescribed for the purposes of Part II;

(c)
prescribing, for the purposes of section 25 records to be kept and retained by financial institutions, or any specified class or classes of financial institutions, and the periods for which those records are to be retained;

(d)
exempting or providing for the exemption of any transaction or class of transactions from all or any of the provisions of this Act;

(e)
prescribing, for the purposes of this Act, or any provision or provisions of this Act, what accounts and arrangements shall be deemed to be or not to be facilities, and the circumstances and conditions in which any account or arrangement shall be deemed to be or not to be a facility;

(f)
prescribing, for the purposes of this Act, or any provision or provisions of this Act, what persons or classes of persons shall be deemed to be or not to be financial institutions, and the circumstances and conditions in which any persons or classes of persons shall be deemed to be or not to be financial institutions;

(g)
prescribing, for the purposes of this Act, or any provision or provisions of this Act, what transactions shall be deemed to be or not to be occasional transactions, and the circumstances and conditions in which any transaction shall be deemed to be or not to be an occasional transaction;

(h)
prescribing the manner in which any notice or other document required by this Act to be given or served by, or to or on, any person is to be so given or served;

(i)
prescribing offences in respect of the contravention of or non-compliance with any provision of any regulations made under this section, and prescribing fines, not exceeding two thousand dollars, that may, on conviction, be imposed in respect of any such offences;

(j)
providing for such matters as are contemplated by or necessary for giving full effect to the provisions of this Act and for their due administration.

FIRST SCHEDULE (Sections 8(6)(c), 9(6)(c), 11(2), 11(3)(b)(iii) and 11(4)(b)(iii))

1. Countries-

Australia
Barbados
Belgium
Bermuda
Brazil
Canada
Cayman Islands
Channel Islands
Denmark
Finland
France
Germany
Gibraltar
Greece
Hong Kong SAR
Ireland
Isle of Man
Italy
Japan
Liechtenstein
Luxembourg
Malta
Netherlands
New Zealand
Norway
Panama
Portugal
Singapore
Spain
Sweden
Switzerland
United Kingdom
United States.

2. The Minister may by order add to, or delete from, the list of countries mentioned in this Schedule.

SECOND SCHEDULE (Section 14(2)(b))

DETAILS TO BE INCLUDED IN SUSPICIOUS TRANSACTION REPORT

1. The name, address, date of birth, and occupation (or, where appropriate, business or principal activity) of each person conducting the transaction (if known to the person making the report).

2. The name, address, date of birth, and occupation (or, where appropriate, business or principal activity) of any person on whose behalf the transaction is conducted (if known to the person making the report).

3. Where an account with a financial institution is involved in the transaction-

(a)
the type and identifying number of the account;

(b)
the name of the person in whose name the account is operated;

(c)
the names of the signatories to the account.

4. The nature of the transaction.

5. The amount involved in the transaction.

6. The type of currency involved in the transaction.

7. The date of the transaction.

8. In relation to the financial institution through which the transaction was conducted, the name of the officer, employee, or agent of that financial institution who handled the transaction.

9. The name of the person who prepared the report.

THE INTERNATIONAL BUSINESS COMPANIES ACT, 2000

(No. 45 of 2000)

PART I PRELIMINARY

1. This Act may be cited as the International Business Companies Act, 2000, and shall come into operation on such date as the Minister may appoint by notice published in the Gazette.

2.

(1) In this Act—

"agent" includes registered agent;

"Articles" means the Articles of Association of a company incorporated under this Act;

"authorised capital", in relation to a company, means the sum of the aggregate par value of all shares which the company is authorised by its Memorandum to issue plus the amount, if any, stated in its Memorandum as authorised capital to be represented by shares without par value which the company is authorised by its Memorandum to issue;

"capital", in relation to a company, means the sum of the aggregate par value of all the outstanding shares with par value of a company and shares with par value held by the company as treasury shares plus—

(a) the aggregate of the amounts designated as capital of all outstanding shares without par value of the company and shares without par value held by the company as treasury shares, and

(b) the amounts as are from time to time transferred from surplus to capital by a resolution of the directors ;

“company” unless the context otherwise requires, means an international business company incorporated under this Act.

"Companies Act" means the Companies Act of The Bahamas;

"continued" means continues in accordance with Part VIII;

"court" means the Supreme Court or a Judge thereof;

"member" includes a person who holds shares in a company;

"Memorandum" means the Memorandum of Association of a company incorporated under this Act;

"Register" means the Register of International Business Companies maintained by the Registrar in accordance with section 15(1);

"registered agent" means the person who is at any particular time performing the functions of registered agent of a company incorporated under this Act;

"Registrar" means the Registrar of Companies;

"Registrar of Companies" means the Registrar General;

"securities" includes shares and debt obligations of every kind, and options, warrants and rights to acquire shares or debt obligations;

"surplus", in relation to a company, means the excess, if any, at the time of the determination, of total assets of the company over the sum of its total liabilities, as shown in the books of account plus its issued and outstanding share capital;

"treasury shares" means shares of a company that were previously issued but were repurchased, redeemed or otherwise acquired by the company and not cancelled.

(2) A company that is incorporated under the Companies Act or under the laws of a jurisdiction outside of The Bahamas shall be a company incorporated under this Act if it is continued as a company incorporated under this Act and references to a "company incorporated under this Act" shall be construed accordingly.

(3) Unless otherwise defined in the Articles "resolution of directors" means—

(a) a resolution approved at a duly constituted meeting of directors or a Committee of directors of a company by affirmative vote of a simple majority or such larger majority as may be specified in the Articles of the directors present at the meeting who voted and did not abstain; or

(b) a resolution consented to in writing by a simple majority or such larger majority as may be specified in the Articles of all the directors or of all the members of the Committee of directors, as the case may be;

but where a director is given more than one vote in any circumstances he shall in the circumstances be counted for the purposes of establishing majorities by the number of votes he casts.

(4) Unless otherwise defined in the Articles "resolution of members" means—

(a) a resolution approved at a duly constituted meeting of the members of a company by the affirmative vote of —

(i) a simple majority, or such larger majority as may be specified in the Articles, of the votes of the shareholders present at the meeting and entitled to vote thereon and who voted and did not abstain, or

(ii) a simple majority, or such larger majority as may be specified in the Articles of the votes of the shareholders of each class or series or shares present at the meeting and entitled to vote thereon as a class or series and who voted and did not abstain and of a simple majority or such larger majority as may be specified in the Articles, of the votes of the remaining shareholders entitled to vote thereon present at the meeting and who voted and did not abstain; or

(b) a resolution consented to in writing by —

(i) a simple majority or such larger majority as may be specified in the Articles, of the shareholders entitled to vote thereon, or

(ii) a simple majority, or such larger majority as may be specified in the Articles, of the votes of the shareholders entitled to vote thereon as a class or series and of a simple majority, or such larger majority as may be specified in the Articles, of the votes of the holders of the remaining shares entitled to vote thereon.

PART II CONSTITUTION OF COMPANIES

3. Subject to the requirements of this Act, two or more persons may, by subscribing to a Memorandum incorporate a company under this Act.

4. No person other than a bank or trust company licensed under the Banks and Trust Companies Regulation Act, 2000 shall incorporate an International Business Company unless such person is licensed and approved under the Financial and Corporate Service Providers Act, 2000.

5. A company shall not be incorporated under this Act-

(a) for the purposes of facilitating any criminal activity; or

(b) for any object or purpose which is prohibited by this Act or by any other law in force in The Bahamas

6. Where a company is incorporated under this Act for any criminal activity including drug trafficking or any relevant offense under the Proceeds of Crime Act, 2000 or for any prohibited purpose the company shall forthwith be struck off the Register by the Registrar publishing notice to that effect in the Gazette but section 164 (5) shall apply to such company for the purposes of liability:

Provided that before being struck off, the Registrar shall give the company the opportunity of being heard within seven days before the striking off.

7. No member, director, officer, agent or liquidator of a company incorporated under this Act shall be liable for any debt, obligation or default of the company unless it is proved that he did not act in good faith or unless it is specifically provided in this Act or in any other law for the time being in force in The Bahamas and except in so far as he may be liable for his own conduct or acts.

8. The liability of the members of a company incorporated under this Act may, according to the Memorandum—

(a) be limited either to the amount, if any, unpaid on the shares respectively held by them (in this Act termed "a company limited by shares");

(b) be limited to such amount as the members may respectively undertake by the Memorandum to contribute to the assets of the company in the event of its being wound up (in this Act termed "a company limited by guarantee"); or

(c) have no limit placed on the liability of its members (in this Act termed "an unlimited liability company").

9. Without affecting anything contained in this Act, a company may be limited both by shares and by guarantee and any reference in this Act to a company limited by shares or to company limited by guarantee shall so far as appropriate include a company limited both by shares and by guarantee.

10. Subject to any limitations in its Memorandum or Articles, this Act or any other law for the time being in force in The Bahamas, a company incorporated under this Act has the power, irrespective of corporate benefit, to perform all acts and engage in all activities necessary or conducive to the conduct, promotion or attainment of the objects or purposes of the company, including the power to do the following —

(a) issue registered shares but not shares issued to bearer;

(b) issue the following —

(i) voting shares,

(ii) non–voting shares,

(iii) shares that may have more or less than one vote per share,

(iv) shares that may be voted only on certain matters or only upon the occurrence of certain events,

(v) shares that may be voted only when held by persons who meet specified requirements,

(vi) no par value shares,

(vii) unnumbered shares;

(c) issue common shares, preferred shares, or redeemable shares;

(d) issue shares that entitle participation only in certain assets;

(e) issue options, warrants or rights, or instruments of a similar nature, to acquire any securities of the company;

(f) issue securities that, at the option of the holder thereof or of the company or upon the happening of a specified event, are convertible into, or exchangeable for, other securities in the company or any property then owned or to be owned by the company;

(g) purchase, redeem or otherwise acquire and hold its own shares;

(h) guarantee a liability or obligation of any person and to secure any of its obligations by mortgage, pledge or other charge, of any of its assets for that purpose; and

(i) protect the assets of the company for the benefit of the company, its creditors and its members, and at the discretion of the directors, for any person having a direct or indirect interest in the company.

11.

(1) No act of a company incorporated under this Act and no transfer of real or personal property by or to a company so incorporated is invalid by reason only of the fact that the company was without capacity or power to perform the act or to transfer or receive the property, but the lack of capacity or power may be pleaded in the following cases—

(a) in proceedings by a member against the company to prohibit the performance of any act or the transfer of real or personal property by or to the company; or

(b) in proceedings by the company, whether acting directly or through a receiver, trustee or other legal representative or through members in a derivative action, against the incumbent or former directors of the company for loss or damage due to their unauthorised act.

(2) For the purposes of subsection (1)(a), the court may set aside and prohibit the performance of a contract if —

(a) the unauthorised act or transfer sought to be set aside or prohibited is being, or is to be, performed or made under any contracts to which the company is a party;

(b) all the parties to the contract are parties to the proceedings; and

(c) it appears fair and reasonable in the circumstances to set aside or prohibit the performance of the contract;

and in so doing the court may, in applying this subsection, award to the company or to the other parties such compensation as may be reasonable except that in determining the amount of compensation the court shall not take into account anticipated profits to be derived from the performance of the contract.

12.

(1) The word "Limited", "Corporation", "Incorporated", "Gesellschaft mit beschränkter Haftung", "Société Anonyme" or "Sociedad Anónima" or its respective abbreviation "Ltd.", "Corp.", "Inc.", "GmbH" or "SA" shall be at the end of the name of every company incorporated under this Act with limited liability, provided that a company incorporated under the laws of a jurisdiction outside The Bahamas and continued as a company incorporated under this Act may use the name designated in the Articles of continuation;

(2) The Minister may by Order add to the list of words and abbreviations contained in subsection (1) words and abbreviations, which would indicate that a company is incorporated with limited liability.

(3) No company shall be incorporated under this Act under a name that -

(a) is identical with that under which a company in existence is already incorporated under this Act or registered under the Companies Act or so nearly resembles the name of another company as to be calculated to deceive, except where the company in existence gives its consent;

(b) contains the words "Assurance", "Bank", "Building Society", "Chamber of Commerce", "Chartered", "Cooperative", "Imperial", "Insurance", "Municipal", "Royal", "Trust", or a word conveying a similar meaning, or any other word that, in the opinion of the Registrar, suggests or is calculated to suggest the patronage of or any connection with Her Majesty or any member of the Royal Family or the Government of The Bahamas, a department thereof, a statutory corporation or board or a local or municipal authority;

(c) is indecent, offensive or, in the opinion of the Registrar is otherwise objectionable.

(4) A company may amend its Memorandum to change its name.

(5) Where a company is incorporated under a name that —

(a) is identical with a name under which a company in existence was incorporated under this Act or registered under the Companies Act; or

(b) so nearly resembles the name of another company in existence which was incorporated under this Act or registered under the Companies Act as to be calculated to deceive or confuse,

the Registrar may, whether or not the consent of the company in existence has been obtained pursuant to subsection (3)(a), give notice to the last registered company to change its name and if it fails to do so within 60 days from the date of the notice the Registrar shall direct the company to change its name to such name as the Registrar deems appropriate, and the Registrar shall publish a notice of the change in the Gazette.

(6) Where a company is incorporated under a name that may be calculated to deceived the public, the Registrar may give notice to the company to change such name and if it fails to

do so within 60 days from the date of the notice the Registrar shall direct the company to be removed from the Register.

(7) Subject to subsections (3) and (5), where a company changes its name, the Registrar shall enter the new name on the Register in place of the former name, and shall issue a new certificate of incorporation indicating the change of name.

(8) A change of name does not affect any rights or obligations of a company, or render defective any legal proceedings by or against a company, and all legal proceedings that have been commenced against a company by its former name may be continued against it in its new name.

(9) Subject to subsection (3), the Registrar may, upon a request made by any person and payment of the prescribed fee, reserve for 90 days a name for future adoption by a company under this Act.

13.

(1) The Memorandum shall include the following particulars —

(a) the name of the company;

(b) the location in The Bahamas of the registered office of the company;

(c) the location in The Bahamas of the registered agent of the company;

(d) subject to subsection (2), the objects or purposes for which the company is to be incorporated;

(e) the currency in which shares in the company shall be issued;

(f) in the case of a company limited by shares, a statement of the authorised capital of the company setting forth the aggregate of the par value, if any, that the company is authorised to issue and the amount, if any, to be represented by shares without par value that the company is authorised to issue;

(g) in the case of a company limited by guarantee, a statement that each member undertakes to contribute to the assets of the company, in the event of a winding up during the time that he is a member, or within one year afterwards, for payment of the debts and liabilities of the company contracted before the time at which he ceases to be a member, and of the costs, charges and expenses of winding up the company and for the adjustment of the rights of the contributors amongst themselves, such amounts as may be required, not exceeding an amount to be specified therein;

(h) in the case of a company limited both by shares and by guarantee, the statements referred to in paragraphs (f) and (g);

(i) in the case of an unlimited liability company, a statement that the liability of the members is unlimited;

(j) a statement of the number of classes and series of shares, the number of shares of each such class and series and the par value of shares with par value and that the shares may be without par value if this is the case;

(k) a statement of the designations, powers, preferences and rights, and the qualifications, limitations or restrictions of each class and series of shares that the company is authorised to issue, unless the directors are to be authorised to fix any such designations, powers, preferences, rights, qualifications, and in that case, an express grant of such authority as may be desired to grant to the directors to fix by resolution any such designations, powers, preferences, rights, qualifications, limitations and restrictions that have not been fixed by the Memorandum.

(2) For the purposes of subsection (1)(d), if the Memorandum contains a statement either alone or with other objects or purposes that the object or purpose of the company is to engage in any act or activity that is not prohibited under any law for the time being in force in The Bahamas, the effect of that statement is to make all acts and activities that are not illegal part of the objects or purposes of the company, subject to any limitations in the Memorandum.

(3) The Memorandum shall be subscribed to by two persons in the presence of another person who shall sign his name as a witness.

(4) The Memorandum, when registered, binds the company and its members from time to time to the same extent as if each member had subscribed his name and affixed his seal thereto and as if there were contained in the Memorandum, on the part of himself, his heirs, executors and administrators, a covenant to observe the provisions of the Memorandum subject to this Act.

14.
The Articles shall be subscribed to by two persons in the presence of another who shall sign his name as a witness and such Articles shall be filed with the Registrar on the same date as the filing of the memorandum

(1) The Articles, when registered, bind the company and its members from time to time to the same extent as if each member had subscribed his name and affixed his seal thereto and as if there were contained in the Articles, on the part of himself, his heirs, executors and administrators, a covenant to observe the provisions of the Articles, subject to this Act.

15.
(1) The Memorandum and the Articles shall be registered by the Registrar in a register to be maintained by him and to be known as the Register of International Business Companies.

(2) Upon the registration of the Memorandum, the Registrar shall issue a certificate of incorporation under his hand and seal certifying that the company is incorporated.

(3) An application for the registration of a company under this Act shall be in such form as may be prescribed and shall be accompanied by such documents as the Registrar may determine.

(4) The Registrar may prohibit the registration of a company where the minimum share capital is less than an amount stated by order of the Minister.

(5) The Registrar shall refuse to register a company if he is of the opinion that the memorandum shows that its minimum share capital will be less than the amount required by the Minister by order under subsection (4).

(6) Any person aggrieved by a decision of the Register under subsection (5) may appeal to the Minister whose decision shall be final.

(7) The Registrar shall not register the memorandum or the articles delivered to him unless he is satisfied that all requirements of this Act in respect of registration has been complied with and-

(a) a counsel and attorney engaged in the formation of the company; or

(b) the registered agent named in the memorandum of the company to be the registered agent, certifies in writing that the requirements of this Act in respect of registration have been complied with and the written certification delivered to the Registrar is sufficient evidence of compliance.

16. Where the Registrar issues a certificate of incorporation of a company, the company is, from the date shown on the certificate of incorporation, a body corporate under the name contained in the Memorandum with the full capacity of an individual who is *sui juris*, subject to any limitations imposed by the Memorandum and to the provisions of this Act.

17. A certificate of incorporation of a company incorporated under this Act issued by the Registrar shall be *prima facie* evidence of compliance with all requirements of this Act in respect of incorporation.

18.

(1) Subject to any limitation in its Memorandum or Articles, a company incorporated under this Act may amend its Memorandum or Articles by a resolution of members or, where permitted by its Memorandum or Articles or by this Act, by a resolution of directors.

(2) A company that amends its Memorandum or Articles shall submit to the Registrar within fourteen days after any amendment a copy of the resolution of members or directors amending the Memorandum or Articles, as the case may be, authenticated, in accordance with subsection (1) of section 72, as a true copy of the resolution amending the Memorandum or Articles and the Registrar shall retain and register such copy of the resolution.

(3) An amendment to the Memorandum or Articles shall not have effect until it is registered by the Registrar.

19. A copy of the Memorandum and a copy of the Articles shall be given to any member who requests a copy on payment by the member of such amount as the directors may determine to be reasonably necessary to defray the costs of preparing and furnishing them.

PART III CAPITAL AND DIVIDENDS

20. Subject to any limitations in the Memorandum or Articles, each share in a company incorporated under this Act shall be issued for money, services rendered, personal property (including other shares, debt obligations or other securities in the company), an estate in real property, a promissory note or other binding obligation to contribute money or property, or any combination thereof.

21.

(1) Subject to any limitations in the Memorandum or Articles, shares in a company incorporated under this Act may be issued for such amount as may be determined from time to time by the directors, and, in the absence of fraud, the decision of the directors as to the value of the consideration received by the company in respect of the issue is conclusive, unless a question of law is involved.

(2) Subject to any limitations in the Memorandum or Articles, treasury shares and unissued shares may be disposed of by a company incorporated under this Act on such terms and conditions as the directors may determine.

22. Subject to any limitations in its Memorandum or Articles, a company incorporated under this Act may issue fractions of a share and unless and to the extent otherwise provided in the Memorandum or Articles, a fractional share has the corresponding fractional liabilities, limitations, preferences, privileges, qualifications, restrictions, rights and other attributes of a share of the same class or series of shares.

23.

(1) Where a company incorporated under this Act issues a share with par value, the consideration in respect of the share constitutes capital to the extent of the par value and the excess constitutes surplus.

(2) Subject to any limitations in the Memorandum or Articles, where a company incorporated under this Act issues a share without par value, the consideration in respect of the share constitutes capital to the extent designated by the directors and the excess constitutes surplus, except that the directors shall designate as capital an amount of the consideration that shall be at least equal to the amount that the share is entitled to as a preference, if any, in the assets of the company upon liquidation of the company.

(3) Upon the disposition by a company incorporated under this Act of a treasury share, the consideration in respect of the share shall be added to surplus.

24.

(1) A share issued as a dividend by a company incorporated under this Act shall be treated for all purposes as having been issued for money equal to the surplus that has been transferred to capital upon the issue of the share.

(2) In the case of a dividend of authorised but unissued shares with par value, an amount equal to the aggregate par value of the shares shall be transferred from surplus to capital at the time of the distribution.

(3) In the case of a dividend of authorised but unissued shares without par value, the amount designated by the directors shall be transferred from surplus to capital at the time of the distribution, except that the directors shall designate as capital an amount that is at least equal to the amount that the shares are entitled to as preference, if any, in the assets of the company upon liquidation of the company.

(4) A division of the issued and outstanding shares of a class or series of shares into a larger number of shares of the same class or series having proportionately small par value does not constitute a dividend of shares.

25.

(1) Subject to any limitations in its Memorandum or Articles, a company incorporated under this Act may, by a resolution of directors, amend its Memorandum to increase or reduce its authorised capital, and in connection therewith, the company may —

(a) increase or reduce the number of shares which the company may issue;

(b) increase or reduce the par value of any of its shares; or

(c) effect any combination under paragraphs (a) and (b).

(2) Where a company reduces its authorised capital under subsection (1), then, for purposes of computing capital of the company, any capital that immediately before the reduction was represented by shares but immediately following the reduction is no longer represented by shares shall be deemed to be surplus transferred from capital to surplus.

26.

(1) A company incorporated under this Act may amend its Memorandum —

(a) to divide the shares, including issued shares, of a class or series into a larger number of shares of the same class or series; or

(b) to combine the shares, including issued shares of a class or series into a smaller number of shares of the same class or series.

(2) where shares are divided or combined under subsection (1), the aggregate par value of the new shares shall be equal to the aggregate par value of the original shares.

27. Shares of a company incorporated under this Act are personal property and are not of the nature of real property.

28.

(1) A company incorporated under this Act shall state in its Articles whether or not certificates in respect of its shares shall be issued.

(2) Where a company incorporated under this Act issues certificates in respect of its shares, the certificates —

(a) shall be signed by two directors or two officers of the company, or by one director and one officer; or

(b) shall be under the common seal of the company evidenced by the signature of a director or officer of the company,

and the Articles may provide for the signatures or common seal to be stamped thereon.

(3) A certificate issued in accordance with subsection (2) specifying a share held by a member of the company shall be *prima facie* evidence of the title of the member to the share specified therein.

29.

(1) A company incorporated under this Act shall cause to be kept at its registered office one or more registers to be known as Share Registers containing —

(a) the names and addresses of the persons who hold registered shares in the company;

(b) the number of each class and series of registered shares held by each person;

(c) the date on which the name of each person was entered in the Share Register; and;

(d) the date on which any person ceased to be a member

(2) The Share Register may be in such form as the directors may approve but if it is magnetic, electronic or other data storage form, the company shall be able to produce legible evidence of its contents.

(3) The Share Register shall be *prima facie* evidence of any matters directed or authorised by this Act to be contained therein.

(4) In the case of a company limited by guarantee the term "Share Register" shall mean "Register of Members" in which shall be entered the names and addresses of the members of such a company, the date of such entry and the date when any person ceases to be a member.

30. (1) If —

(a) information that is required to be entered in the Share Register under section 29 is omitted therefrom or inaccurately entered therein; or

(b) there is unreasonable delay in entering the information in the Share Register,

a member of the company, or any person who is aggrieved by the omission, inaccuracy or delay may apply to the court for an order that the Share Register be rectified, and the court may either grant or refuse the application, with or without costs to be paid by the applicant, or order the rectification of the Share Register and may direct the company to pay all costs of the application and any damages the applicant may have sustained.

(2) The court may, in any proceedings under subsection (1), determine any question relating to the right of a person who is a party to the proceedings to have his name entered in or omitted from the Share Register, whether the question arises between —

(a) two or more members or alleged members; or

(b) between members or alleged members and the company,

and generally the court may in the proceedings determine any question that may be necessary or expedient to be determined for the rectification of the Share Register.

31.

(1) Subject to any limitations in the Memorandum or Articles, registered shares of a company incorporated under this Act may be transferred by a written instrument of transfer signed by the transferor and containing the name and address of the transferee.

(2) In the absence of a written instrument of transfer mentioned in subsection (1), the directors may accept such evidence of a transfer of shares as they consider appropriate.

(3) A company shall not be required to treat a transferee of a registered share in the company as a member until the transferee's name has been entered in the Share Register.

(4) Subject to any limitations in its Memorandum or Articles, a company incorporated under this Act shall, on the application of the transferor or transferee of a registered share in the company, enter in its Share Register the name of the transferee of the share.

(5) A transfer of registered shares of a deceased, or bankrupt member of a company incorporated under this Act made by his personal representative, guardian or trustee, as the case may be, or a transfer of registered shares owned by a person as a result of a transfer from a member by operation of law, is of the same validity as if the personal representative, guardian, trustee or transferee had been the registered holder of the shares at the time of the execution of the instrument of transfer.

32.

(1) Subject to any limitations in its Memorandum or Articles, a company may purchase, redeem or otherwise acquire and hold its own shares.

(2) No purchase, redemption or other acquisition permitted under subsection (1) shall be made unless the directors determine that immediately after the purchase, redemption or other acquisition —

(a) the company will be able to satisfy its liabilities as they become due in the ordinary course of its business; and

(b) the realizable value of the assets of the company will not be less than the sum of its total liabilities, other than deferred taxes, as shown in the books of account;

and, in the absence of fraud, the decision of the directors as to the realizable value of the assets of the company is conclusive unless a question of law is involved.

(3) A determination by the directors under subsection (2) is not required where shares are purchased, redeemed or otherwise acquired —

(a) pursuant to a right of a member to have his shares redeemed or to have his shares exchanged for money or other property of the company;

(b) in exchange for newly issued shares in the company;

(c) by virtue of the provisions of section 80; and

(d) pursuant to an order of the court.

(4) Subject to any limitations in the Memorandum or Articles, shares that a company purchases, redeems or otherwise acquires may be cancelled or held as treasury shares unless the shares are purchased, redeemed or otherwise acquired out of capital pursuant to section 34, in which case they shall be cancelled; and upon the cancellation of a share, the amount included as capital of the company with respect to that share shall be deducted from the capital of the company.

33. Where shares in a company incorporated under this Act —

(a) are held by the company as treasury shares; or

(b) are held by another company of which the first company holds, directly or indirectly, shares having more than 50 percent of the votes in the election of directors of that other company,

the shareholders of the first company are not entitled to vote or to have dividends paid thereon and shall not be treated as outstanding for any purpose under this Act except for the purpose of determining the capital of the first company.

34.

(1) Subject to any limitations in the Memorandum or Articles and subject to subsections (3) and (4), the capital of a company incorporated under this Act may by resolution of directors, be —

(a) increased by transferring an amount out of the surplus of the company to capital; or

(b) reduced by —

(i) returning to members any amount received by the company upon the issue of any of its shares, the amount being surplus to the company;

(ii) canceling any capital that is lost or not represented by assets having a realizable value; or

(iii) transferring capital to surplus for the purpose of purchasing, redeeming or otherwise acquiring shares that the directors have resolved to purchase, redeem or otherwise acquire.

(2) Where a company reduces its capital under subsection (1), the company may —

(a) return to members any amount received by the company upon the issue of its shares;

(b) purchase, redeem or otherwise acquire its shares out of capital; or

(c) cancel any capital that is lost or not represented by assets having a realizable value.

(3) No reduction of capital shall be effected that reduces the capital of the company to an amount that is less than the sum of —

(a) the aggregate of —

(i) all outstanding shares with par value, and

(ii) all shares with par value held by the company as treasury shares; and

(b) the aggregate of the amounts designated as capital of —

(i) all outstanding shares without par value, and

(ii) all shares without par value held by the company as treasury shares that are entitled to a preference, if any, in the assets of the company upon liquidation of the company.

(4) No reduction of capital shall be effected under subsection (1) unless the directors determine that immediately after the reduction —

(a) the company will be able to satisfy its liabilities as they become due in the ordinary course of its business; and

(b) the realizable value of the assets of the company will not be less than its total liabilities, other than deferred taxes, as shown in the books of account, and its remaining issued and outstanding share capital;

and, in the absence of fraud, the decision of the directors as to the realizable value of the assets of the company is conclusive unless a question of law is involved.

35.

(1) Subject to any limitations in its Memorandum or Articles a company incorporated under this Act may, by a resolution of directors, declare and pay dividends in money, shares or other property.

(2) Dividends shall only be declared and paid if the directors determine that immediately after the payment of the dividend —

(a) the company will be able to satisfy its liabilities as they become due in the ordinary course of its business; and

(b) the realizable value of the assets of the company will not be less than the sum of its total liabilities, other than deferred taxes, as shown in the books of account, and its issued and outstanding share capital;

and, in the absence of fraud, the decision of the directors as to the realizable value of the assets of the company is conclusive unless a question of law is involved.

36. Subject to any limitations in its Memorandum or Articles a company incorporated under this Act may, by a resolution of directors, include in the computation of surplus for any purpose under this Act the net unrealized appreciation of assets of the company, and, in the absence of fraud, the decision as to the value of the assets is conclusive, unless a question of law is involved.

PART IV REGISTERED OFFICE AND REGISTERED AGENT

37.

(1) A company incorporated under this Act shall at all times have a registered office in The Bahamas.

(2) The address of the registered office shall be submitted to the Registrar with the Memorandum for registration upon the date of the application for incorporation.

(3) The directors of the company may change the address of the registered office of the company, which change shall be notified to the Registrar within seven days after such change has been made.

38.

(1) A company incorporated under this Act shall at all times have a registered agent in The Bahamas.

(2) No person shall act as registered agent unless he is licensed to carry on the business of financial and corporate services pursuant to section 3 of the Financial and Corporate Service Providers Act, 2000:

Provided that this subsection shall not apply to a company licensed under the Banks and Trust Companies Regulation Act, 2000.

(3) The Minister may by order vary or add to the requirements of subsection (2).

(4) Any person who was acting as a registered agent before the coming into force of this section may continue to so act but only if such person, within 90 days from the commencement of this section obtains a licence pursuant to the Financial and Corporate Service Providers Act, 2000.

(5) The name and address of the registered agent shall be submitted to the Registrar for registration at the date of incorporation of the company.

(6) The company shall notify the Registrar of any change in the name or address of the registered agent.

39.

(1) The Registrar shall maintain a register of licensed registered agents and the register referred to in section 9 of the Financial and Corporate Service Providers Act, 2000 shall be the register for the purposes of this section.

(2) The Registrar shall, during the month of February in each year, publish in the Gazette a list of registered agents on 31st January in that year.

(3) Any change in the details kept by the Registrar in the register of registered agents pursuant to subsection (1) shall be notified immediately by the registered agent to the Registrar, and upon payment of such fee as may be prescribed by the Minister, the Registrar shall record the change in the register of registered agents.

PART V DIRECTORS, OFFICERS, AGENTS AND LIQUIDATORS

40. Subject to any limitations in its Memorandum or Articles or in any unanimous shareholder agreement, the business and affairs of a company incorporated under this Act shall be managed by a board of directors that consists of two or more persons who may be individuals or companies.

41.

(1) All the shareholders of a company among themselves or all the shareholders of a company and a person who is not a shareholder of a company, may by a written agreement restrict in whole or in part, the powers of the directors of the company to manage the business and affairs of the company, and any such agreement if not otherwise invalid, shall be valid.

(2) A shareholder who is a party to any unanimous shareholder agreement has all the rights, powers and duties and incurs all the liabilities of a director of the company to which the agreement relates, to the extent that the agreement restricts the discretion or powers of the directors to manage the business and affairs of the company; and the directors are hereby relieved of their duties and liabilities to the same extent.

(3) If a person who is the beneficial owner of all the issued shares of a company makes a written declaration that restricts in whole or in part the powers of the directors to manage the business and affairs of the company, the declaration shall constitute a unanimous shareholder agreement.

(4) Where any unanimous shareholder agreement is executed or terminated, written notice of that fact, together with the date of the execution or termination thereof, shall be filed with the Registrar within 15 days after the execution or termination and no such agreement shall be legally effective until notice of its execution shall have been filed as aforesaid.

(5) In this section "shareholder" includes "member".

42.

(1) The first directors of a company incorporated under this Act shall be elected by the subscribers to the Memorandum; and thereafter, the directors shall be elected by the members for such term as the members may determine and where permitted by the Memorandum or Articles of a company incorporated under this Act, the directors may also elect directors for such term as the directors may determine.

(2) Each director holds office until his successor takes office or until his earlier death, resignation or removal or in the case of a company upon the making of an order for the winding up or dissolution of the company or upon the removal of a defunct company by the Registrar otherwise than pursuant to a winding–up order.

(3) Subject to any limitations in the Memorandum or Articles or in any unanimous shareholder agreement —

(a) a director shall cease to hold the office of director if a majority requests his resignation in writing;

(b) a director may resign his office by giving written notice of his resignation to the company and the resignation has effect from the date the notice is received by the company or from such later date as may be specified in the notice.

(4) Subject to any limitations in the Memorandum or Articles or in any unanimous shareholder agreement, a vacancy in the board of directors may be filled by a resolution of members or of a majority of the remaining directors.

43. The number of directors shall be fixed by the Articles and, subject to any limitations in the Memorandum or Articles, the Articles may be amended to change the number of directors.

44.

(1) A company incorporated under this Act shall keep a register to be known as a register of directors and officers containing-

(a) the names and addresses of the persons who are directors and officers of the company;

(b) the date on which each person whose name is entered in the register was appointed as a director or officer of the company; and

(c) the date on which each person as a director or officer ceased to be a director or officer of the company.

(2) The register of directors and officers may be in such form as the directors approve, but if it is in magnetic, electronic or other data storage form, the company must be able to produce legible evidence of its contents.

(3) The register of directors and officers, commencing from the date of the registration of the company, shall be kept at the registered office of the company referred to in section 37.

(4) A copy of the register of directors and officers shall be filed with the Registrar and shall be open to inspection by members of the public during official hours.

(5) The register of directors and officers is prima facie evidence of any matters directed or authorised by this Act to be contain therein.

45. The directors shall have all the powers of the company that are not reserved to the members under this Act or in the Memorandum or Articles or in any unanimous shareholder agreement.

46. Subject to any limitations in the Memorandum or Articles or in any unanimous shareholder agreement, the directors may, by a resolution of directors fix the emoluments of directors in respect of services to be rendered in any capacity to the company.

47.

(1) The directors may, by a resolution of directors designate one or more Committees, each consisting of one or more directors.

(2) Subject to any limitations in the Memorandum or Articles or in any unanimous shareholder agreement, each Committee has such powers and authority of the directors, including the power and authority to affix the common seal of the company, as are set forth in the resolution of directors establishing the Committee, except that no Committee has any power or authority with respect to the matters requiring a resolution of directors under section 42 or 53.

48.

(1) Subject to any limitations in the Memorandum or Articles or in an unanimous shareholder agreement, the directors of a company incorporated under this Act may meet at such times and in such manner and places within or outside The Bahamas as the directors may determine to be necessary or desirable.

(2) A director shall be deemed to be present at a meeting of directors if—

(a) he participates by telephone or other electronic means; and

(b) all directors participating in the meeting are able to hear each other and recognise each other's voice and for this purpose participation constitutes *prima facie* proof of recognition.

49.

(1) Subject to a requirement in the Memorandum or Articles or in any unanimous shareholder agreement to give longer notice, a director shall be given not less than 2 days notice of meetings of directors.

(2) Notwithstanding subsection (1) but subject to any limitations in the Memorandum or Articles or in any unanimous shareholder agreement, a meeting of directors held in contravention of that subsection, is valid if all the directors, or such majority thereof as may be specified in the Memorandum or Articles or in any unanimous shareholder agreement entitled to vote at the meeting, have waived the notice of the meeting; and for this purpose, the presence of a director at the meeting shall be deemed to constitute waiver on his part.

(3) The inadvertent failure to give notice of a meeting to a director, or the fact that a director has not received the notice, does not invalidate the meeting.

50. The quorum for a meeting of directors is that fixed by the Memorandum or Articles.

51. Subject to any limitations in the Memorandum or Articles or in any unanimous shareholder agreement, an action that may be taken by the directors or a Committee of directors at a meeting may also be taken by a resolution of directors or a Committee of directors consented to in writing or by telex, telefax, telegram, cable or other written electronic communication, without the need for any notice.

52.

(1) Subject to any limitations in the Memorandum or Articles or in any unanimous shareholder agreement, a director may by a written instrument appoint an alternate who need not be a director and the name of such alternate shall be disclosed and notified to the Registrar.

(2) An alternate for a director appointed under subsection (1) shall be entitled to attend meetings in the absence of the director who appointed him and to vote or consent in the place of the director.

52A. Where there is a single director or a single shareholder of a company incorporated under this Act, any requirement in this Act or in the Articles for a meeting of directors or shareholders for any purpose shall be satisfied where such single director or single shareholder passes a resolution in lieu of such meeting.

53.

(1) The directors may, by a resolution of directors appoint any person, including a person who is a director, to be an officer or agent of the company.

(2) Subject to any limitations in the Memorandum or Articles or in any unanimous shareholder agreement, each officer or agent has such powers and authority of the directors, including the power and authority to affix the common seal of the company, as are set forth in the Articles or in any unanimous shareholder agreement or in the resolution of directors appointing the officer or agent, except that no officer or agent has any power or authority with respect to the matters requiring a resolution of directors under section 46 and this section.

(3) The directors may remove an officer or agent appointed under subsection (1) and may revoke or vary a power conferred on him under subsection (2).

54. Every director, officer, agent and liquidator of a company incorporated under this Act, in performing his functions, shall act honestly and in good faith with a view to the best interests of the company and exercise the care, diligence and skill that a reasonably prudent person would exercise in comparable circumstances.

55. Every director, officer, agent and liquidator of a company incorporated under this Act, in performing his functions, is entitled to rely upon the Share Register kept under section 29, the books of accounts and records and the minutes and copies of consents to resolutions kept under section 66 and any report made to the company by any other director, officer, agent or liquidator or by any person selected by the company to make the report.

56.

(1) Subject to any limitations in the Memorandum or Articles or in any unanimous shareholder agreement, if the requirements of subsection (2) are satisfied, no agreement or transaction between

(a) a company incorporated under this Act; and

(b) one or more of its directors or liquidators, or any person in which any director or liquidator has a financial interest or to whom any director or liquidator is related, including as a director or liquidator of that other person,

is void or voidable for this reason only or by reason only that the director or liquidator is present at the meeting of directors or liquidators, or at the meeting of the Committee of directors or liquidators, that approves the agreement or transaction or that the vote or consent of the director or liquidator is counted for that purpose.

(2) An agreement or transaction referred to in subsection (1) is valid if —

(a) the material facts of the interest of each director or liquidator in the agreement or transaction and his interest in or relationship to any other party to the agreement or transaction are disclosed in good faith or are known by the members entitled to vote at a meeting of members; and

(b) the agreement or transaction is approved or ratified by a resolution of members.

(3) Subject to any limitations in the Memorandum or Articles or in any unanimous shareholder agreement, a director or liquidator who has an interest in any particular business to be considered at a meeting of directors, liquidators or members may be counted for purposes of determining whether the meeting is duly constituted in accordance with section 50 or otherwise.

57.

(1) Subject to subsection (2) and any limitations in its Memorandum or Articles or in any unanimous shareholder agreement, a company incorporated under this Act may indemnify against all expenses, including legal fees, and against all judgements, fines and amounts paid in settlement and reasonably incurred in connection with legal, or administrative proceedings any person who –

(a) is or was a party or is threatened to be made a party to any threatened, pending or completed proceedings, whether civil, or administrative by reason of the fact that the person is or was a director, an officer or a liquidator of the company; or

(b) is or was, at the request of the company, serving as a director, officer or liquidator, or in any other capacity is or was acting for, another company or a partnership, joint venture, trust or other enterprise.

(2) Subsection (1) only applies to a person referred to in that subsection if the person acted honestly and in good faith with a view to the best interests of the company.

58. A company incorporated under this Act may purchase and maintain insurance in relation to any person who is or was a director, a registered agent, an officer or a liquidator of the company, or who at the request of the company is or was serving as a director, a registered agent, and officer or a liquidator of, or in any other capacity is or was acting for, another company or a partnership, joint venture, trust or other enterprise, against any liability asserted against the person and incurred by the person in that capacity, whether or not the company has or would have had the power to indemnify the person against the liability under subsection (1) of section 57.

PART VI PROTECTION OF MEMBERS AND CREDITORS

59.

(1) Subject to any limitations in the Memorandum or Articles or in any unanimous shareholder agreement, the directors of a company incorporated under this Act may convene meetings of the members of the company at such times and in such manner and places within or outside The Bahamas as the directors consider necessary or desirable.

(2) Subject to a provision in the Memorandum or Articles or in any unanimous shareholder agreement for a lesser percentage, upon the written request of members holding more than 50 per cent of the votes of the outstanding voting shares in the company, the directors shall convene a meeting of members.

(3) Subject to any limitations in the Memorandum or Articles, a member shall be deemed to be present at a meeting of members if —

(a) he participates by telephone or other electronic means; and

(b) all members participating in the meeting are able to hear each other and recognise each other's voice and for this purpose participation constitutes *prima facie* proof of recognition.

(4) A member may be represented at a meeting of members by a proxy who may speak and vote on behalf of the member.

(5) The following provisions apply in respect of joint ownership of shares—

(a) if 2 or more persons hold shares jointly each of them may be present in person or by proxy at a meeting of members and may speak as member;

(b) if only one of them is present in person or by proxy, he may vote on behalf of all of them; and

(c) if 2 or more are present in person or by proxy, they shall vote as one.

60.

(1) Subject to a requirement in the Memorandum or Articles or in any unanimous shareholder agreement to give longer notice, the directors shall give not less than 7 days notice of meetings of members to those persons whose names on the date the notice appear as members in the Share Register referred to in section 29and are entitled to vote at the meeting.

(2) Notwithstanding subsection (1) but subject to any limitations in the Memorandum or Articles or in any unanimous shareholder agreement, a meeting of members held in contravention of the requirement to give notice is valid if members holding a 90 per cent majority, or such lesser majority as may be specified in the Memorandum or Articles or in any unanimous shareholder agreement, of

(a) the total number of the shares of the members entitled to vote on all the matters to be considered at the meeting; or

(b) the votes of each class or series of shares where members are entitled to vote thereon as a class or series together with an absolute majority of the remaining votes,

have waived notice of the meeting; and for this purpose, the presence of a member at the meeting shall be deemed to constitute waiver on his part.

(3) The inadvertent failure of the directors to give notice of a meeting to a member, or the fact that a member has not received the notice, does not invalidate the meeting.

61. The quorum for a meeting of members for purposes of a resolution of members is that fixed by the Memorandum or Articles; but where no quorum is so fixed, a meeting of members is properly constituted for all purposes if at the commencement of the meeting there are present in person or by proxy shareholders representing more than one–half of the shares of each class or series thereof.

62.

(1) Except as otherwise provided in the Memorandum or Articles, all shares vote as one class and each whole share has one vote.

(2) The directors of a company incorporated under this Act may fix the date notice is given of a meeting as the record date for determining those shares that are entitled to vote at the meeting.

63. Subject to any limitations in the Memorandum or Articles, an action that may be taken by members at a meeting of members may also be taken by a resolution of all members consented to in writing or by telex, telegram, telefax, cable or other written electronic communication, without the need for any notice.

64.

(1) Any notice, information or written statement required under this Act to be given to members by a company incorporated under this Act shall be served in the case of members holding registered shares —

(a) in the manner prescribed in the Memorandum or Articles, as the case may be, or

(b) in the absence of a provision in the Memorandum or Articles, by personal service or by mail addressed to each member at the address shown in the Share Register; and

65.

(1) Any summons, notice, order, document, process, information or written statement to be served on a company incorporated under this Act may be served by leaving it, or by sending it by registered mail addressed to the company at its registered office or by leaving it with, or by sending it by registered mail to, the registered agent of the company.

(2) Service of any summons, notice, order, document, process, information or written statement to be served on a company incorporated under this Act may be proved by showing that the summons, notice, order, document, process, information or written statement —

(a) was mailed in such time as to admit to its being delivered in the normal course of delivery, within the period prescribed for service; and

(b) was correctly addressed and the postage was prepaid.

66.

(1) A company incorporated under this Act shall keep such financial statements accounts and records as the directors consider necessary or desirable in order to reflect the financial position of the company.

(2) A company incorporated under this Act shall keep at its registered office—

(a) a copy of the Memorandum and Articles and all amendments thereto

(b) a register of all its directors and officers and such other records as the Minister may by order prescribe.

(3) A company incorporated under this Act shall have a common seal and an imprint thereof shall be kept at the registered office of the company.

67.

(1) A member of a company incorporated under this Act may, in person or by attorney and in furtherance of a proper purpose, request in writing specifying the purposes, to inspect during normal business hours the Share Register of the company and the books, records, minutes and consents kept by the company and to make copies or extracts therefrom.

(2) For purposes of subsection (1), a proper purpose is a purpose reasonably related to the member's interest as a member.

(3) If a request under subsection (1) is submitted by an attorney for a member, the request shall be accompanied by a power of attorney authorising the attorney to act for the member.

(4) If the company, by a resolution of directors, determines that it is not in the best interest of the company or of any other members of the company to comply with a request under subsection (1), the company may refuse the request.

(5) Upon refusal by the company of a request under subsection (1), the member may before the expiration of a period of 90 days of his receiving notice of the refusal, apply to the court for an order to allow the inspection.

68.

(1) Contracts may be entered into on behalf of a company incorporated under this Act as follows—

(a) a contract that, if entered into between individuals, is required by law to be in writing and under seal, may be entered into by or on behalf of the company in writing under the common seal of the company, and may, in the same manner, be varied or discharged;

(b) a contract that, if entered into between individuals, is required by law to be in writing and signed by the parties, may be entered into by or on behalf of the company in writing and signed by a person acting under the express or implied authority of the company, and may, in the same manner, be varied or discharged; and

(c) a contract that, if entered into between individuals, is valid although entered into orally, and not reduced to writing, may be entered into orally by or on behalf of the company by a person acting under the express or implied authority of the company, and may, in the same manner, be varied or discharged.

(2) A contract entered into in accordance with this section is valid and is binding on the company and its successors and all other parties to the contract.

(3) Without affecting paragraph (a) of subsection (1), a contract, agreement or other instrument executed by or on behalf of a company by a director or an authorised officer or agent of the company is not invalid by reason only of the fact that the common seal of the company is not affixed to the contract, agreement or instrument.

69.

(1) A person who enters into a written contract in the name of or on behalf of a company incorporated under this Act before the company comes into existence, shall be personally bound by the contract and is entitled to the benefits of the contract, except where —

(a) the contract specifically provides otherwise; or

(b) subject to any provisions of the contract to the contrary, the company adopts the contract, under subsection (2).

(2) Within a period of 90 days after a company incorporated under this Act comes into existence, the company may, by any action or conduct signifying its intention to be bound thereby, adopt a written contract entered into in its name or on its behalf before it came into existence.

(3) When a company adopts a contract under subsection (2) —

(a) the company shall be bound by, and entitled to the benefits of, the contract as if the company had been in existence at the date of the contract and had been a party to it; and

(b) subject to any provisions of the contract to the contrary, the person who acted in the name of or on behalf of the company ceases to be bound by or entitled to the benefits of the contract.

70. A promissory note or bill of exchange shall be deemed to have been made, accepted or endorsed by a company incorporated under this Act if it is made, accepted or endorsed in the name of the company —

(a) by or on behalf or on account of the company; or

(b) by a person acting under the express or implied authority of the company;

and if so endorsed, the person signing the endorsement shall not be liable thereon.

71.

(1) A company incorporated under this Act may, by an instrument in writing, whether or not under its common seal, authorize a person, either generally or in respect of any specified matters, as its agent to act on behalf of the company and to execute contracts, agreements, deeds and other instruments on behalf of the company.

(2) A contract, agreement, deed or other instrument executed on behalf of the company by an agent appointed under subsection (1), whether or not under his seal, is binding on the company and has the same effect as if it were under the common seal of the company.

(3) A power of attorney under this section applies both within and outside The Bahamas.

72.

(1) A document requiring authentication or attestation by a company incorporated under this Act may be signed by a director, a secretary or by an authorised officer or agent of the company, and need not be under its common seal.

(2) If the signature of any director, officer or agent authenticating or attesting any document is verified in writing by the registered agent of a company, the company is bound by the document.

73. If at any time there is no member of a company incorporated under this Act, any person doing business in the name of or on behalf of the company is personally liable for the payment of all debts of the company contracted during the time and the person may be sued therefor without joinder in the proceedings of any other person.

PART VII MERGER, CONSOLIDATION, SALE OF ASSETS, FORCED REDEMPTIONS, ARRANGEMENTS AND DISSENTERS

74. In this Part —

"consolidated company" means the new company that results from the consolidation of 2 or more constituent companies;

"consolidation" means the fusion of 2 or more constituent companies into a new company;

"constituent company" means an existing company that is participating in a merger or consolidation with one or more other existing companies;

"merger" means the merging of 2 or more constituent companies into one of the constituent companies;

"parent company" means a company that owns more than 50 percent of the outstanding voting shares of each class and series of shares in another company:

Provided that for the purposes of section 82 it means a company that owns more than 90 percent of such shares as aforesaid;

"subsidiary company" means a company more than 50 percent of whose outstanding voting shares are owned by another company:

Provided that for the purposes of section 82 it means a company more than 90 per cent of whose shares as aforesaid are owned by another company;

"surviving company" means the constituent company into which one or more other constituent companies are merged.

75.

(1) Two or more companies incorporated under this Act may merge or consolidate in accordance with subsections (3) to (5).

(2) One or more companies incorporated under this Act may merge or consolidate with one or more companies incorporated under the Companies Act in accordance with subsections (3) to (5) if the surviving company or the consolidated company will satisfy the requirements prescribed for an International Business Company by section 4

(3) The directors of each constituent company that proposes to participate in a merger or consolidation shall approve a written plan of merger or consolidation containing, as the case requires—

(a) the name of each constituent company and the name of the surviving company or the consolidated company;

(b) in respect of each constituent company —

(i) the designation and number of outstanding shares of each class and series of shares specifying each such class and series entitled to vote on the merger or consolidation; and

(ii) a specification of each such class and series, if any, entitled to vote as a class or series;

(c) the terms and conditions of the proposed merger or consolidation, including the manner and basis of converting shares in each constituent company into shares, debt obligations or other securities in the surviving company or money or other property, or a combination thereof;

(d) in respect of a merger, a statement of any amendment to the Memorandum or Articles of the surviving company to be brought about by the merger; and

(e) in respect of a consolidation, everything required to be included in the Memorandum and Articles for a company incorporated under this Act except statements as to facts not available at the time the plan of consolidation is approved by the directors.

(4) Some or all shares of the same class or series of shares in each constituent company may be converted into a particular or mixed kind of property and other shares of the class or series, or all shares of other classes or series of shares, may be converted into other property.

(5) The following provisions apply in respect of a merger or consolidation under this section

(a) the plan of merger or consolidation shall be authorised by a resolution of members and the outstanding shares of a class or series of shares are entitled to vote on the merger or consolidation as a class or series if the Memorandum or

Articles so provide or if the plan of merger or consolidation contains any provisions that, if contained in a proposed amendment to the Memorandum or Articles, would entitle the class or series to vote on the proposed amendment as a class or series;

(b) if a meeting of members is to be held, notice of the meeting, accompanied by a copy of the plan of merger or consolidation, shall be given to each member, whether or not entitled to vote on the merger or consolidation;

(c) if it is proposed to obtain the written consent of members, a copy of the plan of merger or consolidation shall be given to each member, whether or not entitled to consent to the plan of merger or consolidation;

(d) after approval of the plan of merger or consolidation by the directors and members of each constituent company, articles of merger or consolidation shall be executed by each company and shall contain

(i) the plan of merger or consolidation and, in the case of consolidation, any statement required to be included in the Memorandum and Articles for a company incorporated under this Act,

(ii) the date on which the Memorandum and Articles of each constituent company were registered by the Registrar,

(iii) the manner in which the merger or consolidation was authorised with respect to each constituent company;

(e) the articles of merger or consolidation shall be submitted to the Registrar who shall retain and register them in the Register;

(f) upon the registration of the articles of merger or consolidation, the Registrar shall issue a certificate under his hand and seal certifying that the articles of merger or consolidation have been registered.

(6) A certificate of merger or consolidation issued by the Registrar shall be *prima facie* evidence of compliance with all requirements of this Act in respect of the merger or consolidation.

76.

(1) A parent company incorporated under this Act may merge with one or more subsidiary companies incorporated under this Act or under the Companies Act without the authorization of the members of any company, in accordance with subsections (2) to (6), if the surviving company is a company incorporated under this Act and will satisfy the requirements prescribed for an International Business Company by section 5.

(2) The parent company shall approve a written plan of merger containing

(a) the name of each constituent company and the name of the surviving company;

(b) in respect of each constituent company —

(i) the designation and number of outstanding shares of each class and series of shares, and

(ii) the number of shares of each class and series of shares in each subsidiary company owned by the parent company; and

(c) the terms and conditions of the proposed merger, including manner and basis of converting shares in each company to be merged into shares, debt obligations or other securities in the surviving company, or money or other property, or a combination thereof.

(3) Some or all shares of the same class or series of shares in each company to be merged may be converted into property of a particular or mixed kind and other shares of the class or all shares of other classes or series of shares, may be converted into other property; but, if the parent company is not the surviving company, shares of each class and series of shares in the parent company may only be converted into similar shares of the surviving company.

(4) A copy of the plan of merger or an outline thereof shall be given to every member of each subsidiary company to be merged unless the giving or that copy of outline has been waived by that member.

(5) Articles of merger shall be executed by the parent company and shall contain —

(a) the plan of merger;

(b) the date on which the Memorandum and Articles of each constituent company were registered by the Registrar;

(c) if the parent company does not own all the shares in each subsidiary company to be merged, the date on which a copy of the plan of merger or an outline thereof was made available to the members of each subsidiary company.

(6) The articles of merger shall be submitted to the Registrar who shall retain and register them in the Register.

(7) Upon the registration of the articles of merger, the Registrar shall issue a certificate under his hand and seal certifying that the articles of merger have been registered.

(8) A certificate of merger issued by the Registrar shall be *prima facie* evidence of compliance with all the requirements of this Act in respect of the merger.

77.

(1) A merger or consolidation is effective on the date the articles of merger or consolidation are registered by the Registrar or such date subsequent thereto, not exceeding 30 days, as is stated in the articles of merger or consolidation.

(2) As soon as a merger or consolidation becomes effective —

(a) the surviving company or the consolidated company insofar as is consistent with its Memorandum and Articles, as amended or established by the articles of merger or consolidation, has all rights, privileges, immunities, powers, objects and purposes of each of the constituent companies;

(b) in the case of a merger, the Memorandum and Articles of the surviving company are automatically amended to the extent, if any, that changes in its Memorandum and Articles are contained in the articles of merger;

(c) in the case of a consolidation, the statements contained in the articles of consolidation that are required or authorised to be contained in the Memorandum and Articles of a company incorporated under this Act, are the Memorandum and Articles of the consolidated company;

(d) property of every description, including choses in action and the business of each of the constituent companies, immediately vests in the surviving company or the consolidated company; and

(e) the surviving company or the consolidated company shall be liable for all claims, debts, liabilities and obligations of each of the constituent companies.

(3) Where a merger or consolidation occurs —

(a) no conviction, judgement, ruling, order, claim, debt, liability or obligation due or to become due, and no cause existing, against a constituent company or against any member, director, officer or agent thereof, is released or impaired by the merger or consolidation; and

(b) no proceedings, whether civil or criminal pending at the time of a merger or consolidation by or against a constituent company, or against any member, director, officer or agent thereof, are abated or discontinued by the merger or consolidation, but —

(i) the proceedings may be enforced, prosecuted, settled or compromised by or against the surviving company or the consolidated company or against the member, director, officer or agent, as the case may be, or

(ii) the surviving company or the consolidated company may be substituted in the proceedings for a constituent company.

(4) The Registrar shall strike off the Register —

(a) a constituent company that is not the surviving company in a merger;

(b) a constituent company that participates in a consolidation.

78.

(1) One or more companies incorporated under this Act may merge or consolidate with one or more companies incorporated under the laws of jurisdictions outside The Bahamas in accordance with subsections (2) to (4), including where one of the constituent companies is a parent company and the other constituent companies are subsidiary companies, if the merger or consolidation is permitted by the laws of the jurisdiction in which the companies incorporated outside The Bahamas are incorporated.

(2) The following provisions apply in respect of a merger or consolidation under this section

(a) a company incorporated under this Act shall comply with the provisions of this Act with respect to the merger or consolidation, as the case may be, of companies incorporated under this Act and a company incorporated under the laws of a jurisdiction outside The Bahamas shall comply with the laws of that jurisdiction; and

(b) if the surviving company or the consolidated company is to be incorporated under the laws of a jurisdiction outside The Bahamas, it shall submit to the Registrar—

(i)an agreement that a service of process may be effected on it in The Bahamas in respect of proceedings for the enforcement of any claim, debt, liability or obligation of a constituent company incorporated under this Act or in respect of proceedings for the enforcement of the rights of a dissenting member of a constituent company incorporated under this Act against a surviving company or the consolidated company,

(ii)an irrevocable appointment of the Registrar as its agent to accept service or process in proceedings referred to in subparagraph (i),

(iii)an agreement that it will promptly pay to the dissenting members of a constituent company incorporated under this Act the amount, if any, to which they are entitled under this Act with respect to the rights of dissenting members, and

(iv)a certificate of merger or consolidation issued by the appropriate authority of the foreign jurisdiction where it is incorporated; or if no certificate of merger is issued by the appropriate authority of the foreign jurisdiction, then, such evidence of the merger or consolidation as the Registrar considers acceptable.

(3) The effect under this section of a merger or consolidation shall be the same as in the case of a merger or consolidation under section 75 if the surviving company or the consolidated company is incorporated under this Act, but if the surviving company or the consolidated company is incorporated under the laws of a jurisdiction outside The Bahamas, the effect of the merger or consolidation shall be the same as in the case of a merger or consolidation under section 75 except insofar as the laws of the other jurisdiction otherwise provide.

(4) If the surviving company or the consolidated company is incorporated under this Act, the merger or consolidation is effective on the date the articles of merger or consolidation are registered by the Registrar or on such date subsequent thereto, not exceeding 30 days, as is stated in the articles of merger or consolidation; but if the surviving company or the consolidated company is incorporated under the laws of a jurisdiction outside The Bahamas, the merger or consolidation is effective as provided by the laws of that other jurisdiction.

79. Any sale, transfer, lease, exchange or other disposition of more than 50 percent, by value, of the assets of a company incorporated under this Act, if not made in the usual manner or regular course of the business carried on by the company, shall be as follows —

(a) the proposed sale, transfer, lease, exchange or other disposition shall be approved by the directors;

(b) upon approval of the proposed sale, transfer, lease, exchange or other disposition, the directors shall submit the proposal to the members for it to be authorised by a resolution of members;

(c) if the meeting of members is to be held, notice of the meeting, accompanied by an outline of the proposal, shall be given to each member, whether or not he is entitled to vote on the sale, transfer, lease, exchange or other disposition; and

(d) if it is proposed to obtain the written consent of members, an outline of the proposal shall be given to each member, whether or not he is entitled to consent to the sale, transfer, lease, exchange or other disposition.

80.
(1) Subject to any limitations in the Memorandum or Articles —

(a) members holding 90 per cent of the votes of the outstanding shares entitled to vote; and

(b) members holding 90 per cent of the votes of the outstanding shares of each class and series of shares entitled to vote as a class or series,

on a merger or consolidation under section 75, may give a written instruction to a company incorporated under this Act directing the company to redeem the shares held by the remaining members.

(2) Upon receipt of the written instruction referred to in subsection (1), the company shall redeem the shares specified in the written instruction irrespective of whether or not the shares are by their terms redeemable.

(3) The company shall give written notice to each member whose shares are to be redeemed stating the redemption price and the manner in which the redemption is to be effected.

81.

(1) In this section "arrangement" means —

(a) a reorganisation or reconstruction of a company incorporated under this Act;

(b) a separation of two or more businesses carried on by a company incorporated under this Act;

(c) any combination of any of the things specified in paragraphs (a) and (b).

(2) The directors of the company may, by a resolution of directors, approve a plan of arrangement that contains the details of the proposed arrangement.

(3) Upon approval of the plan of arrangement by the directors, the company shall make application to the court for approval of the proposed arrangement.

(4) The court may, upon an application made to it under subsection (3), make an interim or final order that is not subject to an appeal unless a question of law is involved and in which case notice of appeal shall be given within the period of 20 days immediately following the date of the order, and in making the order the court may —

(a) determine what notice, if any, of the proposed arrangement is to be given to any person;

(b) determine whether approval of the proposed arrangement by any person should be obtained and the manner of obtaining the approval;

(c) determine whether any holder of shares, debt obligations or other securities in the company may dissent from the proposed arrangement and receive payment of the fair value of his shares, debt obligations or other securities under section 82;

(d) conduct a hearing and permit any interested persons to appear; and

(e) approve or reject the plan of arrangement as proposed or with such amendments as it may direct.

(5) Where the court makes an order approving a plan of arrangement, the directors of the company, if they are still desirous of executing the plan shall confirm the plan of arrangement as approved by the court whether or not the court has directed any amendments to be made thereto.

(6) The directors of the company, upon confirming the plan of arrangement, shall —

(a) give notice to the persons to whom the order of the court requires notice to be given; and

(b) submit the plan of arrangement to those persons for such approval, if any, as the order of the court requires.

(7) After the plan of arrangement has been approved by those persons by whom the order of the court may require approval, articles of arrangement shall be executed by the company and shall contain —

(a) the plan of arrangement;

(b) the order of the court approving the plan of arrangement; and

(c) the manner in which the plan of arrangement was approved, if approval was required by the order of the court.

(8) The articles of arrangement shall be submitted to the Registrar who shall retain and register them in the Register.

(9) Upon registration of the articles of arrangement, the Registrar shall issue a certificate under his hand and seal certifying that the articles of arrangement have been registered.

(10) A certificate of arrangement issued by the Registrar shall be *prima facie* evidence of compliance with all the requirements of this Act in respect of the arrangement.

(11) An arrangement is effective on the date the articles of arrangement are registered by the Registrar or on such date subsequent thereto, not exceeding 30 days, as is stated in the articles of arrangement.

82.

(1) A member of a company incorporated under this Act shall be entitled to payment of the fair value of his shares upon dissenting from —

(a) a merger, if the company is a constituent company, unless the company is the surviving company and the member continues to hold the same or similar shares;

(b) a consolidation, if the company is a constituent company;

(c) any sale, transfer, lease, exchange or other disposition of more than 50 per cent of the assets or business of the company, if not made in the usual or regular course of the business carried on by the company, but not including —

(i) a disposition pursuant to an order of the court, having jurisdiction in the matter,

(ii) a disposition for money on terms requiring all or substantially all net proceeds to be distributed to the members in accordance with their respective interests within one year after the date of disposition, or

(iii) a transfer pursuant to the power described in section 10(2);

(d) a redemption of his shares by the company pursuant to section 80; and

(e) an arrangement, if permitted by the court.

(2) A member who desires to exercise his entitlement under subsection (1) shall give to the company, before the meeting of members at which the action is submitted to a vote, or at the meeting but before the vote, written objection to the action; but an objection is not required from a member to whom the company did not give notice of the meeting in accordance with this Act or where the proposed action is authorised by written consent of members without a meeting.

(3) An objection under subsection (2) shall include a statement that the member proposes to demand payment for his shares if the action is taken.

(4) Within 20 days immediately following the date on which the vote of members authorising the action is taken, or the date on which written consent of members without a meeting is obtained, the company shall give written notice of the authorisation or consent to each member who gave written objection or from whom written objection was not required, except those members who voted for, or consented to in writing, the proposed action.

(5) A member to whom the company was required to give notice who elects to dissent shall, within 20 days immediately following the date on which the notice referred to in subsection (4) is given, give to the company a written notice of his decision to elect to dissent, stating —

(a) his name and address;

(b) the number and classes or series of shares in respect of which he dissents; and

(c) a demand for payment of the fair value of his shares;

and a member who elects to dissent from a merger under section 86 shall give to the company a written notice of his decision to elect to dissent within 20 days immediately following the date on which the copy of the plan of merger or an outline thereof is given to him in accordance with section 86.

(6) A member who dissents shall do so in respect of all shares that he holds in the company.

(7) Upon the giving of a notice of election to dissent, the member to whom the notice relates ceases to have any of the rights of a member except the right to be paid the fair value of his shares.

(8) Within 7 days immediately following the date of the expiration of the period within which members may give their notices of election to dissent, or within 7 days immediately following the date on which the proposed action is put into effect, whichever is later, the company or, in the case of a merger or consolidation, the surviving company or the consolidated company, shall make a written offer to each dissenting member to purchase his shares at a specified price that the company determines to be their fair value; and if, within 30 days immediately following the date on which the offer is made, the company making the offer and the dissenting member agree upon the price to be paid for his shares, the company shall pay to the member the amount in money upon the surrender of the certificates representing his shares.

(9) If the company and a dissenting member fail within the period of 30 days referred to in subsection (8) to agree on the price to be paid for the shares owned by the member, within 20 days immediately following the date on which the period of 30 days expires, the following shall apply —

(a) the company and the dissenting member shall each designate an appraiser;

(b) the 2 designated appraisers together shall designate a third appraiser;

(c) the 3 appraisers shall fix the fair value of the shares owned by the dissenting member as of the close of business on the day prior to the date on which the vote of members authorising the action was taken or the date on which written consent of members without a meeting was obtained, excluding any appreciation or depreciation directly or indirectly induced by the action or its proposal, and that value is binding on the company and the dissenting member for all purposes; and

(d) the company shall pay to the member the amount in money upon the surrender by him of the certificates representing his shares.

(10) Shares acquired by the company pursuant to subsection (8) or (9) shall be cancelled but if the shares are shares of a surviving company, they shall be available for re–issue.

(11) The enforcement by a member of his entitlement under this section excludes the enforcement by the member of a right to which he might otherwise be entitled by virtue of his holding shares, except that this section does not exclude the right of the member to institute proceedings to obtain relief on the ground that the action is illegal.

PART VIII

CONTINUATION

83.

(1) A company incorporated under the Companies Act or incorporated under the laws of a jurisdiction outside The Bahamas may, if it will satisfy the requirements prescribed for an International Business Company by section 4, continue as a company incorporated under this Act as follows

(a) articles of continuation, written in the English language or if written in a language other than the English language, accompanied by a certified translation into the English language, shall be approved —

(i) by a majority of the directors or the other persons who are charged with exercising the powers of the company, or

(ii) in such other manner as may be established by the company for exercising the powers of the company;

(b) the articles of continuation shall contain —

(i) the name of the company and the name under which it is being continued,

(ii) the jurisdiction under which it is incorporated,

(iii) the date on which it was incorporated,

(iv) the information required to be included in a Memorandum under section 13(1), and

(v) the amendments to its Memorandum and Articles, or their equivalent, that are to be effective upon the registration of the articles of continuation;

(c) the articles of continuation, accompanied by a copy of the Memorandum and Articles of the company, or their equivalent, written in the English language or if written in a language other than the English language, accompanied by a certified translation into the English language and, in the case of a foreign company, evidence satisfactory to the Registrar that the company is in good standing, shall be submitted to the Registrar who shall retain and register them in the register; and

(d) upon the registration of the articles of continuation, the Registrar shall issue a certificate of continuation under his hand and seal certifying that the company is incorporated under this Act.

(2) A company incorporated under the laws of a jurisdiction outside The Bahamas shall be entitled to continue as a company incorporated under this Act notwithstanding any provision to the contrary in the laws of the jurisdiction under which it is incorporated.

(3) Notwithstanding any provisions of the Companies Act, a company incorporated under that Act may, by resolution of the directors, continue the incorporation of the company under this Act.

84.

(1) A company incorporated under the laws of a jurisdiction outside The Bahamas may, if it will satisfy the requirements prescribed for an International Business Company by section 4, apply to the Registrar for provisional registration to continue as a company incorporated under this Act by complying with section 77(1) (a) and (b) and by submitting to the Registrar the following documents —

(a) the articles of continuation accompanied by a copy of the Memorandum and Articles of the company, or their equivalent written in the English language or if written in a language other than the English language accompanied by a certified translation into the English language, and evidence satisfactory to the Registrar that the company is in good standing; and

(b) a written authorization designating one or more persons who may give notice to the Registrar by telefax, telex, telegram, cable or other electronic means or by registered mail that the articles of continuation should become effective.

(2) The Registrar shall not, prior to the receipt of the notice referred to in subsection (1), permit any person to inspect the documents referred to in subsection (1) and shall not divulge any information in respect thereof.

(3) Upon receipt of the notice referred to in subsection (1), the Registrar shall —

(a) register the documents referred to in subsection (1) in the Register; and

(b) issue a certificate of continuation under his hand and seal certifying that the company is incorporated under this Act.

(4) For purposes of subsection (3), the Registrar may rely on a notice referred to in subsection (1) sent, or purported to be sent, by a person named in the written authorization.

(5) Prior to the registration of the documents referred to in subsection (1), a company may rescind the written authorization referred to in subsection (1) by delivering to the Registrar a written notice of rescission.

(6) If the Registrar does not receive a notice referred to in subsection (1) from a person named in the written authorization within one year immediately following the date on which the documents referred to in subsection (1) were submitted to the Registrar, the articles of continuation are rescinded.

(7) A company entitled to submit to the Registrar the documents referred to in subsection (1) may authorize the Registrar to accept as resubmitted the documents referred to in that subsection, before or after the documents previously submitted referred to in subsection (1) have been rescinded.

85. A certificate of continuation issued by the Registrar under section 83(1)(d) or under section 84(3) shall be *prima facie* evidence of compliance with all requirements of this Act in respect of continuation.

86.

(1) From the time of the issue by the Registrar of a certificate of continuation under section 83(1)(d) or under section 84(3) —

(a) the company to which the certificate relates —

(i) continues to be a body corporate incorporated under this Act, under the name designated in the articles of continuation,

(ii) is capable of exercising all powers of a company incorporated under this Act, and

(iii) is no longer to be treated as a company incorporated under the Companies Act or a company incorporated under the laws of a jurisdiction outside The Bahamas;

(b) the Memorandum and Articles of the company, or their equivalent as amended by the articles of continuation, are the Memorandum and Articles of the company;

(c) property of every description, including choses in action and the business of the company, continues to be vested in the company; and

(d) the company continues to be liable for all of its claims, debts, liabilities, and obligations.

(2) Where a company is continued under this Act —

(a) no conviction, judgement, ruling, order, claim, debt, liability, or obligation due or to become due and no cause existing, against the company or against any member, director, officer or agent thereof, is released or impaired by its continuation as a company under this Act; and

(b) no proceedings, whether civil or criminal, pending at the time of the issue by the Registrar of a certificate of continuation under section 83(1)(d) or under section 84(3) by or against the company, or against any member, director, officer or agent thereof, are abated or discontinued by its continuation as a company under this Act, but the proceedings may be enforced, prosecuted, settled or compromised by or against the company or against the member, director, officer or agent thereof, as the case may be.

(3) All shares in the company that were outstanding prior to the issue by the Registrar of a certificate of continuation under section 83 (1)(d) or under section 84 (3) in respect of the company shall be deemed to have been issued in conformity with this Act, but a share that at the time of the issue of the certificate of continuation was not fully paid remains unpaid, and until the share is paid up, the member holding the share remains liable for the amount unpaid on the share.

(4) If at the time of the issue by the Registrar of a certificate of continuation under section 83(1)(d) or under section 84(3) in respect of the company any provisions of the Memorandum and Articles of the company do not in any respect accord with this Act —

(a) the provisions of the Memorandum and Articles continue to govern the company until the provisions are amended to accord with this Act or for a period of 2 years immediately following the date of the issue of the certificate of continuation, whichever is the sooner;

(b) any provisions of the Memorandum and Articles of the company that are in any respect in conflict with this Act cease to govern the company when the provisions are amended to accord with this Act or after expiration of a period of 2 years after the date of issue of the certificate of continuation whichever is the sooner; and

(c) the company shall make such amendments to its Memorandum and Articles as may be necessary to accord with this Act within a period that is not later than 2 years immediately following the date of the issue of the certificate of continuation.

87.

(1) Subject to any limitations in its Memorandum or Articles a company incorporated under this Act may, by a resolution of directors or by a resolution of members, continue as a company incorporated under the laws of a jurisdiction outside The Bahamas in the manner provided under those laws.

(2) A company incorporated under this Act that continues as a company incorporated under the laws of a jurisdiction outside The Bahamas, does not cease to be a company incorporated under this Act unless the laws of the jurisdiction outside The Bahamas permit the continuation and the company has complied with those laws.

(3) Where a company incorporated under this Act continues under the laws of a jurisdiction outside The Bahamas —

(a) the company continues to be liable for all of its claims, debts, liabilities and obligations that existed prior to its continuation as a company under the laws of the jurisdiction outside The Bahamas;

(b) no conviction, judgment, ruling, order, claim, debt, liability or obligation due or to become due, and no cause existing against the company or against any member, director, officer or agent thereof, is released or impaired by its continuation as a company under the laws of the jurisdiction outside The Bahamas; and

(c) no proceedings, whether civil or criminal, pending by or against the company, or against any member, director, officer or agent thereof, are abated or discontinued by its continuation as a company under the laws of the jurisdiction outside The Bahamas, but the proceedings may be enforced, prosecuted, settled or compromised by or against the company or against the member, director, officer or agent thereof, as the case may be.

(4) Where a company incorporated under this Act continue under the laws of a jusrisdiction outside The Bahamas, the company shall submit to the Registrar a legal opinion by a person duly qualified in that jurisdiction that –

(a) the laws of the jurisdiction outside The Bahamas permit the continuation; and

(b) the company has complied with those laws; and upon receiving such legal opinion the Registrar shall –

(i) strike the company off the Register; and
(ii) issue a certificate under his hand and seal certifying that the company has ceased to be a company incorporated under this Act.

PART IX WINDING UP, DISSOLUTION AND STRIKING OFF

88. For the purposes of this Part "contributory" means as every person liable to contribute to the assets of a company under this Act in the event of that company being wound up and includes any person alleged to be a contributor in proceedings for determining the persons who are to be deemed contributories and in all proceedings prior to the final determination of such persons.

89.
(1) The liability of any person to contribute to the assets of a company under this Act, in the event of such company being wound up, shall be deemed to create a debt of the nature of a specialty accruing due from such person at the time when his liability commenced, but payable at the time or respective times when calls are made for enforcing such liability.

(2) Without affecting subsection.(I), where a contributory is bankrupt, the estimated value of his liability to future calls, as well as calls already made, may be proved against his estate.

90. Where any contributory dies either before or after he has been placed on the list of contributories, his personal representatives, heirs, and devisees shall be liable in the due course of administration-to contribute to the assets of the company in discharge of the liability of such deceased contributory and such personal representatives, heirs, and devisees shall be deemed to be contributories accordingly.

91. Where any contributory becomes bankrupt, either before or after he has been placed on the list of contributories, his assignees shall be deemed to represent such bankrupt for all the purposes of the winding up, and shall be deemed to be contributories, accordingly, and may be called upon to admit to proof against the estate of such bankrupt, or otherwise to allow to be paid out of his assets in due course of law, any monies due from such bankrupt in respect of his liability to contribute to the assets of the company being wound up.

92. A company under this Act may be wound up by the court in the following circumstances -

(a) when the company has passed a resolution requiring the company to be wound up by the court;

(b) when/ the company does not commence its business within a year from its incorporation, or suspends its business for a period of one year;

(c) where at any time there is no member of the company;

(d) when the company is unable to pay its debts;

(e) if the court is of the opinion that it is just and equitable that the company should be wound up.

93. A company under this Act shall be deemed to be unable to pay its debts where -

(a) a creditor, by assignment or otherwise, to whom the company is indebted, in a sum exceeding one thousand dollars then due, has served on the company, at its registered office, a demand under his hand requiring the company to pay the sum due, and the-company has for three weeks thereafter neglected to pay such sum, or to secure or compound for the same to the reasonable satisfaction of the creditor;

(b) execution of other process issued on a judgment, decree, or order obtained in any court in favour of any creditor in any proceeding instituted by such creditor against the company, is returned unsatisfied in whole or in part;

(c) it is proved to the satisfaction of the court that the company is unable to pay its debts; or

(d) it is proved to the satisfaction of the court that the value of the company's assets is less than the amount of its liabilities, having regard to its contingent and prospective creditors.

94. Any application to the court for the winding up of a company under this Act shall be by petition; and such petition may be presented by the company, a director, or by any one or more creditors, a contributory of the company, or by all or any of the above parties, together or separately; and every order which may be made on any such petition shall operate in favour of all the creditors and all the contributories of the company in the same manner as if it had been made upon the joint petition of a creditor and a contributory.

95. Any judge of a court may do in chambers any act which the court is authorized to do in a winding up by the court.

96. A winding up of a company by the court shall be deemed to commence at the time of the presentation of the petition for the winding up.

97. The court may, at any time after the presentation of a petition for winding up a company under this Act, and before making an order for winding up the company, upon the application of the company, or of any creditor or contributory of the company, restrain further proceedings in any action, suit, or proceeding against the company, upon such terms as the court thinks fit; the court may also at any time after the presentation of such petition, and before the first appointment of liquidators, appoint provisionally an official liquidator of the estate and effects of the company.

98. Upon hearing the petition the court may dismiss the same with or without costs, may adjourn the hearing conditionally or unconditionally, and may make any interim order, or any other order that it deems just.

99. When an order has been made for winding up a company under this Act, or a provisional liquidator has been appointed, no suit, action, or other proceedings shall be proceeded with or commenced against the company except with the leave of the court, and subject to such terms as the court may impose.

100. When an order has been made for winding up a company under this Act, a copy of such order shall be forwarded by the company to the Registrar who shall make a minute thereof in the register of companies.

101. The court may at any time after an order has been made for winding up a company, upon the application by motion of any creditor or contributory of the company, and upon proof to the satisfaction of the court that all proceedings in relation to such winding up ought to be stayed, make an order staying the same, either altogether or for a limited time, on such terms and subject to such conditions as it deems fit.

102. When an order has been made for winding up a company limited by guarantee and having a capital divided into shares, any share capital that may not have been called up shall be deemed to be assets of the company, and to be a debt of the nature of a specialty due to the company from each member to the extent of any sums that may be unpaid on any shares held by him, and payable at such time as may be appointed by the court.

103.

(1) Subject to subsection (2), the court may, as to all matters relating to the winding up, have regard to the wishes of the creditors or contributories, as proved to it by any sufficient evidence, and may, if it thinks it expedient, direct meetings of the creditors or contributories to be summoned, held, and conducted in such manner as the court directs, for the purpose of ascertaining their wishes, and may appoint a person to act as chairman of such meeting, and to report the result of such meeting to the court.

(2) Without affecting subsection (1), in the case of creditors, regard is to be had to the value of the debts due to each creditor, and in the case of contributories to the number of votes conferred on-each contributory by the regulation of the company.

OFFICIAL LIQUIDATORS

104.

(1) For the purpose of conducting the proceedings in winding up a company, and assisting the court therein, there may be appointed a person to be called an official liquidator; and the court having jurisdiction may appoint such person, either provisionally or otherwise, as it thinks fit, to the office of official liquidator; but in either case, if more person than one are appointed to the office of official liquidator, the court may declare whether any act hereby required or authorized to be done by the official liquidator is to be done by all or any one or more of such persons, and the court may also determine whether any and what security is to be given by any official liquidator on his appointment.

105.

(1) If no official liquidator is appointed or during any vacancy in such appointment, all the property shall be deemed to be in the custody of the court.

(2) There shall be .paid to the official liquidator such salary or remuneration, by way of percentages or otherwise, as the court may direct; and if more liquidators than one are appointed such remuneration shall be distributed amongst them in such proportions as the court shall direct.

106. The official liquidator shall be described by the style of the official liquidator of the particular company in respect of which he is appointed, and not by his individual name; and he shall take into his custody, or under his control, all the property, effect, and things in action to which the company is or appears to be entitled, and shall perform such duties in reference to the winding up of the company as may be imposed by the court.

107. The official liquidator may, with the approval of the court, do any or all of the following -

(a) bring or defend any action, suit, or prosecution, or other legal proceedings, civil or criminal, in the name and on behalf of the company;

(b) carry on the business of the company, so far as may be necessary for the beneficial winding up of the same;

(c) sell the real and personal property, effects, and things in action of the company by public auction or private contract, with power to transfer the whole thereof to any person or company, or to sell the same in parcels;

(d) do all acts and execute, in the name and on behalf of the company, all deeds, receipts, and other documents, and for that purpose use, when necessary, the company's seal;

(e) prove, rank, claim and draw a dividend, in the matter of the bankruptcy or insolvency of any contributory, for any balance against the estate of such contributory, and take and receive dividends in respect of such balance, in the matter of bankruptcy or insolvency as a separate debt due from such bankrupt or insolvent, and rateably with the other separate creditors;

(f) draw, accept, make and endorse any bill of exchange or promissory note in the name and on behalf of the company, also to raise upon the security of the assets of the company from time to time any requisite sum or sums of money; and drawing, accepting, making or endorsing of every such bill of exchange or promissory note on behalf of the company shall have the same effect with respect to the liability of such company as if such bill or note had been drawn, accepted, made, or endorsed by or on behalf of such company in the course of carrying on the business thereof;

(g) take out, if necessary, in his official name, letters of administration to any deceased contributory, and do in his official name any other act that may be necessary for obtaining payment of any monies due from a contributory or from his estate, and which act cannot be conveniently done in the name of the company; and in all cases where he takes out letters of administration, or otherwise uses his official name for obtaining payment of any monies due from a contributory, such monies shall for the purposes of enabling him to take out such letters or recover such monies, be deemed to be due to the official liquidator himself; and

(h) do and execute all such other things as may be necessary for winding up the affairs of the company and distributing its assets.

108. The court may provide by any order that the official liquidator may exercise any of the above powers without the approval or intervention of the court, and where an official, liquidator is provisionally appointed may limit and restrict his powers by the order appointing him.

109.

(1) Where a company is being wound up by the court the court may on the application of the liquidator, by order, direct that all or any part of the property belonging to the company or held by trustees on its behalf shall vest in the liquidator by his official name, whereupon the property to which the order relates shall vest accordingly.

(2) The liquidator may, after giving such indemnity, if any, as the court may, direct, bring or defend in his official name any action or other legal proceeding which relates to that property or which is necessary to bring or ,defend for the purpose of effectually winding up the company and recovering its property.

110. The official liquidator may, with the approval of the court, appoint a counsel and attorney to assist him in the performance of his duties.

ORDINARY POWERS OF COURT

111. As soon as may be after making an order for winding up the company, the court shall settle a list of contributories, with power to rectify the register of members in a11 cases where such rectification is required in pursuance or this Act, and shall cause the assets of the company to be collected, and applied in discharge of its liabilities.

112. In settling the list of contributories the court shall distinguish between persons who are contributories in their own right and persons who are contributories as being representatives of or being liable for the debts of others; and it shall not be necessary, where the personal representative of any deceased contributory is placed on the list, to add the heirs or devisees of such contributory, but such heirs or devisees may be added as and when the court thinks fit.

113. The court may, at any time after making an order for winding up a company, require any contributory for the time being settled on the list of contributories, trustee, receiver, banker, or agent, or officer of the company to pay, deliver, convey, surrender, or transfer forthwith, or within such time as the court directs, to or into the hands of the official liquidator, any sum or balance, books, papers, estate, or effects which happen to be in his hands for the time being, and to which the company is prima facie entitled.

114.

(1) Subject to subsections (2) and (3), the court may at any time after making an order for winding up the company, make an order on any contributory, for the time being settled on the list of contributories, directing payment to be made, in respect of any monies due from him or from the estate of the person whom he represents to the company exclusive of any monies which he or the estate of the person whom he represents may be liable to contribute by virtue of any call made or to be made by the court pursuant to this Part.

(2) The court may, in making such order when the company is not limited, allow to such contributory by way of set-off any monies due to him or the estate which he represents from the company on any independent dealing or contract with the company, but not any monies due to him as a member of the company in respect of any dividend or profit.

(3) When all creditors of any company whether limited or unlimited are paid in full, any monies due on account whatever to any contributory from the company may be allowed to him by way of set-off against any subsequent call.

115. The court may, at any time after making an order for winding up a company and either before or after it has ascertained the sufficiency of the assets of the company, make calls on and order payment thereof by all or any of the contributories for the time being settled on the list of contributories, to the extend of their liability, for payment of all or my sums it deems necessary to satisfy the debts and liabilities of the company, and the cost, charges, and expenses of winding it up, and for the adjustment of the rights of the contributories amongst themselves, and it may, in making a call, take into consideration the probability that some of the contributories upon whom the same is made may partly or wholly, fail to pay their respective portions of the same.

116. The court may order any contributory, purchaser or other person from whom money is due to the company to pay the same into a bank to the account of the official liquidator, instead of to the official liquidator and such order may be enforced in the same manner as if it had directed payment to the official liquidator.

117. All monies, bills, notes, and other securities paid and delivered into a bank in the event of a company being wound up by the court shall be subject to such order and regulations for the keeping of the account of such monies and other effects, and for the payment and delivery in, or investment and payment and delivery out of, the same as the court may direct.

118. If any person made a contributory as personal representative of a deceased contributory makes default in paying any sum ordered to be paid by him, proceedings may be taken for administering the personal and real estates of such deceased contributory, or either of such estates, of compelling payment of the monies due.

119. Any order made by the court pursuant to this Act upon any contributory shall, subject to the provisions for appealing against such order, be conclusive evidence that the monies, if any, thereby appearing to be due or ordered to be paid are due, and all other pertinent matters stated in such order are to be taken to be truly stated as against all person, and in all proceedings, with the exception of proceedings taken against the real estate of any deceased contributory, in which case such order shall only be prima facie evidence for the purpose of charging his real estate, unless his heirs or devisees were on the list of contributories at the time of the order being made.

120. The court may fix a day on or within which creditors of the company are to prove their debts or claims, or to be excluded from the benefit of any distribution made before such debts are proved.

121. The court shall adjust the rights of the contributories amongst themselves, and distribute any surplus that may remain amongst the parties entitled thereto.

122. The court may in the event of the assets being insufficient to satisfy the liabilities, make an order as to the payment out of the estate or the company of the costs, charges, and expenses incurred in winding up any company in such order of priority as the court thinks just.

123. When the affairs of the company have been completely wound up, the court may make an order that the company shall be dissolved accordingly.

124. Any order so made shall be reported by the official liquidator to the Registrar who shall make a minute in the register of companies of the dissolution of such company

EXTRAORDINARY POWERS OF COURT

125. The court may, after it has made an order for winding up the company, summon before it any officer of the company or person known or suspected to have in his possession any of the estate or effects of the company, or supposed to be indebted to the company, or any person whom the court may deem capable of giving information concerning the trade, dealings, estate, or effects of the company; and the court may require any such officer or person to produce any books, papers, deeds, writings, or other documents in his custody or power relating to the company; and if any person so summoned after being tendered a reasonable sum for his expenses, refuses to come before the court at the time appointed, having no lawful impediment (made known to the court at the time of its sitting, and allowed by it), the court may cause such person to be apprehended, .and brought before the court for examination; but, in cases where any person claims any lien on papers, deeds, or writings or documents produced by him, such production shall be without prejudice to such lien, and the court shall have jurisdiction in the winding up to determine all questions relating to such lien.

126. The court may examine upon oath, either orally or upon written interrogatories, any person appearing or brought before it concerning the affairs, dealings, estate, or effects of the company, and may reduce into writing the answers of every such person, and require him to subscribe the same.

127. The court may, at ,any time before or after it has made an order for winding up a company, upon proof' being given that there is a probable cause for believing that any contributory to such company is about to leave The Bahamas or otherwise abscond, or to remove or conceal any of his goods or chattels, for the purpose to remove or conceal any of his goods or chattels, for the purpose of evading payment of calls, or for avoiding examination in respect of the affairs of the company, cause such contributory to be arrested, and his books, papers, monies, securities for monies, goods, and chattels to be seized, and him and them to be safely kept until such time as the court may order.

128. Any powers conferred on the court by this Act shall be deemed to be in addition to and not in restriction of any other powers subsisting of instituting proceedings against any contributory, or the estate of any contributory, or against any debtor of the company for the recovery of any call or other sums due form such contributory, or debtor, or his estate, and such proceedings may be instituted accordingly.

129. All orders made by the court under this Act may be enforced in the same manner in which orders of such court made in any suit pending therein may be enforced.

130. A company incorporated under this Act shall commence to wind up and dissolve by a resolution of directors upon the expiration of such time as may be prescribed in its Memorandum or Articles for its existence.

131.

(1) A company incorporated under this Act that has never issued shares may voluntarily commence to wind up and dissolve by a resolution of directors.

(2) Subject to any limitations or provisions to the contrary in its Memorandum or Articles, a company incorporated under this Act that has previously issued shares may voluntarily commence to wind up and dissolve by a resolution of members or by a resolution of directors.

132.

(1) A resolution of members or directors to voluntarily wind up and dissolve a company shall also appoint a liquidator for the purpose of winding up the affairs of the company and distributing its property.

(2) If there is no liquidator acting in the case of a voluntary winding up, the court may, on the application of a contributory, appoint a liquidator and the court may, on due cause shown, remove any liquidator and appoint another liquidator to act in the matter of a voluntary winding up.

133. Upon the commencement of a winding up and dissolution required under section 130 or permitted under section 131 the directors may —

(a) authorize a liquidator, by a resolution of directors, to carry on the business of the company only if the liquidator determines that to do so would be necessary or in the best interests of the creditors or members of the company; and

(b) determine to rescind the articles of dissolution only as permitted under section 139

134.

(1) A liquidator shall, upon his appointment in accordance with this Part and upon the commencement of a winding–up and dissolution, proceed —

(a) to identify all assets of the company;

(b) to identify all creditors of and claimants against the company;

(c) to pay or provide for payment of, or to discharge, all claims, debts, liabilities and obligations of the company;

(d) to distribute any surplus assets of the company to the members in accordance with the Memorandum and Articles;

(e) to prepare or cause to be prepared a statement of account in respect of the actions and transactions of the liquidator; and

(f) to send a copy of the statement of account to members if so required by the plan of dissolution required by section 137.

(2) A transfer, including a prior transfer, described in section 10 of all or substantially all of the assets of a company incorporated under this Act for the benefit of the creditors and members of the company, is sufficient to satisfy the requirements of subsection (1)(c) and (d).

135.

(1) In order to perform the duties imposed on him under section 134, a liquidator has all the powers of the company that are not reserved to the members under this Act or in the Memorandum or Articles, including, but not limited to, the power—

(a) to take custody of the assets of the company and, in connection therewith, to register any property of the company in the name of the liquidator or that of his nominee;

(b) to sell any assets of the company at public auction or by private sale without any notice;

(c) to collect the debts and assets due or belonging to the company;

(d) to borrow money from any person for any purpose that will facilitate the winding up and dissolution of the company and to pledge or mortgage any property of the company as security for any such borrowing;

(e) to negotiate, compromise and settle any claim, debt, liability or obligation of the company;

(f) to prosecute and defend, in the name of the company or in the name of the liquidator or otherwise, any action or other legal proceedings;

(g) to retain counsel and attorneys, accountants and other advisers and appoint agents;

(h) to carry on the business of the company, if the liquidator has received authorization to do so in the plan of dissolution or by a resolution of directors permitted under section 133, as the liquidator may determine to be necessary or to be in the best interest of the creditors or members of the company;

(i) to execute any contract, agreement or other instrument in the name of the company or in the name of the liquidator; and

(j) to make any distribution in money or in other property or partly in each, and if in other property, to allot the property, or an undivided interest therein, in equal or unequal proportions.

(2) Notwithstanding, subsection (1)(h), a liquidator shall not, without the permission of the court, carry on for a period in excess of two years the business of a company that is being wound up and dissolved under this Act.

136. Where a company is being wound up voluntarily the liquidators or any contributory of the company may apply to the court to determine any question arising in the matter of such winding up, or to exercise, as respects the enforcing of calls, or in respect of any other matter, all or any of the powers which the court might exercise if the company were being wound up by the court, and the court if satisfied that the determination of such question, or the required exercise of power will be just and beneficial, may accede, wholly, or partially, to such application, on such terms and subject to such conditions as the court thinks fit, or it may make such other order, interlocutor, or decree on such application as the court thinks just.

137.

(1) The directors of a company required under section 130 or proposing under section 131 to wind up and dissolve the company shall approve a plan of dissolution containing —

(a) a statement of the reason for the winding up and dissolving;

(b) a statement that the company is, and will continue to be, able to discharge or pay or provide for the payment of all claims, debts, liabilities and obligations in full;

(c) a statement that the winding up will commence on the date when articles of dissolution are submitted to the Registrar or on such date subsequent thereto, not exceeding 30 days, as is stated in the articles of dissolution;

(d) a statement of the estimated time required to wind up and dissolve the company;

(e) a statement as to whether the liquidator is authorised to carry on the business of the company if the liquidator determines that to do so would be necessary or in the best interest of the creditors or members of the company;

(f) a statement of the name and address of each person to be appointed a liquidator and the remuneration proposed to be paid to each liquidator; and

(g) a statement as to whether the liquidator is required to send to all members a statement of account prepared or caused to be prepared by the liquidator in respect of his actions or transactions.

(2) If a winding up and dissolution is being effected in a case where section 131(2) is applicable —

(a) the plan of dissolution shall be authorised by a resolution of members or a resolution of directors, as the case may be, and the holders of the outstanding shares of a class or series of shares are entitled to vote on the plan of dissolution as a class or series only if the Memorandum or Articles so provide;

(b) if a meeting of members is to be held, notice of the meeting, accompanied by a copy of the plan of dissolution shall be given to each member, whether or not entitled to vote on to the plan of dissolution; and

(c) if it is proposed to obtain the written consent of members, a copy of the plan of dissolution shall be given to each member, whether or not entitled to consent to the plan of dissolution.

(3) After approval of the plan of dissolution by the directors, and if required, by the members in accordance with subsection (2), articles of dissolution shall be executed by the company and shall contain —

(a) the plan of dissolution; and

(b) the manner in which the plan of dissolution was authorised.

(4) Articles of dissolution shall be submitted to the Registrar who shall retain and register them in the Register and within 30 days immediately following the date on which the articles of dissolution are submitted to the Registrar, the company shall cause to be published, in the Gazette, in a publication of general circulation in The Bahamas and in a publication of general circulation in the country or place where the company has its principal office, a notice stating —

(a) that the company is in dissolution;

(b) the date of commencement of the dissolution; and

(c) the names and addresses of the liquidators.

(5) A winding up and dissolution commences on the date the articles of dissolution are registered by the Registrar or on such date subsequent thereto, not exceeding 30 days, as is stated in the articles of dissolution.

(6) A liquidator shall, upon completion of a winding up and dissolution, submit to the Registrar a statement that the winding up and dissolution has been completed and upon receiving the notice, the Registrar shall —

(a) strike the company off the Register; and

(b) issue a certificate of dissolution under his hand and seal certifying that the company has been dissolved.

(7) Where the Registrar issues a certificate of dissolution under his hand and seal certifying that the company has been dissolved —

(a) the certificate shall be *prima facie* evidence of compliance with all requirements of this Act in respect of dissolution; and

(b) the dissolution of the company is effective from the date of the issue of the certificate.

(8) Immediately following the issue by the Registrar of a certificate of dissolution under subsection (6), the liquidator shall cause to be published in the Gazette, in a publication of general circulation in The Bahamas and in a publication of general circulation in the country or place where the company has its principal office, a notice that the company has been dissolved and has been struck off the Register.

138. Whenever a company is wound up voluntarily all transfers of shares except transfers made to or with the sanction of the liquidators, or alteration in the status of the members of the company taking place, after the commencement of such winding up are void.

139.

(1) In the case of a winding–up and dissolution permitted under section 131, a company may prior to submitting to the Registrar a notice specified in section 137(6), rescind the articles of dissolution by —

(a) a resolution of directors in the case of a winding up and dissolution under section 131(1); or

(b) a resolution of members or a resolution of directors, as the case may be, in the case of winding up and dissolution under section 131(2).

(2) A copy of a resolution referred to in subsection (1) shall be submitted to the Registrar who shall retain and register it in the Register.

(3) Within 30 days immediately following the date on which the resolution referred to in subsection (1) has been submitted to the Registrar, the company shall cause a notice stating that the company has rescinded its intention to wind up and dissolve to be published in the Gazette, in a publication of general circulation in The Bahamas and in a publication of general circulation in the country or place where the company has its principal office.

140.

(a) the directors or, as the case may be, the members of a company that is required under section 130 or permitted under section 131 to wind up and dissolve, at the time of the passing of the resolution to wind up and dissolve the company, have reason to believe that the company will not be able to pay or provide for the payment of or discharge of all claims, debts, liabilities and obligations of the company in full; or

(b) the liquidator after his appointment has reason so to believe,

then, the directors, the members or the liquidator, as the case may be, shall immediately give notice of the fact to the Registrar.

CRIMINAL JUSTICE (INTERNATIONAL CO-OPERATION) ACT

42 of 2000
S.I. 128/2001

An Act to enable The Bahamas to co-operate with other countries in criminal proceedings and investigations; to enable The Bahamas to join with other countries in implementing the Vienna Convention against illicit traffic in narcotic drugs and psychotropic substances; and for connected purposes.

[Commencement 29th December, 2000]

PART I PRELIMINARY

Short title.

1. This Act may be cited as the Criminal Justice (International Co-operation) Act, 2000.

Interpretation.

2. In this Act-

"the Commissioner" means the Commissioner of Police;

"controlled drug" means a drug to which Parts II, III and IV of the Dangerous Drugs Act apply.

PART II CRIMINAL PROCEEDINGS AND INVESTIGATIONS

Mutual Service of Process

3. (1) This section has effect where the Attorney-General receives from the government of, or other authority in, a country outside The Bahamas-

Service of overseas process in The Bahamas.

(a) a summons or other process requiring a person to appear as defendant or attend as a witness in criminal proceedings in that country; or

(b) a document issued by a court exercising criminal jurisdiction in that country and recording a decision of the court made in the exercise of that jurisdiction,

together with a request for that process or document to be served on a person in The Bahamas.

(2) The Attorney-General may cause the process or document to be served by post or, if the request is for personal service, direct the Commissioner to cause it to be personally served on the person concerned.

(3) Service by virtue of this section of any such process or document as is mentioned (1) shall not impose any obligation under the law of The Bahamas to comply with it.

(4) Any such process or document served by virtue of this section shall be accompanied by a notice-

(a) stating the effect of subsection (3);

(b) indicating that the person on whom it is served may wish to seek advice as to the possible consequences of his failing to comply with the process under the law of the country or territory where it was issued; and

(c) indicating that under that law he may not, as a witness, be accorded the same rights and privileges as would be accorded in criminal proceedings in The Bahamas.

(5) Where the Commissioner is directed under this section to cause any process or document to be served, he shall after it has been served forthwith inform the Attorney-General when and how it was served and, if possible, furnish him with a receipt signed by the person on whom it was served; and if the Commissioner has been unable to cause the process or document to be served he shall forthwith inform the Attorney-General of that fact and of the reason.

4. (1) Process of the following descriptions, that is to say-

Service of Bahamian process overseas.

(a) a summons requiring a person charged with an offence to appear before a court in The Bahamas; and

(b) a summons or order requiring a person to attend before a court in The Bahamas for the purpose of giving evidence in criminal proceedings, may be issued or made notwithstanding that the person in question is outside The Bahamas and may be served outside The Bahamas in accordance with arrangements made by the Attorney-General.

(2) Service of any process outside The Bahamas by virtue of this section shall not impose any obligation under the law of The Bahamas to comply with it and accordingly failure to comply shall not constitute contempt of any court nor is it a ground for issuing a warrant to secure the attendance of the person in question.

(3) Subsection (2) is without prejudice to the service of any process (with usual consequences for non-compliance) on the person in question if subsequently effected in The Bahamas.

Mutual Provision of Evidence

Overseas evidence for use in The Bahamas.

5. (1) On an application made in accordance with subsection (2), a Judge or Stipendiary and Circuit Magistrate shall issue a letter ("a letter of request") requesting assistance in obtaining such evidence as is specified in the letter for use in the proceedings or investigation of an offence.

(2) An application under subsection (1) may be made by the Attorney-General or, if proceedings have been instituted, by the person charged in those proceedings.

(3) The Attorney-General may issue a letter of request if he is satisfied-

(a)
that an offence has been committed or that there are reasonable grounds for suspecting that an offence has been committed; and

(b)
that proceedings in respect of the offence have been instituted or that the offence is being investigated.

(4) Subject to subsection (5), a letter of request shall be sent to the Attorney-General for transmission either-

(a)
to a court or tribunal specified in the letter and exercising jurisdiction in the place where the evidence is to be obtained; or

(b)
to any authority recognised by the government of the country in question as the appropriate authority for receiving requests for assistance of the kind of which this section applies.

(5) In cases of urgency a letter of request may be sent directly to such a court or tribunal as is mentioned in subsection (4)(a).

(6) In this section "evidence" includes documents and other articles.

(7) Evidence obtained by virtue of a letter of request shall not without the consent of such an authority as is mentioned in subsection (4)(b) be used for any purpose other than that specified in the letter; and when any document or other article obtained pursuant to a letter of request is no longer required for that purpose (or for any other purpose for which such consent has been obtained), it shall be returned to such authority unless that authority indicates that the document or article need not be returned.

6. (1) This section has effect where the Attorney-General receives-

Bahamian evidence for use overseas.

(a)
from a court or tribunal exercising criminal jurisdiction in a country outside The Bahamas or a prosecuting authority in such a country; or

(b)
from any other authority in such a country which appears to him to have the function of making requests of the kind to which this section applies,

a request for assistance in obtaining evidence in The Bahamas in connection with criminal proceedings that have been instituted, or a criminal investigation that is being carried on, in that country.

(2) If the Attorney-General is satisfied-

(a)
that an offence under the law of the country in question has been committed or that there are reasonable grounds for suspecting that such an offence has been committed; and

(b)
that proceedings in respect of that offence have been instituted in that country or that an investigation into that offence is being carried on there,

he may, after consultation with the Chief Justice, by a notice in writing nominate a court in The Bahamas to receive the evidence to which the request relates.

(3) For the purpose of satisfying himself as to the matters mentioned in subsections (2)(a) and (b) the Attorney-General shall regard as conclusive a certificate issued by such authority in the country in question as appears to him to be appropriate.

(4) In this section "evidence" includes documents and other articles.

(5) The First Schedule shall have effect with respect to the proceedings before a nominated court in pursuance of a notice under subsection (2).

(6) Where it appears to the Attorney-General that the request relates exclusively to a fiscal offence he shall not exercise his powers under subsection (2) unless the request is made pursuant to a treaty to which The Bahamas is a party.

Additional Co-operation Powers

7. (1) The Attorney-General may, if he thinks fit, issue a warrant providing for any person (a "prisoner") serving a sentence in a prison in The Bahamas to be transferred to a country outside The Bahamas for the purpose-

Transfer of Bahamian prisoner to give evidence overseas.

(a)
of giving evidence in criminal proceedings there; or

(b)
of being identified in, or otherwise by his presence assisting in, such proceedings or the investigation of an offence.

(2) No warrant shall be issued under this section in respect of a prisoner unless he has consented to being transferred as mentioned in subsection (1), and that consent may be given either-

(a)
by the prisoner himself; or

(b)
in circumstances in which it appears to the Attorney-General inappropriate, by reason of the prisoner's physical or mental condition or his youth, for him to act for himself, by a person appearing to the Attorney-General to be an appropriate person to act on his behalf;

but a consent once given is not capable of being withdrawn after the issue of the warrant.

(3) The effect of a warrant under this section is to authorise-

(a)
the taking of the prisoner to a place in The Bahamas and his delivery at a place of departure from The Bahamas into the custody of a person representing the appropriate authority of the country to which the prisoner is to be transferred; and

(b)
the bringing of the prisoner back to The Bahamas and his transfer in custody to the place where he is liable to be detained under the sentence to which he is subject.

(4) Where a warrant has been issued in respect of a prisoner under this section he shall be deemed to be in legal custody at any time when, being in The Bahamas or on board a ship or aircraft registered in The Bahamas, he is being taken under the warrant to or from any place or being kept in custody under the warrant.

(5) A person authorised by or for the purposes of the warrant to take the prisoner to or from any place or to keep him in custody has all the powers, authority, protection and privileges of a police officer.

(6) If the prisoner escapes or is unlawfully at large, he may be arrested without warrant by a police officer and taken to any place to which he may be taken under the warrant issued under this section.

(7) This section applies to a person in custody awaiting trial or sentence and a person committed to prison for default in paying a fine as it applies to a prisoner, and the reference in subsection (3)(b) to a sentence shall be construed accordingly.

Transfer of overseas prisoner to give evidence in The Bahamas.

8. (1) This section has effect where-

(a)
a witness order has been made or a witness summons issued in criminal proceedings in The Bahamas in respect of a person (a "prisoner") who is detained in custody in a country outside The Bahamas by virtue of a sentence or order of a court or tribunal exercising criminal jurisdiction in that country; or

(b)
it appears to the Attorney-General that it is desirable for a prisoner to be identified in, or otherwise by his presence to assist in, such proceedings or the investigation in The Bahamas of an offence.

(2) If the Attorney-General is satisfied that the appropriate authority in the country where the prisoner is detained will make arrangements for him to come to The Bahamas to give evidence pursuant to the witness order or witness summons or, as the case may be, for the purpose mentioned in subsection (1)(b), he may issue a warrant under this section.

(3) A warrant shall not be issued under this section in respect of a prisoner unless he has consented to being brought to The Bahamas to give evidence as aforesaid or, as the case may be, for the purpose mentioned in subsection (1)(b); but a consent once given is not capable of being withdrawn after the issue of the warrant.

(4) The effect of the warrant is to authorise-

(a)
the bringing of the prisoner to The Bahamas;

(b)
the taking of the prisoner to, and his detention in custody at, such place or places in The Bahamas as are specified in the warrant; and

(c)
the returning of the prisoner to the country from which he has come.

(5) Subsections (4) to (7) of section 7 shall have effect in relation to a warrant issued under this section as they have effect in relation to a warrant issued under that section.

(6) A person is not subject to the Immigration Act in respect of his entry into or presence in The Bahamas in pursuance of a warrant under this section, but if the warrant ceases to have effect while he is still in The Bahamas he shall be treated for the purposes of that Act as if he has then illegally entered The Bahamas.

Enforcement of overseas forfeiture orders.

9. (1) The Attorney-General may by order provide for the enforcement in The Bahamas of any order which-

(a)
is made by a court in a country outside The Bahamas designated for the purposes of this section by such order;

(b)
is for the forfeiture and destruction, or the forfeiture and other disposal, of anything in respect of which an offence to which this section applies has been committed, or which was used in connection with the commission of such an offence.

(2) Without prejudice to the generality of subsection (1), an order made under this section may provide for the registration by a court in The Bahamas of any order as a condition of its enforcement and prescribe requirements to be satisfied before an order can be registered.

(3) An order made under this section may include such supplementary and incidental provisions as appear to be necessary or expedient and may apply for the purposes of the order, with such modifications as appear to the Attorney-General to be appropriate, any provisions relating to confiscation or forfeiture orders under any other written law.

(4) An order made under this section may make different provisions for different cases.

(5) This section applies to any offence which corresponds to or is similar to an offence under theDangerous Drugs Act, 2000, or an offence as defined in the Proceeds of Crime Act, 2000.

Supplementary

Rules of court.

10. (1) Provision may be made by rules of court for any purpose for which it appears to the authority having power to make the rules that it is necessary or expedient that provision should be made in connection with any of the provisions of this Part.

(2) Rules made for the purposes of the First Schedule may, in particular, make provision with respect to the persons entitled to appear or take part in the proceedings to which that Schedule applies for excluding the public from any such proceedings.

(3) An order made under section 9 may authorise the making of rules of court for any purpose specified in the order.

(4) This section is without prejudice to the generality of any existing power to make rules.

Application to proceedings involving Defence personnel.

11. (1) Section 4 applies also to a summons requiring a person charged with a civil offence to appear before a court-martial or to attend before such a court for the purpose of giving evidence in proceedings for such an offence; and a warrant may be issued under section 8 where-

(a)
such a summons has been issued in respect of a prisoner within the meaning of that section; or

(b)
it appears to the Attorney-General that it is desirable for such a prisoner to be identified in, or otherwise by his presence to assist in, such proceedings or the investigation of such an offence.

(2) Section 7 applies also to a person serving a sentence of detention imposed by a court-martial or detained in custody awaiting trial by such a court.

(3) In this section-

"civil offence" has the meaning assigned to it in section 78 of the Defence Act;

"court-martial" means a court exercising jurisdiction in relation to a civil offence under section 78 of the Defence Act.

PART III THE VIENNA CONVENTION

Interpretation

Interpretation of

12. (1) In this Part-

"Convention state" means a state which is a party to the Vienna Convention; Part III.

"enforcement vessel of a Convention state" means a warship or other ship of that state, authorised by the state to be on its service other than its commercial service, clearly identifiable as being on such service and having on board law enforcement officials of that state and includes any boat or aircraft carried on such ship;

"enforcement vessel of The Bahamas" means a vessel operated by the Royal Bahamas Defence Force, the Royal Bahamas Police Force or by the Customs Department;

"ship" includes any vessel used in navigation;

"the Vienna Convention" means the United Nations Convention against Illicit Traffic in Narcotic Drugs and Psychotropic Substances which was signed in Vienna on 20th December, 1988;

(2) If in any proceedings under this Part of this Act any question arises whether any country is a state or is a party to the Vienna Convention, a certificate issued by or under the authority of the Attorney-General shall be conclusive evidence on that question.

Offences at Sea

Offences on Bahamian registered ships.

13. Anything which would constitute an offence under the Dangerous Drugs Act or an offence within the meaning of the Proceeds of Crime Act, 2000 if done on land in The Bahamas shall constitute that offence if done on a ship registered in The Bahamas.

Ships used for illicit traffic.

14. (1) This section applies to a ship registered in The Bahamas or in a Convention state.

(2) A person is guilty of an offence if on a ship to which this section applies, wherever it may be, he-

(a)
has a controlled drug in his possession; or

(b)
is in any way knowingly concerned in the carrying or concealing of a controlled drug on the ship,

knowing or having reasonable grounds to suspect that the drug is intended to be imported or has been exported contrary to the Dangerous Drugs Act, 2000 or to the law of any state.

(3) A certificate purporting to be issued by or on behalf of the government of any state to the effect that the importation or exportation of a controlled drug is prohibited by law of that state shall be evidence of the matters stated.

(4) A person guilty of an offence under this section is liable-

(a)
in a case where the controlled drug is a Class A drug-

(i)
on summary conviction, to a fine not exceeding two hundred and fifty thousand dollars or to imprisonment for a term not exceeding five years or both;

(ii)
on conviction on indictment, to a fine not exceeding five hundred thousand dollars or to imprisonment for life or both;

(b)
in a case where the controlled drug is a Class B drug-

(i)
on summary conviction, to a fine not exceeding one hundred and fifty thousand dollars or to imprisonment for a term not exceeding four years or both;

(ii)
on conviction on indictment, to a fine not exceeding three hundred thousand dollars or to imprisonment for a term not exceeding twenty years or both;

(c)
in a case where the controlled drug is a Class C drug-

(i)
on summary conviction, to a fine not exceeding seventy-five thousand dollars or to imprisonment for a term not exceeding three years or both;

(ii)
on conviction on indictment, to a fine not exceeding one hundred and fifty, thousand dollars or to imprisonment for a term not exceeding ten years or both.

(5) The Minister of Health may make regulations dividing controlled drugs into classes A, B and C for purposes of subsection (4).

Enforcement powers.

15. (1) The powers conferred on an enforcement officer by the Second Schedule shall be exercisable in relation to any ship to which section 13 or 14 applies for the purpose of detecting and the taking of appropriate action in respect of the offences mentioned in those sections.

(2) The powers shall not be exercised outside the territorial waters of The Bahamas in relation to a ship registered in a Convention state except with the authority of the Attorney-General; and he shall not give his authority unless that state has in relation to that ship-

(a)
requested the assistance of The Bahamas for the purpose mentioned in subsection (1) ; or

(b)
authorised The Bahamas to act for that purpose.

(3) In giving his authority pursuant to a request or authorisation from a Convention state the Attorney-General shall impose such conditions or limitations on the exercise of the powers as may be necessary to give effect to any conditions or limitations imposed by that state.

(4) The Attorney-General may either of his own motion or in response to a request from a Convention state, authorise a Convention state to exercise, in relation to a Bahamian ship, powers corresponding to those conferred on enforcement officers by the Second Schedule but subject to such conditions or limitations, if any, as he may impose.

(5) Subsection (4) is without prejudice to any agreement made, or which may be made, on behalf of The Bahamas whereby The Bahamas undertakes not to object to the exercise by any other state powers corresponding to those conferred by the Second Schedule.

(6) The powers conferred by the Second Schedule shall not be exercised in the territorial waters of any state without the authority of the Attorney-General and he shall not give his authority unless that state has consented to the exercise of those powers.

Enforcement powers of Convention state in territorial waters.

16. (1) Subject to this section, a Convention state may, under an agreement made or which may be made by or on behalf of The Bahamas exercise in relation to a ship in the territorial waters of The Bahamas powers corresponding to those conferred on enforcement officers by the Second Schedule.

(2) A Convention state may exercise those powers in relation to-

(a)
any ship, when so authorised by an enforcement officer of The Bahamas who is embarked on an enforcement vessel of the Convention state;

(b)
any ship which is pursued into the territorial waters of The Bahamas by an enforcement vessel of the Convention state; or

(c)
a ship other than a ship registered in The Bahamas,

for the purpose of detecting and taking appropriate action in respect of drug offences.

(3) A Convention state shall, before exercising the powers referred to in subsection (2)(b) and (c)-

(a)
give advance notice of its proposed action in relation to the ship to an enforcement officer of The Bahamas;

(b)
where it was not practical to do so at the time, notify such officer of any action taken in relation to the ship as soon as possible after its occurrence.

(4) A Convention state shall not exercise the powers referred to in subsections (2)(b) and (c) unless an enforcement vessel of The Bahamas is not immediately available to exercise enforcement powers in relation to the ship.

Jurisdiction and prosecutions.

17. (1) Proceedings under this Part or the Second Schedule in respect of an offence on a ship may be taken, and the offence may for all incidental purposes be treated as having been committed, in any place in The Bahamas.

(2) No proceedings for an offence under section 14 alleged to have been committed outside the territorial waters of The Bahamas on a ship registered in a Convention state shall be instituted except in pursuance of the exercise with the authority of the Attorney-General of the powers conferred by the Second Schedule.

PART IV GENERAL

Expenses and receipts.

18. (1) Any expenses incurred by the Attorney-General under this Act shall be defrayed out of money provided by Parliament.

(2) Any money representing cash forfeited under Part III or accrued interest on any such money shall be paid into the Consolidated Fund.

FIRST SCHEDULE (Section 6(5))

BAHAMIAN EVIDENCE FOR USE OVERSEAS:
PROCEEDINGS OF NOMINATED COURT

Securing Attendance of Witness

1. The court shall have the like powers for securing the attendance of a witness for the purpose of the proceedings before the court as it has for the purpose of other proceedings before the court.

Power to Administer Oaths

2. The court may in the proceedings take evidence on oath.

Privilege of Witnesses

3. (1) A person shall not be compelled to give in the proceedings any evidence which he could not be compelled to give-

(a)
in criminal proceedings in The Bahamas; or

(b)
subject to subparagraph (2) in criminal proceedings in the country from which the request for the evidence has come.

(2) Subparagraph (1)(b) shall not apply unless the claim of the person questioned to be exempt from giving the evidence is conceded by the court, tribunal or authority which made the request.

(3) Where such a claim made by any person is not conceded as aforesaid he may (subject to the other provisions of this paragraph) be required to give the evidence to which the claim relates but the evidence shall not be transmitted to the court, tribunal or authority which requested it if a court in the country in question, on the matter being referred to it, upholds the claim.

(4) Without prejudice to subparagraph (1) a person shall not be compelled under this Schedule to give any evidence if his doing so would be prejudicial to the security of The Bahamas and a certificate signed by or on behalf of the Minister of National Security to the effect that it would be so prejudicial for that person to do so shall be conclusive evidence of that fact.

(5) Without prejudice to subparagraph (1) a person shall not be compelled under this Schedule to give any evidence in his capacity as an officer or

servant of the Crown.

(6) In this paragraph references to giving evidence include references to answering any question and to producing any document or other article and the references in subparagraph (3) to the transmission of evidence given by a person shall be construed accordingly.

Transmission of Evidence

4. (1) The evidence received by the court shall be furnished to the Attorney-General for transmission to the court, tribunal or authority that made the request.

(2) If in order to comply with the request it is necessary for the evidence to be accompanied by a certificate, affidavit or other verifying documents, the court shall also furnish for transmission such document of that nature as may be specified in the notice nominating the court.

(3) Where the evidence consists of a document the original or a copy shall be transmitted, and where it consists of any other article the article itself or a description, photograph or other representation of it shall be transmitted, as may be necessary in order to comply with the request.

Supplementary

5. For the avoidance of doubt it is hereby declared that section 177 of the Evidence Act, 1996 shall not apply to these proceedings.

6. No order for costs shall be made in the proceedings.

SECOND SCHEDULE (Section 15)

ENFORCEMENT POWERS IN RESPECT OF SHIPS

Preliminary

1. (1) In this Schedule "an enforcement officer" means-

(a)
a police officer or a customs officer;

(b)
a captain of any ship belonging to the Royal Bahamas Defence Force and any person acting under the command of such captain; and

(c)
any other person of a description specified in an order made for the purposes of this Schedule by the Attorney-General.

(2) In this Schedule "the ship" means the ship in relation to which the powers conferred by this Schedule are exercised.

Power to Stop, Board, Divert and Detain

2. (1) An enforcement officer may stop the ship, board it and, if he thinks it necessary for the exercise of his functions, require it to be taken to a port in The Bahamas and detain it there.

(2) Where an enforcement officer is exercising his powers with the authority of the Attorney-General given under section 15(2) the officer may require the ship to be taken to a port in the Convention state in question or, if that state has so requested, in any other country willing to receive it.

(3) For any of those purposes in subparagraphs (1) and (2), the enforcement officer may require the member of the crew to take such action as may be necessary.

(4) If an enforcement officer detains a vessel he shall serve on the master a notice in writing stating that it is to be detained until the notice is withdrawn by the service on him of a further notice in writing signed by an enforcement officer.

Power to Search and Obtain Information

3. (1) An enforcement officer may search the ship, anyone on it and anything on it including its cargo.

(2) An enforcement officer may require any person on the ship to give information concerning himself or anything on the ship.

(3) Without prejudice to the generality of those powers an enforcement officer may-

(a)
open any containers;

(b)
make tests and take samples of anything on the ship;

(c)
require the production of documents, books or records relating to the ship or anything on it;

(d)
make photographs or copies of anything whose production he has power to require.

Powers in respect of Suspected Offence

4. If an enforcement officer has reasonable grounds to suspect that an offence mentioned in section 13 or 14 has been committed on a ship to which that section applies he may-

(a)
arrest without warrant anyone whom he has reasonable grounds for suspecting to be guilty of the offence; and

(b)
seize and detain anything found on the ship which appears to him to be evidence of the offence.

Assistants

5. (1) A enforcement officer may take with him, to assist him in exercising his powers-

(a)
any other persons; and

(b)
any equipment or materials.

(2) A person whom an enforcement officer takes with him to assist him may perform any of the officer's functions but only under the officer's supervision.

Use of Reasonable Force

6. An enforcement officer may use reasonable force, if necessary, in the performance of his functions.

Evidence of Authority

7. An enforcement officer shall, if required, produce evidence of his authority.

Protection of Officers

8. An enforcement officer shall not be liable in any civil or criminal proceedings for anything done in the purported performance of his functions under this Schedule if the court is satisfied that the act was done in good faith and that there were reasonable grounds for doing it.

Offences

9. (1) A person is guilty of an offence if he-

(a)
intentionally obstructs an enforcement officer in the performance of any of his functions under this Schedule;

(b)
fails without reasonable excuse to comply with a requirement made by an enforcement officer in the performance of those functions; or

(c)
in purporting to give information required by an enforcement officer for the performance of those functions-

(i)
makes a statement which he knows to be false in a material particular or recklessly makes a statement which he knows to be false in a material particular; or

(ii)
intentionally fails to disclose any material information.

(2) A person guilty of an offence under this paragraph is liable-

(a)
on summary conviction, to a fine not exceeding five thousand dollars or to imprisonment for a term not exceeding two years or both;

(b)
on conviction on indictment, to a fine not exceeding ten thousand dollars or to imprisonment for a term not exceeding ten years, or both.

GUIDELINES FOR ELECTRONIC BANKING

I. INTRODUCTION

The Central Bank of The Bahamas *("the Central Bank")* is responsible for the licensing, regulation and supervision of banks and trust companies operating in and from within The Bahamas pursuant to the Central Bank of The Bahamas Act, 2000 ("the CBA) and the Banks and Trust Companies Regulation Act, 2000 (BTCRA). Additionally, the Central Bank has the duty, in collaboration with financial institutions, to promote and maintain high standards of conduct and management in the provision of banking and trust services.

All licensees are expected to adhere to the Central Bank's licensing and prudential requirements, ongoing supervisory programmes and regulatory reporting requirements, and are subject to periodic onsite inspections. Licensees are expected to conduct their affairs in conformity with all other Bahamian legal requirements.

II. PURPOSE

Electronic banking (e-banking) is defined as the automated delivery of new and traditional banking products and services directly to customers through electronic, interactive communication channels. E-banking includes the systems that enable customers, individuals or businesses, to access accounts, transact business, or obtain information on products and services through a public or private network, including the Internet.

These Guidelines set out the Central Bank's approach to the supervision of licensees' e-banking services, provide licensees with guidance on general principles for risk management of e-banking, outline suggestions for consumer education and security, and introduce the types of internet financial services.

III. APPLICABILITY

These Guidelines apply to all licensees.

IV. SUPERVISORY APPROACH

The Central Bank's supervisory objective is to establish and maintain a prudent regulatory regime for the provision of e-banking services in The Bahamas. The general principle is that licensees are expected to implement the relevant risk management controls that are commensurate with the risks associated with the types, complexity and amounts of transactions allowed (see Appendix 1) and the electronic delivery channels adopted. The risk management controls established for e-banking should be fully integrated into the risk management systems of the licensee.

The Central Bank endorses the principles and recommendations for e-banking outlined by the Basel Committee on Banking Supervision's papers - *"Risk Management Principles for Electronic Banking"* (http://www.bis.org/publ/bcbs98.htm) and the "Management and Supervision of Cross-Border Electronic Banking Activities" (http://www.bis.org/publ/bcbs99.htm) issued July 2003. Licensees are encouraged to read and understand the main principles of these documents.

In keeping with a risk-based supervisory methodology, the Central Bank's supervisory framework for e-banking aims to provide appropriate levels of supervision of its licensees' e-banking activities.

INITIAL DISCUSSIONS

Formal approval is not required to launch new e-banking services or make significant changes to existing services; however as with any other potentially significant change in its operations, licensees should notify and discuss plans with the Central Bank prior to implementing such initiatives in light of the possible implications regarding operational and reputational risk, which may affect capital requirements. The Central Bank will generally require the licensee to present and discuss the strategic outlook for launching e-banking services, demonstrating compatibility with the overall strategy of the licensee's

operations, the risk analysis for the planned project together with details of risk/reward study. Importantly, management is expected to demonstrate that it has reviewed the current risk profile of its operations, considered the impact of implementing an e-banking service and that the board has concluded that there are no undue adverse implications for the safety and soundness of the operations given its resources, risk management systems and technical expertise.

Specifically, the licensee should satisfy the Central Bank that the following issues are properly addressed:-

(1) That there is proper board and senior management oversight;

(2) That major technology-related controls relevant to e-banking have been addressed;

(3) That there are appropriate security measures in place, both physical and logical together with other requisite risk management controls;

(4) That any other relevant supervisory issues related to activities such as outsourcing and cross border e-banking activities have been addressed[1];

(5) That a cost-benefit analysis has been conducted of the provision of the new e-banking service;

(6) That an e-banking strategy has been developed and documented. The strategy should clearly outline the policies, practices and procedures that address and control all of the risks associated with e-banking;

(7) That the effectiveness of the plan will be monitored on an ongoing basis and that it will be updated periodically to take account of changes in technology, legal developments and the business environment including external and internal threats to information security;

(8) That risks are monitored on an ongoing basis; and

(9) That the board is satisfied that the licensee has the necessary level of capital vis-à-vis related risks as denoted in section (V) of these guidelines.

Given the dynamic nature of e-banking and related technology, the Central Bank recognizes that the issues to be dealt with will vary with time and from one licensee to another. The preceding list, therefore, is representative of the issues that should be considered rather than being exhaustive.

ONGOING SUPERVISORY REVIEW

The Central Bank will, in the course of its onsite examinations and offsite reviews, determine, as appropriate, the adequacy of the licensee's risk management of e-banking services based on the requirements set out in these guidelines. The Central Bank may implement other monitoring processes to facilitate its ongoing supervision of e-banking.

Licensees should promptly report any suspected or confirmed cases of fraud relating to e-banking, major security breaches, any material service interruption or other significant issues related to their e-banking services to the Central Bank.

V. RISKS ASSOCIATED WITH E-BANKING ACTIVITIES

Electronic banking creates new risk management challenges for licensees. Typically, all risks associated with traditional banking and products may be impacted with the

[1] (i.e. the necessary supervisory approvals from the Central Bank or overseas regulatory authority have been obtained.

introduction of e-banking services. However, the Central Bank has identified six major categories of risk specifically associated with e-banking for bank supervision purposes. The risks are strategic, operational/transaction, technology, business, reputation and legal.

(1) Strategic Risk is the current and prospective impact on earnings or capital arising from adverse business decisions, improper implementation of decisions, or lack of responsiveness to industry changes. Ideally, an e-banking service should be consistent with the bank's overall financial strategy. The planning and decision making process should focus on how specific business needs are met or enhanced by the e-banking product, rather than focusing on the product as an independent business objective. Strategic vision should determine how the e-banking product is designed, implemented, and monitored. The overall strategic vision of the licensee should influence how the e-banking product is designed and implemented.

(2) Operational/Transaction Risk arises from fraud, processing errors, system disruptions, and the inability to deliver products or services, maintain a competitive position, and manage information. In the provision of e-banking services, banks often rely on outsourced software companies. They require the proper management of information systems and the right capacity to service their customers. Contingency and business resumption planning is necessary for banks to be sure that they can deliver products and services in the event of adverse circumstances.

(3) Technology Risks are risks related to any adverse outcome, damage, loss, disruption, violation, irregularity or failure arising from the use of or reliance on computer hardware, software, electronic devices, online networks, and telecommunications systems. These risks can also be associated with systems failures, processing errors, software defects, operating mistakes, hardware breakdowns, capacity inadequacies, network vulnerabilities, control weaknesses, security shortcomings, malicious attacks, hacking incidents, fraudulent actions and inadequate recovery capabilities.

(4) Business Risk – In some circumstances, due to the more savvy nature of the e-banking consumer, traditional banking risk, such as credit risks, interest rate risk, liquidity risk, and foreign exchange risk are elevated.

(5) Reputation Risk arises from negative public opinion. A licensee's reputation can be damaged by e-banking services that are poorly executed or otherwise alienate customers and the public. It is important that customers understand what they can reasonably expect from a product or service and what special risks and benefits they incur when using the system. Customer education along with formal incident response and management procedures can help lessen reputation risk.

(6) Legal Risk is the risk to earnings or capital arising from violations of, or nonconformance with, laws, rules, regulations, or ethical standards. The need to

ensure consistency between paper and electronic advertisements, disclosures, and notices increases the potential for legal violations. Regular monitoring of the licensee's websites will help ensure compliance with applicable laws, rules, and regulations.

VI. RISK MANAGEMENT OF E-BANKING ACTIVITIES

The board of directors and management of the licensee are responsible for managing its risks, which become more complex following the introduction of electronic banking activities.

RISK ASSESSMENT

The Board of Directors or its designated committee should ensure that the risk management of e-banking is an integral part of the licensee's risk management systems (see Corporate Governance Guidelines issued in December 2001). As a result, the applicable risk management policies and processes, and the relevant internal controls and audits as required in the licensee's risk management system should be enforced and carried out as appropriate for the licensee's e-banking services.

In addition, the Board or its designated committee should ensure that the licensee's risk management controls and systems are modified and enhanced as necessary to cope with the risk management issues associated with e-banking. The e-banking-related risk management controls and policies should cover, at a minimum, the following risk management mechanisms:-

STRATEGIC RISK:

o Cost Benefit Analysis – Licensees should base any decision to implement e-banking products and services on a thorough analysis of the costs and benefits associated with such action (i.e. lower operating costs, improved or sustained competitive position, increased customer demand for e-banking services, and revenue opportunities). The risk management process requires the board and management to decide on what and how much to invest in security and controls in computer systems, telecommunications and networks. In addition to the obvious costs for personnel, hardware, software, and communications, the analysis should also consider:-

- Changes to the licensee's policies, procedures and practices;
- The impact on processing controls for legacy systems[2];
- The appropriate networking architecture, security expertise, and software tools to maintain system availability and to protect and respond to unauthorized access attempts;
- The skilled staff necessary to support and market e-banking services during expanded hours and over a wider geographic area, including possible expanded market and cross-border activity;
- The additional expertise and management information systems needed to oversee e-banking vendors or technology service providers;
- Cost of insurance for e-banking activities;
- Potential losses due to fraud; and
- Opportunity costs associated with allocating capital to e-banking efforts.

[2] A system in which a licensee has already invested considerable time and expense.

1. o **Business Continuity Considerations** – E-banking services should be delivered on a continuous basis with a reasonable system response time in accordance with the licensee's terms and conditions and anticipated customer expectations. In times of disruption, licensees should have the ability to switch to back-up systems which are protected against similar disruptions. Licensees should also have regard to the requirements for business continuity planning requirements addressed in the *"Minimum Standards for the Outsourcing of Material Functions"* Guidelines issued 4th May, 2004. The e-banking business continuity plan should be documented. The plan should:
    1. Set out a process for resuming or replacing e-banking processing capabilities, and reconstructing transaction if necessary, in the event of a business disruption;
    2. Be able to address any dependency on outside service providers (e.g. internet service providers); and
    3. If an alternate service delivery channel is used for contingency arrangements of a critical e-banking service, licensees should ensure that the alternate service delivery channel can provide an appropriate level of continuous service to its customers, taking into account customers' demands and expectations.

b. o **Outsourcing Management** – Some licensees may rely on another unit of the same financial group (e.g. the head office) or outside service providers to operate and maintain IT systems or business processes that support their e-banking services. In these cases, licensees should adhere to the controls specified for outsourcing of material functions in the *"Minimum Standards for the Outsourcing of Material Functions"* Guidelines and the requirement for the prior approval of the Central Bank.

Licensees should perform regular due diligence to evaluate the financial soundness and ability of outside service providers to maintain an adequate level of security and to keep abreast of rapidly changing technologies.

The Central Bank also expects licensees to specifically focus on:

- Adopting appropriate procedures for evaluating decisions to outsource electronic banking systems;
- Conducting appropriate risk analysis and due diligence prior to selecting an e-banking service provider;
- Committing adequate resources, with the required knowledge and clear accountability, for the effective oversight of e-banking services outsourced to e-banking service providers;
- Ensuring that the outsourced service is subject to regular independent assessment. In this regard, licensees should have the right to conduct independent reviews or have the right to obtain confirmation that such reviews or audits have been done by an independent party on the e-banking service provider;
- Assessing the internal capacity necessary to evaluate and oversee outsourcing relationships;
- Implementing necessary controls and reporting processes to effectively monitor the outsourced e-banking activity;
- Defining performance expectations under both normal and contingency circumstances; and
- For cross-border outsourcing, ensuring that the arrangements meet the applicable laws, regulations and supervisory standards.

TECHNOLOGICAL RISK

a. o **Authentication of customers** –Licensees should select reliable and effective authentication techniques to validate the identity and authority of their e-banking customers and should also have regard to the Guidance provided in the Central Bank's Guidelines on the Prevention of Money Laundering and Countering the Financing of Terrorism for verifying customer identity including instances where there is no face to face interaction with a customer;
   1. o **Confidentiality and Integrity of Information** – E-banking services entail transmission of sensitive information over the Internet and licensee's internal
   2. networks. Licensees should therefore implement appropriate technologies to maintain confidentiality and integrity of sensitive information while it is being transmitted over the internal and external networks and also, when it is stored inside the licensee's internal systems. Cryptographic technologies can be used to protect the confidentiality and integrity of sensitive information. Licensees should choose cryptographic technologies that are appropriate to the sensitivity and importance of information and the extent of protection needed.

b. o **Application Security** – Inadequate application security in e-banking systems increases the risk of successful penetration or security attacks. Licensees should ensure an appropriate level of application security in respect of their e-banking systems. When licensees select system development tools or programming languages for developing e-banking application systems, they should evaluate the security features that can be provided by different tools or languages to ensure that effective application security can be implemented. In the case of selecting a third-party developed e-banking system, licensees should take into account the appropriateness of the application security of the system.

c. o **Internet Infrastructure and Security Monitoring** – Licensees should establish an appropriate operating environment that supports and protects their e-banking systems. Licensees should proactively monitor their e-banking systems and internet infrastructure on an ongoing basis to detect and record any security breaches, suspected intrusions or weaknesses.

Licensees should ensure that sufficient physical controls are in place to deter unauthorised access to all critical e-banking systems, servers, databases and applications.

REPUTATIONAL RISK

o Incident Response and Management – Licensees should put in place formal incident response and management procedures for timely reporting and handling of suspected or actual security breaches, frauds or service interruptions of their e-banking services during or outside office hours. The incident response and management procedures should allow the licensee to quickly identify the origin of the weakness and contain the damage, assess the potential scale and impact of the incident, escalate promptly to senior management where warranted, identify and notify affected customers, and collect and preserve forensic evidence as appropriate to facilitate the subsequent investigation and prosecution of suspects and intruders if necessary. Furthermore, the incident response procedures should include strategies for dealing with adverse media and customer reactions in a timely way.

Licensees should report any suspected or confirmed cases relating to e-banking, major security breaches, any material service interruption or other significant issues related to their e-banking services to the Central Bank. Licensees should ensure that the specific mechanisms for ensuring this notification to the regulator are in place.

LEGAL RISK

1. o **Terms and Conditions** - Licensees must set out clearly, in their terms and conditions, the respective rights and obligations between the institutions and their customers. These terms and conditions should protect the interests of both the institutions and the customers.
2. The terms and conditions should be readily available to customers who use the internet banking feature. On initial logon or subscription to a particular service or product, the licensee should require a positive acknowledgement of the terms and conditions from the customer.
3. o Licensees should perform appropriate assessments of the legal and reputation risks associated with their e-banking services. Based on the risk assessment, licensees should have proper controls in place to manage the legal and reputation risks. For example, the controls may include:
   - Proper terms and conditions of e-banking services;
   - Appropriate disclosures and disclaimers prominently posted on the e-banking websites or other relevant documents so as to address the applicable legal requirements and potential reputation issues. In particular, terms and conditions governing outsourced activities and other critical third party relationships; and
   - Consideration of the need to use appropriate insurance coverage to address residual legal risks.

VI. CUSTOMER SECURITY AND EDUCATION

An important aspect of customer security and risk management is customer education. Therefore, licensees should pay special attention to the provision of easy-to-understand and prominent advice to their customers on e-banking security precautions. The Central Bank suggests the use of multiple channels, such as websites, messages printed on customer statements, promotional leaflets, or even direct staff communication with customers, to reinforce certain key precautionary measures.

Security precautionary advice for customers should cover, at a minimum, the following issues:-

- Password and user ID selection and protection;
- Customers should be reminded not to disclose their personal information to unauthorised persons or to any doubtful websites; and
- Reminders not to access e-banking services through public or shared computers.

VII. CROSS BORDER ELECTRONIC BANKING ACTIVITIES

Before engaging in cross-border e-banking transactions, licensees should ensure that adequate information is disclosed on their websites to allow potential customers to make a determination of the licensee's identity, home country, and whether it has the relevant regulatory licence(s) before they establish the business relationship. This information will improve transparency and minimize legal and reputational risk associated with cross border e-banking activities.

APPENDIX 1 TYPES OF INTERNET FINANCIAL SERVICES

Due to the open and dynamic nature of the Internet, the risks associated with providing online services via the Internet are greater and far more extensive than closed networks and proprietary delivery channels.

Specific security and control measures have to be formulated to tie in with the risk management process. It is important that licensees set appropriate control and security benchmarks for the Internet operations.

The level of e-banking risk is directly linked to the type of services provided by licensees. The licensee's management should chose a level of e-banking services provided to various customer segments based on customers needs and the institution's risk assessment considerations. Typically, e-banking services can be classified into information service, interactive information exchange service and transactional service.

1. Information Service

This is the most basic form of online e-banking service. It is a one-way communication whereby information, advertisements or promotional material are provided to the customers. Although the risks associated with such online services are low, these websites are often the targets of hacking which vandalizes and mutilates the original information being provided. A licensee may suffer reputational harm resulting from its website being hacked.

Where a licensee purchases advertising space from a third party, regular monitoring should be made not only of the licensee's advertisement, but also the associated contents of the service provider. Reputational damage may be caused by association with unsavoury advertising being hosted on the same service.

2. Interactive Information Exchange Service

This form of Internet services offers slightly more customer interactions compared with the former. Customers are able to communicate with the bank, make account enquiries and complete application forms for additional services or purchase new products offered. The risks pertaining to these websites depend on whether they have any direct links to the licensee's internal network. These risks range from low to moderate according to the connectivity between the Internet and the internal network and the applications that the customer could access.

3. Transactional Service

This category of Internet services allows customers to execute online transactions such as the transfer of funds, payment of bills and other financials transactions. This is the highest risk category that requires the strongest controls since online transactions are often irrevocable once executed and the bank's internal systems may be exposed to external attacks if controls are inadequate.

GUIDELINES FOR THE ESTABLISHMENT OR ACQUISITION OF OVERSEAS BRANCHES, SUBSIDIARIES AND REPRESENTATIVE OFFICES

I. INTRODUCTION

The Central Bank of The Bahamas ("the Central Bank") is responsible for the licensing, regulation and supervision of banks and trust companies operating in and from within The Bahamas pursuant to The Banks and Trust Companies Regulation Act, 2000 and The Central Bank of The Bahamas Act, 2000. Additionally, the Central Bank has the duty, in

collaboration with financial institutions, to promote and maintain high standards of conduct and management in the provision of banking and trust services.

All licensees are expected to adhere to the Central Bank's licensing and prudential requirements and ongoing supervisory programmes, including periodic on-site inspections, and required regulatory reporting. Licensees are also expected to conduct their affairs in conformity with all other Bahamian legal requirements.

II. PURPOSE

These Guidelines outline the Central Bank's policy with regard to the establishment or acquisition of overseas branches, subsidiaries and representative offices (outward authorization). These Guidelines outline the major considerations of the Central Bank in assessing applications for overseas branches, subsidiaries and representative offices and the information which would normally be required in support of the application. The Central Bank may require the applicant to provide additional information, as necessary, for the proper review of an application for outward authorization.

III. APPLICABILITY

These guidelines apply to all licensees.

IV. DEFINITIONS

An Overseas Branch is defined as an operating entity which does not have a separate legal status and is thus an integral part of the parent bank and/or trust company, which is incorporated in a country other than that of the branch.

An Overseas Subsidiary is defined as a legally independent institution, wholly-owned or majority-owned, by a bank and/or trust company, which is incorporated in a country other than that of the subsidiary.

An Overseas Representative Office is defined as an office engaged solely in carrying out public relations on behalf of a banking and/or trust group. It acts as a liaison between the head office of the group and the banking and financial institutions, private and public companies, and commissions in a country other than that of the head office.

Home Regulator is defined as the regulatory body responsible for the licensing and consolidated supervision of a banking and/or trust organization which has established a branch, subsidiary, or representative office in another country, the "host" country.

Host Regulator is defined as the regulatory body responsible for conducting supervision of branches, subsidiaries and representative offices of foreign banks and/or trust entities which are resident in the host country.

Managed branches, subsidiaries, or representative offices are entities that have no physical presence (as defined in the Central Bank's Physical Presence Guidelines) in the country where they are incorporated and licensed.

V. SUPERVISORY APPROACH TO OUTWARD AUTHORIZATION

In accordance with Section 5 of the Banks and Trust Companies Regulation Act, 2000, no licensee should establish, an overseas branch, subsidiary or representative office without the prior written approval of the Governor.

Applications for outward authorization should be submitted in writing to the Central Bank. The following factors will be considered:-

(**1**) With regards to the licensee (applicant):-

(a) the size, nature and reputation of the applicant;

(b) the fitness, propriety & managerial capacity of the applicant to expand its banking and/or trust business overseas in a prudent and reputable manner;

(c) the business record and experience of the applicant;

(d) the impact on the capital adequacy of the applicant will be assessed together with the ability of the applicant to fund the establishment or acquisition of a branch, subsidiary or representative office abroad;

(e) the nature and sufficiency of the financial resources of the applicant to provide continuing financial support to the branch, subsidiary or representative office overseas, should it be necessary. The financial condition and likely future requirements of the entity in terms of possible injections of capital and liquidity will also be considered to ensure that there will not be undue hardship on the financial resources of the licensee;

(f) the history of compliance of the applicant with Bahamian financial legislation and Central Bank directives, requirements and guidelines;

(g) the applicant must have demonstrated by the quality of their operations in The Bahamas that they are capable of assuming the role of parent to an overseas branch, subsidiary, or representative office. Hence, as a rule, the Central Bank generally requires that:-

(i.) licensees be in good standing with the Central Bank at the time it submits an application to establish a branch, subsidiary or representative office; and

(ii.) licensees have conducted business in The Bahamas over a time period which allows the Central Bank to assess its readiness to establish a branch, subsidiary or representative office abroad.

(h) exceptions to the requirements of (g) above may be made in instances where:-

(i.) the licensee was granted approval at the time of its licensing to establish overseas operations; or

(ii.) the licensee's parent is of sufficient financial strength and has indicated its undertaking to support the licensee's operations in The Bahamas and overseas.

(2) With regards to the proposed overseas branch, subsidiary, or representative office:-

(a)

the soundness and feasibility of the business plan;

(b) the supervisory regime of the host country, particularly its implementation of international regulatory standards and codes; and

(c) the character, competence and experience of those who will operate the branch, subsidiary or representative office overseas.

4. CONSOLIDATED SUPERVISION REQUIREMENT

The Central Bank acknowledges that an essential element of successful supervision is its ability to supervise entire banking groups on a consolidated basis. This includes its ability to review banking and non-banking activities conducted by its licensees, either directly or indirectly (through branches, subsidiaries or representative offices) and activities conducted at both domestic and foreign offices. On an ongoing basis, the Central Bank aims to ensure that entities within banking and/or trust groups, on a consolidated basis:-

(a) are adequately organized;

(b) have adequate risk management systems and appropriately identify, limit and monitor risks inherent in their business activities;

(c) comply with capital adequacy and risk management requirements; and

(d) observe reporting duties and other requirements of the Central Bank and the host supervisory authority.

Effective consolidated supervision of overseas branches, subsidiaries and representative offices can not be achieved without the host regulator's cooperation in the exchange of supervisory and other information. Hence, *the Central Bank may require that the host regulator sign a Memorandum of Understanding with the Central Bank as condition of final approval to the establishment of a branch or subsidiary.* The Memorandum would generally be guided by the Central Bank's Model Memorandum of Understanding (*http://www.centralbankbahamas.com/public/MOU10.08.04.pdf*).

To further ensure the conduct of effective consolidated supervision, the Central Bank will not approve applications for the establishment of managed branches, subsidiaries and representative offices abroad unless:-

(a) the host regulator has no objection to its establishment; and

(b) the mind & management of the operations are conducted from the location of the licensee in The Bahamas.

VI. REQUIREMENTS FOR ESTABLISHING AN OVERSEAS BRANCH

Applications to establish an overseas branch should comprise of the following:-

(1) An application letter advising of:-

(a)

the purpose/rationale for establishing the branch;

(b) the proposed name of the branch;

(c) the proposed location of branch activities and whether a physical presence will be maintained at that location; and

(d) the principle activities which it seeks to carry on through the branch and the targeted clients;

(2) An indication of the level of the applicant's involvement and participation in managing and monitoring the business of the branch, (e.g. management and staff members performing duties);

(3) The pre and post acquisition organizational chart of the applicant's group;

(4) The proposed management[1];

(5) Information on the Statutory Auditors[1];

(6) Information on the Business Rules and Internal Organization[1];

(7) A comprehensive business plan[1];

(8) Board of Directors' Resolution authorizing the establishment of the branch; and

(9) A letter from the host regulator indicating their approval or non-objection to the establishment of a branch in their country.

VII. REQUIREMENTS FOR ESTABLISHING AN OVERSEAS SUBSIDIARY

Applications to establish a subsidiary abroad should comprise of the following:-

(1) An application letter advising of:-

(a) the name of the subsidiary;

(b) the place where it would established and whether it would maintain physical presence at that location;

(c) the rationale for establishing the subsidiary;

(d) the proposed ownership structure; and

(e) the short and long term objectives and business strategy of the subsidiary.;

(2) The business plan of the subsidiary (including primary business activities, projected financial statements, inclusive of balance sheet, profitability, capital adequacy, etc., for the first three years of business activity);

(3) The funding strategy of the subsidiary (including the extent of support from the parent, e.g. by means of injecting capital or issuing guarantees, letters of comfort or other assurances);

(4) The degree of the applicant's involvement and participation in managing and monitoring the business of the subsidiary, e.g. the number, due diligence & qualification particulars regarding the applicant's directors to be appointed to the Board of Directors;

(5) The statutory auditors, (i.e. name and address of proposed auditors and, where appropriate, details of arrangements for the review of the operations of the subsidiary);

(6) Information as to whether the subsidiary will be subject to the supervision of the financial sector regulator in the host country;

(7) Limits, controls and reporting procedures to be established by the applicant over the activities of the subsidiary;

(8) The management structure (e.g. proposed management, any specialised committees, etc.);

(9) The key business rules and internal control systems of the subsidiary;

(10) Organizational chart of the licensee's banking group, inclusive of the proposed subsidiary;

(11) The Board of Directors' Resolution authorizing the establishment of the subsidiary; and

(12) A letter from the host regulator indicating that their approval or non-objection to the establishment of a subsidiary in their country.

[1] *See requirements of the Central Bank of the Bahamas' General Information and Guidelines for Licence Applications for Banking and/or Trust Companies*

VIII. REQUIREMENTS FOR ACQUIRING FIFTY-ONE PERCENT OR MORE OF AN OVERSEAS ENTITY

Applications to acquire 51% or more of an entity abroad should comprise of the following:-

(1) An acquisition letter advising of:-

(a) the name of the entity;

(b) the place and date of incorporation or establishment;

(c) the primary activities of the entity;

(d) the rationale for acquiring the entity;

(e) the percentage of the shareholding to be acquired and the proposed ownership structure;

(f) the location of the operation and whether a physical presence will be maintained at that location; and

(g) the cost of acquisition (including any goodwill) or investment and how it will be funded.;

(2)

Financial information on the entity, inclusive of its audited financial statements for last three years and unaudited financials for the four quarters prior to the application date (e.g. balance sheet, profitability, capital adequacy ratios, etc. should be displayed);

(3)
The short and long term objectives and business strategy for the entity;

(4)
The business plan for the entity (including projected financial statements for the first three years of business activity);

(5)
The funding strategy of the entity (including the extent of support from the parent, e.g. by means of injecting capital or issuing guarantees, letters of comfort or other assurances);

(6)
The degree of the applicant's involvement and participation in managing and monitoring the business of the entity, (e.g. number, due diligence & qualification particulars regarding the applicant's directors to be appointed to the Board of Directors);

(7)
The statutory auditors, i.e. name and address of proposed auditors and, where appropriate, details of arrangements for the review of the operations of the entity;

(8)
Limits, controls and reporting procedures to be established by the applicant over the activities of the entity;

(9)
The proposed management structure (e.g. proposed management and any specialised committees);

(10)
The key business rules and internal control systems of the entity;

(11)
Information as to whether the subsidiary will be subject to the supervision of a banking regulator in its place of incorporation or establishment;

(12)
Organizational chart showing the structure of the direct and indirect shareholdings of the applicant analysed according to holdings of voting rights and/or shares;

(13)
Copy of the act, charter, certificate of incorporation and Memorandum and Articles of Association of the entity, as may be appropriate, verified by statutory declaration made by a director or the secretary duly authenticated under public seal of the jurisdiction in which the applicant has been incorporated;

(14)
The Board of Directors' Resolution authorizing the acquisition;

(15)
Certificate of Good Standing or equivalent document from the host regulator regarding the entity's history of performance and compliance; and

(16)
Letter from the host regulator indicating their approval or non-objection to the acquisition of the entity.

IX. REQUIREMENTS FOR ESTABLISHING AN OVERSEAS REPRESENTATIVE OFFICE

Applications to establish a representative office abroad should comprise of the following:-

(1)
An application letter:-

(a)

detailing the purpose for establishing a representative office and where it would be located (i.e. identification of the host country);and

(b)

describing how the representative office will be operated, i.e. primary functions, proposed personnel resources and administrative arrangements;

(2)

The Board of Directors' Resolution authorizing the establishment of a representative office in the host country;

(3)

Letter from host regulator indicating their approval or non-objection to the establishment of the representative office;

(4)

A written undertaking from the applicant or statement signed by the directors of the applicant that the conditions/requirements to the operation of a representative office will be adhered to;

(5)

Comprehensive information on the proposed resident manager of the representative office, inclusive of curriculum vitae, two character references, one financial reference and a police certificate;

(6)

A written acknowledgement from the resident manager of the representative office that is domiciled in the host country, stating that he/she understands the conditions applicable to the operation of the representative office and that he/she will uphold the conditions; and

(7)

The name and position of the officer in the applicant's office to whom the resident manager will report and an outline of how the operations of the representative office are to be monitored, to ensure that the conditions attached to the operation of the office are observed.

X.

OPERATING CONDITIONS FOR REPRESENTATIVE OFFICES

Where approval has been granted for the establishment of a representative office, the following conditions would normally apply:-

(**1**)

The business of the representative office must be confined to the conduct of purely liaison activities. Examples include conducting research into the host country's economy; liaising with customers of the licensee in the host country; the provision of factual information relating to the licensee's products and services upon request, etc.;

(2)

The representative office must not conduct any form of banking or trust business, such as: soliciting deposits; receiving deposits (which may include allowing customers of the licensee to deposit moneys into any account in the name of the representative office); granting loans; drawing, accepting, endorsing or discounting bills of exchange; establishing letters of credit; dealing in or issuing securities; dealing in derivatives products; buying or selling foreign exchange or executing any documentation for any of the foregoing purposes; acting as trustee or trust administrator;

(3)

The representative office may not engage in any commercial activity (other then pure marketing). It may not issue invoices for the services rendered. This means that the representative office is not allowed to act on its own behalf by using its employees or office for any kind of trading or business; nor may it be granted a power of attorney to act on the behalf of the licensee;

(4)

The representative office must not accept any orders on behalf of the licensee. Accordingly, the representative office's activities must be limited to transferring information to customers on behalf of the licensee, and to transferring offers, bids, acceptance, inquiries, etc., from customers to the licensee;

(5) The representative office must not engage directly in financial transactions (whether within The Bahamas or overseas), except transactions which are necessary for and incidental to the maintenance of its office in the host country;

(6) The name of the licensee should be used by the representative office only in conjunction with the description "representative office". This includes on office signage, letterheads, advertising, business cards, etc;

(7) The activities of the representative office must be kept separate from those of any financial enterprise operating in the host country;

(8) Any proposed closure or change in the location of a representative office, or change in the resident manager, must be advised to the Central Bank;

(9) The resident manager of the representative office must inform the Central Bank of any significant developments adversely affecting its or the licensee's financial soundness and/or reputation globally;

(10) The resident manager of the representative office must provide to the Central Bank a copy its financial accounts (in English) on an annual basis;

(11) The Central Bank must be advised of any change in the licensee's or resident manager's oversight of the representative office;

(12) Evidence that its representative office has been registered in the host country must be provided to the Central Bank as soon as possible after approval to open a representative office has been granted (also annual notification of registration may be necessary should the representative office registration be renewed annually);

(13) The licensee must provide the Central Bank with an annual statement confirming that the representative office is in compliance with the conditions of its approval. This statement should be signed by the executive of the licensee responsible for oversight of the representative office, or by the resident manager of the representative office;

(14) The licensee must ensure that the representative office comply with all applicable laws and must inform the Central Bank in writing of any breach or alleged breach of an applicable law and, in addition, must inform the Central Bank in writing of any event which results or might reasonably be expected to result in the cancellation or suspension of the representative office's registration; and

(15) The representative office must provide the Central Bank with information that it may request from time to time relating to the operations of the office.

XI. NOTICE OF REVOCATION

The Central bank may revoke its approval for the establishment or acquisition of an overseas branch, subsidiary or representative office should the Bank be of the opinion that the licensee's operations/viability and the interests of depositors or potential

depositors or trust clients are threatened by the continuation of the branch, subsidiary or representative office abroad.

XII. REJECTION OF APPLICATION

Notwithstanding submission of all required documents, the Central Bank reserves the right to reject an application if it is considered that the interests of depositors or potential depositors or trust clients of the licensee would be threatened by its establishment of an overseas branch, subsidiary or representative office.

GUIDELINES FOR THE ADMINISTRATION AND ULTIMATE TRANSFER OF DORMANT ACCOUNTS TO THE CENTRAL BANK OF THE BAHAMAS

I. INTRODUCTION

The Central Bank of The Bahamas ("the Central Bank") is responsible for the licensing, regulation and supervision of banks and trust companies operating in and from within The Bahamas pursuant to the Central Bank of The Bahamas Act, 2000 ("the CBA") and the Banks and Trust Companies Regulation Act, 2000 ("BTCRA"). The Central Bank has the duty, in collaboration with financial institutions, to promote and maintain high standards of conduct and management in the provision of banking and trust services.

All licensees are expected to adhere to the Central Bank's licensing and prudential requirements and ongoing supervisory programmes, including periodic on-site examinations, and required regulatory reporting. Licensees are also expected to conduct their affairs in conformity with all other Bahamian legal requirements.

II. PURPOSE

These Guidelines outline the Central Bank's minimum requirements for the identification, administration and investigation of inactive deposit accounts and the ultimate disposition of dormant account balances to the Central Bank.

Banks may develop their own documented internal policies and procedures but these Guidelines should be regarded as the minimum standard by which the Central Bank will assess the adequacy of such internal policies and procedures.

III. APPLICABILITY

Unless a specific exemption is granted by the Central Bank, the information and guidance contained in these Guidelines apply to all bank licensees in The Bahamas and to all deposit accounts for which banks are liable and in respect of which there has been no customer-initiated activity during a period of one (1) to seven (7) years.

IV. DEFINITIONS

For the purposes of these guidelines

"Customer initiated activity" means any transaction undertaken by a bank's customer in respect of a deposit account or any request for a statement or written acknowledgement received by the bank from a such a customer, For the purposes of these Guidelines, the debiting of a fee and the crediting of interest to a deposit account in accordance with any agreement made with the customer are not deemed to be customer-initiated activities.

"Deposit account" refers to the unpaid balance of money or its equivalent received or held by an institution from or on behalf of a person in the usual course of business and for which the institution has given or is obliged to give credit to that person's chequing, savings, demand or time account in respect of which it is primarily liable. Deposit accounts include deposit accounts of gold and silver bullion (section 20(3) of the BTCRA) and include deposit accounts denominated in any currency.

"Dormant account" refers to a deposit account in respect of which no customer-initiated activity has taken place during a period of seven (7) years.

"Inactive account" refers to a deposit account in respect of which no customer-initiated activity has taken place for a period of at least one (1) year and up to six (6) years.

"Statutory period" means the seven (7) year period during which no customer-initiated activity has taken place in respect of a deposit account.

"Transaction" means any customer-initiated deposit, withdrawal, exchange or transfer of funds (in whatever currency denominated), whether in cash, by cheque, payment order or other instrument or by electronic or other non-physical means.

V. INACTIVE ACCOUNTS

A. Administration of Inactive Accounts

Banks' policies and procedures should require that customers be informed, at the time of opening a deposit account and at intervals thereafter as necessary, of the implications of inactivity or dormancy of deposit accounts.

However, where a customer has not undertaken any customer-initiated activity on his or her deposit account for at least one (1) year, banks are expected to take reasonable steps to contact the customer to advise that the deposit account is about to be or has already been classified as inactive and to require that the customer either reactivate the deposit account or collect the funds held to the customer's credit.

If the customer fails to reactivate or close the deposit account the deposit account should be flagged on the client database systems as "inactive". Customers who have more than one deposit account with a bank should be required to undertake some customer-initiated activity in respect of each of the deposit accounts to prevent such deposit accounts from becoming inactive.

Ideally, a bank's systems should have the capability of segregating inactive accounts for reporting purposes. Systems should also have the capability of producing activity exception reporting of items processed through inactive accounts for management's review. Specific internal controls and authorizations should be applied to any transactions that pass through inactive accounts subsequent to their being classified as inactive, including any debit or credit affecting the accounts' inactive classification. Apparent activity on an inactive account should not normally by itself precipitate a change in the account's inactive status. The bank should take necessary steps to determine the validity of any transaction before the account is reclassified as "active".

In all instances, the bank must continue to accrue and pay interest on and manage deposit accounts in accordance with the terms of any agreement made with the customer.

B. Investigation of Inactive Accounts

In accordance with the know-your-customer requirements established by the Financial Transaction Reporting Act, 2000 as amended ("the FTRA"), and to facilitate investigation of deposit accounts that may become inactive, at the account opening stage banks should ensure that they obtain sufficient information to be able to locate persons to whom deposit account facilities are provided. Banks also have an obligation to ensure that they maintain their customers' current contact information throughout the business relationship.

Before a deposit account is initially deemed to be inactive, a thorough investigation should be conducted, with a view to (1) contacting the customer, (2) re-activating the account, and (3) making a final and correct disposition of the funds to the customer, if required. The bank's attempts to contact the customer should be properly documented and should be proportionate to the value of the customer's assets held by the bank. Proportionality is a determination for the bank to make. If the customer cannot be contacted, the bank is expected to continue to hold the funds governed by the controls discussed in these Guidelines and any agreement with the customer.

It is important for banks to ensure that customer confidentiality is upheld, in accordance with section 19 of the BTCRA, when they try to re-establish contact with their customers.

C. Monitoring of Inactive Accounts

Any debit or credit activity on an inactive account should be closely monitored and escalated to supervisory or management personnel for authorization prior to processing a transaction or prior to reclassifying the deposit account as active. As a subsequent review, activity and change-in-status system exception reports should be generated to allow senior management to monitor activity, including accounts entering and exiting inactive status.

All deposit accounts classified as inactive should be properly aged so that the bank and other interested parties would be able to determine the length of time that there has been no customer-initiated activity. As part of its on-going monitoring of inactive accounts a bank should seek to contact its customer pursuant to the following schedule:

- After the account has remained inactive for one (1) year;
- After the account has remained inactive for three (3) years; and
- After the account has remained inactive for six (6) years.

D. Administration Fees

As mandated by section 21 of the BTCRA, banks may only deduct fees related to the administration of inactive deposit accounts pursuant to express and specific agreement between the bank and the customer.

VI. DORMANT ACCOUNTS

A.

Requirements after Seven (7) Years

Banks that have a liability in respect of a deposit account on which no customer-initiated activity has taken place during the statutory period are required to pay to the Central Bank an amount equal to the amount owing by the bank in respect of the deposit account. In the case of a deposit made for a fixed period, the statutory period commences from the date on which the initial contractual period terminates. In the case of any other deposit accounts, the statutory period commences from the date on which the last customer-initiated activity took place in respect of the account. Payment to the Central Bank of an amount equal to the balance held on a dormant deposit account discharges the bank from all liability in respect of the account (section 20(1) of the BTCRA).

Banks are required, within two months after the end of the calendar year in which the statutory period expires, to remit to the Central Bank an amount equal to the amount held by the bank in respect of dormant accounts. Dormant accounts are to be transferred in the same currency in which they were held and the remitted amount should include any interest payable up to the date of transfer to the Central Bank.

B. Record Keeping

Banks transferring dormant account balances to the Central Bank are required, pursuant to section 20(2) of the BTCRA, to retain, until notified that they are no longer required, all registers, signature cards, signing authorities and other records relating to the dormant accounts, or microfilm or electronically stored copies thereof. This requirement is intended to enable banks to verify the entitlement of any person who may subsequently seek to recover the amount transferred to the Central Bank. For these purposes, the Central Bank would normally require the records to be maintained indefinitely or for a reasonable period after a claim is paid out to an entitled person in respect of dormant account balances transferred to the Central Bank.

Dormant account records maintained by banks should include evidence to demonstrate banks' attempts to contact their customers or investigate deposit accounts before or while they were classified as inactive. Such proof might include (1) mail to customers that has been returned and (2) notes to the file regarding the various attempts to make contact with the customer. The bank may wish to use alternative methods of investigation having regard to confidentiality requirements established under section 19 of the BTCRA.

Record Keeping Requirements Under the FTRA

Section 27(2) of the FTRA, as amended in 2008, mandates that a financial institution's liquidator, after the finalisation of a liquidation, is to maintain the records of the institution for the balance of any part of the five (5) year statutory period. For the purposes of the FTRA, the five (5) year statutory period is established under sections 23 and 24 of the FTRA which impose obligations on financial institutions to retain transaction records and identity verification records, respectively for five years after the completion of a transaction and five years after the end of a business relationship. Section 27(2) of the FTRA applies to dormant accounts.

C. Reporting Requirements

Banks are required to submit annual dormant accounts reports to the Central Bank via the Central Bank's Dormant Account Reporting System ('DARS"). This Guideline does not affect the right of confidentiality that currently exists between banks and their customers, and the information required to be submitted in respect of each dormant account is limited to the minimum sensitive information possible. No account holders names or addresses are submitted to the Central Bank.

The information required to be submitted includes: (1) the account type (checking, savings or fixed), (2) the account number, (3) the currency the account is denominated in,

(4) the account balance (include interest to date), (5) the branch code for the branch at which the account is held, and (6) the date of the last customer-initiated activity on the account.

VII. THE CENTRAL BANK'S ADMINISTRATION OF DORMANT ACCOUNTS

A. Payment of Interest

The Central Bank is empowered by section 24 of the CBA to pay interest on dormant account balances that are required to be transferred to it in accordance with section 20 of the BTCRA. As a matter of policy, the Central Bank will only pay interest on dormant accounts balances transferred to it where such balances bore interest up to the time of the transfer to the Central Bank.

B. Investment of Dormant Deposit Account Funds

Dormant account balances transferred to the Central Bank are invested and are accounted for and administered separately from other assets held by the Central Bank.

VIII. CLAIMING DORMANT ACCOUNT BALANCES

The right of entitled persons to claim funds transferred to the Central Bank is preserved under section 24 of the CBA. Persons claiming entitlement to dormant account balances in respect of which payments were made to the Central Bank must satisfy the bank at which the account was originally held of their entitlement to make such claim.

Establishing proof of entitlement may present little difficulty for a claimant who is the customer/account holder since the bank would have retained all signature cards, signing authorities and other records relating to the dormant account. However, difficulties may arise in cases where the claimant is a person other than the customer/account holder. In such cases the bank should take particular care to ensure that the claimant is the entitled person and should require the claimant to provide appropriate documentation in support of the claim.

Once satisfied of the claimant's entitlement to bring the claim, the bank should facilitate the claimant in obtaining the funds from the Central Bank. All claims to the Central Bank must be made in writing by the bank that transferred the funds to the Central Bank. The Central Bank would then confirm whether its records reflect that the payment was received from the bank and the amount of such payment. Once verified, the Central Bank would return the originally remitted amount to the bank together with any interest which may have accrued during the period that the dormant account balance was held at the Central Bank.

Banks should not refer claimants to the Central Bank in reference to dormant account balances transferred to the Central Bank. As pointed out in section VI (C) of these Guidelines, the Central

Bank does not receive any information capable of assisting it in verifying the identity of a claimant.

BUSINESS CONTINUITY GUIDELINES

I. INTRODUCTION

The Central Bank of The Bahamas ("*the Central Bank*") is responsible for the licensing, regulation and supervision of banks and trust companies operating in and from within The Bahamas pursuant to the Central Bank of The Bahamas Act, 2000 ("the CBA") and the Banks and Trust Companies Regulation Act, 2000 ("the BTCRA"). Additionally, the Central Bank has the duty, in collaboration with financial institutions, to promote and maintain high standards of conduct and management in the provision of banking and trust services.

All licensees are expected to adhere to the Central Bank's licensing and prudential requirements and ongoing supervisory programmes, including periodic on-site inspections, and required regulatory reporting. Licensees are also expected to conduct their affairs in conformity with all other Bahamian legal requirements.

II. PURPOSE

The events of September 11, 2001 in the United States, terrorist attacks in London, Madrid, Istanbul and elsewhere, outbreaks of Severe Acute Respiratory Syndrome (SARS) and potentially an Avian Flu epidemic have demonstrated the need for robust business continuity[1] arrangements across the globe. This holds true for The Bahamas, which has been subject to hurricanes and island wide electrical outages in recent times. Licensees could face critical operational disruptions due to natural disasters, island-wide electrical outages, faulty inter-bank electronic linkages and other computer problems, acts of terrorism and system failures among others, hence the need to secure business continuity by formulating action plans in advance to ensure quick recovery.

The quick recovery of business functions after disruptions is therefore crucial to maintaining public confidence in licensees and the financial system as a whole. Failing which, licensees may impair their ability to provide service to clients (i.e. customers, depositors or investors) and honour obligations to other financial sector intermediaries,

[1] **Business Continuity** is a state of continued, uninterrupted operation of a business

which may result in significant financial losses and potentially lead to a contagion effect on the financial system.

Business Continuity Management ("*BCM*") is a comprehensive approach that includes policies, procedures and standards for ensuring that specified operations can be maintained or recovered in a timely fashion in the event of a disruption and by extension, ensures that the functionality of the financial system as a whole is preserved. An important tangible evidence that an institution has embraced BCM is the formulation of an effective and workable Business Continuity Plan ("*BCP*"). The resilience[2] of a financial system to major operational disruptions[3] will be determined by the robustness of the BCPs of all participants within the system.

A BCP is a comprehensive written plan of action that sets out the procedures and establishes the processes and systems necessary to continue or restore the operation of an organization in the event of a disaster or major operational disruption. The BCP provides detailed guidance for implementing the recovery plan and outlines the roles and responsibilities in managing operational disruptions. It also defines triggers for activating licensees' BCPs and establishes business resumption teams for each core business process. An effective BCP should set out the decision-making authority in the event of an operational disruption and provide clear guidance regarding the succession of authority under those circumstances.

The Central Bank endorses the Joint Forum's[4] Paper *"High level principles for business continuity"* issued in August 2006 and has adopted the principles recommended by the Joint Forum in the aforesaid document. These Guidelines outline essential principles that the Central Bank will use as a benchmark in assessing the adequacy of its licensees' BCPs. The Central Bank expects all licensees to develop and implement workable and effective BCPs to ensure that specified operations can be maintained or recovered in a timely manner in the event of a disruption, consistent with the nature, size, and scope of their operations and complexity of their business. Additionally, BCPs are by their nature dynamic, evolving and changing as circumstances dictate and hence should be updated regularly. BCPs should also be flexible to address a broad range of potential disruptions.

III. APPLICABILITY

The Business Continuity Guidelines ("*the Guidelines*") are applicable to all banks and trust companies licensed to do business in and from within The Bahamas. The Guidelines are not intended to be prescriptive, nor does their broad applicability mean a "one-size

[2] **Resilience** is the ability of an organization, network, activity, process or financial system to absorb the impact of a major operational disruption and continue to maintain *critical operations or services*. [3] **A major operational disruption** is a high-impact disruption of normal business operations affecting a large metropolitan or geographic area and the adjacent communities that are economically integrated with it; and subsequently affects physical infrastructure. [4] The **Joint Forum** comprises the **Basel Committee on Banking Supervision**, the **International Organization of Securities Commissions (IOSCO)** and **the International Association of Insurance Supervisors**.

fits-all" approach to business continuity. A licensee's business continuity plan should be flexible, proportionate to its operational risk (arising from both internal and external sources) and tailored to the nature, size, scale and scope of its operations and complexity of its business.

In the case of a licensee that is a branch of a foreign bank, the head office's BCP will suffice, if the plan makes adequate provisions in line with these Guidelines for the licensee. In the case of a licensee that is a subsidiary of a banking group subject to consolidated supervision, the group's BCP will suffice, if the plan makes adequate provisions in line with these Guidelines for the licensee.

With respect to managed licensees, the ultimate responsibility for developing a BCP rests with the parent of the licensee. However, the Central Bank will accept an agreement between such licensees and their managing agents on business continuity and the plans in place to address the same.

Senior management should familiarize themselves with the Guidelines and understand the intent and implications of the principles. Licensees should also read the Guidelines in conjunction with the following documents:

- *Minimum Standards for the Outsourcing of Material Functions*

- *Aide Memoire on Handling Confidential Information Outside The Bahamas*

Licensees are encouraged to conduct a self-assessment of their BCPs against the principles outlined in the Guidelines and rectify deficiencies where applicable.

IV. Board and Senior Management Responsibilities

The Board of Directors of a licensee *("the Board")* is ultimately responsible for risk management and subsequently the BCP and the effectiveness of the same. The Board is also responsible for endorsing policies, standards and principles developed by senior management for business continuity management.

Senior management has ultimate responsibility for developing the BCP and ensuring that sufficient resources are devoted to implementing the plan. They must ensure that the necessary administrative support functions in the recovery effort, such as human resources, insurance, legal, security, etc., are in place. They should also ensure that all levels of staff are cognizant of the importance of BCPs and the role it plays in ensuring the continuous functioning of the institution and preserving the functionality of the financial system as a whole. Further, senior management is to ensure that employees responsible for managing the BCP are adequately trained and aware of their responsibilities.

Senior management should establish clearly which function of the licensee has responsibility for managing the entire process of business continuity planning (*"the BCP function")*. This information should be communicated to the Central Bank and will be the main point of contact between the Central Bank and the licensee with respect to the BCP.

The Board and senior management should ensure that an independent party, such as internal or external audit, tests the BCP and that any shortcomings identified are addressed in an appropriate and timely manner.

In support of the corporate governance process, senior management should submit a formal written annual statement to the Board indicating whether management is satisfied that the recovery strategies adopted are still valid, and whether the BCP management team and/or an independent party have properly tested the BCP during the period. This annual statement should be incorporated into the BCP, as the Central Bank will review it as a part of its on-site examinations.

V. DEVELOPMENT AND IMPLEMENTATION OF AN EFFECTIVE BCP

The development and implementation of a BCP should involve business impact analyses, business recovery strategies, testing, training programs, communications and crisis management.

1. Business Impact Analysis

The objective of the business impact analysis is to identify different kinds of risks to business continuity and to assess the potential impact of system failures on core business processes; assess the risks (infrastructure, operational, credit, liquidity, market, solvency, legal and reputational) arising from the total environment in which the licensee operates; assess the impact of materialized risks, i.e. loss of revenue, impact upon customers, regulatory issues, impact upon employees, and other business interruption consequences. Based on the results of the analysis, the licensee should be able to identify the scope of the critical services to be provided, define the minimum acceptable levels of service/outputs for each core business process and establish time-frames in which the services should be resumed.

2. Business Recovery Strategy

A business recovery strategy sets out recovery objectives and priorities that are based on the business impact analysis. Among other things, it establishes targets for the level of service a licensee would seek to deliver in the event of a disruption and the framework for ultimately resuming business operations. A recovery strategy should indicate the level of services that a licensee is able to provide at various stages during and after operational disruptions.

In formulating a recovery strategy, a licensee should assess the results of the business impact analysis as well as the interdependency among critical services, as these are key factors in determining the recovery priority of individual services and operations. Individual business and support functions should formulate their own recovery strategies on how to achieve the recovery of a minimum level of critical services within a specified time-frame. This involves the determination of an alternate site[5], total number of recovery personnel and the related workspace, applications and technology requirements, office facilities and vital records required for the provision of such levels of service.

3. Testing

The testing of a licensee's ability to recover critical operations and services as intended in the event of a disruption is an important component of an effective BCP. Licensees should test their BCPs, evaluate their effectiveness and update their BCPs as appropriate. The testing programme should validate the business continuity strategy; develop and document continuity test plans; prepare and execute tests; update disaster recovery plans and procedures. Testing should ideally be undertaken by the team who will operate the BCP to ensure effective team working, preparedness and awareness.

Changes in technology, business processes and staffs' roles and responsibilities can affect the appropriateness of the BCP; and ultimately the business continuity preparedness of licensees. Continuous reviews and meaningful testing of all components of the BCP should be undertaken to reflect the risks faced by the licensee, changing circumstances, to familiarize staff with the operation of the plan, to verify that the plan is practically workable, and to identify issues that need to be addressed that were not apparent during the planning stage.

An independent party, such as internal or external audit, should assess the effectiveness of the licensee's testing programme, review test results and report their findings to senior management and the board.

4. Training Programs

The roles and responsibilities of each member of the business continuity team should be clearly defined and delegated and appropriate training should be provided to these employees. All employees should also be cognizant of the importance of the BCP within the licensee's overall risk management framework and emergency contacts in the event of an operational disruption.

5. Communications

[5] An **alternate site** is a site held in readiness for use during a *business continuity* event to maintain an organization's *business continuity*. The term applies equally to work space or technology requirements.

The BCP should outline internal and external communication channels (with regulators, investors, customers, counterparties, business partners, service providers, staff, the media and other stakeholders) in the event of an operational disruption. The BCP should also incorporate comprehensive emergency communication protocols and procedures in the case of a major operational disruption.

Due to the increasing interdependency and interconnectedness among financial institutions within and across jurisdictions, a major operational disruption may extend beyond a licensee's national borders and may consequently affect affiliated institutions in other jurisdictions. This may ultimately impact the financial system of the home and other host countries. Licensees' BCPs should contain communication protocols for contacting relevant non-domestic financial authorities and institutions in these instances.

6. Crisis Management

An effective BCP should set out a crisis management process that serves as documented guidance to assist licensees in identifying potential crisis scenarios and develop procedures for managing these scenarios. Licensees should establish crisis management teams, comprised of senior management and heads of major support functions, to respond to and manage the various stages of a crisis

VI. ALTERNATE SITES FOR BUSINESS CONTINUITY

A useable functional alternate site is an integral component of all BCPs. Where the proposed alternate site is located outside The Bahamas, licensees are advised to assess the appropriateness of the jurisdiction for the temporary relocation of its operations. The First Schedule of the Financial Transactions Reporting Act 2000 (FTRA) provides a list of countries, which the Central Bank regards as being acceptable for this purpose. All other jurisdictions will be assessed by the Central Bank on a case-by-case basis.

In assessing the suitability of an alternate site, emphasis should be placed on location, speed of recovery and adequacy of resources. Alternate sites should be sufficiently distanced to avoid being affected by the same disaster as primary sites and should be readily accessible and available for occupancy within the time requirement specified within the BCP.

Business resumption very often relies on the recovery of technology resources that include applications, hardware equipment and network infrastructure as well as electronic records. Licensees should ensure that alternate sites are adequately equipped with the technology requirements that are needed for the recovery of individual business and support functions. Alternate sites should have sufficient technical equipment of appropriate model, size and capacity to meet recovery requirements. The site should also have adequate telecommunication facilities and pre-installed network connections to handle the expected volume of business. Emphasis should be placed on the resilience of critical technology equipment and facilities such as uninterruptible power supply.

Equipment and facilities at alternate sites should be subject to continuous monitoring and periodic maintenance and testing to keep them operational. Licensees should also ensure that alternate sites are equipped with the necessary personnel/manpower to perform recovery functions.

Copies of vital records should be readily accessible at alternate sites for emergency retrieval by personnel..

VII. CONFIDENTIALITY REQUIREMENTS AND RELOCATION OF OPERATIONS

Licensees are required to ensure that relevant Bahamas statutory requirements relating to client confidentiality continue to be observed, where the BCP will involve the disclosure of customer information to third parties. In this regard, licensees should have controls in place to ensure that the requirements of customer consent and customer data confidentiality are observed and proper safeguards are established to protect the integrity of client information. In the absence of the aforesaid customer consent, the licensee will be expected to enter into an agency agreement subject to the approval of the Central Bank, with the third party prior to the disclosure of customer information to the same.

Where the BCP also requires the temporary physical relocation of Bahamas-based staff and operations to another jurisdiction, licensees should take care in advance to ensure that the operations of those staff are not in breach of local law in that jurisdiction. The Central Bank, for its part, will do everything it can to seek the co-operation of local regulators, particularly in neighbouring jurisdictions; to do all they can to facilitate the smooth temporary transfer of business. Nevertheless, the Central Bank must be in a position continue its regulation/supervision of temporarily relocated functions outside The Bahamas.

VIII. APPROVAL/REPORTING REQUIREMENTS

Licensees are required to confirm to the Central Bank that they have a BCP in place, which should include the name and contact information for the BCP function. Furthermore, licensees are strongly encouraged to seek and obtain legal advice that their BCPs are in compliance with Bahamian legal requirements, particularly with respect to the preservation of client confidentiality. Central Bank approval is not required for activation of BCPs; however, licensees should inform the Inspector of Banks and Trust Companies as soon as possible after activation of the BCP.

In addition, the Board is required to include a statement in the Annual Corporate Governance Certificate confirming that the Board is satisfied that the recovery strategies adopted in the BCP are still valid, and that the licensee's BCP management team and/or an independent party have properly tested the BCP during the period.

The Central Bank will, in the course of its on-site examinations, review the BCP implemented, taking into consideration the extent to which a licensee has observed the Guidelines and its risk profile.

*****End*****

Appendix 1 Examples of Business Continuity Arrangements

- **Use of fault-tolerant or duplicated hardware;**
- **Adequate succession planning and staff orientation;**
- **Arrangements for the cover and accessibility of key staff members;**
- **Regular preventative maintenance of all computer and telecommunications components;**
- **On-site supplies of spare hardware and telecommunications components;**

- **Internally generated or uninterrupted power supplies;**
- **Fire detection and extinguishing systems;**
- **Predetermined emergency responses;**
- **Storage of important documents at both primary and secondary sites;**
- **Use of alternate processes and service providers;**
- **Insurance coverage against foreseeable disruptions;**
- **Developed procedures for the exchange of data by physical media (disks, tape, paper) in the event of telecommunications failure; and**
- **Capability to revert to old technology when new software, hardware or telecommunications component is implemented.**

Appendix 2 Components of an Effective Business Continuity Plan

Institutions should ensure that its business continuity plans are comprehensive, having been based on the business impact analysis and recovery strategies of the institution. Business continuity plans must be documented and should contain a series of key elements:

- a business continuity plan awareness program;
- a risk management program that includes clearly defined roles and responsibilities for resumption of business processes, including support organization functions;
- continuity plans for each core business process;
- procedures for mitigating interdependency risks between departments within the institution and with other institutions;
- trigger points and/or dates to activate the continuity plan;
- data back-up and recovery (hard copy and electronic);
- processes to deal with the loss of information that are not available from backup data;
- manual processes for continuing operations until technology is repaired;
- accessible recovery locations and emergency operations centres;
- a process for automatically switching telephone and date lines;
- testing of the business continuity plans on an end-to-end basis;
- a review process to ensure that the business continuity plan is feasible and up-todate; and
- specific incident/ emergency management responses that identify assembly areas at a safe distance from the site of the incident; and
- annual statement by senior management on whether the recovery strategies adopted are still valid and whether the documented BCPs are properly tested and maintained: and
- regulatory approval.

BUSINESS TRAVEL

BAHAMAS 'BUSINESS CUSTOMS:

The national language of The Bahamas is English, sometimes spoken with a distinctive local accent and the use of colorful local expressions. Due to the proximity of The Bahamas to the US and the extensive familiarity of most Bahamians with Americans and American culture, business customs tend to be similar to those in the United States. Business dress is more formal in The Bahamas than elsewhere in the Caribbean or in Florida; a business suit and tie is recommended for men and conservative business dress for women. Business attire generally follows the standards of the northeastern United States. Bahamians shake hands upon meeting, sometimes exchange business cards, and address first-time business acquaintances by their last names. Conversations generally move to a first-name basis a bit more slowly than in the United States. Firm appointments for business meetings are advisable. Although Bahamians are not punctual for meetings, foreign visitors should be punctual.

In addition, The Bahamas is very much a consensus-driven society, in which people often disguise personal feelings beneath a surface cordiality. Business meetings in The Bahamas tend to be very pleasant and Bahamians often end a meeting with an air of agreement even if real differences remain. Thus, Bahamian partners may still retain some reservations even after meetings that ended with firm handshakes and pleasantries. Bahamians at the middle levels of business or government must often gain final approval from more senior officials.

Bahamian businesses tend to operate on a tighter financial margin than their American counterparts, often juggling financing from one commitment to another. Therefore, for initial or large sales, a businessman should require a deposit against future payment for goods or services delivered, and expect that some delays may occur with subsequent payments.

Business lunches are common in The Bahamas, and invitations to discuss matters over lunch in a quiet restaurant are common practice. Bahamians tend not to drink very much at business lunches and usually expect the lunch to last between an hour and an hour-and-a-half. Business dinners are relatively rare, and Bahamians do not generally invite new acquaintances to their homes. When they do so, dinners at the homes of well-to-do Bahamians tend to be elaborate and formal affairs, at which business attire for men and conservative evening wear for women is appropriate. A small gift for the hostess, such as flowers, and a follow-up thank you note are appropriate acknowledgments.

Acceptable topics of conversation include: sports; the tourist business; the beauty of the islands; the weather; and unique or distinctive aspects of Bahamian culture such as the local cuisine, junkanoo, local music, art, architecture, and history. While Bahamians are comfortable with discussing most topics, visitors to The Bahamas should avoid discussing drug trafficking and race relations during initial contacts.

Since much of Bahamian social life revolves around church, an invitation to a church service is a sign of personal respect and affection. Many churches in The Bahamas have proud traditions of gospel choir singing, and church services can be quite lively. Dress at church services is usually formal with conservative business suits for men and colorful, sometimes elaborate dresses for women.

Travel information and visas: American citizens do not require a passport or visa to enter The Bahamas, but proof of citizenship such as a birth certificate or voter registration card accompanied by a photo ID is required, as well as a return ticket to the United States. In mid-1996 there were no current travel restrictions for The Bahamas. American citizens traveling to an area where they may have some concern about local conditions can contact the State Department's citizens emergency center at tel. (202) 647-5225 for the most up-to-date information.

Business infrastructure: Both Nassau and Freeport boast a wide variety of excellent hotels and resorts. Although Bahamian hotels are more used to catering to the vacationer rather than the business traveler, many large hotels have business centers.

Even hotels without such centers will be happy to arrange for fax transmissions, office and conference facilities, and other business services. Electricity is 110 v, 60 Hz (US standard). Taxis are plentiful near hotels and downtown, and radio taxi services are available. Some taxi drivers are willing, for a prearranged fee, to spend the entire day with a single customer. Rental cars are also available, albeit they are far more expensive than the American norm. Bahamians drive on the left side of the road, as in Great Britain, even though most cars in The Bahamas are imported from or through the United States and have left-hand drive (US standard). Nassau has two large, hospitals, and there is one in Freeport; Nassau's privately-owned Doctors Hospital is widely regarded as the best medical facility in The Bahamas. No special health precautions or vaccinations are necessary.

Tap water is potable but brackish; most Bahamians drink one of the locally-produced brands of bottled water. As major resorts, both Nassau and Freeport have a wide variety of restaurants ranging from local franchises of American fast-food chains to expensive five-star gourmet places. Local cuisine tends to favor freshly-caught seafood, particularly using grouper, lobster (locally known as "crawfish"), and conch (a Caribbean shellfish), but American and ethnic cuisine such as Chinese and Italian are also available.

Bahamian Holidays:

- New Year's Day (January 1)
- Good Friday (Variable)
- Easter Monday (Variable)
- Whit Monday (Seven Weeks After Easter)
- Bahamian Labor Day (First Monday In June)
- Independence Day (July 10)
- Emancipation Day (First Monday In August)
- Discovery Day (October 12)
- Christmas Day (December 25)
- Boxing Day (December 26)

Holidays which fall on Saturday or Sunday are usually observed on the following Monday. Persons present in The Bahamas on the night of December 25-26 or December 31-January 1 can enjoy a unique cultural experience by purchasing tickets to the annual junkanoo parade in downtown Nassau, a carnival similar to Mardi Gras of which Bahamians are justly proud.

SUPPLEMENT

BAHAMAS GOVERNMENT REGISTERED STOCK

Bahamas Government Registered Stock (BGRS), which are issued under the Bahamas Registered Stock Act, 1973, are long-term securities with current maturities ranging up to 30 years. With a minimum investment of B$100, they are issued at par in multiples of 100, and carry varying interest rates, usually tied to the Bahamian prime lending rate. The Central Bank of The Bahamas is the official Registrar of securities for the Bahamas Government. As at end-August 2009, total BGRS outstanding was $2,303.9193 million.

Issue	Name	Amount B$Ms	Interest Rate	Annual Pymt Dates	Maturity Dates
46	BGRS 2010 - 2014 B$30.0 Milllion	10	Prime Rate + 7/8%	26/Feb & 26/Aug	2010-02-26
56	BGRS 2007 - 2018 B$26.0 Million	6	Prime Rate + 5/16%	26/Feb & 26/Aug	2010-02-26
42	BGRS 2007 - 2011 B$55.0 Million	10	6.75%	25/Apr & 25/Oct	2010-04-25
45	BGRS 2010 - 2011 B$29.0 Million	14	Prime Rate + 13/16%	14/Jun 7 & 14/Dec	2010-06-14
40	BGRS 2010 - 2012 B$47.0 Million	5	Prime Rate + 5/8%	24/Feb & 24/Aug	2010-08-24
48	BGRS 2004 - 2016 B$45.0 Million	5	Prime Rate + 7/8%	23/Mar & 23/Sep	2010-09-23
41	BGRS 2009 - 2010 B$20.0 Million	10	Prime Rate + 5/8%	05/Apr & 05/Oct	2010-10-05
42	BGRS 2007 - 2011 B$55.0 Million	10	7.00%	25/Apr & 25/Oct	2011-04-25
47	BGRS 2007 - 2011 B$40.0 Million	10	Prime Rate + 15/16%	07/May & 07/Nov	2011-05-07
45	BGRS 2010 - 2011 B$29.0 Million	15	Prime Rate + 7/8%	14/Jun 7 & 14/Dec	2011-06-14
58	BGRS 2011 - 2019 B$50.0 Million	10	Prime Rate + 7/32%	21/Jan & 21/Jul	2011-07-21
54	BGRS 2011 - 2018 B$50.0 Million	10	Prime Rate + 3/8%	10/Feb & 10/Aug	2011-08-10
40	BGRS 2010 - 2012 B$47.0 Million	15	Prime Rate + 11/16%	24/Feb & 24/Aug	2011-08-24
53	BGRS 2012 - 2014 B$21.0 Million	10	Prime Rate + 7/16%	08/Apr & 08/Oct	2012-04-08
40	BGRS 2010 - 2012 B$47.0 Million	27	Prime Rate + 3/4%	24/Feb & 24/Aug	2012-08-24
18	BGRS 1996 - 2012 B$25.0 Million	20	8.75%	8/Apr & 8/Oct	2012-10-08
46	BGRS 2010 - 2014 B$30.0 Milllion	10	Prime Rate + 1 1/16%	26/Feb & 26/Aug	2013-02-26
19	BGRS 1993 - 2013 B$35.0	20	9.00%	15/Mar & 15/Sep	2013-03-15

	Million				
44	BGRS 2013 B$25.0 Million	25	Prime Rate + 1%	18/May & 18/Nov	2013-05-18
58	BGRS 2011 - 2019 B$50.0 Million	10	Prime Rate + 9/32%	21/Jan & 21/Jul	2013-07-21
48	BGRS 2004 - 2016 B$45.0 Million	10	Prime Rate + 1 1/16%	23/Mar & 23/Sep	2013-09-23
61	BGRS 2013 - 2020 B$25.8 Million	5.8	Prime Rate + 9/32%	25/Apr & 25/Oct	2013-10-25
46	BGRS 2010 - 2014 B$30.0 Milllion	10	Prime Rate + 1 1/8%	26/Feb & 26/Aug	2014-02-26
53	BGRS 2012 - 2014 B$21.0 Million	11	Prime Rate + 1/2%	08/Apr & 08/Oct	2014-04-08
50	BGRS 2014 - 2017 B$40.0 Million	10	Prime Rate + 1 1/16%	22/May & 22/Nov	2014-05-22
51	BGRS 2014 - 2017 B$50.0 Million	10	Prime Rate + 17/32%	15/Jan & 15/Jul	2014-07-15
68	BGRS 2014 - 2023 B$75.0 Million	15	Prime Rate + 3/32%	21/Jan & 21/Jul	2014-07-21
54	BGRS 2011 - 2018 B$50.0 Million	10	Prime Rate + 15/32%	10/Feb & 10/Aug	2014-08-10
43	BGRS 2007 - 2014 B$65.0 Million	15	6.63%	20/Mar & 20/Sep	2014-09-20
49	BGRS 2015 - 2016 B$30.0 Million	15	Prime Rate + 1/8%	26/Feb & 26/Aug	2015-02-26
50	BGRS 2014 - 2017 B$40.0 Million	10	Prime Rate + 1/8%	22/May & 22/Nov	2015-05-22
51	BGRS 2014 - 2017 B$50.0 Million	10	Prime Rate + 9/16%	15/Jan & 15/Jul	2015-07-15
70	BGRS 2015 - 2024 B$100.0 Million	10	Prime Rate + 1/32%	29/Jan & 29/Jul	2015-07-29
48	BGRS 2004 - 2016 B$45.0 Million	10	Prime Rate + 1 3/16%	23/Mar & 23/Sep	2015-09-23
52	BGRS 2015 - 2017 B$50.0 Million	15	Prime Rate + 1/8%	15/Apr & 15/Oct	2015-10-15
71	BGRS 2015 - 2024 #2 B$100.0 Million	10	Prime Rate + 1/32%	22/Apr & 22/Oct	2015-10-22
66	BGRS 2015 - 2022 B$65.0 Million	15	Prime Rate + 3/16%	4/Jun & 4/Dec	2015-12-04
49	BGRS 2015 - 2016 B$30.0 Million	15	Prime Rate + 1 3/16%	26/Feb & 26/Aug	2016-02-26
50	BGRS 2014 - 2017 B$40.0 Million	10	Prime Rate + 1 3/16%	22/May & 22/Nov	2016-05-22
51	BGRS 2014 - 2017 B$50.0 Million	10	Prime Rate + 19/32%	15/Jan & 15/Jul	2016-07-15
58	BGRS 2011 - 2019 B$50.0 Million	10	Prime Rate + 3/8%	21/Jan & 21/Jul	2016-07-21
70	BGRS 2015 - 2024 B$100.0 Million	10	Prime Rate + 1/16%	29/Jan & 29/Jul	2016-07-29

48	BGRS 2004 - 2016 B$45.0 Million	10	Prime Rate + 1 1/4%	23/Mar & 23/Sep	2016-09-23
52	BGRS 2015 - 2017 B$50.0 Million	15	Prime Rate + 3/16%	15/Apr & 15/Oct	2016-10-15
71	BGRS 2015 - 2024 #2 B$100.0 Million	15	Prime Rate + 1/16%	22/Apr & 22/Oct	2016-10-22
59	BGRS 2016 - 2019 B$28.0 Million	8	Prime Rate + 3/8%	23/May & 23/Nov	2016-11-23
50	BGRS 2014 - 2017 B$40.0 Million	10	Prime Rate + 1 1/4%	22/May & 22/Nov	2017-05-22
51	BGRS 2014 - 2017 B$50.0 Million	20	Prime Rate + 5/8%	15/Jan & 15/Jul	2017-07-15
68	BGRS 2014 - 2023 B$75.0 Million	15	Prime Rate + 3/16%	21/Jan & 21/Jul	2017-07-21
54	BGRS 2011 - 2018 B$50.0 Million	10	Prime Rate + 9/16%	10/Feb & 10/Aug	2017-08-10
65	BGRS 2017 - 2022 B$60.0 Million	7	Prime Rate + 1/4%	6/Mar & 6/Sep	2017-09-06
52	BGRS 2015 - 2017 B$50.0 Million	20	Prime Rate + 1/4%	15/Apr & 15/Oct	2017-10-15
71	BGRS 2015 - 2024 #2 B$100.0 Million	15	Prime Rate + 3/32%	22/Apr & 22/Oct	2017-10-22
56	BGRS 2007 - 2018 B$26.0 Million	10	Prime Rate + 9/16%	26/Feb & 26/Aug	2018-02-26
58	BGRS 2011 - 2019 B$50.0 Million	10	Prime Rate + 7/16%	21/Jan & 21/Jul	2018-07-21
70	BGRS 2015 - 2024 B$100.0 Million	10	Prime Rate + 1/8%	29/Jan & 29/Jul	2018-07-29
54	BGRS 2011 - 2018 B$50.0 Million	20	Prime Rate + 19/32%	10/Feb & 10/Aug	2018-08-10
60	BGRS 2018 - 2020 B$30.0 Million	10	Prime Rate + 7/16%	21/Mar & 21/Sep	2018-09-21
55	BGRS 2008 - 2018 B$30 Million	10	Prime Rate + 19/32%	21/Apr & 21/Oct	2018-10-21
59	BGRS 2016 - 2019 B$28.0 Million	10	Prime Rate + 7/16%	23/May & 23/Nov	2018-11-23
83	BGRS 2018, 2020, 2027 & 2030 B$31.5009 Million	10	Prime Rate + 1/32%	28/May & 28/Nov	2018-11-28
63	BGRS 2018 - 2021 B$40.9478 Million	10	Prime Rate + 15/32%	12/Jun & 12/Dec	2018-12-12
67	BGRS 2019 - 2023 B$61.1 Million	15	Prime Rate + 1/4%	8/Apr & 8/Oct	2019-04-08
58	BGRS 2011 - 2019 B$50.0 Million	10	Prime Rate + 15/32%	21/Jan & 21/Jul	2019-07-21
62	BGRS 2019 - 2021 B$34.3 Million	10	Prime Rate + 1/2%	30/Jan & 30/Jul	2019-07-30
65	BGRS 2017 - 2022 B$60.0 Million	8	Prime Rate + 5/16%	6/Mar & 6/Sep	2019-09-06
60	BGRS 2018 - 2020 B$30.0	10	Prime Rate +	21/Mar & 21/Sep	2019-09-21

	Million		15/32%		
71	BGRS 2015 - 2024 #2 B$100.0 Million	15	Prime Rate + 5/32%	22/Apr & 22/Oct	2019-10-22
61	BGRS 2013 - 2020 B$25.8 Million	10	Prime Rate + 15/32%	25/Apr & 25/Oct	2019-10-25
59	BGRS 2016 - 2019 B$28.0 Million	10	Prime Rate + 15/32%	23/May & 23/Nov	2019-11-23
63	BGRS 2018 - 2021 B$40.9478 Million	10	Prime Rate + 1/2%	12/Jun & 12/Dec	2019-12-12
64	BGRS 2020 - 2021 B$20.465 Million	10	Prime Rate + 17/32%	26/Apr & 26/Oct	2020-04-26
73	BGRS 2020 - 2025 B$40.4666 Million	5.4666	Prime Rate + 1/8%	28/Jun & 28/Dec	2020-06-28
70	BGRS 2015 - 2024 B$100.0 Million	10	Prime Rate +3/16%	29/Jan & 29/Jul	2020-07-29
62	BGRS 2019 - 2021 B$34.3 Million	10	Prime Rate + 17/32%	30/Jan & 30/Jul	2020-07-30
65	BGRS 2017 - 2022 B$60.0 Million	15	Prime Rate + 11/32%	6/Mar & 6/Sep	2020-09-06
60	BGRS 2018 - 2020 B$30.0 Million	10	Prime Rate + 1/2%	21/Mar & 21/Sep	2020-09-21
61	BGRS 2013 - 2020 B$25.8 Million	10	Prime Rate + 1/2%	25/Apr & 25/Oct	2020-10-25
83	BGRS 2018, 2020, 2027 & 2030 B$31.5009 Million	6.5009	Prime Rate + 3/32%	28/May & 28/Nov	2020-11-28
66	BGRS 2015 - 2022 B$65.0 Million	15	Prime Rate + 11/32%	4/Jun & 4/Dec	2020-12-04
63	BGRS 2018 - 2021 B$40.9478 Million	10	Prime Rate + 17/32%	12/Jun & 12/Dec	2020-12-12
76	BGRS 2021, 2024, 2025 and 2026 B$75.0 Million	10	Prime Rate + 5/32%	18/Jan. & 18/Jul.	2021-01-18
67	BGRS 2019 - 2023 B$61.1 Million	15	Prime Rate + 5/16%	8/Apr & 8/Oct	2021-04-08
64	BGRS 2020 - 2021 B$20.465 Million	10.465	Prime Rate + 17/32%	26/Apr & 26/Oct	2021-04-26
70	BGRS 2015 - 2024 B$100.0 Million	10	Prime Rate + 7/32%	29/Jan & 29/Jul	2021-07-29
62	BGRS 2019 - 2021 B$34.3 Million	14.3	Prime Rate + 9/16%	30/Jan & 30/Jul	2021-07-30
65	BGRS 2017 - 2022 B$60.0 Million	15	Prime Rate + 3/8%	6/Mar & 6/Sep	2021-09-06
75	BGRS 2021 - 2025 B$75.0 Million	15	Prime Rate + 5/32%	7/Mar & 7/Sep	2021-09-07
78	BGRS 2021-2026 B$100.0 Million	10	Prime Rate + 5/32%	22/Mar & 22/Sep	2021-09-22
66	BGRS 2015 - 2022 B$65.0 Million	15	Prime Rate + 3/8%	4/Jun & 4/Dec	2021-12-04
63	BGRS 2018 - 2021 B$40.9478 Million	10.9	Prime Rate + 9/16%	12/Jun & 12/Dec	2021-12-12

67	BGRS 2019 - 2023 B$61.1 Million	15	Prime Rate + 11/32%	8/Apr & 8/Oct	2022-04-08
72	BGRS 2022 - 2025 B$40.0 Million	10	Prime Rate + 7/32%	27/Apr & 27/Oct	2022-04-27
68	BGRS 2014-2023 B$75.0 Million	20	Prime Rate + 11/32%	21/Jan & 21/Jul	2022-07-21
70	BGRS 2015 - 2024 B$100.0 Million	10	Prime Rate + 1/4%	29/Jan & 29/Jul	2022-07-29
65	BGRS 2017 - 2022 B$60.0 Million	15	Prime Rate + 13/32%	6/Mar & 6/Sep	2022-09-06
75	BGRS 2021-2025 B$75.0 Million	15	Prime Rate + 3/16%	7/Mar & 7/Sep	2022-09-07
78	BGRS 2021-2026 B$100.0 Million	10	Prime Rate + 3/16%	22/Mar & 22/Sep	2022-09-22
71	BGRS 2015 - 2024 #2 B$100.0 Million	15	Prime Rate + 1/4%	22/Apr & 22/Oct	2022-10-22
66	BGRS 2015 - 2022 B$65.0 Million	20	Prime Rate + 13/32%	4/Jun & 4/Dec	2022-12-04
69	BGRS 2023 - 2024 B$23.2898 Million	10	Prime Rate + 11/32%	09/Feb & 09/Aug	2023-02-09
67	BGRS 2019 - 2023 B$61.1 Million	16.1	Prime Rate + 3/8%	8/Apr & 8/Oct	2023-04-08
72	BGRS 2022 - 2025 B$40.0 Million	10	Prime Rate + 1/4%	27/Apr & 27/Oct	2023-04-27
68	BGRS 2014- 2023 B$75.0 Million	25	Prime Rate + 3/8%	21/Jan & 21/Jul	2023-07-21
70	BGRS 2015 - 2024 B$100.0 Million	20	Prime Rate + 9/32%	29/Jan & 29/Jul	2023-07-29
75	BGRS 2021-2025 B$75.0 Million	15	Prime Rate + 7/32%	7/Mar & 7/Sep	2023-09-07
78	BGRS 2021-2026 B$100.0 Million	20	Prime Rate + 7/32%	22/Mar & 22/Sep	2023-09-22
71	BGRS 2015-2024#2 B$100.0 Million	15	Prime Rate + 9/32%	22/Apr & 22/Oct	2023-10-22
76	BGRS 2021, 2024, 2025 and 2026 B$75.0 Million	20	Prime Rate + 1/4%	18/Jan. & 18/Jul.	2024-01-18
69	BGRS 2023 - 2024 B$23.2898 Million	13.2898	Prime Rate + 3/8%	09/Feb & 09/Aug	2024-02-09
72	BGRS 2022 - 2025 B$40.0 Million	10	Prime Rate + 9/32%	27/Apr & 27/Oct	2024-04-27
77	BGRS 2024, 2025 and 2026 B$51.645 Million	11.645	Prime Rate + 1/4%	04/May & 04/Nov	2024-05-04
73	BGRS 2020 - 2025 B$40.4666 Million	10	Prime Rate + 1/4%	28/Jun & 28/Dec	2024-06-28
70	BGRS 2015 - 2024 B$100.0 Million	20	Prime Rate + 5/16%	29/Jan & 29/Jul	2024-07-29
75	BGRS 2021-2025 B$75.0 Million	15	Prime Rate + 1/4%	7/Mar & 7/Sep	2024-09-07
78	BGRS 2021-2026 B$100.0	15	Prime Rate +	22/Mar & 22/Sep	2024-09-22

	Million		1/4%		
71	BGRS 2015 - 2024 #2 B$100.0 Million	15	Prime Rate + 5/16%	22/Apr & 22/Oct	2024-10-22
76	BGRS 2021, 2024, 2025 and 2026 B$75.0 Million	20	Prime Rate + 9/32%	18/Jan. & 18/Jul.	2025-01-18
72	BGRS 2022 - 2025 B$40.0 Million	10	Prime Rate + 5/16%	27/Apr & 27/Oct	2025-04-27
77	BGRS 2024, 2025 and 2026 B$51.645 Million	15	Prime Rate + 9/32%	04/May & 04/Nov	2025-05-04
73	BGRS 2020 - 2025 B$40.4666 Million	25	Prime Rate + 9/32%	28/Jun & 28/Dec	2025-06-28
74	BGRS 2025 B$25.8942 Million	25.8942	Prime Rate + 3/8%	30/Jun & 30/Dec	2025-06-30
75	BGRS 2021-2025 B$75.0 Million	15	Prime Rate + 9/32%	7/Mar & 9/Sep	2025-09-07
78	BGRS 2021-2026 B$100.0 Million	20	Prime Rate + 9/32%	22/Mar & 22/Sep	2025-09-22
76	BGRS 2021, 2024, 2025 and 2026 B$75.0 Million	25	Prime Rate + 5/16%	18/Jan. & 18/Jul.	2026-01-18
79	BGRS 2026 & 2027 B$50.0 Million	25	Prime Rate + 9/32%	28/Mar & 28/Sep	2026-03-28
77	BGRS 2024, 2025 and 2026 B$51.645 Million	25	Prime Rate + 5/16%	04/May & 04/Nov	2026-05-04
78	BGRS 2021-2026 B$100.0 Million	25	Prime Rate + 5/16%	22/Mar & 22/Sep	2026-09-22
79	BGRS 2026 & 2027 B$50.0 Million	25	Prime Rate + 5/16%	28/Mar & 28/Sep	2027-03-28
80	BGRS 2027 B$45.284 Million	45.284	Prime Rate + 5/16%	9/May & 9/Nov	2027-05-09
81	BGRS 2027 & 2035-2037 B$100.0 Million	10	Prime Rate + 5/16%	26/Jan & 26/Jul	2027-07-26
82	BGRS 2027-2029 B$35.0 Million	10	Prime Rate + 5/16%	08/Apr & 08/Oct	2027-10-08
83	BGRS 2018, 2020, 2027 & 2030 B$31.5009 Million	10	Prime Rate + 5/16%	28/May & 28/Nov	2027-11-28
85	BGRS 2028 - 2033 B$107.226 Million	15	Prime Rate + 1/4%	19/Jan & 19/Jul	2028-01-19
86	BGRS 2028 - 2036 B$150.0 Million	20	Prime Rate + 1/8%	27/Feb & 27/Aug	2028-08-27
84	BGRS 2028 - 2033 B$100.0 Million	10	Prime Rate + 9/32%	22/Mar & 22/Sept	2028-09-22
82	BGRS 2027-2029 B$35.0 Million	10	Prime Rate + 11/32%	08/Apr & 08/Oct	2028-10-08
85	BGRS 2028 - 2033 B$107.226 Million	15	Prime Rate + 9/32%	19/Jan & 19/Jul	2029-01-19
86	BGRS 2028 - 2036 B$150.0 Million	20	Prime Rate + 9/64%	27/Feb & 27/Aug	2029-08-27
84	BGRS 2028 - 2033 B$100.0 Million	15	Prime Rate + 5/16%	22/Mar & 22/Sept	2029-09-22

82	BGRS 2027-2029 B$35.0 Million	15	Prime Rate + 3/8%	08/Apr & 08/Oct	2029-10-08
85	BGRS 2028 - 2033 B$107.226 Million	17.226	Prime Rate + 5/16%	19/Jan & 19/Jul	2030-01-19
86	BGRS 2028 - 2036 B$150.0 Million	15	Prime Rate + 5/32%	27/Feb & 27/Aug	2030-08-27
84	BGRS 2028 - 2033 B$100.0 Million	15	Prime Rate + 11/32%	22/Mar & 22/Sept	2030-09-22
83	BGRS 2018, 2020, 2027 & 2030 B$31.5009 Million	5	Prime Rate + 13/32%	28/May & 28/Nov	2030-11-28
85	BGRS 2028 - 2033 B$107.226 Million	20	Prime Rate + 11/32%	19/Jan & 19/Jul	2031-01-19
86	BGRS 2028 - 2036 B$150.0 Million	15	Prime Rate + 11/64%	27/Feb & 27/Aug	2031-08-27
84	BGRS 2028 - 2033 B$100.0 Million	20	Prime Rate + 3/8%	22/Mar & 22/Sept	2031-09-22
85	BGRS 2028 - 2033 B$107.226 Million	20	Prime Rate + 3/8%	19/Jan & 19/Jul	2032-01-19
86	BGRS 2028 - 2036 B$150.0 Million	20	Prime Rate + 3/16%	27/Feb & 27/Aug	2032-08-27
84	BGRS 2028 - 2033 B$100.0 Million	20	Prime Rate + 13/32%	22/Mar & 22/Sept	2032-09-22
85	BGRS 2028 - 2033 B$107.226 Million	20	Prime Rate + 13/32%	19/Jan & 19/Jul	2033-01-19
86	BGRS 2028 - 2036 B$150.0 Million	20	Prime Rate + 13/64%	27/Feb & 27/Aug	2033-08-27
84	BGRS 2028 - 2033 B$100.0 Million	20	Prime Rate + 7/16%	22/Mar & 22/Sept	2033-09-22
86	BGRS 2028 - 2036 B$150.0 Million	20	Prime Rate + 7/32%	27/Feb & 27/Aug	2034-08-27
81	BGRS 2027 & 2035-2037 B$100.0 Million	30	Prime Rate + 9/16%	26/Jan & 26/Jul	2035-07-26
86	BGRS 2028 - 2036 B$150.0 Million	10	Prime Rate + 15/64%	27/Feb & 27/Aug	2035-08-27
81	BGRS 2027 & 2035-2037 B$100.0 Million	30	Prime Rate + 19/32%	26/Jan & 26/Jul	2036-07-26
86	BGRS 2028 - 2036 B$150.0 Million	10	Prime Rate + 1/4%	27/Feb & 27/Aug	2036-08-27
81	BGRS 2027 & 2035-2037 B$100.0 Million	30	Prime Rate + 5/8%	26/Jan & 26/Jul	2037-07-26

SELECTED US AND COUNTRY CONTACTS

BAHAMAS 'US EMBASSY TRADE RELATED CONTACTS

US Embassy Nassau
Economic-Commercial Section
P.O. Box 9009
Miami, FL 33159
Tel:(242)323-7180
Fax:(242)328-3495

US Department of Commerce
Desk Officer for The Bahamas

Room H 3021
Washington, DC 20230
Tel:(202)377-2527

US Department of Agriculture
Office of International Cooperation and Development
Private Sector Relations
McGregor Building
Room 343
14th and Independence Ave., SW
Washington, DC 20250-4300
Tel:(202)653-7917

Overseas Private Investment Corporation
1615 M Street, NW
Washington, DC 20527
Tel:(202)457-7200

Trade and Development Program
US Department of State
2201 C Street, NW
Washington, DC 20523
Tel:(202)875-4357

BAHAMAS 'KEY BAHAMIAN GOVERNMENT OFFICES"

The Bahamas Investment Authority
Office of the Prime Minister
P. O. Box CB-10980
Nassau, Bahamas

Embassy of the Commonwealth of The Bahamas
2220 Massachusetts Avenue, NW
Washington, DC 20008
Tel:(202)319-2660

Bahamas Agricultural and Industrial Corporation
P.O. Box N 4940
Nassau, Bahamas
Tel:(242)322-3740

Bahamian Consulate
Ingraham Building
25 S.E. Second Ave.
Miami, FL 33131
Tel:(305)539-9350

Ministry of Agriculture and Fisheries
P.O. Box N 3028
Nassau, Bahamas
Tel:(242)325-7502

Government of the Commonwealth of The Bahamas
Consulate General
Ingraham Building
25 S.E. Second Avenue
Miami, FL 33131
Tel:(305)373-6295

Bahamas Chamber of Commerce
P.O. Box 665
Nassau, Bahamas
Tel:(242)322-2145

BAGAMAS MASS MEDIA

Bahamas ***'The Nassau GuardianBahamas*** ' (circ. 15,000, morning daily)
P.O. Box N-3011
Nassau, Bahamas
Tel:(242) 323-5655, (242) 3232-6492, or (242) 323-5656.

Bahamas ***'The TribuneBahamas*** ' (circ. 15,000, afternoon daily)
P.O. Box N-3207
Nassau, Bahamas
Tel:(242) 322-1986
Advertising Manager Tel:(242) 322-2768
Fax:(242) 328-2398.

Bahamas ***'The Freeport NewsBahamas*** ' (circ. 5,000, morning daily)
P.O. Box F-40007
Freeport, Bahamas
Tel:(242) 352-8321
Bahamas 'The PunchBahamas ' (circ. 25,000, weekly tabloid)
P.O. Box N-4081
Nassau, Bahamas
Tel:(242) 322-7112
Fax:(242) 323-5268

Bahamas ***'The Bahama Journal Bahamas*** ' (circ. 5,000, weekly)
P.O. Box N-8610
Nassau, Bahamas
Tel: (242) 325-3082

Radio and television advertising can also be purchased on local radio and television stations. The sole television broadcaster is the state-owned ZNS (channel 13). This station, and its Nassau radio stations ZNS-1, ZNS-2, and ZNS-FM, can be contacted at:

Broadcasting Corporation of The Bahamas
P.O. Box N-1347
Nassau, Bahamas
Tel:(242) 322-4623 or (242) 322-4480
Advertising Sales Director:(242) 322-8962

There are three independent FM radio stations in Nassau: 100-Jamz (operated by Bahamas 'The TribuneBahamas '); Love-97 (operated by Bahamas 'The Bahama JournalBahamas '); and 94-More FM.
100-Jamz
P.O. Box N-3207
Nassau, Bahamas
Tel:(242) 328-4771
Fax:(242) 356-5343
Love-97 FM

P.O. Box N 3909
Nassau, Bahamas
Tel: (242) 356-4960
Fax: (242) 356-7256

94-More FM
P. O. Box N-7030
Nassau, Bahamas
Tel: (242) 361-2447
Fax: (242) 341-2448

MUTUAL FUND MANAGERS

Atlantic Bank of Commerce Ltd.
P.O. Box N8865
Nassau, N.P., The Bahamas
Tel: 242-326-0740
Fax: 242-325-1272
Mrs. Hilda Knowles
Deputy General Manager

Bank American & Banking Corporation (Bahamas Ltd.)
P.O. Box N
Nassau, N.P., The Bahamas
Tel: 242-393-7411
Fax: 242-393-3030
Mr. Geoffrey B. Stuart
Assistant manager

Chemical Bank & Trust (Bahamas) Ltd.
P.O. Box N-4723
Nassau, N.P., The Bahamas
Tel: 242-322-1003
Fax: 242-326-7339
Mr. Michael Ranson
Senior Trust Officer

CIBC Trust Company (Bahamas) Ltd.
P.O. Box N3933
Nassau, N.P., The Bahamas
Tel: 242-323-3314
Fax: 242-393-4280
Mr. D. Gilbert Cassar
Senior Manager, Trust Department

Coutts & Company (Bahamas) Ltd.
P.O. Box N7788
Nassau, N.P., The Bahamas
Tel: 242-326-0404
Fax: 242-326-6709
Mr. James D. Graham
Manager

Darier Hentsch Private Bank & Trust Ltd.
P.O. Box N4938
Nassau, N.P., The Bahamas
Tel: 242-322-2721
Fax: 242-326-6983
Mrs. Anna Colebrooke
Vice President

Demachy Worms & Co. International
P.O. Box N3918
Nassau, N.P., The Bahamas
Tel: 242-326-0282
Fax: 242-326-5213
Mr. Ronald W. Springle
Financial Controller

Eastland American Bank Ltd.
P.O. Box N4920
Nassau, N.P., The Bahamas
Tel: 242-325-9170
Fax: 242-325-1002
Mr. Tyrone Fowler
manager

Euro-Dutch Trust Co. (Bahamas) Ltd.
P.O. Box N9205
Nassau, N.P., The Bahamas
Tel: 242-325-1033
Fax: 242-323-7918

Mr. Anthony L.M. Inder Rieden
Managing Director

Fidinam Trust Corporation (Bahamas) Ltd.
P.O. Box N9932
Nassau, N.P., The Bahamas
Tel: 242-326-5084
Fax: 242-328-0541
Mr. Cedric B. Moss
Resident Manager

Laurentian Bank & Trust Company Ltd.
P.O. Box N4883
Nassau, N.P., The Bahamas
Tel: 242-326-5935
Fax: 242-326-5871
Mr. E. Andre Doyon
Managing Director

Lloyds Bank International Private Banking
P.O. Box N4843
Nassau, N.P., The Bahamas
Tel: 242-322-8711
Fax: 242-322-8719
Mr. Sam P. Haven
Assistant Manager, Trust Department

Mees Pierson (Bahamas) Ltd.
P.O. Box SS5539
Nassau, N.P., The Bahamas
Tel: 242-393-8777
Fax: 242-393-0582
Mr. Geoffrey Dyson
Managing Director

Montaque Securities International, Ltd.
Saffrey Square
Bay Street & Bank Lane, 1st Floor
P.O. Box N-7474
Nassau, The Bahamas
Tel: (242) 356-6133
Fax: (242) 356-6144
Owen S. M. Bethel
President & Managing Director

Morgan Trust Company of The Bahamas
P.O. Box N4899
Nassau, N.P., The Bahamas
Tel: 242-326-5519
Fax: 242-326-5520

Mr. Andrew G. Massie
Managing Director

Norshield International, Inc.
Tradewinds Building
P.O. Box N-9645
Nassau, The Bahamas
Tel: (242) 325-4403
Fax: (242) 322-6003

Rawson Trust Company Ltd.
P.O. Box N4465
Nassau, N.P., The Bahamas
Tel: 242-322-7461
Fax: 242-326-6177
Mrs. B. M. Rolle
Manager, Accounts

Sand Ander Investment Bank Ltd.
P.O. Box N1682
Nassau, N.P., The Bahamas
Tel: 242-322-3588
Fax: 242-322-3585
Mrs. R. L. Symonette
Manager

The Chase Manhattan Private Bank
P.O. Box N1576
Nassau, N.P., The Bahamas
Tel: 242-323-6811
Fax: 242-326-8814
Mrs. Eunice E. Smith Manager, Unit Trust Department

The Citibank Private Bank
P.O. Box N1576
Nassau, N.P., The Bahamas
Tel: 242-323-3521
Fax: 242-325-6147
Mr. David N. Tremblay
Managing Director

The Private Trust Corporation Ltd.
P.O. Box N3242
Nassau, N.P., The Bahamas
Tel: 242-323-8574
Fax: 242-326-8388
Mr. Peter B. Evans
Managing Director

Thorand Trust & Management Ltd.
P.O. Box N3242
Nassau, N.P., The Bahamas

Tel: 242-393-8622
Fax: 242-393-3772
Mr. Robert V. Lotmore
Managing Director

Westpac Bank & Trust (Bahamas) Ltd.
P.O. Box N8332
Nassau, N.P., The Bahamas
Tel: 242-328-8064
Fax: 242-326-0067
Mrs. Jacqueline M. Bain
Managing Director

REAL ESTATE COMPANIES

Abaco Homes & Land
General Post Office
Green Turtle Cay, Abaco
The Bahamas
Tel: 242-365-4079
Broker: Ms. Audrey Sattam

Abaco Real Estate Agency
P.O. Box AB20404
Marsh Harbour, Abaco
The Bahamas
Tel: 242-367-2719
Brokers: Mr. Chad Sawyer
Ms. Elaine Thompson

Dorothy Atwood Ltd.
P.O. Box CB11393
Nassau, N.P., The Bahamas
Tel: 242-327-8897
Broker: Ms. Dorothy Atwood

Bahamas Investments
P.O. Box N8877
Nassau, N.P., The Bahamas
Tel: 242-326-3401
Broker: Ms. Paula Augberg

Bahamas Realty Ltd.
P.O. Box N1132
Nassau, N.P., The Bahamas
Tel: 242-393-8618
Fax: 242-393-0326
Brokers: Ms. Robin Brown Rigg
Mr. W. Larry RobertsMr. Gordon Wilde

Belmont Real Estate
P.O. Box EL25009
Governor's Harbour, Eleuthera
The Bahamas
Tel: 242-3322301
Broker: Ms. Enid Bethel

Bethel Estates Ltd.
P.O. Box N3006
Nassau, N.P., The Bahamas
Tel: 242-322-4891
Fax: 242-322-2458
Brokers: Mr. Charles Bethel
Mr. John F. Bethel

Bramble, Bush & Briar Realty
P.O. Box N681
Nassau, N.P., The Bahamas
Tel: 242-324-6164
Fax: 242-394-3391
Broker: Mr. Gerald L.C. Pennerman

Barbara Brown Real Estate
P.O. Box N1110
Nassau, N.P., The Bahamas
Tel: 242-322-2680
Fax: 242-325-6353
Broker: Ms. Barbara Brown

Brown, Morley & Smith Real Estate
P.O. Box N1110
Nassau, N.P., The Bahamas
Tel: 242-322-2683
Fax: 242-325-8468
Brokers: Mr. Geoffrey Brown Sr.
Mr. John R. MorleyMr. Lester Smith

Frank Carey Real Estate
P.O. Box N4764
Nassau, N.P., The Bahamas
Tel: 242-322-4815
Broker: Mr. Frank Carey

Caribbean Marketing Development Ltd.
P.O. Box N3903
Nassau, N.P., The Bahamas
Tel: 242-322-2024
Fax: 242-328-8086
Broker: Mr. Irvin Stubbs

C.A. Christie Real Estate
P.O. Box N8245
Nassau, N.P., The Bahamas
Tel: 242-325-3957
Fax: 242-326-5684
Broker: Mr. Charles Christie

Churchill & Jones Real Estate
P.O. Box F2480
Freeport, Grand Bahama
The Bahamas
Tel: 242-352-7305
Fax: 242-352-3560
Brokers: Mr. David P.L. Hunter
Ms. Hilary Jones

H.G. Christie Ltd.
P.O. Box N8164
Nassau, N.P., The Bahamas
Tel: 242-322-1041
Fax: 242-326-5642
Brokers: Mr. William M. Christie
Ms. Sylvia E. Scriven

Paul Cole Real Estate
P.O. Box N7776
Nassau, N.P., The Bahamas
Tel: 242-362-4380
Broker: Mr. Paul Cole

John Dale Real Estate
P.O. Box CB11413
Nassau, N.P., The Bahamas
Tel: 242-327-8030
Broker: Mr. John Dale

Damianos Realty Company
P.O. Box N732
Nassau, N.P., The Bahamas
Tel: 242-322-2305
Brokers: Mr. George Damianos Sr., Mr. George Damianos Jr.Ms. Virginia Damianos Mr. Alphonso Deleveaux

Eleuthera Adventure
P.O. Box N3709
Nassau, N.P., The Bahamas
Tel: 242-322-7979
Broker: Mr. Brent Symonette

Sloane Farrington Real Estate
P.O. Box N1057
Nassau, N.P., The Bahamas
Tel: 242-324-1058
Broker: Mr. Sloane Farrington

Berkley Ferguson Real Estate
P.O. Box N4278
Nassau, N.P., The Bahamas
Tel: 242-322-4913
Fax: 242-326-0645
Broker: Mr. Berkley Ferguson

Fiduciary Management
P.O. Box N4284
Nassau, N.P., The Bahamas
Tel: 242-327-7522
Broker: Mr. Terence Langford

Ezra Forsythe Real Estate
P.O. Box SS6278
Nassau, N.P., The Bahamas
Tel: 242-393-6235
Broker: Mr. Ezra Forsythe

Gold Circle Company Ltd.
P.O. Box N8998
Nassau, N.P., The Bahamas
Tel: 242-393-8477
Fax: 242-3934508
Brokers: Mr. Kevin Smith
Mr. Philip SmithMr. Patrick Strachan

Laddie Gates Real Estate
P.O. Box SS6339
Nassau, N.P., The Bahamas
Tel: 242-322-8857
Fax: 242-325-4119
Broker: Ms. Laddie Gates

Levi Gibson & Associates
P.O. Box N957
Nassau, N.P., The Bahamas
Tel: 242-322-4654
Fax: 242-322-8730
Brokers: Mr. Levi Gibson
Mr. Wendell Seymour

Grosham Property Ltd.
P.O. Box N8189
Nassau, N.P., The Bahamas
Tel: 242-322-7662
Fax: 242-322-3549
Brokers: Ms. Barbara Brooks
Mr. Jonathan Dean

Sterling T.G. Hanna Real Estate
P.O. Box N4142
Nassau, N.P., The Bahamas
Tel: 242-323-6188
Broker: Mr. Sterling T.G. Hanna

Home Limited
P.O. Box N1591
Nassau, N.P., The Bahamas
Tel: 242-327-7906
Broker: Mr. William J. Smith

Int'l Management & Investment Services
P.O. Box N8160
Nassau, N.P., The Bahamas
Tel: 242-322-2504
Fax: 242-322-6949
Broker: Mr. Graham M. Cooper

Island Real Estate
P.O. Box N1593
Nassau, N.P., The Bahamas
Tel: 242-328-1797
Fax: 242-328-3749
Brokers: Mr. Neil MacTaggard Sr.
Mr. Neil MacTaggard Jr.

Fred Kanitsch & Associates
P.O. Box N1391
Nassau, The Bahamas
Tel: 242-325-6089; 242-365-4042 (Abaco)
Fax: 242-325-2476/2765
Brokers: Mr. Fred Kanitsch
Mr. Vincent Higgs

Michael Lightbourne Real Estate
P.O. Box N4949
Nassau, N.P., The Bahamas
Tel: 242-322-4148
Fax: 242-325-2765
Broker: Mr. Michael Lightbourne

W.T. Lowes & Associates
P.O. Box N3371
Nassau, N.P., The Bahamas
Tel: 242-322-1741
Fax: 242-322-7600
Broker: Ms. Daisy Lowes

Lyford Cay Company Ltd.
P.O. Box N7776
Nassau, N.P., The Bahamas
Tel: 242-327-4280
Broker: Mr. Robert Hepburn

Lyford Cay Real Estate
P.O. Box N4631
Nassau, N.P., The Bahamas
Tel: 242-326-4703
Brokers: Ms. June Disston
Ms. Annie Smith

E.N. Mosko & Sons
P.O. Box N1130
Nassau, N.P., The Bahamas
Tel: 242-322-8808
Broker: Mr. E.N. Mosko

Neymour Rental Company
P.O. Box N4164
Nassau, N.P., The Bahamas
Tel: 242-325-3554
Broker: Mr. Cedric Neymour

Paradise Sales & Rental
P.O. Box SS6299
Nassau, N.P., The Bahamas
Tel/Fax: 242-363-1593
Broker: Ms. Andrea Brown Rigg

PGF Real Estate
P.O. Box N1444
Nassau, N.P., The Bahamas
Tel: 242-326-8017
Fax: 242-328-7508
Broker: Mr. Walter S. Hanchell

Powell's Mktg. & Mgmt. Services Ltd.
P.O. Box N4225
Nassau, N.P., The Bahamas
Tel: 242-328-8618
Fax: 242-326-2491
Broker: Ms. Edith Powell

Leslie W. Roberts Real Estate
P.O. Box SS5959
Nassau, N.P., The Bahamas
Tel: 242-393-2492
Broker: Ms. Leslie W. Roberts

Thomas V.A. Roberts Real Estate
P.O. Box N918
Nassau, N.P., The Bahamas
Tel: 242-324-2015
Broker: Mr. Thomas V.A. Roberts

Sandy Port Development Company
P.O. Box N8585
Nassau, N.P., The Bahamas
Tel: 242-327-8500
Broker: Mr. Hugh Buckner

Peter Shaw-Sadler Real Estate
P.O. Box N1516
Nassau, N.P., The Bahamas
Tel/Fax: 242-327-7500
Broker: Mr. Peter Shaw-Sadler

Oris Symonette Real Estate Sales & Appraisal Co.
P.O. Box N7795
Nassau, N.P., The Bahamas
Tel: 242-325-8280
Fax: 242-325-1739
Broker: Mr. Oris E. Symonette

Janet Taylor-Rich Real Estate
(Great Harbour Cay, Berry Islands)
c/o Pierce, P.O. Box N907
Nassau, N.P., The Bahamas
Broker: Ms. Janet Taylor-Rich

Chester Thompson Real Estate
P.O. Box N1688
Nassau, N.P., The Bahamas
Tel: 242-322-4777
Fax: 242-322-4385
Broker: Mr. Chester Thompson

Curtis Thompson Real Estate
P.O. Box N10333
Nassau, N.P., The Bahamas
Tel: 242-325-0318
Fax: 242-323-8015
Broker: Mr. Curtis Thompson

Tropical Realty Company
P.O. Box N1121
Nassau, N.P., The Bahamas
Tel: 242-393-2449
Broker: Mr. Freeman Smith

Westerwale Investments Ltd.
P.O. Box N8892
Nassau, N.P., The Bahamas
Tel: 242-393-2741
Broker: Mr. Donald H. Smith

World Development Ltd.
P.O. Box CB10964
Nassau, N.P., The Bahamas
Tel: 242-327-7721
Fax: 242-327-8948
Brokers: Ms. Astrid Fraser
Mr. Alan Winner

ACCOUNTING FIRMS

NEW PROVIDENCE ISLAND

Atkinson, Ronald & Company
P.O. Box N8326
Nassau, N.P., The Bahamas
Tel: 242-325-7355
Fax: 242-326-5602
Mr. Ronald Atkinson
Senior Partner

Butler & Taylor
P.O. Box N7777
Nassau, N.P., The Bahamas
Tel: 242-393-0224
Fax: 242-393-7570
Mr. Darryl Butler
Partner

Specialties: Provides a full range of business and offshore corporate services and is fully conversant in computerized accounting, auditing, and management systems.

Coopers & Lybrand
P.O. Box N596

Nassau, N.P., The Bahamas
Tel: 242-322-1061
Fax: 242-326-7668
Mr. Ishmael Lightbourne
Managing Partner
(Branch in Freeport, Grand Bahama Island)

Deloitte & Touche
P.O. Box N7120
Nassau, N.P., The Bahamas
Tel: 242-322-4393
Fax: 242-328-8006
(Branch in Freeport, Grand Bahama Island)

Specialties: Management and computer consulting, bank and trust audits and operations, liquidations, receiverships and estate management, new business ventures, services to offshore investors, capital markets. Staff are fluent in Spanish, German and French..

Ernst & Young
P.O. Box N-3231
Nassau, N.P., The Bahamas
Tel: 242-322-3805
Fax: 242-326-8180
Sen. Hon. Philip Galanis
Managing Partner

Specialties: Full range of accounting, auditing, receivership, insolvency and business advisory services to both local and international clients.

Gomez & Gomez
P.O. Box N8285
Nassau, N.P., The Bahamas
Tel: 242-322-7516
Fax: (242) 322-7517
Mr. Paul Gomez
Partner

Hepburn, Michael & Co.
P.O. Box N7250
Nassau, N.P., The Bahamas
Tel: 242-322-8814
Fax: 242-322-8285
Mr. Michael Hepburn
Partner

Specialties: Accounting, auditing, management services. Staff are fluent in German, Swiss German, French and Spanish.

KPMG Peat Marwick
P.O. Box N123
Centreville House, Collins Avenue

Nassau, N.P., The Bahamas
Tel: 242-322-8551
Fax: 242-326-5622
Mr. Michael Fielder
Managing Partner
(Branch in Freeport, Grand Bahama Island

Specialties: Auditing and accounting to financial institutions. Other industry experience includes hotels and casinos, construction, retailers and wholesalers, insurance and real estate development.

Mann Judd
P.O. Box N10144
Nassau, N.P., The Bahamas
Tel: 242-325-6591
Fax: 242-325-6592
Mr. Clifford Culmer
Partner

Specialties: Services include auditing, accounting, and feasibility studies for local clients. Offers administration of corporations and trusts to offshore clients.

Pannel Kerr Forster
P.O. Box N-8335
Nassau, N.P., The Bahamas
Tel: 242-322-8560
Fax: 242-326-8796
Mr. Basil Sands
Senior Partner
(Branch in Freeport, Grand Bahama Island)

Specialties: Provides services to a number of government agencies and corporations. Also provides services to the tourism, hospitality, banking, and finance industries.

Price Waterhouse
P.O. Box N3910
Nassau, N.P., The Bahamas
Tel: 242-322-8543
Fax: 242-326-7308
Mr. Lenworth Smith
Partner
(Branch in Freeport, Grand Bahama Island)

Specialties: Provides auditing, accounting and other business advisory services to numerous clients, which include banks and trust companies, insurance companies, hotels and casinos, retailers and wholesalers. Also provides corporate and company formation services.

F.R. Wilson & Co. Ltd.
P.O. Box N3739
Nassau, N.P., The Bahamas
Mr. Franklin Wilson
Senior Partner

Specialties: Insolvency services, financial advisors, corporate managers and investors.

BASIC TITLES ON BAHAMAS

IMPORTANT!
All publications are updated annually!
Please contact IBP, Inc. at ibpusa3@gmail.com for the latest ISBNs and additional information

TITLE
Bahamas A "Spy" Guide - Strategic Information and Developments
Bahamas A Spy" Guide"
Bahamas Banking & Financial Market Handbook
Bahamas Banking & Financial Market Handbook
Bahamas Business and Investment Opportunities Yearbook
Bahamas Business and Investment Opportunities Yearbook
Bahamas Business and Investment Opportunities Yearbook Volume 1 Strategic Information and Opportunities
Bahamas Business Intelligence Report - Practical Information, Opportunities, Contacts
Bahamas Business Intelligence Report - Practical Information, Opportunities, Contacts
Bahamas Business Law Handbook - Strategic Information and Basic Laws
Bahamas Business Law Handbook - Strategic Information and Basic Laws
Bahamas Business Law Handbook - Strategic Information and Basic Laws
Bahamas Business Law Handbook - Strategic Information and Basic Laws
Bahamas Business Success Guide - Basic Practical Information and Contacts
Bahamas Company Laws and Regulations Handbook
Bahamas Company Laws and Regulations Handbook - Strategic Information and Basic Laws
Bahamas Constitution and Citizenship Laws Handbook - Strategic Information and Basic Laws
Bahamas Country Study Guide - Strategic Information and Developments
Bahamas Country Study Guide - Strategic Information and Developments
Bahamas Country Study Guide - Strategic Information and Developments Volume 1 Strategic Information and Developments
Bahamas Criminal Laws, Regulations and Procedures Handbook - Strategic Information, Regulations, Procedures
Bahamas Customs, Trade Regulations and Procedures Handbook
Bahamas Customs, Trade Regulations and Procedures Handbook
Bahamas Diplomatic Handbook - Strategic Information and Developments
Bahamas Diplomatic Handbook - Strategic Information and Developments
Bahamas Ecology & Nature Protection Handbook
Bahamas Ecology & Nature Protection Handbook
Bahamas Ecology & Nature Protection Laws and Regulation Handbook
Bahamas Electoral, Political Parties Laws and Regulations Handbook - Strategic Information, Regulations, Procedures
Bahamas Energy Policy, Laws and Regulation Handbook
Bahamas Export-Import Trade and Business Directory
Bahamas Export-Import Trade and Business Directory
Bahamas Fishing and Aquaculture Industry Handbook - Strategic Information, Regulations, Opportunities

TITLE
Bahamas Foreign Policy and Government Guide
Bahamas Foreign Policy and Government Guide
Bahamas Immigration Laws and Regulations Handbook - Strategic Information and Basic Laws
Bahamas Industrial and Business Directory
Bahamas Industrial and Business Directory
Bahamas Insolvency (Bankruptcy) Laws and Regulations Handbook - Strategic Information and Basic Laws
Bahamas Investment and Business Guide - Strategic and Practical Information
Bahamas Investment and Business Guide - Strategic and Practical Information
Bahamas Investment and Business Guide - Strategic and Practical Information
Bahamas Investment and Business Guide - Strategic and Practical Information
Bahamas Investment and Business Profile - Basic Information and Contacts for Succesful investment and Business Activity
Bahamas Investment and Trade Laws and Regulations Handbook
Bahamas Investment, Trade Strategy and Agreements Handbook - Strategic Information and Basic Agreements
Bahamas Labor Laws and Regulations Handbook - Strategic Information and Basic Laws
Bahamas Land Ownership and Agriculture Laws Handbook
BAHAMAS Offshore Investment and Business Guide - Strategic and Practical Information
Bahamas Offshore Investment and Business Guide - Strategic and Practical Information
Bahamas Offshore Tax Guide
Bahamas Offshore Tax Guide
Bahamas Offshore Tax Guide - Strategic Information, Regulations, Contacts
Bahamas Recent Economic and Political Developments Yearbook
Bahamas Recent Economic and Political Developments Yearbook
Bahamas Recent Economic and Political Developments Yearbook
Bahamas Ship Registration, Merchant Shipping Regulations and Rules Handbook
Bahamas Starting Business (Incorporating) in....Guide
Bahamas Tax Guide Volume 1 Strategic Information and Basic Regulations
Bahamas Taxation Laws and Regulations Handbook
Bahamas Telecommunication Industry Business Opportunities Handbook
Bahamas Telecommunication Industry Business Opportunities Handbook
Bahamas: How to Invest, Start and Run Profitable Business in Bahamas Guide - Practical Information, Opportunities, Contacts

NEW! WORLD OFFSHORE, LAW, INVESTMENT & BUSINESS LIBRARY

Detailed Information on conducting business and investment activity in the countries with special offshore status
Price: $149.95 each

Andorra Offshore Investment and Business Guide
Anguilla Offshore Investment and Business Guide
Bahamas Offshore Investment and Business Guide
Barbados Offshore Investment and Business Guide
Belize Offshore Investment and Business Guide
Bermuda Offshore Investment and Business Guide
British Virgin Islands Offshore Investment and Business Guide
Cayman Islands Offshore Investment and Business Guide
Cook Islands Offshore Investment and Business Guide
Costa Rica Offshore Investment and Business Guide
Cyprus Offshore Investment and Business Guide
Dubai Offshore Investment and Business Guide
Gibraltar Offshore Investment and Business Guide
Grenada Offshore Investment and Business Guide
Guernsey Offshore Investment and Business Guide
Hong Kong Offshore Investment and Business Guide
Ireland Offshore Investment and Business Guide
Isle of Man Offshore Investment and Business Guide
Jersey Offshore Investment and Business Guide
Labuan Offshore Investment and Business Guide
Liechtenstein Offshore Investment and Business Guide
Luxembourg Offshore Investment and Business Guide
Madeira Offshore Investment and Business Guide
Malta Offshore Investment and Business Guide
Mauritius Offshore Business and Investment Opportunities Handbook
Mauritius Offshore Investment and Business Guide
Monaco Offshore Investment and Business Guide
Nauru Offshore Investment and Business Guide
Netherlands Antilles Offshore Investment and Business Guide
Panama Offshore Investment and Business Guide
Seychelles Offshore Investment and Business Guide
Switzerland Offshore Investment and Business Guide
Turks & Caicos Islands Offshore Investment and Business Guide
Vanuatu Offshore Investment and Business Guide

To order and for additional analytical and marketing information, please contacrt
International Business Publications, USA at:
P.O. Box 15343, Washington, DC 20003, USA. Phone: (202) 546-2103. Fax: (202) 546-3275.
E-mail: rusric@erols.com

Basic Laws and Regulations for conducting business and investment activity in the countries with special offshore status

Andorra Offshore Business Law Handbook
Anguilla Offshore Business Law Handbook
Bahamas Offshore Business Law Handbook
Barbados Offshore Business Law Handbook
Belize Offshore Business Law Handbook
Bermuda Offshore Business Law Handbook
British Virgin Islands Offshore Business Law Handbook
Cayman Islands Offshore Business Law Handbook
Cook Islands Offshore Business Law Handbook
Costa Rica Offshore Business Law Handbook
Cyprus Offshore Business Law Handbook
Dubai Offshore Business Law Handbook
Gibraltar Offshore Business Law Handbook
Grenada Offshore Business Law Handbook
Guernsey Offshore Business Law Handbook
Hong Kong Offshore Business Law Handbook
Ireland Offshore Business Law Handbook
Isle of Man Offshore Business Law Handbook
Jersey Offshore Business Law Handbook
Labuan Offshore Business Law Handbook
Liechtenstein Offshore Business Law Handbook
Luxembourg Offshore Business Law Handbook
Madeira Offshore Business Law Handbook
Malta Offshore Business Law Handbook
Mauritius Offshore Business and Investment Opportunities Handbook
Mauritius Offshore Business Law Handbook
Monaco Offshore Business Law Handbook
Nauru Offshore Business Law Handbook
Netherlands Antilles Offshore Business Law Handbook
Panama Offshore Business Law Handbook
Seychelles Offshore Business Law Handbook
Switzerland Offshore Business Law Handbook
Turks & Caicos Islands Offshore Business Law Handbook
Vanuatu Offshore Business Law Handbook

www.ingramcontent.com/pod-product-compliance
Ingram Content Group UK Ltd.
Pitfield, Milton Keynes, MK11 3LW, UK
UKHW051458290926
15471UKWH00008B/1284

9 781433 003707